ACT®

Strategies, Practice, and Review

2010 Edition

RELATED TITLES FOR COLLEGE-BOUND STUDENTS

ACT Strategies for Super Busy Students

Spotlight ACT
Spotlight SAT
SAT Premier Live Online 2010
SAT Strategies, Practice, and Review 2010
12 Practice Tests for the SAT
SAT Strategies for Super Busy Students
Inside the SAT: 10 Strategies to Help You Score Higher
SAT Advanced
SAT Critical Reading Workbook
SAT Math Workbook
SAT Writing Workbook
SAT in a Box Flashcards

The Ring of McAllister: A Score-Raising Mystery Featuring 1,046 Must-Know SAT Vocabulary Words
Frankenstein: A Kaplan New SAT Score-Raising Classic
The Tales of Edgar Allan Poe: A Kaplan New SAT Score-Raising Classic
Dr. Jekyll and Mr. Hyde: A Kaplan New SAT Score-Raising Classic
War of the Worlds: A Kaplan New SAT Score-Raising Classic
Wuthering Heights: A Kaplan New SAT Score-Raising Classic
Domina El SAT: Prepárate para Tomar el Examen para Ingresar a la Universidad

AP Biology
AP Calculus AB & BC
AP Chemistry
AP English Language & Composition
AP English Literature & Composition
AP Environmental Science
AP European History
AP Human Geography
AP Macroeconomics/Microeconomics
AP Physics B & C
AP Psychology
AP Statistics
AP U.S. Government & Politics
AP U.S. History
AP U.S. History in a Box
AP World History

SAT Subject Test: Biology E/M
SAT Subject Test: Chemistry
SAT Subject Test: Literature
SAT Subject Test: Mathematics Level 1
SAT Subject Test: Mathematics Level 2
SAT Subject Test: Physics
SAT Subject Test: Spanish
SAT Subject Test: U.S. History
SAT Subject Test: World History

ACT®

Strategies, Practice, and Review

2010 Edition

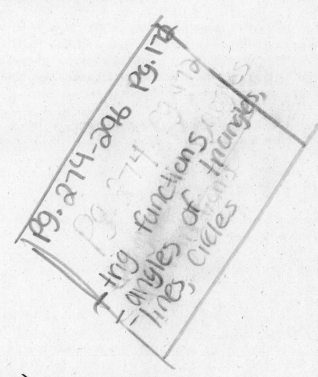

KAPLAN) PUBLISHING

New York

© 2010 by Kaplan, Inc.

Published by Kaplan Publishing, a division of Kaplan, Inc.
1 Liberty Plaza, 24th Floor
New York, NY 10006

Printed in the United States of America

10 9 8 7 6 5 4

ISBN-13: 978-1-4195-5326-4

Kaplan Publishing books are available at special quantity discounts to use for sales promotions, employee premiums, or educational purposes. For more information or to purchase books, please call the Simon & Schuster special sales department at 866-506-1949.

Table of Contents

WELCOME TO *KAPLAN ACT: STRATEGIES, PRACTICE, AND REVIEW*

Are you ready to conquer the ACT?

Kaplan knows the ACT exam is important to you. A great score on the ACT can help you stand out from the crowd when applying to colleges and can also help you get scholarships and financial aid to pay for it all.

Kaplan has nearly 70 years of experience getting students ready exams. We've spent decades building a powerful arsenal of test-taking tools designed with *you* in mind, and the book you now hold in your hands contains everything you need to score higher on the ACT.

The name of this book says it all: the 2010 edition of *Kaplan ACT: Strategies, Practice, and Review* has proven ACT strategies, realistic test practice, and in-depth review of all tested material. Kaplan's exclusive ACT tools work. Use them to your advantage and get ready to score higher on the ACT!

LET'S GET STARTED!

Kaplan ACT: Strategies, Practice, and Review has everything you need to get ready for Test Day, but how you use it is *your* choice. Kaplan realizes that no one knows your test-prep needs better than you, so we've designed this book to put you in control of the variety and amount of study that best suits your needs.

This book is designed to allow you to determine the path your test prep takes. Use it front to back or jump around and focus on the test sections that you need the most help with—it's your call.

On top of all the great test prep inside the book, we've put a diagnostic test online to help you determine your test strengths and weaknesses and focus your study plan. This is a great place to get started.

TAKE THE ONLINE DIAGNOSTIC TEST

Taking the online diagnostic test is a great way to figure out where your ACT skills stand and how to structure your study time between now and test day. Take the test and see what test sections are your strongest and which may require the most prep.

Here's how to access your ACT Diagnostic test online:

1. **Locate the serial number in your book.** You'll find it on the lower left corner of the inside back cover. Have this when you go online to register.
2. **Go to kaptest.com/ACTbooksonline.** The address is case sensitive, so enter it carefully!
3. **Follow the directions and register.** Once you register, you can access your diagnostic test whenever you want to. Just jump on your computer, got to **kaptest.com**, and select the "My Page" link.

BUILD YOUR ACT STUDY PLAN

Okay, so you've taken the online diagnostic test. Now what? Well, now that you have a good idea which test sections are your strongest and which need the most attention, you are ready to make the most of this book and build your study plan.

YOUR ACT STUDY PLAN—5 STEPS TO SUCCESS

1. Carefully go through the lessons in this book, paying close attention to the ones that focus on the test sections you were weakest in on your diagnostic test.

2. Take the end of chapter practice sets to see how well you're progressing. Be sure to read the answer explanations carefully—they'll help you figure out where you might have gone wrong during your problem solving.

3. Don't be afraid to review challenging lessons and concepts more than once. Isn't doing well on the ACT worth the extra study time?

4. Take time to practice your writing skills for the ACT essay. Use the strategies provided in this book to wow the scoring judges on test day!

5. Once you're comfortable with the various ACT question types and test material, dive into the full-length practice tests at the back of the book. Test yourself under realistic test day conditions and chart your progress. If your strengths and weaknesses change, adjust your study plan.

KAPLAN'S GOT YOU COVERED!

In addition to all the proven test-prep material in this book, based on decades of experience preparing students for the ACT, we've asked some of Kaplan's premier test experts to provide you with exclusive advice, tips, and strategies for scoring higher on the ACT.

Whenever you see:

We recommend you read the quote carefully and follow the advice given as you get ready for test day.

These helpful hints come from the following sources:

KAPLAN EXPERT TUTOR TIPS

One of Kaplan's expert ACT tutors provides valuable insight on how you can make the most of your ACT prep and score higher.

Good luck on test day!

NOTE FOR INTERNATIONAL STUDENTS

If you are an international student considering attending an American university, you are not alone. Over 600,000 international students pursued academic degrees at the undergraduate, graduate, or professional school level at U.S. universities during the 2004–2005 academic year, according to the Institute of International Education's Open Doors report. Almost 50 percent of these students were studying for a bachelor's or first university degree. This number of international students pursuing higher education in the United States is expected to continue to grow. Business, management, engineering, and the physical and life sciences are particularly popular majors for students coming to the United States from other countries.

If you are not a U.S. citizen and you are interested in attending college or university in the United States, here is what you'll need to get started.

- **If English is not your first language, you'll probably need to take the TOEFL® (Test of English as a Foreign Language) or provide some other evidence that you are proficient in English.** Colleges and universities in the United States will differ on what they consider to be an acceptable TOEFL score. Because American undergraduate programs require all students to take a certain number of general education courses, all students—even math and computer science students—need to be able to communicate well in spoken and written English.

- **You may also need to take the SAT® or the ACT®.** Many undergraduate institutions in the United States require both the SAT and TOEFL for international students.

- There are over 3,400 accredited colleges and universities in the United States, so selecting the correct undergraduate school can be a confusing task for anyone. **You will need to get help from a good advisor or at least a good college guide that gives you detailed information on the different schools available.** Since admission to many undergraduate programs is quite competitive, you may want to select three or four colleges and complete applications for each school.

- **You should begin the application process at least a year in advance.** An increasing number of schools accept applications year round. In any case, find out the application deadlines and plan accordingly. Although September (the fall semester) is the traditional time to begin university study in the United States, you can begin your studies at many schools in January (the spring semester).

- **In addition, you will need to obtain an I-20 Certificate of Eligibility from the school you plan to attend if you intend to apply for an F-1 Student Visa to study in the United States.**

KAPLAN ENGLISH PROGRAMS*

If you need more help navigating the complex process of university admissions, preparing for the SAT, ACT, or TOEFL, or building your English language skills in general, you may be interested in Kaplan's programs for international students.

Kaplan English Programs were designed to help students and professionals from outside the United States meet their educational and career goals. At locations throughout the United States, international students take advantage of Kaplan's programs to help them improve their academic and conversational English skills, raise their scores on the TOEFL, SAT, ACT, and other standardized exams, and gain admission to the schools of their choice. Our staff and instructors give international students the individualized attention they need to succeed. Here is a brief description of some of Kaplan's programs for international students:

GENERAL INTENSIVE ENGLISH

Kaplan's General Intensive English course is the fastest and most effective way for students to improve their English. This full-time program integrates the four key elements of language learning—listening, speaking, reading, and writing. The challenging curriculum and intensive schedule are designed for both the general language learner and the academically bound student.

TOEFL AND ACADEMIC ENGLISH

Our world-famous TOEFL course prepares you for the TOEFL and also teaches you the academic language and skills needed to succeed in a university. Designed for high-intermediate to advanced-level English speakers, our course includes TOEFL-focused reading, writing, listening, speaking, vocabulary, and grammar instruction.

GENERAL ENGLISH

Our General English course is a semi-intensive program designed for students who want to improve their listening and speaking skills without the time commitment of an intensive program. With morning class time and flexible computer lab hours throughout the week, our General English course is perfect for every schedule.

*Kaplan is authorized under federal law to enroll nonimmigrant alien students. Kaplan is accredited by ACCET (Accrediting Council for Continuing Education and Training).

OTHER KAPLAN PROGRAMS

Since 1938, more than three million students have come to Kaplan to advance their studies, prepare for entry to American universities, and further their careers. In addition to the above programs, Kaplan offers courses to prepare for the ACT, GMAT®, GRE®, MCAT®, DAT®, USMLE®, NCLEX-RN®, and other standardized exams at locations throughout the United States.

APPLYING TO KAPLAN ENGLISH PROGRAMS

To get more information, or to apply for admission to any of Kaplan's programs for international students and professionals, contact us at:

KAPLAN ENGLISH PROGRAMS

700 South Flower, Suite 2900

Los Angeles, CA 90017, USA

Phone (if calling from within the United States): 800-818-9128

Phone (if calling from outside the United States): (213) 452-5800

Fax: (213) 892-1364

Website: www.kaplanenglish.com

Email: world@kaplan.com

FREE Services for International Students

Kaplan now offers international students many services online—*free of charge*! Students may assess their TOEFL skills and gain valuable feedback on their English language proficiency in just a few hours with Kaplan's TOEFL Skills Assessment. Log onto www.kaplanenglish.com today.

Part One

ACT BASICS

CHAPTER 1: INTRODUCTION TO THE ACT

IF YOU LEARN ONLY FIVE THINGS IN THIS CHAPTER . . .

1. The ACT consists of four required subject tests (English, Math, Reading, and Science) plus an optional Writing test.

2. Total testing time is about three hours, plus half an hour for Writing.

3. All questions are multiple choice except on the Writing test (one essay question).

4. There is no penalty for a wrong answer so you should **always** guess.

5. ACT composite scores range from 1–36.

Before you plunge into studying for the ACT, let's take a step back and look at the big picture. What's the ACT all about? How can you prepare for it? How's it scored? This chapter will answer these questions and more.

The ACT is an opportunity, not a barrier. In fact, you should be grateful that you have to take it. Really. Because a strong ACT score is one credential that doesn't depend on things you can't control. It doesn't depend on how good or bad your high school is. It doesn't depend on how many academic luminaries you know, or how rich and famous your family is, or whether any of your teachers are gullible enough to swear in a letter of recommendation that you're the greatest scientific mind since Isaac Newton. No, your ACT score depends on only you.

Granted, the ACT is a tough exam. It's probably one of the toughest exams you'll ever take. But you should be grateful for that too. Really. If the ACT were easy, everyone would do well. A good score wouldn't mean much. But because it's such a bear of a test, the ACT can be your single best opportunity to show what you can do,

EXPERT TUTOR TIP

" If you have two weeks or fewer to prep for the ACT, don't panic. The first thing you should do is become familiar with the test. This chapter is the place to start. "

to prove to colleges that you are the candidate of choice—for admission, for advanced placement, for scholarships.

It's important, though, that you take the test in the right spirit. Don't be timid in the face of the ACT. Don't let it bully you. You've got to take control of the test. Our mission in this book is to show you exactly how to do that.

It helps to think of the ACT challenge as a contest—not only between you and the test, but also between you and that other person trying to get your spot in college. The ACT, after all, is meant to provide a way for all college applicants to compete on an even playing field. How do you compete successfully in a fair academic fight? You train—harder and smarter than the next person. First, you learn whatever knowledge and skills you need to know. But then, just as important, you learn how to show what you know, in ways that the test is designed to reward. You learn how to be a savvy test taker.

FOUR KEYS TO ACT SUCCESS

There are four basic commandments for achieving ACT success. Following any of these by itself will improve your score. Following all four together will make you nothing less than awesome.

1. THOU SHALT LEARN THE TEST

The ACT is very predictable. You'd think the test makers would get bored after a while, but they don't. The same kinds of questions, testing the same skills and concepts, appear every time the ACT is given.

Because the test specifications rarely change, you should know in advance what to expect on every section. Just a little familiarity can make an enormous difference on the ACT. Here are a few ways in which learning the test will boost your score:

- **You'll learn the directions.** Why waste valuable time reading directions when you can have them down pat beforehand? You need every second during the test to answer questions and get points.

- **You'll learn the difficulty range of questions.** It's a fact that a typical ACT test taker gets only about half the questions right. Knowing this will stop you from panicking when you hit an impossible science passage or trigonometry question. Relax! You can skip many tough questions on the ACT and still get a great score! And once you know that the questions aren't arranged in order of difficulty, you'll know that just beyond that awful question will be one, two, or even three easy questions that you can score on with no sweat at all.

- **You'll learn how to get extra points by guessing.** Unlike some other standardized tests, the ACT has no wrong-answer penalty. Knowing that simple fact can boost your score significantly. If you can't answer a question, guess.

- **You'll learn what makes a high-scoring essay.** If you are taking the optional Writing test, learning how it is scored will help you craft a good essay.

We'll help you get a better understanding of the ACT in the chapter following this one, entitled "The Subject Tests: A Preview."

2. THOU SHALT LEARN THE STRATEGIES

The ACT isn't a normal exam. Most normal exams test your memory. The ACT isn't like that. The ACT tests problem-solving skills rather than memory, and it does so in a standardized-test format. That makes the test highly vulnerable to test-smart strategies and techniques.

Most students miss a lot of ACT questions for no good reason. They see a tough-looking question, say to themselves, "Uh-oh, I don't remember how to do that," and then they start to gnaw on their No. 2 pencils.

But many ACT questions can be answered without perfect knowledge of the material being tested. Often, all you need to do to succeed on the ACT is to think strategically and creatively. We call this kind of strategic, creative frame of mind "The ACT Mind-set."

How do you put yourself into the ACT Mind-set? You continually ask yourself questions like: "What does this mean? How can I put this into a form I can understand and use? How can I do this faster?" Once you develop some savvy test-taking skills, you'll find yourself capable of working out problems that at first reading might have scared you half to death! In fact, we'll show you how you can sometimes get right answers when you don't even understand the question or the passage it's attached to!

There are many, many specific strategies you can use to boost your score. For instance, here are just a couple of things you'll learn:

- **You'll learn the peculiarities of the ACT format.** Except for the Writing test, the ACT is a multiple-choice test. The correct answer is **always** right there in front of you. We'll show you how to develop specific tactics for each question type to maximize the chances of selecting the correct answer. The wrong answers are often predictable. For example, in English the shortest answer is the correct answer with surprising frequency. Strange, but true. Knowing statistical information like this can give you an important edge.

- **You'll learn a plan of attack for each subject test.** We'll show you some really useful ways of attacking each subject test. You'll learn how to do "question triage"—deciding which questions to do now and which to save for later. You'll learn a strategic method for each subject test designed to get you points quickly and systematically. You'll learn gridding techniques to avoid any answer-sheet disasters.

- **You'll learn "unofficial" ways of getting right answers fast.** On the ACT, nobody cares how you decide which choice to select. The only thing that matters is picking the right answer. That's different from the way it works on most high school tests, where you get credit for showing that you've done the questions the "right" way (that is, the way you were taught to do them by Mrs. Crabapple in high school). We'll show you how to find creative shortcuts to the correct answers—"unofficial" methods that will save you precious time and net you extra points.

The basic test-smart techniques and strategies for the whole test are covered in the chapter called "Taking Control: The Top Ten Strategies." General strategies for each subject test, plus specific hints, techniques, and strategies for individual question types, are found in the Skill-Building Workouts. These are then summarized in the Strategic Summaries.

3. THOU SHALT LEARN THE MATERIAL TESTED

The ACT is designed to test skills and concepts learned in high school and needed for college. Familiarity with the test, coupled with smart test-taking strategies, will take you only so far. For your best score you need to sharpen up the skills and knowledge that the ACT rewards. Sometimes, in other words, you've just got to eat your spinach.

The good news is that most of the content on the ACT is pretty basic. You've probably already learned most of what the ACT expects you to know. But you may need help remembering. That's partly what this book is for—to remind you of the knowledge you already have and to build and refine the specific skills you've developed in high school. Here are just a few of the things we'll "remind" you of:

- **You'll learn how to read graphs and tables.** Many Science questions rely on your ability to use data presented in the form of graphs and tables. (We'll teach you how to read graphs and tables in Science Workout 1.)

- **Have you met any FANBOYS lately?** Don't know? Well, this is the acronym for the conjunctions that connect two independent clauses in a sentence. We know you want to know more about this, so here's a sneak preview: FANBOYS help you remember **F**or, **A**nd, **N**or, **B**ut, **O**r, **Y**et, **S**o. For more grammar rules, check out English Workout 3.

- **If your math "engine" is rusty when it comes to triangles, probabilities, algebraic expressions,** and more, we'll get you up and running. The three Math Workout chapters and the 100 Key Math Concepts for the ACT will have that engine purring again in no time.

- **You'll learn how to do trigonometry problems.** Do you remember exactly what a cotangent is? A cosine? We didn't think so. But there are four trig problems on every ACT. (You can learn about trigonometry problems in 100 Key Math Concepts for the ACT, items 96–100.)

- **You'll learn the difference between** *lie* **and** *lay***.** Is it "I lay down on the couch" or "I lie down on the couch"? You may want to lie down yourself if you encounter such issues on the ACT. But don't fret. We'll remind you of the common grammar traps the test lays for you (or is it *lies* for you ???). (For a discussion of this conundrum, see Classic Grammar Error #9 in English Workout 3.)

4. THOU SHALT PRACTICE, PRACTICE, PRACTICE

Practice creates confidence. On test day, you need to have all the strategies and concepts in your brain and to be relaxed and ready to go. Reading and understanding the contents of this book is key. But there's one more step. For Kaplan's methods to be most effective on test day, you need to make them part of your everyday routine. The best way to do that is to practice as much as possible.

Test day often becomes THE DAY. You're in a room full of people, all in a state of anticipation and nervousness—it's contagious. Don't let the moment take over and make you forget your methods. Your best ally in this excitement is the confidence that practice gives you.

Note: If you don't have time to practice with all of the sections, you *can* (and should!) practice in the areas you feel weakest.

Specifics like those mentioned above comprise what we call the ACT "knowledge base." The components of this knowledge base are reviewed along the way throughout this book. The ACT Resources in the book and in your online syllabus summarize this information for the two sections of the ACT that explicitly test knowledge: English and Math.

In sum, then, follow these four commandments:

1. **Thou shalt learn the test.**
2. **Thou shalt learn the strategies.**
3. **Thou shalt learn the material tested.**
4. **Thou shalt practice, practice, practice.**

If you do, you'll find yourself just where you should be on test day: in full command of your ACT test-taking experience. Count on it.

WHAT IS THE ACT?

It was Attila the Hun who first coined this epigram: knowing the enemy is the first step in conquering the enemy. Attila, of course, was talking about waging wars on the steppes of Central Asia, but his advice also works for taking standardized tests in central Illinois. In fact, that's probably why Attila got a composite score of 30 on the ACT.

Well, to be honest, we haven't fact-checked Attila the Hun's ACT score, but the point remains valid. To succeed on the ACT, you've got to know the ACT.

But is the ACT really your enemy? Only in a manner of speaking. The test is more like an adversary in a game of chess. If you know your adversary's entire repertoire of moves and clever stratagems, you'll find it that much easier to beat him. Myths about the ACT are common.

Even high school teachers and guidance counselors sometimes give out inaccurate information (we know you're shocked to hear this). To earn your best score, you need to know how the ACT is really put together.

So, before anything, take some time and get to know this so-called adversary. Let's start with the basics. The ACT is a three-hour exam (three and a half hours if you take the optional Writing test) taken by high school juniors and seniors for admission to college. It is not an IQ test; it's a test of problem-solving skills—which means that you can improve your performance by preparing for it.

Speaking of myths, you may have heard that the ACT is really the only thing colleges look at when deciding whether to admit you. Untrue. Most admissions officers say the ACT is only one of several factors they take into consideration. But let's be realistic about ACT scores. Here's this neat and easy way of comparing all students numerically, no matter what their academic backgrounds and no matter how much grade inflation exists at their high schools. You know the admissions people are going to take a serious look at your test scores.

The ACT consists of four subject tests: English, Math, Reading, and Science, as well as the optional Writing test. All the subject tests are primarily designed to test skills rather than knowledge, though some knowledge is required—particularly in English, for which a familiarity with grammar and writing mechanics is important, and in Math, for which you need to know the basic math concepts taught in a regular high school curriculum. The Writing test tests your ability to communicate clearly your position on an issue.

OVERVIEW OF THE ACT

- The ACT is about three hours long (three and a half with the Writing test).
- There will be a short break between the second and third subtests.
- The ACT consists of a total of 215 scored multiple-choice questions, and one optional essay
- The exam is composed of four subject tests and an optional Writing test:
  — English (45 minutes, 75 questions)
  — Math (60 minutes, 60 questions)
  — Reading (35 minutes, 40 questions)
  — Science (35 minutes, 40 questions)
  — Writing (30 minutes, 1 essay question)

ACT FAQS

Here are some quick answers to the questions students ask most frequently about the ACT.

To be fair, no school uses the ACT as an absolute bar to admission, no matter how low it is. But for most applicants, a low ACT score is decisive. As a rule, only students whose backgrounds are extremely unusual or who have overcome enormous disadvantages are accepted if their ACT scores are below the benchmark. It also sometimes helps if you can convince your parents to donate a gymnasium to the school you're aiming for.

Should You Take the Optional Writing Test?

You should decide whether to take the ACT Writing test based on the admissions policies of the schools you will apply to and on the advice of your high school guidance counselors. A list of colleges requiring the test is maintained on the ACT website, www.act.org/aap/writing. If you are unsure about what schools you will apply to, you should plan to take the Writing test. However, testing will be available later if you decide not to take the Writing test and discover later that you need it.

How Do Schools Use the Optional Writing Test?

The ACT Writing test may be used for either admissions or course placement purposes, or both. Students who take the Writing test will receive an English score, a Writing subscore, and a combined English-Writing score on a 1–36 scale. (The combined English-Writing score is not averaged into the composite score.) Copies of the essay (with the graders' comments) will also be available online for downloading. Schools that do not require the Writing test will also receive the combined English-Writing score for students who have taken the Writing test, unless the school specifically asks *not* to receive those results.

Should You Guess on the ACT?

The short answer? Yes! The long answer? Yes, of course!

As we saw, ACT scores are based on the number of correct answers only. This means that questions that you leave blank and questions you answer incorrectly simply don't count. Unlike some other standardized tests, the ACT has no wrong-answer penalty. That's why you should **always** take a guess on every ACT question you can't answer, even if you don't have time to read it. Though the questions vary enormously in difficulty, harder questions are worth exactly the same as easier ones, so it pays to guess on the really hard questions and spend your time breezing through the really easy ones. We'll show you just how to do this in the chapter called "Taking Control: The Top Ten Strategies."

Can You Retake the Test?

You can take the ACT as many times as you like. You can then select whichever test score you prefer to be sent to colleges when you apply. However, you cannot take advantage of this option if, at the time you register for the test, you designate certain colleges to receive your scores. Thus, it is crucial that you not designate any colleges at the time you register for the test. You can (for a small additional fee) have ACT scores sent to colleges at any time you desire after the scores are reported.

Unless you don't have enough money for that small extra fee or if you're taking the ACT under the wire and you need your scores to reach the schools you're applying to ASAP, give yourself the freedom to retake the test. What this means, of course, is that even if you blow the ACT once, you can give yourself another chance without the schools of your choice knowing about it. The ACT is one of the few areas of your academic life in which you get a second chance.

ACT REGISTRATION OVERVIEW

- **To get a registration packet, see your guidance counselor, or contact:**

  ACT Registration
  301 ACT Drive
  P.O. Box 414
  Iowa City, IA 52243-0414
  Phone: (319) 337-1270
  Web: www.act.org

- **You can also register online at www.actstudent.org.**
- **Students with disabilities or with other special circumstances can call (319) 337-1332.**
- **The basic fee at press time for the ACT is $32 without the Writing test,** and $47 with the Writing test, in the United States. For students testing outside the 50 United States, the fee is $58 ($73 for the ACT with Writing test). Call (319) 337-1448 for more information on taking the test outside the United States.

  This price includes reports for you, your high school, and up to four college choices. There are additional fees for late registration, standby testing, changing test centers or test dates, and for additional services and products.

- **In the United States, the ACT is administered in September, October, December, February, April, and June.** (The February date is not available in the state of New York.) Register early to secure the time you want at the test center of your choice and to avoid late registration fees.
- **You may take the ACT assessment as often as you wish.** Many students take it twice, once as a junior and again as a senior. There are no limitations on how many times you can take the ACT, but there are some restrictions on how often you can test. For example, you can test only once per national test date.

GO ONLINE

" Visit the test maker's website at www. act. org for the latest information on test registration, fees, and content. "

- **Be sure you take your test center admission ticket and acceptable identification with you to the test center.** Acceptable forms of identification are a photo ID or a recent published photo with your full name printed. Unacceptable forms of identification are a birth certificate, Social Security card, or any other ID without photo. You will not be admitted without acceptable identification.

- **Check with ACT, Inc., for all the latest information on the test.** Every effort is made to keep the information in this book up-to-date, but changes may occur after the book is published.

- **Go online (act.org) to make sure you know ALL the ACT regulations for test day.** For example, all electronic devices (including cell phones) must be turned off from the time you're admitted to the test until you're dismissed after testing concludes.

Note: Violations of these rules, such as an alarm going off or a phone ringing in the test room, may result in your dismissal from the room and the nonscoring of your answer sheet.

- **You might be considering whether to take the ACT, the SAT, or both.** For more information on the SAT, go to the College Board's website at www.collegeboard.com.

TAKING THE PLAN EXAM

Students should also be aware of the PLAN exam, which offers a preview of the format and content of the material found on the ACT. A student's success on this exam is often an accurate predictor of success on the ACT. PLAN scores help students decide which courses to take their junior and senior years of high school in addition to helping students consider certain career paths prior to college, based on their strengths or weaknesses as indicated by their scores. The PLAN is generally offered to students in the fall of their sophomore year. To learn more, visit PLAN's website for student information at www.actstudent.org/plan.

CHAPTER 2: THE SUBJECT TESTS: A PREVIEW

IF YOU LEARN ONLY FIVE THINGS IN THIS CHAPTER . . .

1. The ACT English test includes 75 questions to be answered in 45 minutes. It tests your knowledge of grammar and usage. You'll be asked to fix errors in passages and sometimes to comment on the passage as a whole.

2. The ACT Math test consists of 60 questions to be answered in 60 minutes. Topics include pre-algebra, elementary and intermediate algebra, coordinate and plane geometry, and trigonometry. Questions are not given in order of difficulty.

3. The ACT Reading test includes 40 questions to be answered in 35 minutes. The questions refer to four passages: Prose Fiction, Humanities, Social Sciences, and Natural Sciences.

4. The ACT Science test is comprised of 40 questions to be answered in 35 minutes. There are seven passages with related questions which ask you to analyze and interpret experiments, figures, and scientists' viewpoints. There will only be one to three questions which call on you to use your existing science knowledge.

5. The ACT Writing test consists of one essay prompt that asks you to take a stand on an issue. You have 30 minutes to write a clear and persuasive essay, supported with evidence from your experience, reading, current events, or other sources.

Okay, you've seen how the ACT is set up. But to really know your adversary, you've got to know something about the ACT subject tests (which, by the way, **always** appear in the above order).

As we'll see, the questions in every subject test vary widely in difficulty. Some are so easy that most elementary school students could answer them. Others would give even Einstein a little trouble. But, again: **the questions are not arranged in order of difficulty.** That's different from some

EXPERT TUTOR TIP

" If you have two weeks or fewer to prep for the ACT, you should spend time getting familiar with the test. Be sure to read this chapter. You'll learn the directions and how the tests are organized. "

other tests, in which easier questions come first. Skipping past hard questions is very important, since otherwise you may never reach easy ones toward the end of the exam.

Here's a preview of the types of questions you'll see on the subject tests. We'll keep them toward the easy end of the difficulty scale here, but later, in the Skill-Building Workouts, we'll be less kind.

After we look at the four required subject tests, we'll give you a preview of the optional Writing test.

ENGLISH

The English test lasts 45 minutes and includes 75 questions. That works out to about 30 seconds per question. When it comes down to it, though, you should spend less time on easier questions and more on harder questions. The test is divided into five passages, each with about 15 questions.

Note: You're not tested on spelling or vocabulary here. Rather, the ACT is designed to test your understanding of the conventions of English—punctuation, grammar, sentence structure—and of rhetorical skills. Rhetorical skills are more strategic things like organizing the text and making sure it's styled clearly.

Students nearly always get more questions correct in English than in any other section. That tends to make them think that English is a lot easier than the rest of the ACT. But, alas, it's not that simple. Because most students do well, the test makers have much higher expectations for English than for other parts of the test. They know that it's generally easier to get English questions right than, say, Science questions. They've got a whole department of little statistician elves who keep track of things like this. That's why, to earn an average English subscore (a 20, say), you have to get almost two-thirds of the questions right, while on the rest of the test you need to get only about half right.

EXPERT TUTOR TIP

" ACT questions are not arranged in order of ascending difficulty. Skip past the tough questions and spend your first minutes on the test piling up some easy points. "

THE FORMAT

Almost all of the English questions follow a standard format. A word, phrase, or sentence in a passage is underlined. You're given four options: to leave the underlined portion alone ("NO CHANGE," which is **always** the first choice), or to replace it with one of three alternatives.

The correct answer for this question is F. Though G correctly states that the sentence doesn't belong in the passage, it offers a pretty inappropriate reason. The passage is concerned with Pike's achievements. Choices H and J are wrong because they recommend including a sentence that is clearly redundant.

Many of the nonstandard questions occur at the end of a passage. Some ask about the meaning, purpose, or tone of individual paragraphs or of the passage as a whole. Others ask you to evaluate the passage. And still others ask you to determine the proper order of words, sentences, or paragraphs that have been scrambled in the passage.

We think you'll like the English subject test. It can actually be fun, which is probably why the test makers put it first. We'll cover strategies for the English question types in the English Workouts.

MATH

The Math test is 60 minutes long and includes 60 questions. That works out to one minute per question, but you'll want to spend less time on easy questions and more on the tough ones.

THE FORMAT

All of the Math questions have the same basic multiple-choice format. They ask a question and offer five possible choices (unlike questions on the other subject tests, which have only four choices each). Why the Math test has five choices while the other tests have only four is one of those mysteries that only the ACT makers understand.

The questions cover a full range of math topics, from pre-algebra and elementary algebra, to plane geometry and even a little bit of trigonometry. We'll tell you the exact number of questions in each area later, in Math Workout 1. If you have specific weaknesses in any of these areas, the 100 Key Math Concepts for the ACT section at the end of this book will help.

Although the Math questions, like those in other sections, aren't ordered in terms of difficulty, questions drawn from elementary school or junior high tend to come earlier in the section, while those from high school math curricula tend to come later. But this doesn't mean that the easy questions come first and the hardest ones come later. We've found that high school subjects tend to be fresher in most students' minds than things they were taught years ago, so you may actually find the later questions easier. (Do *you* remember the math you learned in seventh grade?)

THE DIRECTIONS

Here's what the Math directions will look like:

Directions: Solve each of the following problems, select the correct answer, and then fill in the corresponding space on your answer sheet.

Don't linger over problems that are too time-consuming. Do as many as you can, then come back to the others in the time you have remaining.

Calculator use is permitted, but some problems can best be solved without a calculator.

Note: Unless otherwise noted, all of the following should be assumed:

1. Illustrative figures are *not* necessarily drawn to scale.
2. All geometric figures lie in a plane.
3. The term *line* indicates a straight line.
4. The term *average* indicates arithmetic mean.

Again, when it comes to directions on the ACT, the golden rule is: ***don't read them on test day!*** You'll already know what they say by the time you take the test.

The Math directions don't really tell you much anyway. Of the four special notes at the end of the Math directions, #2, #3, and #4 almost go without saying. Note #1—that figures are not necessarily drawn to scale—seems pretty scary, but in fact the vast majority of ACT figures are drawn to scale, a fact that, as we'll see, has significant implications for how to guess on geometry questions.

Reading and Drawing Diagrams

We find that about a third of the Math questions either give you a diagram or describe a situation that should be diagrammed. For these questions, the diagrams are crucial.

Example

1. The figure below contains five congruent triangles. The longest side of each triangle is 4 meters long. What is the area of the whole figure?

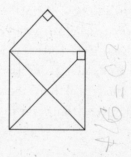

   A.   12.5 square meters
   B.   15 square meters
   C.   20 square meters
   D.   30 square meters
   E.   Cannot be determined from the given information.

Nothing stupefying here. But nothing very substantive either. We'll be a little more specific and strategic than the test makers when we suggest a plan of attack in the three Reading Workouts.

NAILING DOWN THE DETAILS

Specific Detail Questions ask about things stated explicitly in the passage.

Your challenge is to:

1. Find the exact place in the passage where the answer can be found. If the question doesn't give line references to help, you will be glad you marked up the passage (Remember: **A**bbreviating margin notes, **B**racketing key sentences, and **C**ircling key words and phrases).

2. Match the text in the passage with the correct answer (by locating either similar words or antonyms).

Many wrong choices will be designed to trip you up by including details from other parts of the passage or by using the same wording as the passage while distorting the meaning.

Two important points to keep in mind:

1. There is a "best" answer, which means there may be other tempting answers.

2. "Refer to the passage" in the Reading directions means that it's a good idea to look at the text before you try to answer the question.

Example

When we say "Bach" we almost always refer to Johann Sebastian Bach (1685–1750), but in fact the name "Bach" belongs to a whole family of Baroque German musicians . . .

(*7 paragraphs and 950 words omitted*)

The works of Johann Christian Bach, J. S. Bach's son, clearly prefigure the rich musical developments that followed the Baroque period. Thus, it is both surprising and unfortunate that the rest of J. S. Bach's family isn't more well known.

6. According to the author, J. S. Bach is the best-known:

   F.   German Baroque musician.

   G.   member of a musical family.

   H.   organist in German history.

   J.   composer of Lutheran hymns.

7. Johann Christian Bach was:

   A.   born earlier than Johann Sebastian Bach.

   B.   a composer of the "Romantic" school of music.

   C.   a composer whose works are transitional in style.

   D.   well known during his own lifetime.

The answer for question 6 is G. Both the first and last sentences in the passage refer to J. S. Bach as the most famous member of a whole family of musicians. You might think J. S. Bach is the best-known "German Baroque musician" (choice F), but that's not what the passage says, so it's wrong.

The answer for question 7 is C. At the end of the passage, the author says that Johann Christian's work "prefigure[d]" the music that followed the Baroque. Thus, it must have had some Baroque characteristics and some new aspects. In other words, it was transitional.

MAKING AN INFERENCE

We find that **most Reading passages also include a large number of Inference Questions, which require you to make an inference from the passage (to "read between the lines").** They differ somewhat from Specific Detail Questions. For one thing, students usually consider them harder. An example of each can be found below.

Example

EXPERT TUTOR TIP

" Be sure you know what the Reading question is asking. Sometimes you'll need to find what is **not** in the passage or the least likely situation. "

. . . though schizophrenia and multiple personality disorder (M.P.D.) may be related, and are often confused by laymen, the two terms have radically different meanings . . .

32. Which of the following best expresses the relationship between schizophrenia and multiple personality disorder?

    F. They are two terms that describe essentially the same phenomenon.

    G. The two disorders have nothing in common.

    H. Though the two have some similarities, they are fundamentally different.

    J. The two are not exactly alike, but are very close.

33. Suppose that a patient has been diagnosed with schizophrenia. Based on the passage, which of the following is least likely?

    A. The patient's doctors immediately assume that the patient also suffers from M.P.D.

    B. The patient is a layman.

    C. The patient denies that he has M.P.D.

    D. The patient is related to someone with M.P.D.

Note the differences between Specific Detail and Inference Questions: Question 32, a Specific Detail Question, requires that you understand the explicitly stated idea that schizophrenia and M.P.D. have some connection, but are not the same. That's what choice H says. Question 33, on the other hand, requires you to apply the idea that the two disorders are different. If they are, it's highly unlikely that doctors would simply assume that a patient suffering from one disorder must suffer from the other. Therefore, choice A is least likely—and therefore correct. The other choices may or may not be true, and nothing in the passage leads us to think one way or the other about them. Question 33 is what we'd call a garden-variety Inference Question.

GETTING THE BIG PICTURE

Although the majority of Reading questions are Specific Detail and Inference Questions, the Reading subtest also includes another type of question that we call Big Picture Questions. Some Big Picture Questions ask about the passage as a whole, requiring you to find the theme, tone, or structure of the passage. Others ask you to evaluate the writing. Here's a typical Big Picture Question that might have appeared with the Bach family passage we talked about earlier.

Example

9. The author's main point in the passage is to:
   A. show that many of the lesser-known members of the Bach family also influenced music history.
   B. argue that J. C. Bach was actually a greater composer than his father, J. S. Bach.
   C. demonstrate that musical talent always runs in families.
   D. dispute the claim that the Bach family was the best-known family of German Baroque musicians.

In order to answer this kind of question, you've got to have a good sense of the Big Picture—of the shape and flow of the whole passage. Of course, we printed only a few selected lines from the passage, but that should have been enough to lead you to A as the answer. The first line definitely indicates that the subject of the passage is going to be the entire Bach family, with a focus on the ones who aren't as well known as the big cheese, J. S. himself.

SCIENCE

The Science test is 35 minutes long and includes 40 questions. It has seven passages, each with five to seven questions. This breaks down to approximately five minutes per passage.

No, you don't have to be a scientist to succeed on the ACT Science test. You don't have to know the atomic number of cadmium or the preferred mating habits of the monarch butterfly. All that's required is common sense (though a knowledge of standard scientific processes and procedures sure does help). You'll be given passages containing various kinds of scientific information—drawn from the fields of biology, chemistry, physics, geology, astronomy, and meteorology—which you'll have to understand and use as a basis for inferences.

THE FORMAT

On the Science section of the test, the seven passages are broken down as follows:

- Three passages about tables and graphs
- Three passages about experiments
- One passage that presents opposing viewpoints on the same issue

Each passage will generate between five and seven questions. A warning: some passages will be very difficult to understand, but they'll usually make up for that fact by having many easy questions attached to them. The test makers do show some mercy once in a while.

THE DIRECTIONS

Here's what the Science directions will look like:

> **Directions:** There are seven passages in this test. Each passage is followed by several questions. After reading each passage, decide on the best answer to each question and fill in the corresponding oval on your answer sheet. You may refer to the passages as often as necessary. You are NOT permitted to use a calculator on this test.

Sounds a lot like the set of directions for Reading, doesn't it? Not much substance here, either. But don't worry. We'll show you the best strategic way to attack this subject test in the three Science Workouts.

ANALYZING DATA

About two-thirds of the questions on the Science subtest require you to read data from graphs or tables. In easier questions, you need only report the information. In harder questions, you may need to draw inferences or note patterns in the data. For example:

17. Which of the following discoveries would most weaken the theory of V-shaped valley formation given in the passage?

   A. Certain parts of many valleys formed by water that are U-shaped

   B. A group of V-shaped valleys almost certainly formed by wind erosion

   C. A group of U-shaped valleys formed by water erosion in hard rock

   D. A group of valleys on Mars that appear to be V-shaped but that are not near any running water

In question 16, the correct answer is J, since this is consistent with the passage as described. The correct answer in question 17 is B. Finding V-shaped valleys not formed by water erosion would tend to weaken the theory that they are formed this way. The other answers do not offer evidence about V-shaped valleys on Earth, and thus are irrelevant to a theory about them.

We'll be showing you strategies for each kind of Science question in the three Science Workouts.

WRITING

The Writing test is 30 minutes long and includes one essay. You'll be given a topic or issue and expected to take a position on it, supporting your point of view with examples and evidence.

You don't have to be a great creative writer to succeed on the ACT Writing test. Instead, you have to show that you can focus on an issue and argue your point of view in a coherent, direct way with concrete examples. Furthermore, the essay graders are not primarily concerned with your grammar and punctuation skills. In terms of writing, clarity is what they are looking for. You are being tested on your ability to communicate in writing.

One of the biggest challenges of the Writing test is the time frame. With only 30 minutes to read about the issue, plan your response, draft the essay, and proofread it, you have to work quickly and efficiently. Coming up with a plan and sticking to it are key to succeeding on the Writing test.

THE FORMAT

The Writing test consists of one prompt that lays out the issue and gives directions for your response. There are no choices of topic; you have to respond to the topic that's there. Don't worry too much about not knowing anything about the issue you have to write about. Test makers try to craft topics that will be relevant to high school students and about which they can be expected to have a point of view.

THE DIRECTIONS

Here's what the Writing test directions will look like:

> In many high schools, the administration has provided guidelines for the publication of student newspapers. These guidelines often determine which topics can and cannot be discussed in the newspaper and prohibit what the administration deems inappropriate language. Many administrators and teachers feel that these restrictions enable them to provide a safe learning environment for students. Others feel that any restriction on the student newspaper is a violation of freedom of speech. In your opinion, should high schools place restrictions on student newspapers?

> In your essay, take a position on this question. You may write about either one of the two points of view given, or you may present a different point of view on this question. Use specific reasons and examples to support your position.

The first paragraph gives some background on the issue about which you must write. The final paragraph giving directions is always the same. Notice that there are two distinct parts to the assignment: (1) state a position and (2) provide support for your position.

That's not much guidance, is it? But don't worry. In the Writing Workout, we'll show you how to plan and draft a high-scoring essay. You'll learn what the essay readers will be looking for and how to give it to them.

WRITING TEST SKILLS

The readers realize you're writing under time pressure and expect you to make some mistakes. **The content of your essay is not relevant; readers are not checking your facts. Nor will they judge you on your opinions. What they want is to see how well you can communicate a relevant, coherent point of view.**

The test makers identify the following as the skills tested in the Writing test:

- **Stating a clear perspective on an issue.** This means answering the question in the prompt.

- **Providing supporting evidence and logical reasoning.** This means offering relevant support for your opinion, and building an argument based on concrete details and examples.

- **Maintaining focus and organizing ideas logically.** You've got to be organized, avoid digressions, and tie all your ideas together in a sensible way.

- **Writing clearly.** This is the only skill addressing your ability to write directly, and it's limited to clarity.

The Writing test is not principally a test of your grammar and punctuation (which are tested in the English test)—colleges want a chance to see your reasoning and communication skills. To learn more about doing well on the Writing test, review the Writing Workout.

CHAPTER 3: TAKING CONTROL: THE TOP TEN STRATEGIES

IF YOU LEARN ONLY TWO THINGS IN THIS CHAPTER . . .

1. Remember the ACT Mind-set: take control of your test experience.

2. Know the four commandments and the top ten strategies.

Now that you've got some idea of the kind of adversary you face in the ACT, it's time to start developing strategies for dealing with this adversary. In other words, you've got to start developing your ACT Mind-set.

The ACT, as we've just seen, isn't a normal test. A normal test requires that you rely almost exclusively on your memory. On a normal test, you'd see questions like this:

The "golden spike," which joined the Union Pacific and Central Pacific Railroads, was driven in Ogden, Utah, in May 1869. Who was president of the United States at the time?

To answer this question, you have to resort to memory dredging. Either you know the answer is Ulysses S. Grant or else you don't. No matter how hard you think, you'll **never** be able to answer this question if you can't remember your history.

But the ACT doesn't test your long-term memory. The answer to every ACT question can be found in the test. Theoretically, if you read carefully and understand the words and concepts the test uses, you can get almost any ACT question right. Notice the difference between the regular-test question above and the ACT-type question that follows:

EXPERT TUTOR TIP

❝ This chapter will help you to take control of the ACT. You should read this chapter even if you have two weeks or fewer to prep. ❞

Example

1. What is the product of n and m^2, where n is an odd number and m is an even number?

   A.   An odd number

   B.   A multiple of four

   C.   A noninteger

   D.   An irrational number

   E.   The square of an integer

Aside from the obvious difference (this question has answer choices, while the other one does not), there's another difference: the ACT question mostly tests your ability to understand a situation rather than your ability to passively remember a fact. Nobody expects you to know off the top of your head what the product of an odd number and the square of an even number is. But the ACT test makers do expect you to be able to roll up your sleeves and figure it out (as we'll do below).

THE ACT MIND-SET

Most students take the ACT with the same mind-set that they use for normal tests. Their brains are on "memory mode." Students often panic and give up because they can't seem to remember enough. **But you don't need to remember a ton of picky little rules for the ACT. Don't give up on an ACT question just because your memory fails.**

On the ACT, if you understand what a question is really asking on the test, you can **almost** always answer it. For instance, take the Math problem above. You might have been thrown by the way it was phrased. "How can I solve this problem?" you may have asked yourself. "It doesn't even have numbers in it!"

The key here, as in all ACT questions, is taking control. Take the question (by the throat, if necessary) and wrestle it into a form you can understand. Ask yourself: What's really being asked here? What does it mean when they say something like "the product of n and m^2"?

Well, you might start by putting it into words you might use. You might say something like this: "I've got to take one number times another. One of the numbers is odd and the other is an even number squared. Then I've got to see what kind of number I get as an answer." Once you put the question in your own terms like this, it becomes much less intimidating—and much easier to get right. You'll realize that you don't have to do complex algebraic computations with variables. All you have to do is substitute numbers.

So do it! Try picking some easy-to-use numbers. Say that n is 3 (an odd number) and m is 2 (an even number). Then m^2 would be 4, because 2^2 is 4. And $n \times m$ would be 3×4, which is 12—a multiple of four, but not odd, not a noninteger, not an irrational number, and not a perfect square. The only answer that can be right, then, is B.

See what we mean about figuring out the answer creatively rather than passively remembering it? True, there are some things you had to remember here—what even and odd numbers are, how variables and exponents work, and maybe what integers and irrational numbers are. But these are very basic concepts. Most of what you're expected to know on the ACT is like that: basic. (By the way, you'll find such concepts gathered together in the very attractive 100 Key Math Concepts for the ACT section at the end of this book.)

Of course, basic doesn't always mean easy. Many ACT questions are built on basic concepts, but are tough nonetheless. The problem above, for instance, is difficult because it requires some thought to figure out what's being asked. This isn't only true in Math. It's the same for every part of the ACT.

The creative, take-control kind of thinking we call the ACT Mind-set is something you want to bring to virtually every ACT question you encounter. As we'll see, being in the ACT Mind-set means reshaping the test-taking experience so that you are in the driver's seat.

It means:

- Answering questions **if you** want to (by guessing on the impossible questions rather than wasting time on them).

- Answering questions **when you** want to (by skipping tough but "doable" questions and coming back to them after you've gotten all of the easy questions done).

- Answering questions **how you** want to (by using "unofficial" ways of getting correct answers fast).

And that's really what the ACT Mind-set boils down to: Taking control. Being creative. Solving specific problems to get points as quickly and easily as you can.

What follows are the top ten strategies you need to do just that.

TEN STRATEGIES FOR MASTERING THE ACT

1. DO QUESTION TRIAGE

In a hospital emergency room, the triage nurse is the person who evaluates each patient and decides which ones get attention first and which ones should be treated later. You should do the same thing on the ACT.

Practicing triage is one of the most important ways of controlling your test-taking experience. It's a fact that there are some questions on the ACT that most

> **EXPERT TUTOR TIP**
>
> " ACT questions are puzzles to solve, not quizzes for which you must remember the answers. Don't think: "Can I remember?" Think: "Let me figure this thing out!" "

students could **never** answer correctly, no matter how much time or effort they spent on them.

Example

57. If $\sec^2 x = 4$, which of the following could be $\sin x$?

    A.   1.73205

    B.   3.14159

    C. $\sqrt{3}$

    D. $\dfrac{\sqrt{3}}{2}$

    E.   Cannot be determined from the given information.

Clearly, even if you could manage to come up with an answer to this question, it would take some time (if you insist on doing so, refer to the explanation below). But would it be worth the time? We think not.

> **EXPERT TUTOR TIP**
>
> " The key to question triage is to evaluate questions quickly. If you linger over these decisions, you will lose valuable time on test day. "

This question clearly illustrates our point: do question triage on the ACT. The first time you look at a question, make a quick decision about how hard and time-consuming it looks. Then decide whether to answer it now or skip it and do it later.

- If the question looks comprehensible and reasonably doable, do it right away.

- If the question looks tough and time-consuming, but ultimately doable, skip it, circle the question number in your test booklet, and come back to it later.

- If the question looks impossible, forget about it. Guess and move on, **never** to return.

This triage method will ensure you spend the time needed to do all the easy questions before getting bogged down with a tough problem. Remember, every question on a subject test is worth the same number of points. You get no extra credit for test machismo.

Answering easier questions first has another benefit: it gives you confidence to answer harder ones later. Doing problems in the order you choose rather than in the order imposed by the test makers gives you control over the test. Most students don't have time to do all of the problems, so you've got to make sure you do all of the ones you can easily score on!

DO YOU KNOW YOUR TRIG?

Okay, since you're reading this, it's obvious that you want to know the answer to the trig question we just looked at. The answer is D. Here's how we got it:

Example

Isaac Newton was born in 1642 in the hamlet of Woolsthorpe in Lincolnshire, England. But he is more famous as a man of Cambridge, where he studied and taught…

7. Which of the following does the author imply is a fact about Newton's birth?

    A. It occurred in Lincoln, a small hamlet in England.

    B. It took place in a part of England known for raising sheep.

    C. It did not occur in a large metropolitan setting.

    D. It caused Newton to seek his education at Cambridge.

You might expect the right answer to be that Newton was born in a hamlet, or in Woolsthorpe, or in Lincolnshire. But none of those is offered as a choice. Choice A is tempting, but wrong. Newton was born in Lincolnshire, not Lincoln. Choice B is actually true, but it's wrong here. As its name suggests, Woolsthorpe was once known for its wool—which comes from sheep. But the question asks for something implied in the passage.

The correct answer here is C, because a hamlet is a small village. That's not a large metropolitan setting. (It's also a famous play, but that's not among the choices.)

Checking back is especially important in Reading and Science, because the passages leave many people feeling adrift in a sea of details. Often, the wrong answers will be "misplaced details"—details taken from different parts of the passage. They are things that don't answer the question properly but that might sound good to you if you aren't careful. By checking back with the passage, you can avoid choosing such devilishly clever wrong choices.

There's another important lesson here: **Don't pick a choice just because it contains "key words" you remember from the passage.** Many wrong choices, like D in the question above, are distortions—they use the right words but say the wrong things about them. Look for answer choices that contain the same ideas you find in the passage.

One of the best ways to avoid choosing misplaced details and distortions is to check back with the passage.

5. ANSWER THE RIGHT QUESTION

This strategy is a natural extension of the last. As we said, **the ACT test makers often include among the wrong choices for a question the correct answer to a different question.** Under time pressure, it's easy to fall for one of these red herrings, thinking that you know what's being asked for when really you don't.

EXPERT TUTOR TIP

"Researching Reading questions is important because the correct answer directly relates to the passage. Incorrect answers, **even if true,** don't relate well to either the passage OR the question."

Example

7. What is the value of $3x$ if $9x = 5y + 2$ and $y + 4 = 2y - 10$?

     A.   5
     B.   8
     C.   14
     D.   24
     E.   72

To solve this problem, we need to find y first, even though the question asks about x (because x here is given only in terms of y). You could solve the second equation like this:

$$y + 4 = 2y - 10 \qquad \text{given}$$
$$4 = y - 10 \qquad \text{by subtracting } y \text{ from both sides}$$
$$14 = y \qquad \text{by adding 10 to both sides}$$

But choice C, 14, isn't the right answer here, because the question doesn't ask for the value of y—it asks about x. We can use the value of y to find x, however, by plugging the calculated value of y into the first equation:

$$9x = 5y + 2 \qquad \text{given}$$
$$9x = 5(14) + 2 \qquad \text{because } y = 14$$
$$9x = 70 + 2$$
$$9x = 72$$

But E, 72, isn't the answer either, because the question doesn't ask for $9x$. It doesn't ask for x either, so if you picked B, 8, you'd be wrong as well. Remember to refer to the question! The question asks for $3x$. So we need to divide $9x$ by 3:

$$9x = 72 \qquad \text{from above}$$
$$3x = 24 \qquad \text{dividing by 3}$$

Thus, the answer is D.

Always check the question again before choosing your answer. Doing all the right work but then getting the wrong answer can be seriously depressing. So make sure you're answering the right question.

6. LOOK FOR THE HIDDEN ANSWER

On many ACT questions, the right answer is hidden in one way or another. An answer can be hidden by being written in a way that you aren't likely to expect. For example, you might work out a problem and get .5 as your answer, but then find that .5 isn't among the answer choices. Then you notice that one choice reads "$\frac{1}{2}$." Congratulations, Sherlock. You've found the hidden answer.

There's another way the ACT can hide answers. **Many ACT questions have more than one possible right solution, though only one correct answer choice is given. The ACT will hide that answer by offering one of the less obvious possible answers to a question. For example:**

Example

2. If $3x^2 + 5 = 17$, which of the following could be the value of x?

    A.   −3
    B.   −2
    C.   0
    D.   1
    E.   4

You quickly solve this very straightforward problem like so:

$3x^2 + 5 = 17$	given
$3x^2 = 12$	by subtracting 5
$x^2 = 4$	dividing by 3
$x = 2$	taking square root of both sides

Having gotten an answer, you confidently look for it among the choices. But 2 isn't a choice. The explanation? This question has two possible solutions, not just one. The square root of 4 can be either 2 or −2. B is thus the answer.

Keep in mind that though there's only one right answer choice for each question, that right answer may not be the one that occurs to you first. A common mistake is to pick an answer that seems "sort of" like the answer you're looking for even when you know it's wrong. Don't settle for second best. If you don't find your answer, don't assume that you're wrong. Try to think of another right way to answer the question.

7. GUESS INTELLIGENTLY

An unanswered question is always wrong, but even a wild guess may be right. On the ACT, a guess can't hurt you, but it can help. In fact, smart guessing can make a big difference in your score. **Always** guess on every ACT question you can't answer. **Never** leave a question blank.

EXPERT TUTOR TIP

"If you guess blindly, you have one chance in four (or one in five, on the Math) of getting the question right. But if, before guessing, you can eliminate one or two choices as definitely wrong, you can improve those odds."

EXPERT TUTOR TIP

"Get used to the idea of guessing—you don't learn how to do it in school. *Pick one letter and go with it.* Correct guesses will increase your score just as much as the other answers do."

You'll be doing two different kinds of guessing during your two sweeps through any subject test:

- Blind guessing (which you do mostly on questions you deem too hard or time-consuming even to try).

- Considered guessing (which you do mostly on questions that you do some work on, but can't make headway with).

When you guess blindly, you just choose any letter you feel like choosing (many students like to choose B for Bart; few choose H for Homer). When you guess in a considered way, on the other hand, you've usually done enough work on a question to eliminate at least one or two choices. If you can eliminate any choices, you'll up the odds that you'll guess correctly.

Here are some fun facts about guessing: If you were to work on only half of the questions on the ACT but get them all right, then guess blindly on the other half of the questions, you would probably earn a composite ACT score of around 23 (assuming you had a statistically reasonable success rate on your guesses). A 23 would put you in roughly the top quarter of all those who take the ACT. It's a good score. And all you had to do was answer half the questions correctly.

On the other hand, if you were to hurry and finish all the questions, but get only half of them right, you'd probably earn only a 19, which is below average.

How? Why are you better off answering half and getting them all right instead of answering all and getting only half right?

Here's the trick. The student who answers half the questions right and skips the others can still take guesses on the unanswered questions—and odds are this student will have enough correct guesses to move up 4 points, from a 19 to a 23. But the student who answers all the questions and gets half wrong doesn't have the luxury of taking guesses.

In short: **guess if you can't figure out an answer for any question!**

8. Be Careful with the Answer Grid

Your ACT score is based on the answers you select on your answer grid. Even if you work out every question correctly, you'll get a low score if you misgrid your answers. So be careful! Don't disdain the process of filling in those little "bubbles" on the grid. Sure, it's mindless, but under time pressure it's easy to lose control and make mistakes.

It's important to **develop a disciplined strategy for filling in the answer grid.** We find that it's smart to grid the answers in groups rather than one question at a time. What this means is this: as you figure out each question in the test booklet, circle the answer choice you come up with. Then transfer those answers to the answer grid in groups of five or more (until you get close to the end of the section, when you start gridding answers one by one).

Gridding in groups like this cuts down on errors because you can focus on this one task and do it right. It also saves time you'd otherwise spend moving papers around, finding your place, and redirecting your mind. Answering ACT questions takes deep, hard thinking. Filling out answer grids is easy, but you have to be careful, especially if you do a lot of skipping around. Shifting between "hard thinking" and "careful bookkeeping" takes time and effort.

In English, Reading, and Science, the test is divided naturally into groups of questions—the passages. For most students, it makes sense to circle your answers in your test booklet as you work them out. Then, when you're finished with each passage and its questions, grid the answers as a group.

In Math, the strategy has to be different because the Math test isn't broken up into natural groups. Mark your answers in the test booklet and then grid them when you reach the end of each page or two. Since there are usually about five math questions per page, you'll probably be gridding five or ten math answers at a time.

No matter what subject test you're working on, though, if you're near the end of a subject test, start gridding your answers one at a time. You don't want to be caught with ungridded answers when time is called.

During the test, the proctor should warn you when you have about five minutes left on each subject test. But don't depend on proctors! Yes, they're usually nice people, but they can mess up once in a while. **Rely on your own watch.** When there's five minutes left in a subject test, start gridding your answers one by one. With a minute or two left, start filling in everything you've left blank. Remember: even one question left blank could cut your score.

9. USE THE LETTERS OF THE CHOICES TO STAY ON TRACK

One oddity about the ACT is that even-numbered questions have F, G, H, J (and, in Math, K) as answer choices, rather than A, B, C, D (and, again, E in Math). This might be confusing at first, but you can make it work for you. **A common mistake with the answer grid is to accidentally enter an answer one row up or down. On the ACT, that won't happen if you pay attention to the letter in the answer.** If you're looking for an A and you see only F, G, H, J, and K, you'll know you're in the wrong row on the answer grid.

Another advantage of having answers F through K for even-numbered questions is that it makes you less nervous about patterns in the answers. It's common to start worrying if you've picked the same letter twice or three times in a row. Since the questions have different letters, this can't happen on the ACT. Of course, you could pick the first choice (A or F) for several questions in a row.

This shouldn't worry you. It's common for the answers in the same position to be correct three times in a row, and even four times in a row isn't unheard of.

10. Keep Track of Time

During each subject test, you really have to pace yourself. On average, English, Reading, and Science questions should take about 30 seconds each. Math questions should average less than one minute each. Remember to take into account the fact that you'll probably be taking two passes through the questions.

Set your watch to 12:00 at the beginning of each subject test, so it will be easy to check your time. Again, don't rely on proctors, even if they promise that they will dutifully call out the time every 15 minutes. Proctors get distracted once in a while.

For English, Reading, and Science questions, it's useful to check your timing as you grid the answers for each passage. English and Reading passages should take about nine minutes each. Science passages should average about five minutes.

More basic questions should take less time, and harder ones will probably take more. In Math, for instance, you need to go much faster than one per minute during your first sweep. But at the end, you may spend two or three minutes on each of the harder problems you work out.

Take Control

You are the master of the test-taking experience. A common thread in all ten strategies above is: take control. That's Kaplan's ACT Mind-set. Do the questions in the order you want and in the way you want. Don't get bogged down or agonize. Remember, you don't earn points for suffering, but you do earn points for moving on to the next question and getting it right.

The ACT Is Not School

You have spent at least 11 years in school at this point. There, you learned some techniques that won't help you on the ACT. (Want two good examples? "Don't guess on a test" and "If you show your work on math problems, you'll get partial credit.") Many of these school-driven methods don't work well on the ACT. In fact, they work *against* you.

Don't fall into the trap of familiar school habits on ACT test day. Test day is an exciting and stressful event. We strongly suggest that you practice using the ten strategies in this chapter, so that you're rehearsed and confident for test day.

EXPERT TUTOR TIP

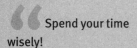

Spend your time wisely!

English: About 30 seconds per question

Reading: About nine minutes on three passages, eight minutes on the fourth one

Science: About five minutes per passage/question set

Math: About 30–60 seconds each, depending on difficulty

Just reading and understanding these strategies before the test doesn't mean you'll remember to do them effectively on test day. These techniques will only work if you use them, so practice!

As you practice, time yourself. Buy or borrow a digital watch, and get used to working with it so it doesn't beep at the wrong moment. Your cell phone will be turned off during the test, so you won't be able to use that as a timekeeper.

Practicing the various sections of the test at home and taking at least one entire Practice Test in one sitting are the best ways to make sure you're comfortable with the test and ready to get your highest scores on test day.

BASIC STRATEGY REFERENCE SHEET

THE FOUR COMMANDMENTS

1. THOU SHALT LEARN THE TEST

- Learn the directions before test day.

- Become familiar with all the subject tests.

- Get a sense of the range of difficulty of the questions.

2. THOU SHALT LEARN THE STRATEGIES

- Develop a plan of attack for each subject test.

- Develop a guessing strategy that works for you.

- Find "unofficial" ways of finding answers fast.

3. THOU SHALT LEARN THE MATERIAL

- Bone up on weak areas.

- Find out what is and isn't part of the ACT knowledge base.

- Use the ACT Resources section to review important Math and English concepts.

4. THOU SHALT PRACTICE, PRACTICE, PRACTICE

THE TOP TEN STRATEGIES

1. Do question triage.
2. Put the material into a form you can understand and use.
3. Ignore irrelevant issues.
4. Check back.

5. Answer the right question.

6. Look for the hidden answer.

7. Guess intelligently.

8. Be careful with the answer grid.

9. Use the letters of the choices to stay on track.

10. Keep track of time.

Part Two

SKILL-BUILDING WORKOUTS

CHAPTER 4: ENGLISH WORKOUT 1: WHEN IN DOUBT, TAKE IT OUT

IF YOU LEARN ONLY THREE THINGS IN THIS CHAPTER . . .

1. Many English questions test redundancy, verbosity, and irrelevance. Start with the shortest answer.

2. When approaching questions, ask yourself, "Do these words belong here? Do these words make sense? Is there an error in grammar here? How does this idea (or these words) sound in context?"

3. Read the passage as far as you find necessary to answer each question, and then answer each one in turn.

Think back to the last paper you had to write. Maybe your teacher assigned something like ten pages. You wrote and you wrote, and ended up with six pages.

It was the night before the paper had to be turned in. You were out of research and ideas. But you knew what to do: pad it.

You're not alone. Almost all of us have padded papers at one time or another. The recipe for padding, in fact, is practically universal: You repeat yourself a few times. You trade short phrases for long-winded verbiage. You add a few offbeat ideas that don't really belong. And presto! Your six-page paper is transformed into a ten-page paper.

The ACT test makers know that most students pad. And they know how to punish you for it. In fact, almost a third of the English questions on the ACT are testing for the very same bad writing habits—long-windedness, repetitiousness, irrelevance— that padders tend to cultivate.

EXPERT TUTOR TIP

The ACT English test includes:

- 10 punctuation questions
- 12 grammar and usage questions
- 18 sentence structure questions
- 12 strategy questions
- 11 organization questions
- 12 style questions

EXPERT TUTOR TIP

If you don't have much time, learn the Kaplan Method for ACT English. Try the practice passage that follows. If you need more help, go back and read the whole chapter.

But there's hope. Once you know what ACT English is testing for, you can easily avoid making these common English mistakes. More than any other part of the exam, the ACT English subject test is predictable.

ANSWERS

1. B
2. F
3. D
4. J
5. B
6. J
7. A
8. F
9. D
10. J
11. A
12. J

The shortest answer happens to be correct in all 12 of the questions above. Note that OMIT, where it is an option, is the shortest answer, since taking the material out leaves a shorter text than leaving anything in. In question 12, answer J is the shortest answer, since it leaves the proposed final sentence off entirely.

REDUNDANCY

In questions 1–4 above, the wrong (long) answers are redundant. This means that they make the passage say the same thing twice. **The ACT is very strict about redundancy: never let the text in a sentence repeat itself.**

VERBOSITY

In questions 5–8, the wrong (long) answers are verbose. They force the reader to read more words, but they are no clearer than the short answers and don't add meaning. **This is another rule the ACT is very strict about: the best way to write something is the shortest way, as long as it doesn't violate any rules of writing mechanics (like grammar or punctuation) or contain vulgarities inappropriate to civilized discourse.**

IRRELEVANCE

Questions 9–12 test relevance. The wrong (long) answers introduce irrelevant concepts. The paragraph is about ACT English questions and how to answer them—it's not about history or science classes, the necessity of taking the ACT, or that lovely translucence of clear water. **Omit the ideas that are not directly and logically tied in with the purpose of the passage.**

EXPERT TUTOR TIP

On recent ACT English sections, the shortest answer has been correct about half the time.

With Economy Questions, the shortest answer is correct with great frequency. What that means is:

- If you're not sure whether an idea is redundant, it probably is, so take it out.

- If you're not sure whether a certain way to say something is too verbose, it probably is, so take it out.

- If you're not sure whether an idea is relevant, it probably isn't, so take it out.

In other words: **when in doubt, take it out.**

KEEP IT SHORT—ON ALL ENGLISH QUESTIONS

Questions in which the lengths of the answers vary greatly, or questions that contain the answer choice OMIT, are usually Economy Questions. For these questions, you should be especially inclined to choose the shortest choice. For the other questions, the shortest answer is not nearly as often correct.

As we'll see in later workouts, the other English questions mostly test your ability to spot nonsense, bad grammar, and bad punctuation. But even in these cases, the rule "when in doubt, take it out" still holds. Most grammatical mistakes can be solved by removing the offending words.

Because these issues of writing economy are so important to English questions of all kinds, we've made them the linchpin for our recommended approach to the English subject test. **When approaching English questions, the very first question you should ask yourself is: "Does this stuff belong here? Can the passage or sentence work without it?"**

READING AS YOU GO

Read the passage as far as you find necessary to answer each question, and then answer each one in turn. *Don't skip over sentences without questions in them*—you'll need to understand the whole passage when you answer the questions at the end.

THE KAPLAN THREE-STEP METHOD FOR ACT ENGLISH

Here's our three-step (or really, three-question) approach to ACT English questions. (Note: Steps 2 and 3 will be covered more thoroughly in English Workouts 2 and 3.)

STEP 1. DO THESE WORDS BELONG HERE?

As we've seen, writing economy is very near to the hearts of ACT test makers. So ask yourself: Does the underlined section belong? Is it expressed as succinctly as possible? If the answer is no, choose the answer that gets rid of the stuff that doesn't belong. If the answer is yes, move on to . . .

Step 2. Do These Words or Sentences Make Sense?

The ACT test makers want simple, easy-to-understand prose. They expect everything to fit together logically. Does the underlined part of the passage make logical sense? If the answer is no, select the choice that turns nonsense into sense. If the answer is yes, go on to…

Step 3. Do I Hear or See an Error?

Many grammar errors will sound wrong to your ear. Even the ones that don't will be recognizable to you if you study our 19 Classic Grammar Errors in English Workout 3 and create a "flag list" of the ones you're shaky on. Choose the answer that corrects the error and makes the sentence sound right.

Most ACT English test takers are so worried about grammar and punctuation that they don't think about anything else. That's the wrong mind-set. Don't think too much about technical rules. As indicated in the approach above, the first thing to think about is getting rid of unnecessary or irrelevant words. Only after you've decided that the underlined selection is concise and relevant do you go on to Steps 2 and 3. Note that this means you won't necessarily be going through all three steps on any English question. The answer can come at any point in the three-step method.

PRACTICE BEING ECONOMICAL

Now try the next practice passage, keeping in mind the approach you just learned:

Example

The Phoenix Cardinals are the oldest, most long-

established, longest-playing football club in the
¹

National Football League (NFL). They began as the

Racine Avenue Cardinals on Chicago's South Side

sometime in the 1870s or 1880s, during the nineteenth
²

century. At that time, the Cardinals were an amateur
²

team that did not play for money.
³

There was nothing in the world which so much as
⁴

resembled pro football in those days. The Racine
⁴

Avenue Cardinals played amateur ball all through the

late 1800s and the game they played was football, no
⁵

doubt about it.
⁵

1. A. NO CHANGE
    B. oldest
    C. most long-established
    D. longest-playing

2. F. NO CHANGE
    G. 1880s.
    H. the nineteenth century.
    J. during the 1880s.

3. A. NO CHANGE
    B. that played for the pure joy of the sport.
    C. that played on a nonprofessional level.
    D. OMIT the underlined portion and end the sentence with a period.

4. F. NO CHANGE
    G. nothing anything like
    H. no such thing as
    J. not even a dream of

5. A. NO CHANGE
    B. no doubt about it.
    C. to be assured it was football.
    D. OMIT the underlined portion and end the sentence with a period.

ANSWERS

1. B
2. G
3. D
4. H
5. D
6. G
7. C
8. J
9. A
10. J
11. C
12. J
13. D
14. G
15. D

Did you see the point? On every regular format question except number 11, you shouldn't have gotten past the first step of the three-step method, because all of the questions test economy errors. In fact, the shortest answers are correct on every question here except that one. In 11, if you omit the phrase "is the place in which," the sentence doesn't make any sense, meaning that you'd correct it in Step 2 of the three-step approach. (Note: This passage is not typical—most ACT passages don't consist exclusively of Economy Questions—but we used this passage to drive home the point about choosing concise answers on the English subject test.)

Many students might object to answer J in question 10, because the word *successful* alone does not indicate the kind of success meant. But use common sense. What would make a professional football team successful? Winning and making money. Thus, the concepts of "winning" and "profitability" are implicit in the notion that the Cardinals are (now) a successful team. **The ACT expects you to cut anything that isn't absolutely needed.**

EXPERT TUTOR TIP

" Remember that OMIT is **always** the shortest answer. For instance, D is "shorter" than A and B in question 15 because not including a new paragraph makes the passage shorter than including it. "

CHAPTER 5: MATH WORKOUT 1: THE END JUSTIFIES THE MEANS

IF YOU LEARN ONLY FOUR THINGS IN THIS CHAPTER . . .

1. Look for the quickest ways to solve problems. Sometimes this requires creative thinking.

2. Use the answer choices to help you. If you are stuck, can you plug numbers in for the variables or use the numbers in the answer choices to get to the correct answer?

3. Follow Kaplan's Two-Pass Plan: skip problems that are more difficult, and come back to them after you've finished the easy ones.

4. Practice with your calculator so you are comfortable using it—and understand when it is faster not to use it.

Your goal on the Math subject test is to get as many correct answers as you can in 60 minutes. It doesn't matter what you do (short of cheating, naturally) to get those correct answers.

You don't have to do every problem the way your math teacher would. **Be open to clever and original solution methods.** All that matters is that your methods be quick and that they get you a solid number of correct answers. How many correct answers you need depends on what kind of score you're aiming for, but chances are you don't have to get so many right as you might think to get a good score. Yes, it's a tough test, but it's graded "on a curve."

As we've pointed out, the ACT is different from the typical high school test. On a typical high school math test, you get a series of problems just like the ones you've been doing in class. Since you're being tested on a relatively narrow scope of topics, you're expected to get almost every question right.

EXPERT TUTOR TIP

" Here's how to use this chapter if you don't have much time. Learn the Kaplan Method for ACT Math, trying the sample questions that follow. Read the sidebars throughout the whole chapter for quick ACT strategy tips. "

ACT Math is different. The scope of what's tested is deliberately wide so that every student will get an opportunity to demonstrate his or her strengths, wherever they may lie.

The average ACT student gets fewer than half of the Math questions right. **You need only about 40 correct answers to get your Math score over 25—just two right out of every three questions gets you a great score!**

THE ACT MATH MIND-SET

According to an old legend at MIT, a physics professor once asked the following question on a final exam: *How could a barometer be used to determine the height of a tower?*

To answer the question, most students worked out complex equations based on the fact that air pressure (which is what a barometer measures) decreases at higher altitudes. But one student made three suggestions instead:

1. Measure the length of the barometer, then use the barometer as a ruler and measure the tower.
2. Drop the barometer and time its fall, keeping in mind that the acceleration of falling objects is about 32 ft/sec^2.
3. Find the person who built the tower and say, "I'll give you a nice barometer if you tell me how tall your tower is."

Guess which student got an A . . .

On the ACT, as in college and beyond, you'll sometimes be called upon to do more than merely regurgitate memorized facts and unquestioningly follow prepackaged procedures. True, some ACT Math questions are straightforward: as soon as you understand what the question's asking, you know what to do. But more challenging—and more fun (really)—are the ACT Math questions that aren't what they seem at first glance. These are the questions that call for creative solutions.

DON'T BE OBEDIENT

On the ACT, there's no partial credit. All that matters is the right answer. It makes no difference how you find it. In fact, as we'll see, it's sometimes safer and faster if you don't do ACT problems the "right" way—the way you've been taught in school. For a lot of ACT Math problems there's more than one way to find the answer. And many of these other ways are faster than the so-called right way.

It seems that when you convert $\frac{4}{11}$ to a decimal, there are at least 50 digits after the decimal point. The question asks for the 50th. One way to answer this question would be to divide 11 into 4, carrying the division out to 50 decimal places. That method would work, but it would take forever. It's not worth spending that much time on one question.

No ACT Math question should take more than a minute to take care of, if you know what you're doing. There has to be a faster way to solve this problem. There must be some kind of pattern you can take advantage of. And what kind of pattern might there be with a decimal? How about a *repeating* decimal?!

In fact, that's exactly what you have here. The decimal equivalent of $\frac{4}{11}$ is a repeating decimal: $\frac{4}{11} = .3636363636\ldots$

The 1st, 3rd, 5th, 7th, and 9th digits are each 3. The 2nd, 4th, 6th, 8th, and 10th digits are each 6. Put simply, odd-numbered digits are 3s and even-numbered digits are 6s. The 50th digit is an even-numbered digit, so it's a 6 and the answer is E.

What looked at first glance like a "fractions and decimals" problem turned out to be something of an "odds and evens" problem. If you don't use creative shortcuts on problems like this one, you'll get bogged down, you'll run out of time, and you won't get a lot of correct answers.

Question 3 demonstrates how the ACT designs problems to reward clever thinking and to punish students who blindly "go through the motions." But how do you get yourself into a creative mind-set on the Math test? For one thing, you have to take the time to understand each problem you decide to work on. Most students are so nervous about time that they skim each math problem and almost immediately start computing with their pencils. But that's the wrong way of thinking. **Sometimes you have to *take* time to *save* time.** A few extra moments spent understanding a math problem can save many extra moments of computation or other drudgery.

THE KAPLAN THREE-STEP METHOD FOR ACT MATH

At Kaplan, we've developed this take-time-to-save-time philosophy into a three-step method for ACT Math problems. The approach is designed to help you find the fast, inventive solutions that the ACT rewards. The steps are:

STEP 1: UNDERSTAND

Focus first on the question stem (the part before the answer choices) and make sure you understand the problem. Sometimes you'll want to read the stem twice or rephrase it in a way you can better understand. Think to yourself: "What kind

> **EXPERT TUTOR TIP**
>
> " Don't rely on your calculator for every operation. It's there to supplement your skills, not to replace them. "

> **EXPERT TUTOR TIP**
>
> " Underlining what the question is asking will help you to make sure you choose the correct answer. "

of problem is this? What am I looking for? What am I given?" Don't pay too much attention to the answer choices yet, though you may want to give them a quick glance just to see what form they're in.

To understand an ACT Math problem, you first have to understand the language. Mathematicians are generally very precise in their use of language. They choose their words carefully and mean exactly what they say.

In everyday life we can be a little loose with math terminology. It doesn't really matter that Harvard Square is not a square or that a batting average is not an average.

In an ACT Math problem, however, words have precise meanings. You don't need to memorize definitions (you'll **never** have to recite one on the ACT) but you do need to understand what the question writer means.

> **EXPERT TUTOR TIP**
>
> " Examine the diagram if you are given one, or make your own. "

STEP 2: ANALYZE

Think for a moment and decide on a plan of attack. Don't start crunching numbers until you've given the problem a little thought. There are three ways to solve the problem:

1. **Use your math skills.** If you know what to do, go for it!
2. **Picking numbers.** Are there variables in the answer choices that you can pick numbers for?
3. **Back-solving.** Are there numbers in the answer choices that you can use to figure out which one has to be the correct answer?

STEP 3. SELECT

Once you get an answer, check the answer choices. If your answer matches one of the answer choices, double-check that it answered what the question was asking, and then circle the answer in your test book and fill in the answer grid.

If you are stuck: skip the problem on the first pass through the test. Go get all your "easy" points first! When you come back, if you still don't know how to approach the problem, try guessing strategically. In other words, are there any answer choices that you know could not possibly be the answer? Eliminate as many as you can before you choose an answer. Each answer choice you eliminate gets you one step closer to the correct answer!

Each of these steps can happen in a matter of seconds. And it may not **always** be clear when you've finished with one step and moved on to the next. Sometimes you'll know how to attack a problem the instant you read and understand it.

USING THE KAPLAN METHOD

Here's how the Three-Step Method could be applied to Question 3 above.

STEP 1: UNDERSTAND

First, we made sure we understood what the problem was asking for: the 50th digit after the decimal point in the decimal equivalent of the fraction. Because we knew what digit and decimal equivalent mean, it took only a second to understand what the problem was asking.

STEP 2: ANALYZE

Second, and most crucially, we analyzed the situation and thought about a plan of attack before we tried to solve the problem. We realized that the "obvious" method would take too long, so we figured out a creative approach that got us an answer of 6 in just a few seconds.

STEP 3: SELECT

Third, we looked at the answer choices, found 6, and selected choice E.

The Three-Step Method isn't a rigid procedure; it's a set of guidelines that will keep you on track, moving quickly, and evading pitfalls.

Example

4. If the sum of five consecutive even integers is equal to their product, what is the greatest of the five integers?

    F.   4
    G.   10
    H.   14
    J.   16
    K.   20

STEP 1: UNDERSTAND

Before you can begin to solve this problem, you have to figure out what it's asking, and to do that you need to know the meanings of *sum, product, consecutive, even,* and *integer.* Put the question stem into words you can understand. What the question stem is really saying here is that when you add up these five consecutive even integers you get the same thing as when you multiply them.

STEP 2: ANALYZE

How are we going to figure out what these five numbers are? We could set up an equation:

$$x + (x-2) + (x-4) + (x-6) + (x-8) = x(x-2)(x-4)(x-6)(x-8)$$

EXPERT TUTOR TIP

" If you don't have any idea how to solve this problem, ask yourself, "Can I pick numbers? Can I back-solve?" There are numbers in the answer choices, so you should back-solve. "

But there's no way you'll have time to solve an equation like this! So don't even try. Come up with a better way.

Let's stop and think logically about this one for a moment. When we think about sums and products, it's natural to think mostly of positive integers. With positive integers, we would generally expect the product to be *greater* than the sum.

But what about negative integers? Hmm. Well, the sum of five negatives is negative, and the product of five negatives is also negative, and generally the product will be "more negative" than the sum, so with negative integers the product will be less than the sum.

So when will the product and sum be the same? How about right at the boundary of positive and negative—that is, around 0? The five consecutive even integers with equal product and sum are: -4, -2, 0, 2, and 4.

$$(-4) \times (-2) \times 0 \times 2 \times 4 = (-4) + (-2) + 0 + 2 + 4$$

The product and sum are both 0. Ha! We've done it!

How to back-solve: The question asks about which is the greatest of the integers, so you start with the greatest answer choice: K. If the largest number is 20, than the other numbers must be 18, 16, 14, 12. Their sum is $20 + 18 + 16 + 14 + 12 = 80$. 20 times 18 is already 360, so we know that K is not correct, and that it is WAY too big! Let's try choice H (14). We want to add: $14 + 12 + 10 + 8 + 6 = 50$. Still too big, because 10 times 6 is already 60. So let's try 4, choice F. $4 + 2 + 0 + (-2) + (-4) = 4 \times 2 \times 0 \times (-2) \times (-4) = 0$. It works!

Step 3: Select

The question asks for the greatest of the five integers, which is 4, choice F.

You've probably encountered every math term that appears on the ACT sometime in your high school math career, but you may not remember exactly what every one of them means. The Math Glossary in the ACT Resources section of your online syllabus is a complete but compact list of the terminology you need for ACT Math problems. Look it over. Jot down the ones you're not sure of for future reference. And be sure to use the Glossary to look up any unfamiliar term you encounter while practicing with ACT Math questions.

Definition Alert

As you refresh your memory of key terminology, watch out for technicalities. Here are a few examples of such technicalities (by the way, these are great for stumping your know-it-all friends):

- *"Integers" include 0 and negative whole numbers.* If a question says "x and y are integers," it's not ruling out numbers like 0 and −1.

- *"Evens and odds" include 0 and negative whole numbers.* Zero and −2 are even numbers; −1 is an odd number.

- *"Prime numbers" do not include 1.* The technical definition of a prime number is: "a positive integer with exactly two distinct positive integer factors." Two is prime because it has exactly two positive factors: 1 and 2. Four is not prime because it has three positive factors (1, 2, and 4)—too many! And 1 is not prime because it has only one positive factor (1)—too few!

- *"Remainders" are integers.* If a question asks for the remainder when 15 is divided by 2, don't say "15 divided by 2 is 7.5, so the remainder is .5." What you should say is: "15 divided by 2 is 7 with a remainder of 1."

- *The $\sqrt{}$ symbol represents the positive square root only.* The equation $x^2 = 9$ has two solutions: 3 and −3. But when you see $\sqrt{9}$, it means positive 3 only.

- *"Rectangles" include squares.* The definition of a rectangle is a four-sided figure with four right angles. It doesn't matter if the length and width are the same or not—if it has four right angles, it's a rectangle. When a question refers to "rectangle ABCD," it's not ruling out a square.

Example

5. What is the value of $x^2 + 3x - 9$ when $x = -3$?

   A.   −27
   B.   −9
   C.   −6
   D.   0
   E.   9

STEP 1: UNDERSTAND

You've probably seen dozens of problems just like this. If so, then you realize right away that what it's asking is, "What do you get when you plug $x = -3$ into $x^2 + 3x - 9$?"

STEP 2: ANALYZE

So that's what you do—plug it in and "solve":

$$x^2 + 3x - 9 = (-3)^2 + 3(-3) - 9$$
$$= 9 + (-9) - 9$$
$$= -9$$

> **EXPERT TUTOR TIP**
>
> " Whenever plugging negative numbers into your calculator, always make sure to put them in parentheses. Not using them will lead to a wrong answer! "

STEP 3: SELECT

The answer is B.

So this is a case where you knew exactly what to do as soon as you understood what the question was asking. Sometimes you're not so lucky. Let's look at a case where the method of solution is not so obvious, even after you "understand" the stem:

Example

6. What is the greatest of the numbers $1^{50}, 50^1, 2^{25}, 25^2, 4^{10}$?

    F. 1^{50}
    G. 50^1
    H. 2^{25}
    J. 25^2
    K. 4^{10}

STEP 1: UNDERSTAND

It's not hard to figure out what the question is asking: which of five numbers is the greatest? But the five numbers are all written as powers, some of which we don't have time to calculate. Yikes! How are we going to compare them?

STEP 2: ANALYZE

If all the powers had the same base or the same exponent, or if they could all be rewritten with a common base or exponent, we could compare all five at once. As it is, though, we should take two at a time.

Compare 1^{50} and 50^1 to start: $1^{50} = 1$, while $50^1 = 50$, so there's no way choice F could be the biggest.

Next, compare 50^1 and 2^{25}. We don't have time to calculate 2^{25}, but we can see that it doesn't take anywhere near 25 factors of 2 to get over 50. In fact, 2^6 is 64, already more than 50, so 2^{25} is much more than 50. That eliminates G.

Choice J, 25^2, doesn't take too long to calculate: $25 \times 25 = 625$. How does that compare to 2^{25}? Once again, with a little thought, we realize that it doesn't take 25 factors of 2 to get over 625. That eliminates J.

The last comparison is easy because choice K, 4^{10}, can be rewritten as $(2^2)^{10} = 2^{20}$, in that form clearly less than 2^{25}. That eliminates K.

STEP 3: SELECT

So the answer is H.

EXPERT TUTOR TIP

" Use your calculator to fly right through example 6. If you don't use a calculator all the time in school, start practicing so you are familiar with it by test day. "

KNOW WHEN TO SKIP

At any time during the three-step process, you could choose to cut bait and skip the question. **Almost everyone should skip at least some questions the first time through.**

If you know your own strengths and weaknesses, you can sometimes choose to skip a question while still in Step 1: "Understand." For example, suppose you **never** studied trigonometry. Maybe you think that a secant is something that sailors sing while climbing up the yardarms. Well, the ACT includes exactly four trigonometry questions, and it's not hard to spot them. Why waste a second on such a question? Skip it! You don't need those four measly questions to get a great score. And since you know a second visit later won't help any, you might as well go ahead and make some random guesses.

It can be harder to decide when to skip a question if you understand it, but then get stuck in Step 2: "Analyze." Suppose you just don't see how to solve it. Don't give up too quickly. Sometimes it takes 30 seconds or so before you see the light. But don't get bogged down either. **Never** spend more than a minute on a question the first time through the section. No single question is worth it. Be prepared to leave a question and come back to it later. Often, on the second try, you'll see something you didn't see before. That old lightbulb will light up over your head and you'll be on your way.

Of course, eventually you're going to grid in an answer choice for every question, even the ones you don't understand. **The first time through the section, however, you should concentrate on the questions you understand.**

KAPLAN'S TWO-PASS PLAN FOR ACT MATH

We recommend that you plan two "passes" through the Math test.

- **First Pass:** Examine each problem in order. Do every problem you understand. Don't skip too hastily—sometimes it takes a few seconds of thought to see how to do something—but don't get bogged down. **Never** spend more than a minute on any question in the first pass. This first pass should take about 45 minutes.

- **Second Pass:** Use the last 15 minutes to go back to the questions that stumped you the first time. Sometimes a fresh look is all you need—after going away and then coming back you'll sometimes suddenly see what to do.

Be sure to select an answer for every question, even if it's just a blind guess.

Don't plan on visiting a question a third time; it's inefficient to go back and forth that much. Every time you leave a question and come back to it, you have to

> **EXPERT TUTOR TIP**
>
> " The fastest way to a higher score on the ACT is to get all your easy points first—skip those hard problems, and go back to them later if you have time. "

> **EXPERT TUTOR TIP**
>
> " If you need to take a random guess, guess the same letter for every question you need to guess on throughout the ACT. This will increase your chance of getting some points off of those guesses. "

take at least a few seconds to refamiliarize yourself with the problem. **Always** grid in an answer choice on the second pass—even if it's just a wild guess. At the end of the second pass, every question should be answered.

Don't worry if you don't work on every question in the section. The average ACT test taker gets fewer than half of the problems right. You can score in the top quarter of all ACT test takers if you can do just *half* of the problems on the test, get every single one of them right, and guess blindly on the other half. If you did just *one-third* of the problems and got every one right, then guessed blindly on the other 40 problems, you would still earn an average score.

DON'T MAKE CARELESS MISTAKES

Most students don't worry much about careless errors. Since in school (where you show your work) you can earn partial credit, many students think that careless errors somehow "don't count." Not so on the ACT. There are only so many problems you'll know how to do. Some of the problems will be impossible for you, so you'll make or break your score on the problems you can do. You can't afford to miss one easy problem!

Unless math is a very strong area for you, the best way to maximize your score is to work on the questions you deserve to get correct. Don't worry about getting to every problem (though, of course, you should mark an answer for every problem on your answer grid, even if it's a blind guess).

Even if math is a strong area for you, don't get complacent on easy problems—that causes careless errors. For strong students, the easy problems may be the most challenging. You have to find a way to answer them quickly and accurately in order to have time for the tougher ones. You won't have time for the hard problems unless you save some time on the easy ones.

Here's a question that's not hard to understand but is hard to solve if you don't remember the rules for simplifying and adding radicals:

Example

7. $\dfrac{\sqrt{32} + \sqrt{24}}{\sqrt{8}} = ?$

    A. $\sqrt{7}$

    B. $\sqrt{2} + \sqrt{3}$

    C. $2 + \sqrt{3}$

    D. $\sqrt{2} + 3$

    E.   7

EXPERT TUTOR TIP

This problem can also be solved using a calculator. If you plug this into your calculator, you get 3.73. Then put each of the answer choices into your calculator to see which one matches.

Example

12. Which of the following fractions is greater than 0.68 and less than 0.72?

   A. $\dfrac{5}{9}$

   B. $\dfrac{3}{4}$

   C. $\dfrac{7}{11}$

   D. $\dfrac{2}{3}$

   E. $\dfrac{5}{7}$

Here you have to convert the fractions to decimals and see which one falls in the range of values given in the question. If you're familiar with common decimal/fraction conversions you might know that choice B, $\dfrac{3}{4}$, is equal to 0.75 (too large) and choice D, $\dfrac{2}{3}$, is approximately 0.67 (too small). But you'd still have to check out the other three choices. Your calculator can make short work of this, showing you that choice A, $\dfrac{5}{9}$, equals $0.\overline{55}$, choice C, $\dfrac{7}{11}$, equals $.\overline{63}$, and choice E, $\dfrac{5}{7}$, is approximately 0.71. Only 0.71 falls between 0.68 and 0.72, so E is correct.

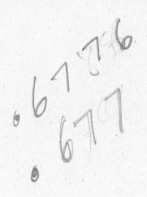

CHAPTER 6: READING WORKOUT 1: KNOW WHERE YOU'RE GOING

IF YOU LEARN ONLY THREE THINGS IN THIS CHAPTER . . .

1. Follow structural clues and content to figure out the overall passage using the ABCs of Active Reading: **A**bbreviate margin notes, **B**racket key sentences, and **C**ircle key words and phrases.

2. Carefully read the question stems (*only*) to determine the type of question being asked.

3. Look for the correct answer in the passage—don't try to answer from memory. Predict an answer, and look for the answer that best matches your prediction.

Reading skills are crucial on every part of the ACT, not just on the Reading test. Savvy ACT-style reading is certainly useful for the English and Science tests, and even your work on many of the Math problems will benefit from the skills discussed below. So don't ignore the Reading Workouts, even if you think you're an ace reader.

The kind of reading rewarded by the ACT is special. You probably know how to do it already, but you may be reluctant to do it on a standardized test. You may think that success on a test like this requires that you read very slowly and deliberately, making sure you remember everything. Well, we at Kaplan have found that this kind of reading won't work on the ACT. In fact, it is a sure way to run out of time halfway through the Reading test.

THE KEY TO ACTIVE ACT READING

The real key to ACT Reading is to read quickly but actively, getting a sense of the gist or "main idea" of the passage and seeing how everything fits together to support that main idea. You should constantly try to think ahead. Look for the general outline of the passage—determine how it's structured. Don't worry about the details. You'll come back for those later.

Fast, active reading, of course, requires a little more mental energy than slow, passive reading. But it pays off. Those who dwell on details—who passively let the passage reveal itself at its own pace—are sure to run out of time. Don't be that kind of reader! Make the passage reveal itself to you on your schedule, by skimming the passage with an eye to structure rather than detail. Look for key words that tell you what the author is doing so that you can save yourself time. For instance, read examples very quickly, just glancing over the words. When an author says "for example," you know that what follows is an example of a general point. Do you need to understand that specific example? Maybe, maybe not. If you do, you can come back and read the verbiage when you're attacking the questions. You'll know exactly where the author gave an example of general point *x* (or whatever). If you *don't* need to know the example for any of the questions, great! You haven't wasted much time on something that won't get you a point.

You actually do this kind of "reading" all the time, and not just when you're reading a book or newspaper. When you watch TV or see a movie, for instance, you can often figure out much of what's going to happen in advance. You see the bad guys run out of a bank with bags of money in their hands, and you can guess that the next thing they'll do is get into a car and drive away in excess of the speed limit. You see a character in an old sitcom bragging to his friends about how great a driver he is, and you know that he's bound to get into a fender bender before the next commercial. **This ability to know where something is going is very valuable. Use it on the ACT.**

To help you know where an author is going, pay careful attention to "structural clues." Words like *but, nevertheless,* and *moreover* help you get a sense of where a piece of writing is going. Look for signal phrases (like *clearly, as a result,* or *no one can deny that*) to determine the logic of the passage. The details, remember, you can come back for later, when you're doing the questions. **What's important in reading the passage is getting a sense of how those details fit together to express the point or points of the passage.**

PRACTICE KNOWING WHERE YOU'RE GOING

In the following exercise, try to fill in the word or phrase that should come next. For most, there are many possible answers, so don't worry about getting the "right" answer.

1. You'd think that the recipe for a strawberry soufflé would be complicated, but my friend's version was _____.

EXPERT TUTOR TIP

The ACT Reading test includes:

- One Prose Fiction passage with ten questions
- One Humanities passage with ten questions
- One Social Sciences passage with ten questions
- One Natural Sciences passage with ten questions

EXPERT TUTOR TIP

Here's how to use this chapter if you don't have much time. Learn the Kaplan Method for ACT Reading. Try the sample passage that follows. Check your answers. If you need more help, go back and read the whole chapter.

MENTAL NOTE

Read actively, with an eye toward where the author is going. **Don't worry about remembering the details. You can (and should) always refer to them later.**

2. I can't believe my good luck! The one time in my life I buy a lottery ticket, I _____.

3. A parked car burns no fuel and causes no pollution. Once the ignition is turned on, however, _____.

4. As their habitat is destroyed, wild animals _____.

5. The new word-processing program was far easier to use than the old one. Moreover, the accompanying instruction booklet explained the commands in a _____ way.

6. The new word-processing program was far easier to use than the old one. On the other hand, the accompanying instruction booklet explained the commands in a _____ way.

ANSWERS

- In Sentence 1, the active reader would probably complete the sentence by saying that the friend's version was "actually quite simple" or something similar. How do you know what's coming next here? The structural clue *but* tips you off. *But* tells you that a contrast is coming up. You'd think the recipe would be complicated, *BUT* it's "actually quite simple."

- In Sentence 2, on the other hand, there's no real structural clue to help you out, but the *meaning* of the sentence should make clear what's coming up. The speaker here is marveling at his good luck, right? That means that he must have won some money. So a likely completion would be something like: The one time in my life I buy a lottery ticket, I "win the jackpot."

- In Sentence 3, we have another contrast, signaled by the clue *however*. A parked car doesn't burn fuel or pollute. *HOWEVER*, once you turn on the ignition . . . The answer has to be something like "the car starts burning gas and polluting." That's the clear contrast that was anticipated by the structural clue *however*.

- Sentence 4 demonstrates again that you don't need explicit structural clues to stay ahead. Sometimes all you need is common sense. What do you think would happen to animals whose habitat had been destroyed? Would they thrive? Celebrate? Buy a condo in Florida? No, they'd probably "start dying out." They might even "become extinct."

- Sentences 5 and 6 show clearly how you can use an author's language to anticipate what point he or she is going to make next. Here, we have identical sentences, except for one small (but very important) difference. The sentences in #5 include the word *moreover*, indicating continuation or addition of similar information. The blank should be something close to "in a clear and easy-to-understand" way. It makes sense that, "The program was easy to use; moreover, the instructions were easy to understand." The sentences in #6 have an *on the other hand* connection, indicating contrast. So the sentences make sense only if you fill the blank with "a confusing and unclear" way.

CREATE A PASSAGE MAP

The best way to read actively is to take quick notes, marking up the passage as you go. You don't have time to write extensively in the margin, nor do you want to underline too many sentences.

After all, *if you underline everything, nothing stands out on the page*. Your goal is to create flags that wave at you when you are looking for the answers to the questions in the passage.

The fastest way to create your passage map is to follow the ABCs of Active Reading:

> **A**bbreviate margin notes.
>
> **B**racket key sentences.
>
> **C**ircle key words and phrases.

Abbreviate margin notes. Develop your own shorthand notes, such as *opin* (opinion), *contr* (contrast or comparison), *hist* (history), *bio* (early years). You must be able to understand what you've written. Otherwise, the notes won't be helpful.

Bracket key sentences. These may (or may not) be the first and last sentences of a paragraph. You are looking for any sentences that express key themes, conclusions, or opinions (of either the author or of the "characters" in the passage). If you string these bracketed sentences together, you will have highlighted the author's train of thought.

Circle key words and phrases. These are the structural clues or flags (*however, therefore, on one hand... on the other hand*), as well as proper names, dates, key actions, etc.—the signposts of each paragraph. For example, if a passage were about child development, you'd want to circle the key ages discussed in each paragraph. Thus, circling *six months, one year, age two through five* would help you know where to look for the answers to questions about those ages.

THE KAPLAN FIVE-STEP METHOD FOR ACT READING

These steps are tried-and-true. If you learn and practice them, you'll be able to read all four passages successfully and have time to answer all the questions. This is your goal, and when test day rolls around, you'll be glad you've got these steps to follow.

The key to this section is being in control of timing—meaning how much time you spend reading the passage (about three minutes) and answering the questions (an average of 30 seconds per question).

If you divide 40 questions into 35 minutes, you'll see that you have $8\frac{3}{4}$ minutes per passage. As you practice, it will be clear that one or two passages take more (or less) time than the others. So your goal is an average of just under 9 minutes per passage. How do you learn to do this? Practice. Practice. Practice.

For the ACT, however, you have a special purpose: to answer specific multiple-choice questions. And we've found that the best way to do that is initially to read a passage quickly and actively for general understanding, then refer to the passage to answer individual questions. Not everybody should use the exact same strategy, but we find that almost every ACT test taker can succeed by following these basic steps:

1. **Preread the passage.**
2. **Consider the question stem.**
3. **Refer to the passage (before looking at the choices).**
4. **Answer questions in your own words.**
5. **Match your answer with one of the choices.**

For most students, these five tasks should together take up about nine minutes per passage. Less than three of those nine minutes should be spent prereading. The remaining time should be devoted to considering the questions and referring to the passage to check your answers. As we mentioned in the ACT Basics section, you'll probably want to take two sweeps through the questions for each passage, getting the doable ones the first time around, coming back for the harder ones.

STEP 1: PREREAD THE PASSAGE

Prereading means quickly working through the passage before trying to answer the questions. Remember to "know where you're going," anticipating how the parts of the passage fit together. In this preread, the main goals are to:

- Understand the "gist" of the passage (the main idea).
- Create a road map of the passage, using the ABCs of Active Reading: **A**bbreviate margin notes, **B**racket key sentences, and **C**ircle key words.

You may want to underline key points, jot down notes, circle structural clues— whatever it takes to accomplish the two goals above. You may even want to label each paragraph, to fix in your mind how the paragraphs relate to one another and what aspect of the main idea is discussed in each. That could be your road map.

Two important reminders: ***don't*** **read slowly, and** ***don't*** **get bogged down in individual details.** Most of the details in the passage aren't required for answering the questions, so why waste time worrying about them?

STEP 2: CONSIDER THE QUESTION STEM

Approaching the questions requires self-discipline in Reading. Most test takers have an almost irresistible urge to immediately jump to the answer choices to see what "looks okay." That's not a good idea. Don't peek at the answer choices.

> **EXPERT TUTOR TIP**
>
> " The reading questions are not arranged from easy to hard. Make sure you consider each question. Don't spend more than 30 seconds (average) on any one question. "

> **EXPERT TUTOR TIP**
>
> " Mark up the passages! Have a system worked out where you use different symbols to mean different things. For example, circle names, box numbers and dates, underline key sentences, and draw arrows to lists of details. Once you know your system, you can find the facts you are looking for faster. "

Read the question stem to identify what the test maker is asking. Is it about:

A detail (what happened)

The passage as a whole (the Big Idea)

A conclusion (reading between the lines)

A specific word or phrase used in the passage

Analyzing what the question stem is asking is very important because the test maker will offer you answers that don't answer the question at hand. These wrong answers are tempting—but only to someone who hasn't taken time to predict an answer. It is easy to get the right answer—if you know what you are looking for.

In Reading, think about the question stem without looking at the choices. In most questions, you won't be able to remember exactly what the passage said about the matter in question. That's okay. In fact, even if you do think you remember, don't trust your memory. Instead . . .

STEP 3: REFER TO THE PASSAGE

Now's the time when your marked-up passage comes to your aid. You have **A**bbreviated margin notes, **B**racketed key sentences, and **C**ircled key words and phrases—these are all waiting to help you find the answers to ten questions.

In Step 3 these become the flags which catch your eye as you look to the passage for help with answers. This road map is especially helpful when the question doesn't give you any specific line references.

STEP 4: ANSWER THE QUESTION IN YOUR OWN WORDS

It's extremely important in Reading to **make a habit of answering the question in your own words** (based on your checking of the passage) *before* looking at the answer choices. Most students waste enormous amounts of time thinking about answer choices in Reading. If you do that, you'll never finish, and you'll get so confused you'll probably get many questions wrong.

STEP 5: MATCH YOUR ANSWER WITH ONE OF THE CHOICES

When you look at answer choices in Reading, your mental process should be "matching." You've got an answer in your head based on what you've read and rechecked in the passage. You need to match it to one of the answer choices. Avoid trying to see if they "look right." **You don't want to think very hard about the choices if you can help it.** They're intended to confuse you, after all, so don't think about them any more than you absolutely have to.

EXPERT TUTOR TIP

Remember to read around any lines given in the question stem. The answer may be above or below the actual lines cited.

EXPERT TUTOR TIP

Keep track of time. If you can, try to devote only nine minutes to each passage and its questions.

Now practice the Kaplan Method on the full-length ACT passage that follows. We're going to give you added incentive to use it by first showing you the questions *without* answer choices. That way you can't give in to the temptation to look at the choices before you think about the questions. The same questions in ACT style, *with* answer choices, will follow the passage. But try to answer them in "fill-in-the-blank" format first.

Example   **Your Answers**

Questions

1. The description of the near starvation of the oxen (lines 70–74) serves to:

2. According to the passage, the fact that the peasants' individual strips of land were unfenced subdivisions of larger fields required each peasant to:

3. According to the second paragraph (lines 4–31), the fallow part of the arable had to be plowed a total of how many times in any given calendar year?

4. The passage suggests that the practice of peasants owning strips "scattered through the three fields in different parts" (lines 37–38) was instituted in order to:

5. On the basis of the information in the passage, it may be inferred that people in medieval times did not think of sowing hay because:

6. As it is used in line 53, the word *garnered* means:

7. According to the passage, if one of the arable's three great fields were left fallow one year, it would be:

8. Which of the following conclusions is suggested by the fourth paragraph (lines 41–58)?

9. According to the passage, a manor's value might be judged according to the number of its plows because:

10. According to the passage, summer pasture for a manor's geese would be provided:

PASSAGE I

By the tenth century most of northern Europe was divided into farming units known as manors . . .

Line [Almost always a manor comprised four parts:
(5) arable, meadow, waste, and the village area itself.] The arable was of course the land which grew the crops on which the inhabitants of the manor subsisted. To maintain fertility and keep down weeds it was necessary to fallow a part of the cultivated
(10) land each year. It was, therefore, usual (though not universal) to divide the arable into three fields. One such field was planted with winter grain, a second with spring grain, and the third left fallow; the following year, the fallow field would be planted
(15) with winter grain, the field in which winter grain had been raised was planted with spring grain, and the third field left fallow. By following such a rotation, the cycle was completed every three years. [Since the fallow field had to be plowed twice
(20) in the year in order to keep down the weeds, and the others had to be plowed once, work for the plow teams extended almost throughout the year.] Plowing stopped only at times when all hands were needed to bring in the harvest, or when the
(25) soil was too wet to be plowed, or was frozen. The amount of land that could be tilled was fixed fairly definitely by the number of plows and plow teams which the manor could muster; and official documents sometimes estimated the wealth and value
(30) of a manor in terms of the number of plows it possessed.

The three great fields lay open, without fences, but were subdivided into numerous small strips (often one acre in size, i.e., the amount of one
(35) day's plowing) which individual peasants "owned." [The strips belonging to any one individual were scattered through the three fields in different parts, perhaps in order to assure that each peasant would have strips plowed early and late, in fertile
(40) and infertile parts of the arable land.]

Custom severely restricted the individual's rights over his land. The time for plowing and planting was fixed by custom and each peasant

had to conform, since he needed his neighbor's
(45) help to plow his strips and they needed his. Uniform cropping was imperative, since on a given day the village animals were turned into the fields to graze after the harvest had been gathered, and if some individual planted a crop which did
(50) not ripen as early as that of his neighbors, he had no means of defending his field from the hungry animals. If his crop ripened sooner, on the other hand, it could not be garnered without trampling neighboring fields. Moreover, the very idea of
(55) innovation was lacking: men did what custom prescribed, cooperated in the plowing and to some extent in the harvesting, and for many generations did not dream of trying to change.

The meadow was almost as important as the
(60) arable for the economy of the village. Hay from the meadow supported the indispensable draught animals through the winter. The idea that hay might be sown did not occur to men in medieval times; consequently they were compelled to rely
(65) on natural meadows alone. One result was that in many manors shortage of winter fodder for the plow teams was a constant danger. It was common practice to feed oxen on leaves picked from trees, and on straw from the grain harvest; but despite
(70) such supplements the draught animals often nearly starved in winter. In some cases oxen actually had to be carried out from their winter stalls to spring pastures until some of their strength was recovered and plowing could begin. Thus on
(75) many manors meadow land was even more valuable than the arable and was divided into much smaller strips (often the width of a scythe stroke).

The waste provided summer pasture for various animals of the manor: pigs, geese, cattle, and
(80) sheep. The animals of the whole manor normally grazed together under the watchful eyes of some young children or other attendants who could keep them from wandering too far afield, and bring them back to the village at night. The waste
(85) also was the source of wood for fuel and for building purposes, and helped to supplement the food supply with such things as nuts, berries, honey, and rabbits . . .

land use

plowing

indiv. owned parts

harvest

grazing animals

The fourth segment of the manor was the vil-
(90) lage itself, usually located in the center of the
arable near a source of drinking water, and perhaps along a road or path or footpath leading to
the outside world. The cottages of medieval peasants were extremely humble, usually consisting of
(95) a single room, with earthen floor and thatched
roof. Around each cottage normally lay a small
garden in which various vegetables and sometimes
fruit trees were planted. In the village streets
chickens, ducks, and dogs picked up a precarious
(100) living.

From *History of Western Civilization, A Handbook*, Sixth
Edition, copyright ©1986 by William H. McNeill. Reprinted by
permission of the University of Chicago Press.

1. The description of the near starvation of the
   oxen (lines 70–74) serves to:

   A. demonstrate how difficult life on the manor
      was in tenth century northern Europe;
   B. showcase how important work animals
      were to medieval manors.
   C. emphasize how important natural mead-
      ows were to feeding the work animals.
   D. explain why uniform cropping was a
      critical practice that ensured survival on
      the medieval manor.

2. According to the passage, the fact that the
   peasants' individual strips of land were
   unfenced subdivisions of larger fields required
   each peasant to:

   F. follow a fixed planting schedule so as to
      be able to harvest crops at the same time
      as the other peasants.
   G. harvest crops independently of his
      neighbors.
   H. limit the size of strips to what could be
      plowed in a single day.
   J. maintain small garden plots in order to
      provide his family with enough food.

3. According to the second paragraph
   (lines 4–31), the fallow part of the arable had
   to be plowed a total of how many times in any
   given calendar year?

   A. One
   B. Two
   C. Four
   D. Six

4. The passage suggests that the practice of
   peasants owning strips "scattered through the
   three fields in different parts" (lines 37–38)
   was instituted in order to:

   F. divide resources fairly evenly.
   G. preserve the wealth of elite landowners.
   H. protect the three fields from overuse.
   J. force neighbors to work only their own
      lands.

5. On the basis of the information in the passage,
   it may be inferred that people in medieval
   times did not think of sowing hay because:

   A. hay sowing had not been done in the past.
   B. the need for more hay was not great
      enough to warrant the extra work.
   C. northern Europeans did not yet have the
      necessary farming techniques for suc-
      cessful hay cultivation.
   D. the tight schedule of cultivating the ara-
      ble meant that the peasants had no time
      to cultivate extra crops.

6. As it is used in line 53, the word *garnered*
   means:

   F. planted.
   G. watered.
   H. gathered.
   J. plowed.

7. According to the passage, if one of the arable's three great fields were left fallow one year, it would be:

    A. left fallow for two more years in succession.

    B. planted the next year with winter grain only.

    C. planted the next year with spring grain only.

    D. planted with either winter or spring grain the next year.

8. Which of the following conclusions is suggested by the fourth paragraph (lines 41–58)?

    I.   An individual was free to cultivate his own land in any way he wished.

    II. The manor was run according to tradition.

    III. Successful farming required cooperative methods.

    F. I and II only

    G. I and III only

    H. II and III only

    J. I, II, and III

9. According to the passage, a manor's value might be judged according to the number of its plows because:

    A. the more plows a manor had, the less land had to be left fallow.

    B. plows, while not in themselves valuable, symbolized great wealth.

    C. manors with sufficient plows could continue plowing throughout the year.

    D. the number of plows a manor owned determined how much land could be cultivated.

10. According to the passage, summer pasture for a manor's geese would be provided:

    F. next to cottages, within the village.

    G. on the fallow field of the arable.

    H. on the communal ground of the waste.

    J. on the whole of the meadow.

THE LAY OF THE LAND

Well, how'd you do? Did you remember to refer to the passage? You probably found that you had to do a more thorough check for some questions than for others.

This passage, like most nonfiction passages on the ACT, is organized in a fairly logical way around the main idea, which you might have expressed as "the structure and common practices of the medieval manor." Here's one possible road map you might have come up with:

- Paragraph 1 (just a single sentence, really): Intro to the topic of medieval manors (divided, as cited in the first line of next paragraph, into arable, meadow, waste, and village)

- Paragraphs 2, 3, and 4: Discussion of the arable and the practices associated with it

- Paragraph 5: Discussion of the meadow

- Paragraph 6: Discussion of the waste

- Paragraph 7: Discussion of the village

It should be obvious why, in your prereading step, you really need to get some sense of the layout of the passage like this. **Many questions don't contain specific line references to help you locate information, and if you don't have a road map of the passage in your head or on paper, you might get lost.**

Following is a key to the ten questions attached to this passage.

KEY TO PASSAGE I

(Nonfiction—Social Studies)

Answer	Refer to	Type	Comments
1. C	Lines 59–77	Function	The entire paragraph supports this claim.
2. F	Lines 46–52	Detail	"Uniform cropping was imperative . . ."
3. B	Lines 19–21	Detail	Don't confuse fallow with planted fields.
4. F	Lines 36–40	Inference	Every peasant got some fertile and some infertile land—inferably, to be fair to each.
5. A	Lines 54–58, 62–64	Inference	No line reference so you had to have a sense of the structure to find this.
6. H	Lines 52–54	Vocab in Context	Use context. The crop is ripe, and so must be ready to be gathered.
7. B	Lines 14–15	Detail	No line reference; otherwise no problem.

Answer	Refer to	Type	Comments
8. H	Lines 41–58	Inference	I: lines 42–44 say the opposite II: lines 41–46 III: lines 49–54 Statement I is false, so that means F, G, and J are wrong. That means H must be the answer.
9. D	Lines 26–28	Detail	No line reference; number of plows = amount of land.
10. H	Lines 78–80	Detail	Whole paragraph devoted to describing waste.

CHAPTER 7: SCIENCE WORKOUT 1: LOOK FOR PATTERNS

IF YOU LEARN ONLY THREE THINGS IN THIS CHAPTER . . .

1. The information you need is given in the passages—**don't** rely on your outside knowledge of science.

2. Approach Science passages like Reading passages: preread to get the sense of a passage, focus on the question stem, and find the answer in the data or scenario given.

3. When reading graphs and tables, determine what's being represented, the units of measurement, and any patterns or trends.

The Science subject test causes a lot of unnecessary anxiety among ACT takers. Many people get so overwhelmed by the terminology and technicality of the passages that they just give up. What they fail to realize is that **Science is a little like the reverse of Math.** In Math, you'll remember, we said that many of the questions are difficult problems based on elementary principles. In Science, on the other hand, many of the questions are elementary problems based on difficult material. So it's important not to panic if you don't understand the passage in Science. You can often get many of the questions right on a passage, even if you find it virtually incomprehensible!

Many ACT takers also tend to rely too heavily on what they've learned in school when approaching the Science subject test. But as we've said, "remembering" is not the mind-set the ACT will reward. You couldn't possibly know the answers to ACT Science questions in advance: you have to pull them out of the passages. **All the information you need to answer the questions is right on the page.**

EXPERT TUTOR TIP

" The ACT Science test covers biology, chemistry, earth/space sciences, and physics. It includes:

- Three Data Representation passages with five questions each

- Three Experiment passages with six questions each

- One Conflicting Viewpoints passage with seven questions "

EXPERT TUTOR TIP

" Here's how to use this chapter if you don't have much time. Learn the Kaplan Method for ACT Science on the next page. Try the sample passage that follows. Then read the section called Reading Tables and Graphs. "

EXPERT TUTOR TIP

" You will only need to use your knowledge of science on one to three questions on the ACT. The remaining questions will all be based on the information in the passages. "

Worrying about science knowledge can be a problem no matter how good or bad your science background is. Students who have done poorly in science tend to panic because they think they don't know enough. Students who have done well in science might know **too** much. Some questions include wrong choices that are scientifically correct but don't relate to the passages. Choosing such answers will not earn you points on the ACT. So try not to rely primarily on your knowledge of science. Instead, use your ability to refer to the passages.

ACT Science requires many of the same skills that ACT Reading does. The strategies discussed in Reading Workout I will therefore also work well for many Science passages. The most important difference between Reading and Science is that the "details" you have to find in the Science passages almost all relate to numbers or scientific processes, and they are often contained in graphs and tables rather than in paragraph form.

- **Reading graphs, tables, and research summaries.** Many questions involve only accurately retrieving data from a single graph or table. Others involve combining knowledge from two different graphs or tables. Still others involve understanding experimental methods well enough to evaluate information contained in summaries of experiments.

- **Looking for patterns in the numbers that appear.** Do these numbers get bigger or smaller? Where are the highest numbers? the lowest? At what point do the numbers change? A little calculation is sometimes required, but not much. In Science, you won't be computing with numbers so much as thinking about what they mean.

In Science, as in Reading, it's crucial to consider the questions and at least try to answer them before looking at the answer choices. Refer to the passage to find the answer, and try to match it with one of the choices. **Use the process of elimination as a fallback strategy for hard questions—but don't make it your main approach.**

THE KAPLAN FIVE-STEP METHOD FOR ACT SCIENCE

The same Kaplan Method for Reading is also useful in Science. The steps, you'll remember, are:

1. **Preread the passage (one minute).**
2. **Consider each question stem.**
3. **Refer to the passage (before looking at the choices).**
4. **Answer the question in your own words.**
5. **Match your answer with one of the choices.**

In Science, you have seven shorter passages to do instead of the four longer ones in Reading. Each passage should average five minutes. We recommend using just about one minute or so to preread the passage, and then a total of about four minutes to consider the questions and refer to the passage (that's about 40 seconds per question). Notice that this is less time prereading than in the Reading test.

STEP 1: PREREAD THE PASSAGE

It's especially important in Science not to get bogged down in the details (we'll see that this is also critical in the Natural Sciences passage in Reading). Some of the material covered is extremely technical, and you'll just get frustrated trying to understand it completely. So it's crucial that you skim, to get a general idea of what's going on and—just as important—to get a sense of where certain types of data can be found.

Almost all Science passages have the same general structure. They begin with an introduction. **Always** read the introduction first to orient yourself. Some passages relate to material you may have already studied in high school. If you're familiar with the concepts, you may not need to do more than skim the introduction. If not, you'll want to read the introduction more carefully. But remember, don't focus on details. In the introduction, mark the purpose of the experiment. Whether you bracket it, circle it, or put a "P" next to it doesn't really matter. The only important thing is that somehow you note where it is in case a question refers to it. The purpose will answer the question "Why was this experiment performed?"

After reviewing the introduction, quickly scan the rest of the passage. Take note of the method of the experiment(s). The method will answer the question "How was the experiment set up?" How is the information presented? Graphs? Diagrams? Are there experiments? What seems to be important? Size? Shape? Temperature? Speed? Chemical composition? Don't worry about details and don't try to remember it all. Plan to refer to the passage just as you would in Reading.

Example

> Scientists researching the relationship between birds and dinosaurs have chosen to carefully examine three fossils dating from the Jurassic period: an *archaeopteryx* (the oldest known bird) at the British Museum in London, a *compsognathus* (a dinosaur) at the Field Museum in Chicago, and a *teleosaurus* (a crocodile) at the National Museum in Beijing. All three creatures were about the same size as a turkey.

Remember to read actively. Ask yourself: why would the scientists choose these three creatures? Since the scientists are studying birds and dinosaurs, the first two choices seem natural. But why should they include a crocodile? Maybe the National Museum in Beijing had a special deal on crocodile bones? More likely it's because crocodiles are somewhat like dinosaurs, but not extinct.

EXPERT TUTOR TIP

" If you need to know the meaning of a special scientific term, the test will normally define it. If the test doesn't tell you what a word means, you can usually figure it out from the context (or else you won't need to know it). "

As you preread the passage, you also want to make sure you know what any tables and graphs in the passage are meant to represent. Feel free to take notes, mark up the test booklet, or circle important information. Get a sense of what kind of data is contained in each graph and table, but don't read the data carefully yet! You may want to take note of general trends in the data, but don't waste time taking in information that may not be relevant to the questions. **Remember, your goal is to answer questions, *not* to learn and remember everything that goes on in the passage.**

STEP 2: CONSIDER THE QUESTION STEM

Most of your time in Science will be spent considering questions and referring to the passage to find the answers. Here's where you should do most of your really careful reading. **It's essential that you understand exactly what the question is asking.** Then, go back to the passage and get a sense of what the answer should be before looking at the choices.

There are three basic kinds of Science questions:

- **Figure Interpretation Questions.** For these questions, you'll almost certainly be going back to the graphs. They are usually among the easiest on the Science test. Knowing the headings of each figure will help make these questions that much easier.

- **Patterns Questions.** These are usually medium difficulty. You have to look beyond just the data that is presented in the figures to see what the patterns are in the data.

- **Scientific Interpretation Questions.** These questions are usually among the hardest on the test, because they are based on what is in the text versus what is in the figures. Here you must apply a scientific principle or identify ways of defending or attacking a principle. This includes making predictions based on a given theory or showing how a hypothesis might be strengthened or weakened by particular findings. (These questions will be especially important for the Conflicting Viewpoints passage, discussed in Science Workout 3.)

As we mentioned, one possible pitfall in answering the questions is relying too heavily on your own knowledge of science. In answering questions, use your knowledge of scientific *methods* and *procedures*. But don't rely heavily on any knowledge of specific *facts*. For example, the following question might have appeared with the passage excerpted above:

Example

1. The dinosaur studied by the scientists, *compsognathus*, was:

    A.   definitely a reptile.

    B.   definitely a bird.

    C.   about the size of a turkey.

    D.   larger than *archaeopteryx* or *teleosaurus*.

If you know that dinosaurs are usually classified as reptiles, choice A would be very tempting. But it's wrong. The passage doesn't say that. In fact, if we had seen the rest of this passage, we would have learned that the researchers were questioning whether dinosaurs should be classified as reptiles or birds. What the passage *does* say is that all three of the creatures tested are turkey sized, making the correct choice C.

STEP 3: REFER TO THE PASSAGE

As in Reading, you have to be diligent about referring to the passage. Your prereading of the passage should have given you an idea of where particular kinds of data can be found. Sometimes the questions themselves will direct you to the right place.

Be careful not to mix up units when taking information from graphs, tables, and summaries. Don't confuse *decreases* and *increases*: many questions will hinge on whether you can correctly identify the factors that decrease and the ones that increase. The difference between a correct and an incorrect answer will often be a "decrease" where an "increase" should be. Read the questions carefully!

STEP 4: ANSWER THE QUESTION IN YOUR OWN WORDS

The answers to the Science questions are there in the passage. As we mentioned in Step 2 above, don't rely too much on your own knowledge of science. Instead think of paraphrasing the information in the passage.

STEP 5: MATCH YOUR ANSWER WITH ONE OF THE CHOICES

Once you've paraphrased the information and matched it to an answer choice, double-check the question to make sure that you've actually answered the question asked. **Many of the questions in Science are reversal questions. Always look for words like *not* and *except* in the questions.**

READING TABLES AND GRAPHS

Most of the information in ACT Science passages is presented in tables or graphs, usually accompanied by explanatory material. Knowing how to read data from tables and graphs is critical to success on the Science subject test! In order to read most graphs and tables, ask yourself three questions:

- **What does the figure show?**
- **What are the units of measurement?**
- **What is the pattern in the data?**

> **EXPERT TUTOR TIP**
>
> " Reading the question carefully is the most important step. If you miss a little word like *not*, you will get the question wrong. "

> **EXPERT TUTOR TIP**
>
> " If the answer that you want is not there, eliminate answer choices that you know are wrong, and then pick the best answer that remains. "

Let's say you saw the following graph in a Science passage:

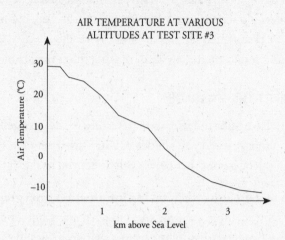

AIR TEMPERATURE AT VARIOUS
ALTITUDES AT TEST SITE #3

- **What does the figure show?** Most graphs and tables have titles that tell you what they represent. For some, though, you may have to get that information from the introduction. Here, the graph is representing how cold or hot the air is at various altitudes above a certain Test Site #3.

- **What are the units of measurement?** Note that distance here is measured in *kilometers*, not miles or feet. Temperature is measured in degrees *Celsius*, not Fahrenheit.

- **What is the pattern in the data?** The "pattern" of the data in this graph is pretty clear. As you rise in altitude, the temperature drops—the higher the altitude, the lower the temperature.

The sloping line on the graph represents the various temperatures measured at the various altitudes. To find what the measured temperature was at, say, 2 km above sea level, find the 2 km point on the *x*-axis and trace your finger directly up from it until it hits the line. It does so at about the level of 3° C. In other words, at an altitude of 2 km above sea level at Test Site #3, the air temperature was about 3° C.

Be careful with units of measurement! Most passages use the metric system, but a few may use traditional or British units of measure. You won't be expected to remember oddball unit conversions like 8 furlongs = 1 mile or 2.54 cm = 1 in, and passages that use special units of measure such as microns or parsecs will define these units if necessary. But don't assume that all the units in the graphs match the units in the questions. For instance, try the following question:

EXPERT TUTOR TIP

" Many students race through the section and do not read the questions carefully. If you just slow down and make sure of what you are being asked, you will find that these problems are not so bad after all. "

Example

2.   At what altitude did the meteorologists measure an air temperature of 10° C?

F.   1.4 m

G.   140 m

H.   1,400 m

J.   14 km

Many test takers solving the problem above would find the point on the line at the level of 10° C on the *y*-axis, trace their fingers down to the *x*-axis, see that the altitude would be about halfway between 1 and 2 (a little closer to 1, maybe), and then quickly choose F. But F is wrong, since F gives you 1.4 *meters*, while the graph figures are given in *kilometers*. Remember to translate the data! A kilometer is 1,000 meters, so 1.4 kilometers would be 1.4 times 1,000 meters = 1,400 meters. That's choice H.

You should follow a similar procedure with tables of information. For instance, in the introduction to the passage in which the following table might have appeared, you would have learned that scientists were trying to determine the effects of two pollutants (Pb and Hg, lead and mercury) on the trout population of a particular river.

Table 1

Location	Water Temperature (°C)	Presence of Pb (parts per million)	Presence of Hg (parts per million)	Population Density of Speckled Trout (# per 100 m³)
1	15.4	0	3	7.9
2	16.1	0	1	3.5
3	16.3	1	67	0
4	15.8	54	3	5.7
5	16.0	2	4	9.5

- **What does the figure show?** Here, each row represents the data from a different numbered location on the river. Each column represents different data: water temperature, presence of the first pollutant, presence of the second pollutant, population of one kind of trout.

- **What are the units of measurement?** Temperature is measured in degrees Celsius. The two pollutants are measured in parts per million (or ppm). The trout populations are measured in average number per 100 cubic meters of river.

- **What is the pattern in the data?** Glancing at the table, it looks like locations where the Hg concentration is high (as in Location 3), the trout population is virtually nonexistent. This would seem to indicate that trout find a high Hg concentration incompatible. But notice the location where the other pollutant is abundant—in Location 4. Here, the trout population seems to be more in line with other locations. That would seem to indicate that this other pollutant—Pb—is NOT quite so detrimental to trout populations (though we'd have to do more studies if it turned out that all of the trout in that location had three eyes).

HOW TABLES AND GRAPHS RELATE

To really understand tables and graphs, it helps to see how the same information can be represented in both. For instance, look at the next table and graph:

Concentration of *E. coli* in Cooling Pool B	
DISTANCE FROM EFFLUENT PIPE 3	1000s OF *E. COLI* PER CENTILITRE
zero m	.4
5 m	5.6
10 m	27.6
15 m	14.0
20 m	7.5

Concentration of *E. coli* in Cooling Pool B

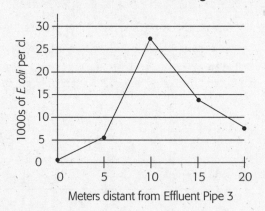

The table and graph above represent the exact same data. And here's yet another way of depicting the same data, in a bar chart:

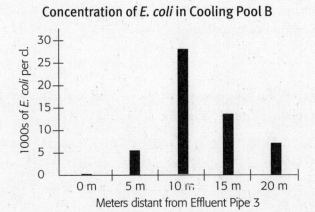

Concentration of *E. coli* in Cooling Pool B

Remember that data can be represented in many different ways. But however it appears in the passage, whether it be in tables, graphs, or charts, you'll have to read and translate it to answer the questions.

Look for Patterns and Trends

When you first examine a graph or table, don't focus on exact numbers. **Look for patterns in the numbers. But don't assume that there is *always* a pattern or trend:** finding that there isn't a pattern is just as important as finding that there is one. When looking for patterns and trends, you should keep three things in mind.

1. Extremes

Extremes—or maximums and minimums—are merely the highest and lowest points that things reach. In tables, the minimums and maximums will be represented by relatively high and low numbers. In graphs, they will be represented by highs and lows on the *x*- and *y*-axes. In bar charts, they will be represented by the tallest and shortest bars.

Look back at Table 1. What location on the river has the maximum concentration of Hg? Of Pb? A glance at the numbers tells you that Location 3—with 67 ppm—represents the maximum for Hg, while Location 4—with 54 ppm—represents the maximum for Pb.

How can taking note of maximums and minimums help you spot patterns in the data? Look again at Table 1. Notice that the maximum concentration of Hg, 67 ppm, just happens to coincide with the *minimum* for trout population—0 per 100 m^3. That's a good indication that there's some cause and effect going on here. Somehow, a maximum of Hg concentration correlates with a minimum of trout population. The obvious (though not airtight) conclusion is that a high concentration of Hg is detrimental to trout populations. And this kind of finding is much more evident when you look at maximums and minimums.

2. CRITICAL POINTS

To find out how critical points can help you evaluate data, take another look at the graph representing the concentration of *E. coli* (a common type of bacterium) in Cooling Pool B.

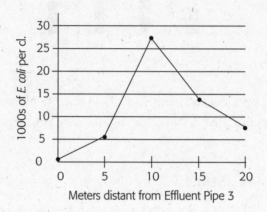

Notice how the concentration is low very near Effluent Pipe 3. From there, it rises until about 10 meters away from the pipe, then it falls again, tapering off as you get farther from the pipe. There's a critical point, then, right around 10 meters from Effluent Pipe 3. Somehow, that vicinity is most conducive to the growth of *E. coli*. As you move closer to or farther away from that point, the concentration falls off. So, in looking to explain the data, you'd want to focus on that location—10 meters from the pipe. What is it about that location that's so special? What makes it the hot new place for *E. coli* to see and be seen?

3. RELATIONSHIPS

Being able to recognize relationships within a figure will lead directly to earning more points on test day. Look at the figure below.

Hours of Sunlight	Air Temperature (Fahrenheit)		
	Chamber 1	Chamber 2	Chamber 3
2	73.23	75.67	78.87
4	71.23	75.79	79.78
6	69.23	74.76	81.34
8	67.23	79.87	82.12
10	65.23	80.65	83.06

What happens in Chamber 1? What do you think the temperature is going to be after 12 hours of sunlight? Do you notice the pattern? The temperature goes down by 2 degrees for every two hours of sunlight. The temperature is going to be 63.23 degrees.

As the number of hours of sunlight increases, what happens to the temperature in Chamber 2? When you look at the data, there doesn't appear to be a relationship! This is a valid answer.

Based on the data, what do you think the temperature will be after one hour of sunlight in Chamber 3? Well, as the number of hours of sunlight increases, the temperature in the chamber increases. So, if you had to predict what would happen after only one hour of sunlight, then according to the table, it is going to be less than 78.87 degrees.

Before you tackle a "real" Science passage, let's review the Kaplan Method for the Science section. Note how similar it is to the steps for the Reading section. However, here you spend only one minute prereading (actively reading) the passage.

THE REAL THING: PRACTICE PASSAGE

Let's take a look at a full-fledged Science passage that requires these skills. Give yourself about seven minutes to do the passage and the questions (on the actual test, you'll want to move a bit faster).

PASSAGE I

Although the effective acceleration due to gravity at the earth's surface is often treated as a constant ($g = 9.80$ m/sec^2) its actual value varies from place to place because of several factors.

First, a body on the surface of any rotating spheroid experiences an effective force perpendicular to the rotational axis and proportional to the speed of rotation. This centrifugal force, which counteracts gravity, varies with latitude, increasing from zero at the poles to a maximum at the equator. In addition, because the earth "bulges" at the equator, a body at equatorial sea level is farther from the center of the earth than is a body at polar sea level. Figure 1 shows the variation of mean values of g at sea level resulting from both effects; the contribution from "bulging" is about half that from rotation.

> **EXPERT TUTOR TIP**
>
> " If the terminology in the passage scares you, just concentrate on the figures to answer the questions. "

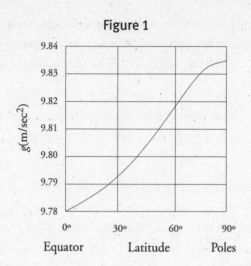

Figure 1

Measurements of *g* also vary depending on local rock density and altitude. Table 1 shows the effect of altitude on *g* at various points above sea level.

Table 1

Altitude above Sea Level (km)	g (m/sec^2)
1	−0.0031
5	−0.0154
10	−0.0309
25	−0.0772
30	−0.1543

Example

3. If the earth's density were uniform, at approximately what latitude would calculations using an estimated value at sea level of $g = 9.80$ m/sec^2 produce the least error?

   A. 0°

   B. 20°

   C. 40°

   D. 80°

4. According to Table 1, what would the change in gravity (in m/s^2) be at 2 km above sea level?

   F. −0.0001

   G. −0.0030

   H. −0.0081

   J. −0.0165

5. Given the information in the passage, which of the following figures most closely approximates the value of g at a point 10 km high along the equator?

    A. 9.75 m/sec^2
    B. 9.80 m/sec^2
    C. 9.81 m/sec^2
    D. 9.87 m/sec^2

6. Suppose that the earth stopped rotating but still "bulged." Based on information from the passage, the value of g at sea level at the equator would be:

    F. exactly 9.80 m/sec^2.
    G. greater than 9.78 m/sec^2.
    H. exactly 9.78 m/sec^2.
    J. less than 9.78 m/sec^2.

7. According to the information in Figure 1, the value of g:

    A. changes by a greater average amount per degree latitude between 30° and 60° than it does near the equator or poles.
    B. changes by a greater average amount per degree latitude near the equator or poles than it does between 30° and 60°.
    C. increases by an average of 5.8 m/sec^2 per degree latitude from the equator to the poles.
    D. decreases by an average of 3.1×10^{-3} m/sec^2 per degree latitude from the equator to the poles.

ANSWERS

3. C
4. J
5. A
6. G
7. A

ANSWERS AND EXPLANATIONS

This was actually a relatively simple, straightforward Science passage, but the terminology may have been intimidating nonetheless. The introduction tells you that the issue here is gravity and how its pull (in other words, the acceleration due to gravity) changes because of several factors. Those factors—and the changes they

TEST TIP

" Remember, you score points by answering the questions right, not by understanding the passages completely. You can get points on a Science passage, even if you don't understand it! "

cause—are represented in Figure 1, which deals with the factor of latitude, and Table 1, which deals with the factor of altitude.

Analyzing Figure 1 as described above, you should have seen that the graph is supposed to show how g (the acceleration due to gravity) is affected by latitude (i.e., north-south location on the globe). The higher the latitude (the greater the distance from the equator), the greater the value of g. As the curves at the beginning and ending of the line in Figure 1 tell you, the increase in g is "slower" near the equator and near the poles.

Notice how you could have answered **question 3** just by understanding Figure 1. Question 3 asks, assuming the earth's density were uniform, "at what latitude would calculations using an estimated value at sea level of $g = 9.80$ m/sec^2 produce the least error?" First, figure out what that question is asking. You remember this question; we mentioned it in ACT Basics. It's simply asking you: where would you get an actual value of g closest to 9.80 m/sec^2? Find 9.80 on the y-axis of the graph, follow across until you intersect with the curved line, and see where you are on the x-axis. That turns out to be about a third of the way from $30°$ to $60°$ latitude. In other words, choice C, $40°$, is the answer.

Question 4 is simply asking you to figure out the pattern in Table 2. To find out what the change in g at 2 km is, you would need to look at the table between 1 km and 5 km. There is only one answer choice that falls between the values of -0.0031 and -0.0154, and that is answer H, -0.0081.

We'll get to **question 5** below.

Question 6 requires more applications of principles and is yet another question that can be answered by simply reading Figure 1. It asks you to suppose that rotation effects (one of the two factors affected by latitude) ceased, but that the earth still bulged at the equator. What would be the value of g? Well, again, rotation tends to "counteract" gravity, so it would have a depressing effect on g. Without rotation, then, g would be less depressed—it would go up, in other words. That means (reading from Figure 1 again) that g at $0°$ latitude (the equator) would, in the absence of rotation, go up from its current value of 9.78. That's why G is correct.

Question 7 (not to get monotonous) is another that can be answered just by a proper reading of Figure 1. It asks you to describe what the graph tells you about the value of g. As we saw, the value rises slowly as you head away from $0°$ latitude (the equator), rises more rapidly in the middle latitudes, and slows down again near $90°$ latitude (the poles). That's best described by choice F. (Choice B gets it backwards—remember to read the choices carefully!) Choices C and D would involve you in some extensive calculations, at the end of which you'd realize that they were not true. But there's no reason to get that far. If you find yourself doing extensive calculation, you should know that you're on the wrong track. ACT Science will involve simple calculation only.

Notice how you could have answered four of the five questions with just a rudimentary grasp of the introduction and an understanding of how to "read" Figure 1 and Table 1.

The other question, **question 5,** requires that you read both Figure 1 and Table 1 properly. It asks for the value of g at the equator (that information comes from Figure 1), but at an altitude of 10 km above sea level (that information comes from Table 1). Figure 1 tells you that the value of g at the equator at sea level would be 9.78 m/sec². But at 10 km above sea level, according to Table 1, g would be slightly lower—0.0309 m/sec² lower, to be precise. So, 9.78 minus 0.0309 would be about 9.75 m/sec². That's choice A.

LOOK FOR PATTERNS

The passage and questions above should convince you of one thing: to do well on Science, you have to be able to read graphs and tables, paying special attention to trends and patterns in the data. Sometimes, that's all you need to do to get most of the points on a passage.

CHAPTER 8: ENGLISH WORKOUT 2: MAKE IT MAKE SENSE

IF YOU LEARN ONLY TWO THINGS IN THIS CHAPTER . . .

1. Consider the meaning of a sentence. If it doesn't make sense, there's probably a grammatical mistake. The correct answer will make sense.

2. Nonstandard-Format Questions ask you to judge the passage and consider it as a whole. You may be asked about paragraph structure and function.

In English Workout 1, we saw that the ACT expects you to use your words efficiently, and that, in fact, the shortest answer is often correct. However, the shortest answer is often wrong. What could make it wrong? It may not mean what it says.

Take this example: "Abraham Lincoln's father was a model of hardworking self-sufficiency. He was born in a log cabin he built with his own hands." Well, that's a cute trick, being born in a cabin you built yourself. Presumably the writer means that Abe was born in a cabin that his father built. But the literal meaning of the example is that the father somehow managed to be born in a cabin that he himself had built.

It's possible, of course, to analyze this example in terms of the rules of apostrophe use and pronoun reference. But that's not practical for the ACT, even for a student who has good grammar skills. There isn't time to carefully analyze every question, consider all the rules involved, and decide on an answer. You have to do 75 English questions in only 45 minutes—that's almost 2 questions per minute.

But there is plenty of time to approach examples like this one in a more pragmatic way. Ask yourself, *Do these words make sense?*

For the ACT, it's important to care. You need to adjust your mind-set. After deciding whether or not the selection in a question is concise and relevant (Step 1 in the

EXPERT TUTOR TIP

In the ACT English section, make sure that what is written is the same as what the writer wanted to say. Choose answers that correct the differences you find.

Three-Step Method), the next step is to make sure that the sentence *says* exactly what it's supposed to mean. If it doesn't, your job is to make it so. In other words, make it make sense.

We at Kaplan have a name for questions that test errors of meaning—**Sense Questions.** Once you get the hang of them, these questions can actually be fun. They're often funny once you see them. The following passage gives examples of the most common kinds of Sense Questions you'll find on the ACT.

Example

PASSAGE 1

Most people—even those who've never read

Daniel Defoe's *Robinson Crusoe*—are familiar with the

strange story of the sailor shipwrecked on a far-flung

Pacific island. Relatively few of them, however, know

that Crusoe's <u>story. It was</u> actually based on the real-life
₁

adventures of a Scottish seaman, Alexander Selkirk.

Selkirk came to the Pacific as a member of a 1703

privateering expedition led by a captain named William

Dampier. During the voyage, Selkirk became

dissatisfied with conditions aboard ship. <u>After a bitter</u>
₂
<u>quarrel with his captain, he put Selkirk ashore</u> on tiny
₂
Mas a Tierra, one of the islands of Juan Fernandez, off

the coast of Chile. Stranded, Selkirk lived there alone—

in much the <u>same manner as</u> Defoe's Crusoe—until
₃
1709, when he was finally rescued by another English

privateer. Upon his return to England, Selkirk found

himself a <u>celebrity, his</u> strange tale had already become
₄
the talk of pubs and coffeehouses throughout the

British Isles. The story even reached the ears of

1. A. NO CHANGE
   B. story: was
   C. story, was
   D. story was

2. F. NO CHANGE
   G. Quarreling with his captain, the boat was put ashore
   H. Having quarreled with his captain, Selkirk was put ashore
   J. Having quarreled with his captain, they put Selkirk ashore

3. A. NO CHANGE
   B. same manner that
   C. identical manner that
   D. identical way as

4. F. NO CHANGE
   G. celebrity, but his
   H. celebrity. His
   J. celebrity his

Richard Steele, who featured it in his periodical,

The Tatler. Eventually, <u>he became</u> the subject of a
5

best-selling book, *A Cruizing Voyage Round the World*, by

Woodes Rogers. <u>And while</u> there is some evidence that
6

Defoe, a journalist, may actually have interviewed

Selkirk personally, most literary historians believe

that it was the reprinting of the Rogers book in 1718

that served as the real stimulus for Defoe's novel.

In *Crusoe*, which <u>has been published</u> in 1719,
7

Defoe took substantial liberties with the Selkirk story.

For example, while Selkirk's presence on the island was

of course <u>known for many people</u> (certainly everyone
8

in the crew that stranded him there), no one in the

novel is aware of Crusoe's survival of the wreck and

presence on the island. Moreover, while Selkirk's exile

lasted just six years, Crusoe's goes on for a much more

dramatic, though less credible, twenty-eight <u>(over four
9

times as long)</u>. But Defoe's most blatant embellishment
9

of the tale is the invention of the character of Friday,

for whom there was no counterpart whatsoever in the

real-life story.

<u>Because</u> of its basis in fact, Robinson Crusoe is
10

often regarded as the first major novel in English

5. A. NO CHANGE
   B. Selkirk became
   C. his became
   D. he becomes

6. F. NO CHANGE
   G. But since
   H. And therefore
   J. OMIT the underlined portion and start
      the sentence with "There."

7. A. NO CHANGE
   B. was published
   C. had been published
   D. will have been published

8. F. NO CHANGE
   G. widely known among people
   H. known about many people
   J. known to many people

9. A. NO CHANGE
   B. (much longer)
   C. (a much longer time, of course)
   D. OMIT the underlined portion.

10. F. NO CHANGE
    G. Despite
    H. Resulting from
    J. As a consequence of

literature. <u>Still popular today, contemporary audiences</u>
                                    11
<u>enjoyed the book as well.</u> In fact, two sequels, in which
                11
Crusoe returns to the island after his rescue, were

eventually <u>published. Though</u> to little acclaim.
                    12
Meanwhile, Selkirk himself never <u>gave a hoot</u>
                                          13
<u>about returning</u> to the island that had made him
      13
famous. Legend has it that he never gave up his

eccentric living habits, spending his last years in a cave

teaching alley cats to dance in his spare time. One

wonders if even Defoe himself could have invented a

more fitting end to the bizarre story of his shipwrecked

sailor.

11. A. NO CHANGE
    B. Still read today, Defoe's contemporaries also enjoyed it.
    C. Viewed by many even then as a classic, the book is still popular to this day.
    D. Much read in its day, modern audiences still find the book compelling.

12. F. NO CHANGE
    G. published, though
    H. published although
    J. published; although

13. A. NO CHANGE
    B. evinced himself as desirous of returning
    C. could whip up a head of steam to return
    D. expressed any desire to return

Items 14–15 ask about the passage as a whole.

---

14. Considering the tone and subject matter of the preceding paragraphs, is the last sentence an appropriate way to end the essay?

    F. Yes, because it is necessary to shed some doubt on Defoe's creativity.
    G. Yes, because the essay is about the relationship between the real Selkirk and Defoe's fictionalized version of him.
    H. No, because there is nothing "bizarre" about Selkirk's story as it is related in the essay.
    J. No, because the focus of the essay is more on Selkirk himself than on Defoe's fictionalized version of him.

15. This essay would be most appropriate as part of a:

    A. scholarly study of eighteenth-century maritime history.
    B. study of the geography of the islands off of Chile.
    C. history of privateering in the Pacific.
    D. popular history of English literature.

ANSWERS

1. D
2. H
3. A
4. H
5. B
6. F
7. B
8. J
9. D
10. G
11. C
12. G
13. D
14. G
15. D

Sense Questions vs. Economy Questions

Most of the time, we don't usually care much if an author isn't clear. We have learned to interpret what the writer meant to say and move on. On the ACT, test takers *must* care and make sure that what is written is the same as what the author meant. Sense Questions may seem harder than the Economy Questions—the shortest answers aren't necessarily right.

Step 1 is all you needed in question numbers 1, 3, 7, 8, 9, 10, and 13. When in doubt, take it out worked for these. As we saw in English Workout 1, questions that include an OMIT option, and those in which some of the answers are much longer than others, are usually testing writing economy.

In the rest of the questions in this passage, the answers differ in other ways. They may join or fragment sentences, rearrange things, or add words that affect the meaning of the sentences. When the answers are all about the same length, as in most of the questions here, the question is more likely to test sense. Consider the shortest answer first, but don't be as quick to select it and move on. Think about the effect each choice has on the meaning of the sentence and pick longer answers if the shortest one doesn't make sense.

Note: Students tend to reject informal writing as "incorrect." But ACT passages are written at various levels of formality. Some are as stiff as textbooks. Others are as casual as a talk with friends. Pay attention to the tone of the words. Are they serious? Are they laid back? Stay with the author's tone. Don't always stay formal.

GRAMMAR RULES AND SENSE QUESTIONS

The ACT test makers include questions like those in Passage I to test many different rules of writing mechanics. Though it's not *necessary* to think about rules to answer the questions, being familiar with them will help. **The more ways to think about a question you have, the more likely you are to find the right answer.**

We'll discuss some of these examples in groups based on what they're designed to test. That way we can briefly discuss the rules, but also show you how the basic strategic approach of "make it make sense" can help you find the answers without a lot of technical analysis. Let's start with **question 1.**

COMPLETENESS

Rule at work: Every sentence must stand alone as a complete thought.

…Relatively few of them, however,

know that Crusoe's <u>story. It was</u> actually
1
based on the real-life adventures of a

Scottish seaman, Alexander Selkirk.

1. A. NO CHANGE
    B. story: was
    C. story, was
    D. story was

If the underlined section for question 1 were left as it is, the second sentence of the passage would be incomplete. It wouldn't make sense. "Relatively few people know that Crusoe's story" what? To make it make sense, you've got to continue the sentence so that it can tell us what it is that few people know about Crusoe's story. The three alternatives all do that, but B introduces a nonsensical colon, while C adds a comma when there's no pause in the sentence. D, however, continues the sentence—adding nothing unnecessary, but making it complete.

When you are testing a sentence for completeness, don't just look to see if it has a subject and verb.

Question 12 tests the same concept:

…In fact, two

sequels, in which Crusoe returns to the

island after his rescue, were eventually

<u>published. Though to</u> little acclaim.
12

12. F. NO CHANGE
     G. published, though
     H. published although
     J. published; although

Here, the fragment should be more obvious, since the clause that's trying to pass itself off as a sentence—"Though to little acclaim"—contains neither a subject nor a verb. That's the technical reason it's wrong, and if you recognized this, great. But on a more intuitive level, it just doesn't make sense to say, as a complete thought: "Though to little acclaim."

Clearly, that fragment has to be connected to the sentence before it, so F and J are wrong, since both would leave the fragment isolated. H goes too far in the other direction, omitting any punctuation at all between the fragment and the main body of the sentence, and that's no good. But the correct choice, G, does just what we need it to do: it connects the fragment logically to the main sentence, but it provides a comma to represent the pause between the two.

SENTENCE STRUCTURE

Rule at work: A sentence can have two thoughts, but they must be combined correctly (see below). If none of the answer choices does this, select the choice that creates two separate sentences.

…Upon his return to England, Selkirk

found himself a <u>celebrity, his</u> strange
4
tale had already become the talk of

pubs and coffeehouses throughout the

British Isles.

4. F. NO CHANGE
   G. celebrity, but his
   H. celebrity. His
   J. celebrity his

Here we have two complete thoughts: (1) Selkirk found himself a celebrity upon his return, and (2) his tale was bandied about the pubs and coffeehouses. You can't just run these two complete thoughts together with a comma, as the underlined portion does. And you certainly can't just run them together *without* a comma or anything else, as choice J does. You can relate the two thoughts with a comma and a linking word (*and*, for instance), but choice G's inclusion of the word *but* makes no sense. It implies a contrast, while the two complete thoughts are actually very similar. Thus, you should create two sentences, one for each thought. That's what correct choice H does.

Rule at work: There are three ways to connect complete thoughts.

1. Use a semicolon.
2. Use a comma with a FANBOY (For, And, Nor, But, Or, Yet, So) conjunction.
3. Make one of the two thoughts *IN*complete (or dependent).

Working with these three possibilities for question 4, you might have seen any of these correct answer choices:

1. …Selkirk found himself a celebrity; his strange tale had already…

2. …Selkirk found himself a celebrity, *for* his strange tale had already…

3. …Selkirk found himself a celebrity *because* his strange tale had already…

MODIFIERS

Question 2 tests modifier problems:

. . . After a bitter quarrel with his captain,
                           2
he put Selkirk ashore on tiny Mas a
                  2
Tierra, one of the islands of Juan

Fernandez . . .

2. F.   NO CHANGE

   G.   Quarreling with his captain, the boat was put ashore

   H.   Having quarreled with his captain, Selkirk was put ashore

   J.   Having quarreled with his captain, they put Selkirk ashore

Rule at work: A modifier, or "describer," is any word, or *group of words*, that describe another. Any and all describers must clearly relate to (be close to) whatever they are referring to.

Sentences become confused if a descriptive word, phrase, or clause is separated from the verb, noun, pronoun, etc. that it should be connected to. In the underlined portion of question 2, the clause "after a bitter quarrel with his captain" should describe the person (or pronoun) that follows next. It doesn't. The *he* who put Selkirk ashore must be the captain, but it can't be the captain who had "a bitter quarrel with his captain." That doesn't make sense (unless the captain quarrels with himself). So put the thing modified next to the thing modifying it. The person who quarreled with his captain was Selkirk—not the boat and not "they," whoever they are—so H is correct.

If you recognized the problem with question 2 as a "misplaced modifier," that's great. Fantastic, even. But you didn't have to know the technicalities to get the right answer here. You just had to make the sentence make sense.

Question 11 tests a similar problem:

. . . Still popular today, contemporary
                          11
audiences enjoyed the book as well.
                  11

11. A.   NO CHANGE

   B.   Still read today, Defoe's contemporaries also enjoyed it.

   C.   Viewed by many even then as a classic, the book is still popular to this day.

   D.   Much read in its day, modern audiences still find the book compelling.

The way the sentence is written, it basically means that contemporary audiences are "still popular today." That doesn't make sense. The *intended* meaning is that the *book* is still popular today, as it was then. Choice C fixes the sense problem by putting its modifier—"viewed by many even then as a classic"—next to the thing it modifies—"the book." Notice that the other choices all misplace their modifiers in the same way, making them modify "Defoe's contemporaries" (in B) and "modern audiences" (in D).

As a rule of thumb, you should **always** make sure that modifiers are as close as possible to the things they describe.

IDIOM (ACCEPTED WORD FORM AND CHOICE)

Rule at work: The correct preposition can vary depending on the sense of the sentence. Many other phrases in English are correct because people have agreed to use them in a certain way. No overall rules apply. To master these, listen to what sounds right, or if English is not your native language, remember them one by one.

Question 3 tests idiom, or unusual but accepted uses of English words. Many words have special rules.

. . . Stranded, Selkirk lived there alone—

in much the <u>same manner as</u> Defoe's
                          3
Crusoe—until 1709, when he was

finally rescued by another . . .

3. A. NO CHANGE
    B. same manner that
    C. identical manner that
    D. identical way as

The sentence as written actually makes sense. Selkirk lived in "much the same manner as" Defoe's Crusoe. The idiom "much the same" calls for as to complete the comparison between Selkirk's and Crusoe's ways of life. Note how B and C would create completeness problems—in much the same (or identical) manner as Defoe's Crusoe what? Choice D, meanwhile, sounds strange. In English, we just don't say "in much the identical way as," because the word *identical* is an absolute. You can't be more or partially identical; you either are or aren't identical to something else. But even if you didn't analyze D this carefully, it should have just sounded wrong to your ear. (In English Workout 3 we'll show you how "trusting your ear" can be a great way to get correct answers on the English subject test.)

Question 8 tests another idiom problem:

. . . For example, while Selkirk's presence

on the island was of course known for
                                    8

many people (certainly everyone in the
        8

crew that stranded him there), no one

in the novel is aware of Crusoe's survival

of the wreck and presence on the island.

8. F. NO CHANGE
    G. widely known among people
    H. known about many people
    J. known to many people

The underlined portion as written uses a preposition that is wrong in context. Selkirk's presence wasn't known *for* many people—it was known *by*, or known *to*, many people. When you're "known *for*" something, that means you have a reputation for doing such and such. That makes no sense in this context. Answer J *does* make sense, since it points out that Selkirk's presence on the island was known *to* many people—that is, it was something that many people knew about. G sounds as if we're talking about people as a species. Answer choice H means that something is true about many people—not the point of the sentence.

PRONOUNS

Rule at work: A pronoun must agree with the person or thing it is referring to, in person, gender, and number (singular or plural). The reference must be clear; if there is *any* confusion, the sentence must be fixed.

Sometimes, the test will throw you a sentence in which the meaning of a pronoun is unclear. You won't be sure to whom or what the pronoun is referring. That's the kind of problem you were given in **question 5:**

. . . The story even reached the ears of

Richard Steele, who featured it in his

periodical, *The Tatler*. Eventually, he
                                      5

became the subject of a best-selling
    5

book . . .

5. A. NO CHANGE
    B. Selkirk became
    C. his became
    D. he becomes

The *intended* meaning of the pronoun *he* here is "Selkirk." But what's the closest male name to the pronoun? Richard Steele, the publisher of *The Tatler*. Your job is to make it clear whom the pronoun is refering to. Choice B takes care of the problem by naming Selkirk explicitly. C would create a sense problem—his *what* became the subject of a book? Meanwhile, D shifts the verb tense into the present, which makes no sense since this book was written over 250 years ago!

Mistakes of sense often involve pronouns. Make a habit of checking every underlined pronoun as you go along. What does the pronoun stand for? Can you tell? If not, there's an error. Does it make sense? If not, there's an error. Make sure it's perfectly clear to what or to whom all pronouns refer.

LOGIC

Remember when we talked about structural clues back in Reading Workout 1? (C'mon, it wasn't *that* long ago!) Structural clues are words that signal where an author is going in a piece of writing. They show how all of the pieces logically fit together. If the author uses the structural clue *on the other hand*, that means a contrast is coming up; if he or she uses the clue *moreover*, that means that a continuation is coming up—an addition that is more or less in the same vein as what came before.

Many ACT English questions mix up the logic of a piece of writing by giving you the wrong structural clue or other logic word. That's what happened in **question 10:**

. . . <u>Because of</u> its basis in fact,
      10
Robinson Crusoe is often regarded as

the first major novel in English literature.

10. F.   NO CHANGE
    G.   Despite
    H.   Resulting from
    J.   As a consequence of

As written, this sentence means that *Crusoe* was regarded as the first major novel because it was based on fact. But that makes no sense. If it was based on fact, that would work against its being regarded as a novel. There's a contrast between "basis in fact" (which implies nonfiction) and "first major novel" (which implies fiction). To show that contrast logically, you need a contrast word like *despite*. That's why G is correct here.

Question 6 also tests logic:

. . . the subject of a best-selling book, *A*

Cruizing Voyage Round the World, by

Woodes Rogers. <u>And while</u> there is
          6
some evidence that Defoe, a journalist,

may actually have interviewed Selkirk

personally, most literary historians

believe that it was the reprinting of the

Rogers book in 1718 that served as the

real stimulus for Defoe's novel.

6. F.   NO CHANGE
    G.   But since
    H.   And therefore
    J.   OMIT the underlined portion and start the sentence with "There."

The structural clue should convey a sense of continuation from the preceding sentence (since we're still talking about the book *A Cruizing Voyage*) and a sense of contrast with the latter part of the sentence. Even though Defoe may have interviewed Selkirk, many believe Defoe's main source was the book by Rogers. *And* provides the continuation; *while* provides the needed contrast, making NO CHANGE the correct answer.

Answers G and H have *since* and *therefore* which are cause-and-effect words, which make no sense in context. Answer J omits key words and creates a run-on sentence—two independent clauses that are combined improperly. Remember, don't pick OMIT simply because it's there!

VERB USAGE

Rules at work:

1. Use the simplest tense possible. In most cases, the present, past, and future tenses are all you need.

2. Change tenses only if the sentence doesn't make sense as written.

3. Make sure the verb is singular if it has a singular subject and plural if the subject is plural.

Verbs have an annoying habit of changing form depending on who's doing the action and when that person is doing it. Example: "I hate verbs; he hates verbs; and we both have hated verbs ever since we were kids." **You have to be very careful to make sure verbs match their subject and the tense of the surrounding context.**

…In *Crusoe*, which <u>has been published</u>
                                    7
in 1719, Defoe took substantial liberties

with the Selkirk story.

7. A. NO CHANGE
   B. was published
   C. had been published
   D. will have been published

The publication of *Robinson Crusoe* is something that took place in 1719—the past, in other words. So the underlined portion, which puts the verb in the present perfect tense, is flawed. Choices C and D, meanwhile, would put the verb into bizarre tenses normally used to convey a complex time relationship. C makes it seem as if publication of the book happened before Defoe took his liberties with the story. But that's nonsensical. The liberties were taken in the writing of the book. D, meanwhile, does strange things with the time sequence. The book was published in the past; Defoe also took his substantial liberties in the same past. So just use the simple past tense, choice B.

TONE

Rule at work: Every writer of an ACT English passage has a voice, or tone. This voice is usually either casual (conversational) or factual (informational). Be sure to make choices that fit the author's voice.

If a passage contains slang, a few exclamation marks, and a joke or two, the tone is casual and informal; if it sounds like something your teacher would say, it is factual or formal.

As we said earlier, the passages in the English subject test vary in tone. Some are formal; others are informal. Usually, you'll know which is which without having to think about it.

Good style requires that the tone of a piece of writing be at the same level throughout. Sometimes the underlined portion might not fit the tone of the rest of the passage. If so, it's up to you to correct it. Look at **question 13:**

…Meanwhile, Selkirk himself never gave
                                  13
a hoot about returning to the island
          13
that had made him famous.

13. A.   NO CHANGE
     B.   evinced himself as desirous of returning
     C.   could whip up a head of steam to return
     D.   expressed any desire to return

> **EXPERT TUTOR TIP**
>
> " Don't pick an answer just because it sounds "fancy." Pick commonsense, everyday words that express the meaning the author intends. Don't worry if it sounds plain. "

Selkirk "never gave a hoot" about going back? No. Slang doesn't belong in this passage. Choose answer D because it uses a straightforword, factual tone that fits the passage. The NO CHANGE choice is silly; choice B is too wordy and formal; choice C is also slang.

NONSTANDARD-FORMAT QUESTIONS

The Nonstandard-Format Questions ask about the passage as a whole. Keep in mind the main point of the passage—the "gist"—as well as the overall tone and style. For an entire passage to "make sense," it has to be consistent throughout, both in content and in tone and style.

JUDGING THE PASSAGE

Question 14 asks you to judge the passage. Was the last sentence an appropriate ending or not?

14. Considering the tone and subject matter of the preceding paragraphs, is the last sentence an appropriate way to end the essay?

    F.   Yes, because it is necessary to shed some doubt on Defoe's creativity.

    G.   Yes, because the essay is about the relationship between the real Selkirk and Defoe's fictionalized version of him.

    H.   No, because there is nothing "bizarre" about Selkirk's story as it is related in the essay.

    J.   No, because the focus of the essay is more on Selkirk himself than on Defoe's fictionalized version of him.

Think of the passage as a whole. It has been comparing Selkirk's real life with the one that Defoe made up for the character of Robinson Crusoe. Therefore, ending in this way, with an ironic reference wondering whether Defoe could write a more fitting end to Selkirk's life, is perfectly appropriate. The answer is yes (eliminating choices H and J). Choice G restates the point of the passage and is the best answer.

READING COMPREHENSION QUESTIONS

If you thought **question 15** looked like a Reading question hiding in the English part of the exam, you were right. As mentioned in ACT Basics, one reason that you should keep thinking about what the passage means—rather than focusing on picky rules of grammar or punctuation—is that **the English section includes Reading Comprehension Questions.**

15. This essay would be most appropriate as part of a:

    A.   scholarly study of eighteenth-century maritime history.

    B.   study of the geography of the islands off of Chile.

    C.   history of privateering in the Pacific.

    D.   popular history of English literature.

What was this passage principally about? How Defoe's *Robinson Crusoe* was loosely based on the life of a real shipwrecked sailor, Alexander Selkirk. Would that kind of thing belong in a study of geography (choice B)? No. The focus is on the fictionalization of a historical life, not on the physical features of the islands off Chile. The passage isn't principally about privateering or maritime history either, so C and A are wrong as well. This passage is about the relationship between a true story and a famous fictionalized story. And its tone isn't overly scholarly either. So it probably belongs in a popular history of English literature (choice D).

STRUCTURE AND PURPOSE

The English section will also have questions that test your grasp of overall structure and purpose in a piece of prose. The test makers scramble the order of the sentences in a paragraph (or of the paragraphs in a passage). The question then asks you to decide on the best order for the scrambled parts. Take a look at **question 16:**

[1] Only recently has new evidence led many scientists to question the accepted division between birds and dinosaurs. [2] Traditionally, they have been placed in entirely separate classes within the subphylum *Vertebrata*. [3] Birds and dinosaurs don't have many obvious similarities. [4] Birds formed the class *Aves*, while dinosaurs constituted two orders, *Saurischia* and *Ornithischia*, within the class *Reptilia*.

16. To best fulfill the author's purpose, the order of the sentences in the paragraph above should be:

   F.   1, 2, 3, 4

   G.   2, 3, 4, 1

   H.   3, 2, 4, 1

   J.   3, 2, 1, 4

> **EXPERT TUTOR TIP**
>
> " Don't know where to start on an organization question? Look at the answers that begin with the same number (H and J), compare the two, and eliminate one or both answers. "

Here again, the goal is to make it make sense. All of the sentences in this paragraph relate to the differences between birds and dinosaurs. Sentence 3 best introduces this idea. Notice that two of the answer choices begin with Sentence 3—H and J. The other two can be eliminated.

Look again at the logic of the sentences. Since Sentence 4 elaborates on the distinction introduced in Sentence 2, Sentence 4 should immediately follow Sentence 2. Only H has them in that order, so H looks like the answer.

Just to check, you'll want to read the entire paragraph in the order suggested by H. And if you do, you'll notice that the paragraph makes perfect sense, with Sentence 3 introducing the topic, Sentences 2 and 4 showing how that topic has been traditionally viewed, and Sentence 1 coming in naturally to show how that traditional view is no longer valid.

For questions like this, it's usually a good idea to start by trying to figure out the first (and sometimes the last) sentence, because first and last sentences usually have the most obvious functions in an ACT-style paragraph.

CHAPTER 9: MATH WORKOUT 2: SHAKE IT UP!

> ## IF YOU LEARN ONLY THREE THINGS IN THIS CHAPTER . . .
>
> 1. You should be familiar with the ten textbook algebra and coordinate geometry problems.
>
> 2. Some ACT Math problems will be disguised so that their method of solution isn't obvious.
>
> 3. Be familiar with the formulas for calculating percentages and averages.

The main idea of Math Workout 1 was: don't jump in headfirst and start crunching numbers until you've given a problem some thought. Make sure you know what you're doing—*and* that what you're doing won't take too long.

As we saw in Math Workout 1, sometimes you'll know how to proceed as soon as you understand the question. A good number of ACT algebra and coordinate geometry questions are straightforward textbook questions you may already be prepared for.

TEN TEXTBOOK ALGEBRA AND COORDINATE GEOMETRY QUESTIONS

When you take the ACT, you can be sure you'll see some of the following questions with only slight variations. You'll find answers and explanations for these questions in the 100 Key Math Concepts for the ACT section.

1. **Evaluate an algebraic expression.** *(See 100 Key Math Concepts for the ACT, #52)*

   Example: If $x = -2$, then $x^2 + 5x - 6 = ?$

2. **Multiply binomials.** *(See 100 Key Math Concepts for the ACT, #56)*

   Example: $(x + 3)(x + 4) = ?$

3. **Factor a polynomial.** *(See 100 Key Math Concepts for the ACT, #61)*

   Example: What is the complete factorization of $x^2 - 5x + 6$?

4. **Simplify an algebraic fraction.** *(See 100 Key Math Concepts for the ACT, #62)*

   Example: For all $x \neq \pm 3$, $\dfrac{x^2 - x - 12}{x^2 - 9} = ?$

5. **Solve a linear equation.** *(See 100 Key Math Concepts for the ACT, #63)*

   Example: If $5x - 12 = -2x + 9$, then $x = ?$

6. **Solve a quadratic equation.** *(See 100 Key Math Concepts for the ACT, #66)*

   Example: If $x^2 + 12 = 7x$, what are the two possible values of x?

7. **Solve a system of equations.** *(See 100 Key Math Concepts for the ACT, #67)*

   Example: If $4x + 3y = 8$ and $x + y = 3$, what is the value of x?

8. **Solve an inequality.** *(See 100 Key Math Concepts for the ACT, #69)*

   Example: What are all the values of x for which $-5x + 7 < -3$?

9. **Find the distance between two points in the (x, y) coordinate plane.**

   (See 100 Key Math Concepts for the ACT, #71)

   Example: What is the distance between the points with (x, y) coordinates $(-2, 2)$ and $(1, -2)$?

10. **Find the slope of a line from its equation.** *(See 100 Key Math Concepts for the ACT, #73)*

    Example: What is the slope of the line with the equation $2x + 3y = 4$?

These questions are all so straightforward and traditional, they could have come out of a high school algebra textbook. Do these questions the way you were taught. In case you'd like to review them, you'll find all the standard approaches succinctly summarized in 100 Key Math Concepts for the ACT. We're not so concerned in these workouts with problems you may already know how to solve. Here we're going to focus on several situations where the quick and reliable solution method is not so obvious.

THREE WAYS TO SHAKE IT UP

It's bound to happen at some point on test day. You look at a math problem and you don't see what to do. Don't freak out. Think about the problem for a few seconds before you give up. **When you don't see the quick and reliable approach right away, shake the problem up a little.** Try one of these "shake-it-up" techniques:

1. **Restate.**

2. **Remove the disguise.**

3. **Try eyeballing.**

1. RESTATE THE PROBLEM

Often, the way to get over that stymied feeling is to change your perspective. Have you ever watched people playing Scrabble®? In their search to form high-scoring words with the letters on their seven tiles, they continually move the tiles around in their racks. Sometimes a good word becomes apparent only after rearranging the tiles. One might not see the seven-letter word in this arrangement:

R E B A G L A

But reverse the tiles and a word almost reveals itself:

A L G A B E R

The tiles can spell "ALGEBRA."

The same gimmick works on the ACT too. **When you get stuck, try looking at the problem from a different angle.** Try rearranging the numbers, or changing fractions to decimals, or factoring, or multiplying out, or redrawing the diagram, or anything that might give you the fresh perspective you need to uncover a good solution method.

Here's a question you might not know what to do with at first glance:

Example

1. Which of the following is equivalent to $7^{77} - 7^{76}$?

    A.   7

    B. 7^{77-76}

    C. $7^{77 \div 76}$

    D. $7(77 - 76)$

    E. $7^{76}(6)$

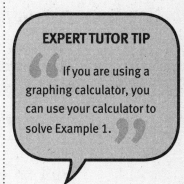

EXPERT TUTOR TIP

If you are using a graphing calculator, you can use your calculator to solve Example 1.

Here's a hint: *think of an easier problem testing the same principles.* The important thing to look for is the basic relationships involved—here, we have exponents and subtraction. That subtraction sign causes trouble, because none of the ordinary rules of exponents (see 100 Key Math Concepts for the ACT, #47–48) seem to apply when there is subtraction of "unlike" terms.

Another hint: how would you work with $x^2 - x$? Most test takers could come up with another expression for $x^2 - x$: they'd factor to $x(x - 1)$. Or if the problem asked for $x^{77} - x^{76}$, they'd factor to $x^{76}(x - 1)$. The rule is no different for 7 than for x. Factoring out the 7^{76} gives you: $7^{76}(7 - 1)$, which is $7^{76}(6)$, or choice E.

Sometimes an ACT algebra question will include an expression that isn't of much use in its given form. The breakthrough in such a case may be to restate the expression by either simplifying it or factoring it.

Example

2. If $\dfrac{x}{2} - \dfrac{x}{6}$ is an integer, which of the following statements must be true?

    F. x is positive.

    G. x is odd.

    H. x is even.

    J. x is a multiple of 3.

    K. x is a multiple of 6.

Reexpress: $\dfrac{x}{2} - \dfrac{x}{6} = \dfrac{3x}{6} - \dfrac{x}{6} = \dfrac{2x}{6} = \dfrac{x}{3}$

This form of the expression tells us a lot more. If $\dfrac{x}{3}$ is an integer, then x is equal to 3 times an integer:

$$\dfrac{x}{3} = \text{an integer}$$
$$x = 3 \times (\text{an integer})$$

In other words, x is a multiple of 3, choice J.

2. REMOVE THE DISGUISE

Sometimes it's hard to see the quick and reliable method immediately because the true nature of the problem is hidden behind a disguise. Look at this example:

Example

3. What are the (x, y) coordinates of the point of intersection of the line representing the equation $5x + 2y = 4$ and the line representing the equation $x - 2y = 8$?

    A. $(2, 3)$

    B. $(-2, 3)$

    C. $(2, -3)$

    D. $(-3, 2)$

    E. $(3, -2)$

This may look like a coordinate geometry question, but do you really have to graph the lines to find the point of intersection? Remember, the ACT is looking for creative thinkers, not mindless calculators! Think about it for a moment—what's the special significance of the point of intersection, the one point that the two lines have in common? That's the one point whose coordinates will satisfy *both* equations.

So what we realize now is that this is not a coordinate geometry question at all, but a "system-of-equations" question. All it's really asking you to do is solve the pair of equations for x and y. The question has nothing to do with slopes, intercepts, axes, or quadrants. It's a pure algebra question in disguise.

Now that we know we're looking at a system of equations, the method of solution presents itself more clearly. The first equation has a $+2y$, and the second equation has a $-2y$. If we just add the equations, the y terms cancel:

$$\begin{array}{r} 5x + 2y = 4 \\ x - 2y = 8 \\ \hline 6x = 12 \end{array}$$

If $6x = 12$, then $x = 2$. Plug that back into either of the original equations and you'll find that $y = -3$. The point of intersection is $(2, -3)$, and the answer is C.

Example

4. A geometer uses the following formula to estimate the area A of the shaded portion of a circle as shown in the figure below when only the height h and the length of the chord c are known:

$$A = \frac{2ch}{3} + \frac{h^3}{2c}$$

What is the geometer's estimate of the area, in square inches, of the shaded region if the height is 2 inches and the length of the chord is 6 inches?

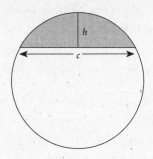

F.   6

G. $6\frac{2}{3}$

H. $7\frac{1}{2}$

J. $8\frac{2}{3}$

K.   12

> **EXPERT TUTOR TIP**
>
> When you have a system of equations, you can solve it by:
>
> • Combination
>
> • Substitution
>
> • Graphing
>
> This example demonstrates combination.

At first glance, this looks like a horrendously esoteric geometry question. Who ever heard of such a formula? But when you think about the question a bit, you realize that you don't really have to understand the formula. You certainly don't have to remember it—it's right there in the question.

In fact, this is not really a geometry question at all. It's just an "evaluate the algebraic expression" question in disguise. All you have to do is plug the given values $h = 2$ and $c = 6$ into the formula:

$$A = \frac{2ch}{3} + \frac{h^3}{2c}$$
$$= \frac{2(6)(2)}{3} + \frac{(2)^3}{2(6)}$$
$$= 8 + \frac{2}{3} = 8\frac{2}{3}$$

> **EXPERT TUTOR TIP**
>
> " If you look at this problem and you freak out the first time through the test, skip it. Hopefully you'll realize how easy it is on your second pass. Don't waste valuable time freaking out about one problem. "

Choice J is correct.

The people who wrote this question wanted you to freak out at first sight and give up. Don't give up on a question too quickly just because it looks like it's testing something you never saw before. In many such cases, it's really a familiar problem in disguise.

3. STUCK? TRY EYEBALLING

There is another simple but powerful strategy that should give you at least a 50-50 chance on almost any diagram question: **when in doubt, use your eyes. Trust common sense and careful thinking; don't worry if you've forgotten most of the geometry you ever knew.** For almost half of all diagram questions, you can get a reasonable answer without solving anything: just eyeball it.

The Math directions say, "Illustrative figures are NOT necessarily drawn to scale," but in fact they almost **always** are. You're **never** really *supposed* to just eyeball the figure, but it makes a lot more sense than random guessing. Occasionally, eyeballing can help you narrow down the choices.

"favorable" outcomes is 2 (the number of black ties). The probability of choosing a black tie at random is $\frac{2}{7}$.

WHAT TO DO NEXT

Because more than half the Math questions on the ACT involve algebra, it's a good idea to solidify your understanding of the basics before test day. Focus on #52–70 in 100 Key Math Concepts for the ACT. Keep things in perspective. **Geometry questions are important, too, but algebra questions are more important.**

CHAPTER 10: READING WORKOUT 2: LOOK IT UP!

IF YOU LEARN ONLY THREE THINGS IN THIS CHAPTER . . .

1. Preread the passage and make a "road map": know what each paragraph is saying.

2. Refer to your road map when you attack the questions, and always refer back to the passage to find the answer.

3. Reading questions can ask about specific details of a passage, what a passage implies, and its overall structure and argument. It's important to know what type of question you are researching.

In Reading Workout 1, we discussed general strategies for approaching ACT Reading. Now let's look more closely at the types of questions you'll encounter.

The three main types of Reading questions are:

1. Specific Questions

    Detail

    Vocab-in-Context

    Function (Why)

2. Conclusion Questions

    Inference

    Writer's View

3. Generalization Questions

THE KAPLAN FIVE-STEP METHOD (AGAIN)

Don't forget to use the Kaplan Five-Step Method for ACT Reading which we discussed in Reading Workout 1. Here's a reminder of how it works:

STEP 1: PREREAD THE PASSAGE

In other words, work through the passage before trying to answer the questions in less than three minutes. Read actively, and assemble a mental road map, or overall idea of how the passage is organized.

STEP 2: CONSIDER THE QUESTION STEM

Before plunging into the answer choices take a moment to understand what kind of question it is. They are:

Detail: Specific "what" questions

Vocab-in-Context: The meaning of a word or words in context

Function: Specific "why" questions about a word, sentence, or example—the purpose it has in the passage

Inference: Asking you to read between the lines of the passage

Writer's View: What tone of voice does the author use?

Generalization: The overall point or argument of the passage

STEP 3: REFER TO THE PASSAGE

You don't need to refer to the whole passage. Just refer to the passage by finding the place where the answer to a question can be found. Sometimes a line reference will be included in the question; otherwise, rely on your road map of the passage.

STEP 4: ANSWER THE QUESTION IN YOUR OWN WORDS

Do this before looking at the answer choices.

STEP 5: MATCH YOUR ANSWER WITH ONE OF THE CHOICES

With an answer in mind, it'll be easier to spot the best choice.

IMPORTANT QUESTION TYPES

Try the following typical ACT nonfiction passage, this one from the Humanities. Afterward, we'll discuss selected questions from this set as examples of Specific Detail, Inference, and Big Picture Questions.

PASSAGE II

[Tragedy was the invention of the Greeks. In their Golden Age, the fifth century before Christ, they produced the world's greatest dramatists, new forms

Line of tragedy and comedy that have been models ever
(5) since, and a theatre that every age goes back to for rediscovery of some basic principle . . .]

Since it derived from primitive religious rites, with masks and ceremonial costumes, and made use of music, dance, and poetry, the Greek drama was at
(10) the opposite pole from the modern realistic stage. [In fact, probably no other theatre in history has made fuller use of the intensities of art.] The masks, made of painted linen, wood, and plaster, brought down from primitive days the atmosphere of gods, heroes,
(15) and demons. Our nineteenth- and twentieth-century grandfathers thought masks must have been very artificial. Today, however, we appreciate their exciting intensity and can see that in a large theatre they were indispensable. If they allowed no fleeting
(20) change of expression during a single episode, [they could give for each episode in turn more intense expression than any human face could.] When Oedipus comes back with bleeding eyes, the new mask could be more terrible than any facial makeup
(25) the audience could endure, yet in its sculpted intensity more beautiful than a real face.

Most essential of all intensities, and hardest for us to understand, was the chorus. Yet many playwrights today are trying to find some equivalent to do for a
(30) modern play what the chorus did for the Greeks. [During the episodes played by the actors, the chorus would only provide a background of group response, enlarging and reverberating the emotions of the actors, sometimes protesting and opposing
(35) but in general serving as ideal spectators to stir and lead the reactions of the audience. But between episodes, with the actors out of the way, the chorus took over.] We have only the words, not the music or

dance, and some translations of the odes are in such
(40) formal, old-fashioned language that it is hard to guess that they were accompanied by vigorous, sometimes even [wild dances and symbolic actions that filled an orchestra which in some cities was sixty to ninety feet in diameter. Sometimes the cho-
(45) rus expressed simple horror or lament.] Sometimes it chanted and acted out, in unison and in precise formations of rows and lines, the acts of violence the characters were enacting offstage. When Phaedra rushes offstage in *Hippolytus* to hang herself from
(50) the rafters, the members of the chorus, all fifteen of them, perform in mime and chant the act of tying the rope and swinging from the rafters. Sometimes the chorus tells or reenacts an incident of history or legend that throws light on the situation in the play.
(55) Sometimes the chorus puts into specific action what is a general intention in the mind of the main character. When Oedipus resolves to hunt out the guilty person and cleanse the city, he is speaking metaphorically, but the chorus invokes the gods of
(60) vengeance and dances a wild pursuit.

On the printed page, the choral odes seem static and formal, lyric and philosophical, emotional letdowns that punctuate the series of episodes, like intermissions between two acts of a play. The reader
(65) who skips the odes can get the main points of the play. A few are worth reading as independent poems, notably the famous one in *Antigone* beginning, "Many are the wonders of the world, but none is more wonderful than man." [Some modern acting
(70) versions omit the chorus or reduce it to a few background figures.] Yet to the Greeks the odes were certainly more than mere poetic interludes: the wild Dionysian words and movements evoked primitive levels of the subconscious and at the same time
(75) [served to transform primitive violence into charm and beauty and to add philosophical reflections on the meaning of human destiny.]

use many arts (margin note)

roles of chorus (margin note)

study today (margin note)

impt to ancient Greeks (margin note)

(For production today,) we can only improvise some partial equivalent. In Athens the entire popula-
(80) tion was familiar with choral performances. Every year each of the tribes entered a dithyramb in a con-test, rehearsing five hundred men and boys for weeks. [Some modern composers have tried to write dramatic music for choruses:] the most notable
(85) (examples) are the French composer Darius Milhaud, in the primitive rhythms, shouts, and chants of his operatic version of the *Oresteia*; George Gershwin, in the Negro funeral scenes of *Porgy and Bess*; and Kurt Weill, in the African choruses for *Lost in the Stars*,
(90) the musical dramatization of Alan Paton's novel, *Cry, the Beloved Country*. For revivals of Greek tragedies we have not dared use much music beyond a few phrases half shouted, half sung, and drum-beats and suggestive melodies in the background.

From *Invitation to the Theatre*, Third Edition, copyright © 1985 by George Kernodle. Reprinted by permission of Wadsworth, a division of Thomson Learning: www.thomsonlearning.com. Fax 800-730-2215.

A quick preread of the passage should have given you a sense of its general organization:

- First paragraph: introduces the topic of Greek tragedy

- Second paragraph: discusses use of masks (artificial but intense)

- Third paragraph: discusses use of chorus (also artificial but intense)

- Fourth paragraph: expands discussion to choral odes

- Fifth paragraph: concludes with discussion of how Greek tragedy is performed today and how it has influenced some modern art

That's really all the road map you need going into the questions. Aside from that, you should take away the author's main point: Greek tragedy included many artificial devices, but these devices allowed it to rise to a high level of intensity.

1. Combined with the passage's additional information, the fact that some Greek orchestras were sixty to ninety feet across suggests that:

   A. few spectators were able to see the stage.

   B. no one performer could dominate a performance.

   C. choruses and masks helped overcome the distance between actors and audience.

   D. Greek tragedies lacked the emotional force of modern theatrical productions.

2. The phrase "fuller use of the intensities of art" (line 12) most nearly means:

   F. employment of brightly illuminated effects.

   G. good use of powerful, dramatic effects of music, dance, and poetry.

   H. the enjoyment of strong elements of effects on stage.

   J. the utilization of dramatic interactions.

3. The description of the chorus's enactment of Phaedra's offstage suicide (lines 48–52) shows that, in contrast to modern theater, ancient Greek theater was:

   A. more violent.

   B. more concerned with satisfying an audience.

   C. more apt to be historically accurate.

   D. less concerned with a realistic portrayal of events.

4. It can be inferred that one consequence of the Greeks' use of masks was that:

   F. the actors often had to change masks between episodes.

   G. the characters in the play could not convey emotion.

   H. the actors wearing masks played non-speaking roles.

   J. good acting ability was not important to the Greeks.

5. Which of the following is supported by the information in the second paragraph (lines 7–26)?

   A. Masks in Greek drama combined artistic beauty with emotional intensity.

   B. The use of masks in Greek drama was better appreciated in the nineteenth century than it is now.

   C. Masks in Greek drama were used to portray gods but never human beings.

   D. Contemporary scholars seriously doubt the importance of masks to Greek theater.

6. The author indicates in lines 57–58 that Oedipus's resolution "to hunt out the guilty person and cleanse the city" was:

   F. at odds with what he actually does later in the performance.

   G. misinterpreted by the chorus.

   H. dramatized by the actions of the chorus.

   J. angrily condemned by the chorus.

7. According to the passage, when actors were present on stage, the chorus would:

   A. look on as silently as spectators.

   B. inevitably agree with the actors' actions.

   C. communicate to the audience solely through mime.

   D. react to the performance as an audience might.

8. The main point of the fifth paragraph (lines 61–77) is that choral odes:

   F. should not be performed by modern choruses.

   G. have a meaning and beauty that are lost in modern adaptations.

   H. can be safely ignored by a modern-day reader.

   J. are only worthwhile in *Antigone*.

9. The passage suggests that modern revivals of Greek tragedies "have not dared use much music" (line 92) because:

   A. modern instruments would appear out of place.

   B. to do so would require a greater understanding of how choral odes were performed.

   C. music would distract the audience from listening to the words of choral odes.

   D. such music is considered far too primitive for modern audiences.

10. The author discusses *Porgy and Bess* and *Lost in the Stars* in order to:

   F. show how two modern plays reenact ancient Greek tragedies.

   G. demonstrate the sue of music in modern plays.

   H. give examples of two modern-day playwrights who used musical choruses in their dramas.

   J. illustrate how music evokes subconscious emotions in modern-day plays.

Now let's take a look at selected questions, which fall into three categories.

SPECIFIC QUESTIONS

Questions 2, 6, 7, and 10 are typical Specific Questions. Some Specific Questions give you a line reference to help you out; others don't, forcing you either to start tearing your hair out (if you're an unprepared test taker) or else to seek out the answer based on your sense of how the passage is laid out (one of the two key reasons to preread the passage).

Question 2 is a Vocab-in-Context question. This stem refers to a word or phrase in the passage and asks you to select the answer that is closest to the meaning in *context*.

Note: The best answer is not a direct definition of the words. Look instead for the answer that would make the most sense. To check your answer, plug it into the sentence.

Question 6 provides a line reference (lines 57–58), but to answer the question confidently, you should have also read a few lines *before* and a few lines *after* the cited lines. There you would have read: "Sometimes the chorus puts into action what is a general intention in the mind of the main character. When Oedipus resolves . . ." Clearly, the Oedipus example is meant to illustrate the point about the chorus acting out a character's intentions. So H is correct—they are "dramatizing" (or acting out) Oedipus's resolution. (By the way, G might have been tempting, but there's no evidence that the chorus is "misinterpreting," just that they're "putting a general intention into specific action.")

Question 7 is a Specific Question *without* a line reference. Such questions are common on the ACT, and they require that you have a good sense of the structure of the passage as a whole so that you can locate the place where the question is answered. The mention of the chorus in the question should send you to paragraph 3. We have marked this paragraph with the ABC method we've discussed. A quick glance over the marked-up version leads you to the sentence that begins on line 31, where the author claims that the chorus serves to "lead the reactions of the audience"—captured by correct choice D.

Question 10 is another type of Specific Question: Function. These questions ask why an author uses a word, phrase, or detail in the passage. You can spot these questions because you'll see phrases like, "is used to," "is meant to," and "in order to" in the question stem.

Question 10 asks why the author mentions the modern plays *Porgy and Bess* and *Lost in the Stars* in the passage. It is important to remember that WHY something is discussed is different from WHAT is discussed. Choice H is the right answer.

Note: While G and J may be true, they are not the reason why the author mentions these plays. F is false—they are not reenactments of Greek tragedies.

INFERENCE QUESTIONS

With Inference Questions, your job is to combine ideas logically to make an inference—something that's not stated explicitly in the passage but that is definitely said implicitly. Often, you'll see a word like *suggest, infer, inference,* or *imply* in the question stem to tip you off.

To succeed on Inference Questions, you have to "read between the lines." Common sense is your best tool here. You use various bits of information in the passage as evidence for your own logical conclusion.

Questions 1, 3, and **5** require that you combine information from more than one place in the passage. **Question 1** has no line references to help; a quick survey of the passage tells you that C is the only answer compatible with the passage. **Question 3** research might lead to a prediction of "the chorus emphasizes what's happening on stage," pointing you to answer D. **Question 5** research leads you to the key word *intensity*, which you examined previously for question 2.

Note: The relationship between questions 2 and 5 is a good example of how answering one question can help you with the answer to another. Thus, you may find that if you skip a question the first time, you can answer it during a second pass.

Question 4 provides no line reference, but the mention of masks should have sent you to the second paragraph of the passage. Lines 19–20 explain that masks "allowed no fleeting change of expression during a single episode." Treat that as your first piece of evidence. Your second comes in lines 20–22: "they [the masks] could give for each episode in turn more intense expression than any human face could." Put those two pieces of evidence together—masks can't change expression *during* a single episode, but they can give expression for each episode in *turn*.

Clearly, the actors must have changed masks between episodes so that they could express the different emotions that different episodes required. Choice F is correct.

Question 9 refers to line 92, but you really have to keep the context of the entire paragraph in mind when you make your inference. Why would modern revivals not have "dared" to use much music? Well, the paragraph opens by saying that modern productions "can only improvise some partial equivalent" to the choral odes. Since we can only improvise the odes, we don't understand very much about them. That's why the use of music would be considered daring, and why choice B is correct.

One warning: keep your inferences as "close" to the passage as possible. Don't make wild inferential leaps. An inference should follow naturally and inevitably from the evidence provided in the passage.

BIG PICTURE QUESTIONS

About one-third of the ACT Reading questions are Detail Questions and most of the rest are Inference Questions. But there are also a few questions that test your understanding of the theme, purpose, and organization of the passage as a whole. **Big Picture Questions tend to look for:**

- **Main point or purpose of a passage or part of a passage**
- **Author's attitude or tone**
- **Logic underlying the author's argument**
- **How ideas in different parts of the passage relate to each other**
- **Difference between fact and opinion**

> **EXPERT TUTOR TIP**
>
> If a Big Picture question stumps you, circle it and tackle the Detail and Inference Questions. Then go to the overall question—you may see the answer right away.

One way to see the Big Picture is to read actively. As you read, ask yourself, "What's this all about? What's the point of this? Why is the author saying this?"

Question 8 asks for the main idea of a particular paragraph—namely, the fifth, which our general outline indicates is the paragraph about choral odes. Skimming that paragraph, you find reference to how the odes seem to us modern people—"static and formal" (line 61–62), "like intermissions between two acts of a play" (lines 63–64). Later, the author states, by way of contrast (note the use of the clue word *yet*): "Yet to the Greeks the odes were certainly more than mere poetic interludes." Clearly, the author wants to contrast our modern static view of the odes with the Greeks' view of them as something more. That idea is best captured by choice G.

> **EXPERT TUTOR TIP**
>
> If you're still stumped on a Big Picture Question after reading the passage, try doing the Detail and Inference Questions first. They can help you fill in the Big Picture.

FIND AND PARAPHRASE . . . AND OTHER TIPS

The examples above show that your real task in Reading is not what you might expect. **Your main job is to *find* the answers.** Perhaps a better name for the Reading subtest would be "find and paraphrase." But students tend to think that their task in Reading is to "comprehend and remember." That's the wrong mind-set.

DON'T BE AFRAID TO SKIP

Now that you've done a couple of full-length passages and questions, you've probably encountered at least a few questions that you found unanswerable. **What do you do if you can't find the answer in the passage, or if you can find it but don't understand, or if you do understand but can't see an answer choice that makes sense? Skip the question.** Skipping is probably more important in Reading than in any other ACT subject test. Many students find it useful to skip as many as half of the questions on the first pass through a set of Reading questions. That's fine.

CHAPTER 11: SCIENCE WORKOUT 2: THINK LIKE A SCIENTIST

IF YOU LEARN ONLY THREE THINGS IN THIS CHAPTER . . .

1. When you encounter Experiment Questions, identify the factor being varied, the control group (if any), and how results vary between groups.

2. Look for Figure Interpretation Questions first—they'll get you the quickest points.

3. Some scenarios ask you to make inferences about data (specific-to-general); others ask you to use general ideas to determine what will happen in a particular case (general-to-specific).

In Science Workout 1, you learned that to succeed on the ACT Science subtest, you've got to be able to spot trends and patterns in the data of graphs and tables. But that's not all you need to do well. You've also got to learn how to think like a scientist. You don't have to know very much science (though it certainly helps), but you should at least be familiar with how scientists go about getting and testing knowledge.

HOW SCIENTISTS THINK

Scientists use two very different kinds of logic, which (to keep things nontechnical) we'll call:

- General-to-Specific Thinking
- Specific-to-General Thinking

GENERAL-TO-SPECIFIC

In some cases, scientists have already discovered a law of nature and wish to apply their knowledge to a specific case. For example, a scientist may wish to know how fast a pebble (call it Pebble A) will be falling when it hits the ground three seconds after being dropped. There is a law of physics from which it can be determined that on Earth, falling objects accelerate at a rate of about 9.8 m/sec^2. The scientist could use this known general principle to calculate the specific information she needs: after three seconds, the object would be falling at a rate of about 3 sec $\times$ 9.8 m/sec^2, or roughly 30 m/sec. You could think of this kind of logic as *general-to-specific*. The scientist uses a *general* principle (the acceleration of any object falling on Earth) to find a *specific* fact (the speed of Pebble A).

SPECIFIC-TO-GENERAL

But scientists use a different kind of thinking in order to discover a new law of nature. In this case, they examine many specific facts and then draw a general conclusion about what they've seen. For example, a scientist might watch hundreds of different kinds of frogs live and die, and might notice that all of them developed from tadpoles. She might then announce a conclusion: all frogs develop from tadpoles. You could think of this kind of logic as *specific-to-general*. The scientist looks at many *specific* frogs to find a *general* rule about all frogs.

This conclusion is called a "hypothesis," not a fact or a truth, because the scientist has not checked every single frog in the universe. She knows that there theoretically *could* be a frog somewhere that grows from pond scum or from a Dalmatian puppy. But until she finds such a frog, it is reasonable to think that her hypothesis is correct. Many hypotheses, in fact, are so well documented that they become the equivalent of laws of nature.

In your science classes in school, you mostly learn about general-to-specific thinking. Your teachers explain general rules of science to you and then expect you to apply these rules to answer questions and solve problems. Some ACT Science questions are like that as well. But a majority are not. Most ACT Science questions test specific-to-general thinking. The questions test your ability to see the kinds of patterns in specific data that, as a scientist, you would use to formulate your own general hypotheses. We did something like this in Science Workout 1, when we theorized— based on the trends we found in a table of data—that the pollutant Hg was in some way detrimental to trout populations.

EXPERT TUTOR TIP

❝ Only one to three questions on the entire test will be based on your science knowledge. Everything else is based on what's in the passage. ❞

HOW EXPERIMENTS WORK

PURPOSE

Many ACT passages describe experiments and expect you to understand how they're designed. Experiments help scientists do specific-to-general thinking in a reliable and efficient way. Consider the tadpole researcher above. In a real-world situation, what would probably happen is that she would notice some of the frogs develop from tadpoles and wonder if maybe they all did. Then she'd know what to look for and could check all the frogs systematically. This process contains the two basic steps of any experiment:

1. **Forming a hypothesis (guessing that all frogs come from tadpoles)**
2. **Testing a hypothesis (checking the frogs to see if this guess was right)**

Scientists are often interested in cause-and-effect relationships. Having formed her hypothesis about tadpoles, a scientist might wonder what *causes* a tadpole to become a frog. To test causal relationships, a special kind of experiment is needed. She must test one possible cause at a time in order to isolate which one actually produces the effect in question. For example, the scientist might inject tadpoles with several different kinds of hormones. Some of these tadpoles might die. Others might turn into frogs normally. But a few—those injected with Hormone X, say—might remain tadpoles for an indefinite time. One reasonable explanation is that Hormone X in some way inhibited whatever causes normal frog development.

In other words, the scientist would hypothesize a causal relationship between Hormone X and frog development.

METHOD

The relationship between Hormone X and frog development, however, would not be demonstrated very well if the scientist also fed different diets to different tadpoles, kept some in warmer water, or allowed some to have more room to swim than others—or if she didn't also watch tadpoles who were injected with no hormones at all but who otherwise were kept under the same conditions as the treated tadpoles. Why? Because if the "eternal tadpoles" had diets that differed from that of the others, the scientist wouldn't know whether it was Hormone X or the special diet that kept the eternal tadpoles from becoming frogs. Moreover, if their water was warmer than that of the others, maybe it was the warmth that somehow kept the tadpoles from developing. And if she didn't watch untreated tadpoles (a control group), she couldn't be sure whether under the same conditions a normal, untreated tadpole would also remain undeveloped.

> **EXPERT TUTOR TIP**
>
> " Many ACT Science questions ask you to determine the purpose of an experiment or to design one yourself. To figure out the purpose of an experiment, look to see what factor was allowed to change: that's what's being tested. To design an experiment yourself, keep everything constant except the factor you must investigate. "

Thus, a scientist creating a well-designed experiment will:

- Ensure that there's a single variable (like Hormone X) that varies from test to test or group to group

- Ensure that all other factors (diet, temperature, space, etc.) remain the same

- Ensure that there is a control group (tadpoles who don't get any Hormone X at all) for comparison purposes

RESULTS

One of the advantages to knowing how experiments work is that you can tell what a researcher is trying to find out about by seeing what she allows to vary. That's what is being researched—in this case, Hormone X. Data about things other than hormones and tadpole-to-frog development would be outside the design of the experiment. Information about other factors might be interesting, but could not be part of a scientific proof.

For example, if some of the injected tadpoles that did grow into frogs later actually turned into princes, the data from experiments about the hormone they were given would not prove what causes frogs to become princes, though the data *could* be used to design another experiment intended to explore what could make a frog become a prince.

Therefore, whenever you see an experiment in Science, you should ask yourself:

1. **Find the factor that's being varied.** That is what is being tested.

2. **Identify the control group.** It's the group that has nothing special done to it.

3. **Analyze the results.** What differences exist between the results for the control group and those for the other group(s)? Or between the results for one treated group and those for another, differently treated group?

HANDLING EXPERIMENT QUESTIONS

Below is a full-fledged Science passage organized around two experiments. Use the Kaplan Method, but this time, ask yourself the three questions above. Take about five or six minutes to do the passage and its questions.

PASSAGE II

A *mutualistic* relationship between two species increases the chances of growth or survival for both of them. Several species of fungi called *mycorrhizae* form mutualistic relationships with the roots of plants. The benefits to each species are shown in the figure that follows.

ANSWERS

1. B
2. G
3. A
4. H
5. D

ANSWERS AND EXPLANATIONS

Notice how many diagrams and tables were used here. That's common in experiment passages, where information is given to you in a wide variety of forms. Typically, though, the experiments themselves are clearly labeled, as Study 1 and Study 2 were here.

A quick preread of the introduction would have revealed the topic of the experiments here—the "mutualistic relationship" between some fungi and some plant roots, the fungi called mycorrhizae ("myco" for short). The first diagram just shows you who gets what out of this relationship. The benefit accruing to the plant (the arrow pointing to the word *plant*) is an increased ability to absorb water and minerals. The benefit accruing to the *fungus* (the other arrow) is the plant-synthesized sugars on which the fungus feeds. That's the mutual benefit that the myco association creates.

Notice, by the way, that reading this first diagram alone is enough to answer **question 4.** The question is asking: what do the plants get out of the association? And we just answered that—increased ability to absorb water and minerals. Statement III is obviously correct, but so is Statement II, since increased water absorption would indeed enhance the plant's ability to survive drought (a drought is a shortage of water, after all). Statement I, though, is a distortion. We know that the *fungi* benefit from sugars produced by the plants, but we don't have any evidence that the association actually causes plants to produce sugar more efficiently. So I is out; II and III are in, making H the answer.

Can't Live without Those Fungi

Let's get back to the passage. We've just learned who gets what out of the myco association. Now we get a table that shows what *kinds* of plants enter into such associations. Some (those in the first column) are so dependent on myco associations that they can't live without them. Others (those in the second column) merely grow better with them; presumably they could live without them.

Here again, is a question we can answer based solely on information in this one table. **Question 2** tells us that mycos are highly susceptible to acid rain, and then

EXPERT TUTOR TIP

" Every Science passage will have easy and hard questions. Make sure you do the easy questions first to get all of the easy points that you can! "

asks what kind of plant communities would be most harmed by acid rain. Well, if acid rain hurts mycos, then the plants that are most dependent on myco fungi (that is, the ones listed in the first column) would be the most harmed by acid rain. Of the four choices, only birch forests—choice G—correspond to something in column 1 of the table. Birch trees can't even *survive* without myco fungi, so anything that hurts myco fungi would inferably hurt birch forests. (Grapevines and orange groves—which are citrus trees—would also be hurt by acid rain, but not as much, since they *can* survive without myco fungi; meanwhile, we're told nothing about wheat in the passage.)

STUDY 1

Now look at the first experiment. Three plots, each with differently treated soil, are planted with pine seedlings. Plot A gets soil with cultivated myco fungi; Plot B gets untreated soil with only naturally occurring myco fungi; and Plot C gets no myco fungi at all, since the soil has been sterilized and isolated (via the concrete lining and the fabric covering). Now ask yourself the three important Experiment Questions.

1. **Find the factor being varied.** The factor being varied is the amount of myco fungi in the soil. Plot A gets lots; Plot B gets just the normal amount; Plot C gets none at all. It's clear, then, that the scientists are testing the effects of myco fungi on the growth of pine seedlings.

2. **Identify the control group.** The plants in Plot B, since they get untreated soil. To learn the effects of the fungi, the scientists will then compare the results from fungi-rich Plot A with the control, and the results from fungi-poor Plot C with the same control.

3. **Analyze the results.** The results are listed in the first column of the table. And they are decisive: no seedlings at all survived in Plot C; 34 did in Plot B; and 107 did in Plot A. The minimums and maximums coincide. Minimum fungi = minimum number of surviving seedlings; maximum fungi = maximum number of surviving seedlings. Clearly, there's a cause-and-effect relationship here. Myco fungi probably help pine seedlings survive.

Questions 1 and 3 can be answered solely on the basis of Study 1. **Question 1** is merely a procedural question: why the concrete liner in Plot C? Well, in the analysis of the experiment above, we saw that the factor being varied was the amount of myco fungi. Plot C was designed to have none at all. Thus, one can safely assume that the concrete liner was probably there to prevent any stray myco fungi from entering the sterilized soil—choice B.

Question 3 actually sets up an extra experiment based on Study 1. The soils were prepared in the exact same way, except that the soil came from a different location. The results? The number of surviving seedlings from Plots A and B were almost identical. What can that mean? Well, Plot A was supposed to be the fungi-rich plot, whereas Plot B (the control) was supposed to be the fungi-normal plot. But here they have the same results. However, notice that we're *not* told what those results are; it could be that no seedlings survived in any plots this time around.

The question—a reversal question—is phrased so that the three wrong choices are things that *could* explain the results; the correct choice will be the one that *can't*. Choices B, C, and D all *can* explain the results, since they all show how similar results could have been obtained from Plots A and B. If the new soil just couldn't support life—fungi or no fungi—well, Plots A and B would have gotten similar results; namely, no seedlings survive. On the other end of the spectrum, choices C and D show how the two plots might have gotten similar *high* survival rates. If there were lots of myco fungi naturally in this soil (that's choice D), then there wouldn't be all that much difference between the soils in Plots A and B. And if the soil were naturally extremely fertile for the pine seedlings (that's choice C), there must have been lots of fungi naturally present in the soil because pine trees (conifers) don't grow without fungi. So all three of these answers would help to explain similar results in Plots A and B.

Choice A, however, wouldn't help, since it talks about the sterilized soil that's in Plot C. The soil in Plot C won't affect the results in Plots A and B, so choice A is the answer here—the factor that *doesn't* help to explain the results.

STUDY 2

This study takes the surviving seedlings from Plots A and B in Study 1 and just tests how much potassium (K) and phosphorus (P) the roots have used. The results are listed in the second and third columns of the table. (Notice the "N/A"—not applicable—for Plot C in these columns, since there were no surviving seedlings to test in Plot C!) The data shows much better utilization of both substances in the Plot A seedlings, the seedlings that grew in a fungi-rich soil. This data would tend to support a theory that the myco fungi aid in the utilization of K and P and that this in turn aids survival in pine seedlings.

The only question that hinges on Study 2 is **question 5.** It asks what generalization would be supported by the specific results of Study 2. Notice that Study 2 involved only measuring K and P. It did not involve survival rates (that was Study 1), so choice A can't be right. And *neither* study measured growth rates, so B is out. The minerals K and P were in the control group's soil, which was natural, untreated pine forest soil, so choice C is clearly unsupported.

But the *data* did show that not all of the potassium (K) could be absorbed by pine seedlings. Only 18 percent was absorbed in Plot A, while only 10 percent was absorbed in Plot B. That's a long way from 100 percent, so choice D seems a safe generalization to make.

THE REAL THING: PRACTICE PASSAGE

Now that we've taken you step-by-step through a Science passage based on an experiment, it's time to try one on your own. Give yourself about six minutes for the next passage and questions. This time the explanations at the end will be very short:

PASSAGE III

The following flowchart shows the steps used by a chemist in testing sample solutions for positive ions of silver (Ag), lead (Pb), and mercury (Hg).

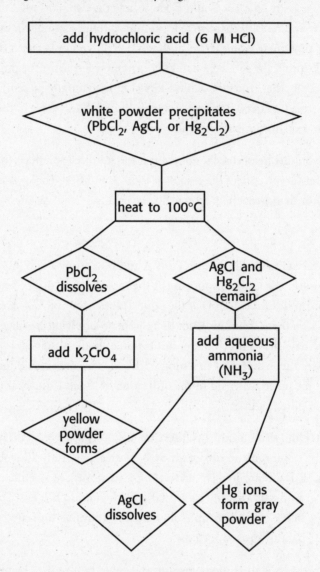

The following experiments were performed by the chemist:

Experiment 1

Hydrochloric acid (6 M HCl) was added to samples of four unknown solutions labeled 1, 2, 3, and 4. A white powder precipitated out of solutions 1, 2, and 3; no precipitate formed in solution 4.

Experiment 2

Each of the sample solutions from Experiment 1 was placed in a 100°C water bath for 15 minutes. The precipitate in solution 1 redissolved completely; solutions 2 and 3 still contained a white powder; solution 4 was unchanged. Solutions 2 and 3 were centrifuged to remove the precipitates, which were retained for further testing. Potassium chromate (K_2CrO_4) was then added to each sample. A bright yellow precipitate formed in solutions 1 and 2; none formed in solutions 3 or 4.

Experiment 3

The white powder centrifuged from solutions 2 and 3 in Experiment 2 was treated with aqueous ammonia (NH_3). The precipitate from solution 2 returned into solution, while that from solution 3 produced a gray powder.

6. Which conclusion is best supported by the results of Experiment 1 alone?

F. Silver ions are present only in solution 3.

G. No ions are present in solution 4.

H. Lead ions are present in solutions 1, 2, and 3.

J. No positive ions of silver, mercury, or lead are present in solution 4.

7. Based on the experimental results, which ions did solution 2 contain?

A. Lead ions only

B. Lead and silver ions only

C. Silver and mercury ions only

D. Silver ions only

8. The yellow precipitate that formed in Experiment 2 was most likely:

F. AgCl

G. Hg_2Cl_2

H. $PbCrO_4$

J. Ag_2CrO_4

9. The experimental results suggest that if lead chloride ($PbCl_2$) were treated with aqueous ammonia (NH_3), the results would be:

A. a bright yellow precipitate.

B. a light gray precipitate.

C. a powdery white precipitate.

D. impossible to determine from the information given.

10. A student proposed that the analysis could be carried out more efficiently by heating the samples to 100° C before adding the 6 M HCl. This suggestion is:

F. a bad idea; since $PbCl_2$ will not precipitate out of solution at this temperature, lead ions would be undetectable.

G. a bad idea; the hot solutions could not be safely centrifuged.

H. a good idea; the number of steps would be reduced from 3 to 2, saving much time and effort.

J. a good idea; the chloride-forming reaction would proceed faster, eliminating the necessity for a 15-minute water bath.

ANSWERS

6. **J**
7. **B**
8. **H**
9. **D**
10. **F**

ANSWERS AND EXPLANATIONS

This experiment passage was somewhat different from the preceding one. In the mycorrhiza experiment, the scientists were thinking in specific-to-general terms (observing the growth of *specific* pine seedlings to come to a conclusion about the general effect of myco fungi on pine seedlings). In this series of experiments, the general principle is known—silver, lead, and mercury will precipitate or dissolve when certain things are done to them—and the scientists are using this principle to test certain substances in order to identify them. In fact, this is more like a procedure than an experiment, since there's no control group. But the same kind of experimental thinking—using the results of varying procedures to make reasonable inferences about what's happening—will get you your answers.

This passage also introduces the idea of a flowchart. Basically, the flowchart indicates an order of procedures. You follow the flowchart from top to bottom. The things in squares indicate what's done to a specimen; the things in diamonds indicate possible results.

Let's say you have an unknown substance. Following the flowchart, the first thing you do is add hydrochloric acid. If a white powder precipitates, that means there are positive ions of silver, lead, and/or mercury. (If nothing precipitates, the experiment is over; the substance is not of interest here.)

But, assuming you do get a white powder, how do you identify exactly which kind of white powder you have? You do the next procedure—heat it to 100°C. When you do this, any lead ions will dissolve, but any silver or mercury ions will remain as a powder. So the flowchart has to divide here.

If part of your specimen dissolved when heated, that doesn't necessarily mean you have lead ions. To test for that, you add K_2CrO_4. If a yellow powder forms, then you know you've got lead; if not, you've got something else.

But what about the other branch? That tells you what has to be done if you do have some powder remaining after heating. And what you do is add NH_3. If the powder dissolves, you've got silver ions. If it forms a gray powder, on the other hand, what you've got are mercury (Hg) ions.

The three experiments here are actually three parts of a single experiment or procedure, each one using the results of the former in the way outlined in the flowchart. The questions ask for results at various points in the procedure, so let's look at them briefly now.

KEY TO PASSAGE III

	Answer	Refer to	Comments
6.	J	Experiment 1 only	If any Ag, Pb, or Hg ions were present, they would have precipitated out as powder. Note that G is too extreme (could be ions of a fourth type not within scope of the experiment). Not enough testing in Exp. 1 to determine F or H.
7.	B	All 3 experiments	Heating left powder, so has to have Ag or Hg or both, so cut A. Addition of K_2CrO_4 left yellow precipitate, so must contain Pb (cut C and D).
8.	H	Experiment 2	Must be lead-based, because Ag and Hg precipitates were already removed (cut F, G, and J).
9.	D	Flowchart	No evidence for what would happen—two different branches of the flowchart.
10.	F	Flowchart	If the solutions were heated first, and then the HCl was added, the $PbCl_2$ would never form, and the chemist would not know whether lead ions were present.

> **EXPERT TUTOR TIP**
>
> " If you get stuck on a problem, see what answer choices you can eliminate. The more you eliminate, the closer you are to the correct answer. "

As you've seen, not all experiments on the ACT Science subject test are specific-to-general experiments; some are general-to-specific procedures. But the same kind of strict thinking—manipulating factors to narrow down possibilities—can get you points, no matter what direction you're thinking in.

CHAPTER 12: ENGLISH WORKOUT 3: LOOK AND LISTEN

IF YOU LEARN ONLY THREE THINGS IN THIS CHAPTER . . .

1. You can recognize some grammar mistakes because they sound strange. Listening is a great tool in the English section.

2. Other grammar mistakes break rules in context. To find these, you must read the sentence carefully to determine the correct punctuation, word, phrase, or clause.

3. Grammar rules tested by the ACT are relatively few. Refer to the quick outline provided in this chapter to learn them.

In the first two English Workouts, we discussed English questions that hinged mostly on common sense. But there are also some English questions—we call them Technicality Questions—that may seem harder because they test for the technical rules of grammar, requiring you to correct errors that don't necessarily affect the economy or sense of the sentence. But don't worry. You don't have to be a grammar whiz to get these questions right. Luckily, you can often detect these errors because they "sound funny" or see the errors right on the page.

LISTEN TO THE CHOICES

Which of the following "sounds right" and which "sounds funny"?

- Bob doesn't know the value of the house he lives in.
- Bob don't know the value of the house he lives in.

EXPERT TUTOR TIP

" You can spot questions that test grammar rules because the answers are roughly the same length. Read the sentences carefully, looking and listening for clues to the error. "

The first sounds a lot better, right? For many of these questions, all you need to do is "listen" carefully in this way.

Your ear can help you determine the tone of a passage. For example, if the passage starts off "You'll just love Bermuda—great beaches, good living . . . " it won't end like this: "and an infinitely fascinating array of flora and fauna which may conceivably exceed, in range and scope, that of any alternative . . . " It's too formal. Pick something like this: "You'll just love Bermuda—great beaches, good living, and lots of awesome plants and animals."

Although ACT passages differ in level of formality, they all are designed to test "standard" English—the kind used by people in most of America. Test takers who speak regional or ethnic dialects may therefore find it more difficult to follow their ears on some ACT questions. In much of the South, for instance, it's common to use the word *in* with the word *rate*, like this: "Mortality declined *in* a rate of almost 2 percent per year." Most speakers of English, however, use the word *at* with *rate*, like this: "Mortality declined *at* a rate of . . . " Fortunately, ACT questions testing issues like this are rare. And even if you do speak a "nonstandard" dialect, you probably know what standard English sounds like. The dialect used on most television and radio programs would be considered "standard."

In the following short passage, use your eyes and ears.

Example

PASSAGE II

Halloween was first celebrated among various Celtic
                                    1
tribes in Ireland in the fifth century B.C. It traditionally

took place on the official last day of summer—October

31, and was named "All-Hallows' Eve." It was believed
 2

that all persons who had died during the previous year

returned on this day to select persons or animals to

inhabit for the next twelve months, until they could

pass peaceful into the afterlife.
 3

1. A. NO CHANGE
   B. among varied
   C. between the various
   D. between various

2. F. NO CHANGE
   G. 31—and
   H. 31. And
   J. 31; and

3. A. NO CHANGE
   B. pass peacefully
   C. passed peacefully
   D. be passing peaceful

On All-Hallows' Eve, the Celts were dressing up as
                                         4
demons and monsters to frighten the spirits away, and

tried to make their homes as coldest as possible to
                           5
prevent any stray ghosts from crossing their thresholds.

Late at night, the townspeople typically gathered outside

the village, where a druidic priest would light a huge

bonfire to frighten away ghosts and to honor the sun

god for the past summer's harvest. Any villager whom was
                                                  6
suspected of being possessed would be captured, after

which they might be sacrificed in the bonfire as a
      7
warning to other spirits seeking to possess the living.

When the Romans invaded the British Isles, they

adopted Celtic—not Saxon—Halloween rituals, but

outlawed human sacrifice in A.D. 61. Instead, they used

effigies for their sacrifices. In time, as belief in spirit
                                        8

possession waned, Halloween rituals lost their serious

aspect and had been instead performed for amusement.
            9

Irish immigrants, fleeing from the potato famine in

the 1840s, brought there Halloween customs to the
            10
United States. In New England, Halloween became a

night of costumes and practical jokes. Some favorite

4. F. NO CHANGE
   G. were dressed
   H. dressed
   J. are dressed

5. A. NO CHANGE
   B. colder
   C. coldest
   D. as cold

6. F. NO CHANGE
   G. whom were
   H. who was
   J. who were

7. A. NO CHANGE
   B. it
   C. he or she
   D. those

8. F. NO CHANGE
   G. belief for
   H. believing about
   J. belief of

9. A. NO CHANGE
   B. having been
   C. have been
   D. were

10. F. NO CHANGE
    G. brought they're
    H. brought their
    J. their brought-in

pranks <u>included unhinging</u> front gates and overturning
    11
out houses. The Irish also introduced the custom of

carving jack-o'-lanterns. The ancient Celts probably

began the tradition by hollowing out a large turnip,

carving it with a demon's face, and lighting it from

inside with a candle. Since there were <u>far less</u> turnips
                                         12
in New England than in Ireland, the Irish immigrants

were forced to settle for pumpkins.

   Gradually, Halloween celebrations spread to other

regions of the United States. Halloween has been a

popular holiday ever since, <u>although these days it's</u>
                                        13
principal celebrants are children <u>rather than</u> adults.
                                       14

11. A. NO CHANGE
    B. include unhinging
    C. had included unhinged
    D. includes unhinged

12. F. NO CHANGE
    G. lots less
    H. not as much
    J. far fewer

13. A. NO CHANGE
    B. although these days its
    C. while now it's
    D. while not it is

14. F. NO CHANGE
    G. rather then
    H. rather
    J. else then

KEY TO PASSAGE II

Answer	Problem
1. A	*among/between* distinction
2. G	commas and dashes mixed
3. B	use of adjectives and adverbs
4. H	unnecessary *-ing* ending
5. D	comparative/superlative
6. H	*who/whom* confusion
7. C	pronoun usage error
8. F	preposition error
9. D	tense problem with *to be*
10. H	*they're/there/their* mix-up
11. A	verb tense problem
12. J	*less/fewer* confusion
13. B	*it's/its* confusion
14. F	*then/than* confusion

GRAMMAR RULES TO KNOW

The rest of this workout is designed to help you build your own "flag list" of common errors on the ACT that your ear might not catch. Consider each classic error. If it seems like common sense to you (or, better, if the error just sounds like bad English to you, while the correction sounds like good English), you probably don't have to add it to your flag list. On the other hand, if it doesn't seem obvious, add it to your list.

As we'll see, making things match works in two ways. Some rules force you to match one part of the sentence with another part. Other rules force you to match the right word or word form with the intended meaning.

ERROR 1: PROBLEM SENTENCES

The most tested "matching" rule on the ACT is this: singular nouns must match with singular verbs and pronouns, and plural nouns must match with plural verbs and pronouns. The most common error in this area involves the use of the word *they*. It's plural, but in everyday speech, we often use it as a singular.

Wrong: "If a student won't study, they won't do well."

Problem: A *student* (singular) and *they* (plural) don't match.

Correction: "If students won't study, they won't do well" or "If a student won't study, he or she won't do well."

ERROR 2: *AND* (COMPOUND PHRASES)

Another common matching error concerns "compound subjects" (lists).

Wrong: "The fool gave the wrong tickets to Bob and I."

Problem: *I* is a subject; it can't be the object of the preposition *to*.

Correction: "The fool gave the wrong tickets to Bob and me."

Hint: Try dropping the rest of the list (Bob and). "The fool gave the wrong tickets to I" should sound funny to you.

ERROR 3: COMMAS OR DASHES (PARENTHETICAL PHRASES)

Parenthetical phrases must begin and end with the same punctuation mark. Such phrases can be recognized because without them the sentence would still be complete. For instance: "Bob, on his way to the store, saw a large lizard in the street." If you dropped the phrase "on his way to the store," the sentence would still be complete. Thus, this phrase is parenthetical. It could be marked off with commas, parentheses, or dashes. But the same mark is needed at both ends of the phrase.

Wrong: "Bob—on his way to the store, saw a lizard."

Problem: The parenthetical phrase starts with a dash but finishes with a comma.

Correction: "Bob, on his way to the store, saw a lizard."

ERROR 4: COMMAS (RUN-ONS AND COMMA SPLICES)

You can't combine two sentences into one with a comma (though you can with a semicolon or conjunction).

Wrong: "Ed's a slacker, Sara isn't."

Problem: Two sentences are spliced together with a comma.

Correction: "Ed's a slacker, but Sara isn't."

ERROR 5: FRAGMENT

This rule goes hand in hand with the one above. **A sentence must have at least one "major event."** A "fragment" is writing that could be a subordinate part of a sentence, but not a whole sentence itself.

Wrong: "Emily listened to music. While she studied."

Problem: "She studied" would be a sentence, but *while* makes this a fragment.

Correction: "Emily listened to music while she studied."

ERROR 6: ANY PUNCTUATION MARK

The ACT doesn't test tricky rules of punctuation. But it does expect you to know what the punctuation marks mean and to match their use to their meanings. Here are some common punctuation marks and their uses:

Period (.):	means "full stop" or "end of sentence."
Question mark (?):	serves the same purpose, but for questions.
Exclamation mark (!):	can be used instead of a period, but is generally inappropriate for all but very informal writing because it indicates extreme emotion.
Comma (,):	sets off items in a list of three or more items;
	separates two independent clauses with a FANBOY conjunction (For, And, Nor, But, Or, Yet, So);
	separates an introductory phrase from the rest of the sentence;
	separates nonessential information from the rest of the sentence, called a parenthetical phrase.
Semicolon (;):	joins two independent clauses (another option for run-on sentences);
	separates items in a series or list if those items already include commas.
Colon (:):	introduces an important short phrase, quotation, explanation, example, or list.
Dash (–):	sets off an explanatory element in a sentence;
	indicates a hesitation or a break in thought.
Apostrophe (')	indicates the possessive form of a noun;
	stands in for a letter or letters in a contraction (*don't = do not; can't = cannot*)

ERROR 7: *-LY* ENDINGS (ADVERBS AND ADJECTIVES)

The ACT expects you to understand the difference between adverbs (the *-ly* words) and adjectives. The two are similar because they're both "modifiers." They modify, or refer to, or describe, another word or phrase in the sentence. The trick is that nouns and pronouns must be modified by adjectives, while other words, especially verbs and adjectives themselves, must be modified by adverbs.

Wrong:	"Anna is an extreme gifted child, and she speaks beautiful too."
Problem:	*Extreme* and *beautiful* are adjectives, but they're supposed to modify an adjective (*gifted*) and a verb (*speaks*) here, so they should be adverbs.
Correction:	"Anna is an extremely gifted child, and she speaks beautifully too."

ERROR 8: *GOOD* OR *WELL*

In everyday speech, we often confuse the words *good* and *well*. But *good* is an adjective (it modifies a noun or pronoun); *well* is an adverb (it can modify verbs and adjectives).

Wrong: "Joe did good on the ACT."

Problem: *Good* is an adjective, but here it's modifying a verb (*did*), so use an adverb.

Correction: "Joe did well on the ACT."

One exception: *Well* can also be used as an adjective, when it means "healthy." So: "Joe was well again by the morning of the ACT" is correct, even though *well* is modifying the noun *Joe*.

ERROR 9: *LIE, LAY, LAID, LAIN*

The words *lay* and *lie* are easy to confuse because they look alike and have similar meanings. The key difference in meaning is point of view. If the speaker is doing something without a direct object, he is "lying." If the speaker is doing it to something else, he is "laying." So, for example, "I will go lie down" (not *lay down*), but "I will lay this pencil on the desk" (not *lie* it).

It gets worse. The past tense of *lay* is *laid*. That's not too hard. The confusing word is *lie*. The past tense of *lie* is *lay*; when used for special tenses (with the words *had*, *have*, or *been*, for example), the form is *lain*. Thus, you'd say "I lay down" (meaning you, yourself, took a rest at some time in the past), or "I have lain down for a nap every afternoon for years now." But you'd say, "I laid that pencil on the desk yesterday, just as I have laid it on the desk every day for years now."

Don't confuse *lie* with the word *lie* that relates to dishonesty. The past tense of *lie* (meaning to tell an untruth) is *lied*.

Wrong: "I lied. I said that I had lain down, but I hadn't. In fact, I had just laid the pencil down. After I lied, though, I lay down to repent for having lied."

Problem: None. All uses of *lie*, *lied*, *lay*, *laid*, and *lain* above are correct.

Try not to get bogged down with *lie* and *lay*. If you don't get it, don't sweat it. It will account for one point if it appears at all.

ERROR 10: *IN, OF, TO, FOR* (IDIOMATIC PREPOSITION USE)

Whenever you see a preposition, double-check to make sure it makes sense and that it "matches" the other words. Many words require particular prepositions.

Wrong: "She tried to instill on me a respect to the law." "I want to protect you in all dangers."

Problem: The prepositions don't match the verbs.

Corrections: "She tried to instill in me a respect for the law." "I want to protect you from all dangers."

ERROR 11: *WHO* OR *WHOM*

Many students fear the words *who* and *whom* more than any other grammatical conundrum. Fear no more. There's an easy way to remember when to use them: they work the same way *he* and *him* work. Turn the sentence into a question as we've done in the example below. If the answer to the question is *he*, the form should be *who*. If the answer is *him*, the form should be *whom*. Notice that the *ms* go together.

> Wrong: "Always remember who you're speaking to."
>
> Problem: *Who* is wrong. Ask: Speaking to who? Speaking to him, not to he. So, it should be *whom*.
>
> Correction: "Always remember whom you're speaking to."

Some students try to avoid the who/whom problem by using the word *which* instead. Nope. It's not nice to call people "whiches." **Never** use the word *which* for a person.

ERROR 12: *ITS* OR *IT'S* (APOSTROPHE USE)

Probably the trickiest rule on the ACT is the proper use of apostrophes. Apostrophes are used primarily for two purposes: possessives and contractions. When you make a *noun* (not a pronoun) possessive by adding an *s*, you use an apostrophe. Examples: *Bob's, the water's, a noodle's.* You **never** use an apostrophe to make a pronoun possessive—pronouns have special possessive forms. You'd never write *her's*. When you run two words together to form a single word, you use an apostrophe to join them. For example: *you'd, he's, they're.*

Apostrophes also have a few unusual uses, but luckily they're almost never tested on the ACT. So master the basics and you're in good shape. The most common apostrophe issue on the ACT is usage of the words *its* and *it's*. A good way to remember which is which is that *its* and *it's* follow the same rule as do *his* and *he's*. Both *its* and *his* are possessive pronouns: so they have *no* apostrophes. Both *it's* and *he's* are contractions—so they *do* have apostrophes.

> Wrong: "The company claims its illegal to use it's name that way."
>
> Problem: *It's* is a contraction of *it is*; *its* is the possessive form of *it*.
>
> Correction: "The company claims it's illegal to use its name that way."

ERROR 13: *THERE, THEIR,* OR *THEY'RE* AND *ARE* OR *OUR* (PROPER WORD USAGE)

Some students confuse the words *there, their,* and *they're*. **A good way to remember which is *they're* is to remember that contractions use apostrophes—so *they're* is the contraction for *they are*.** You can tell which is *there* because it's spelled like *here*, and the words *here* and *there* match. (*Their* means "of or belonging to them"; you'll just have to remember that one the old-fashioned way.)

Students also frequently confuse the words *are* (a verb) and *our* (a possessive). You can remember that *our* is spelled like *your*, another, less confusing possessive.

ERROR 14: *SANG, SUNG, BRANG, BRUNG*, ETC. (VERB FORMS)

When the answers differ because of different forms of the same or similar verbs (for example, *live, lives, lived*), ask yourself *who* did it and *when* did they do it? We would say "I now live" but "he now lives." In these sentences, the *who* is different—and so the verb changes. Similarly, we would say "I now live" but "I lived in the past." In these sentences, the *when* is different—so the verb changes.

Most verbs are "regular" in this way, with only the endings *s* and *d* to worry about. You use the *s* when the point of view is *he, she, or it* and the time is now (present tense). You use the *d* for times in the past. For times in the future, or several steps backward in time, there are no special endings. You use the words *will, will have, have,* and *had* for these time sequences. "I *will* live. I *will have* lived for 25 years by the time the next century begins. I *had* lived in Nebraska, but we moved. I *have* lived in Indiana since then."

But a few verbs are irregular. They have special forms. For example, we say *sang* rather than *singed* and *have sung* rather than *have singed* or *have sang*. Each of these verbs must be learned separately.

One irregular verb commonly tested on the ACT is *bring*.

Wrong: "I've brung my umbrella to work."

Problem: *Brang* and *brung* aren't used in standard English.

Correction: "I've brought my umbrella to work."

ERROR 15: *BE* AND *WAS* (FORMS OF THE VERB *TO BE*)

The ACT tests the use of proper verb forms, especially of the verb *to be*. You must use the following forms. Memorize them if you have to:

Present Tense:	I *am*, we *are*, you *are*, they *are*, he *is*, she *is*, it *is*
Past Tense:	I *was*, we *were*, you *were*, they *were*, he/she/it *was*
Future Tense:	I/we/you/they/he/she/it *will be*
Perfect Tense:	I/we/you *have been*, he/she/it *has been*
Past Perfect:	I/we/you/he/she/it *had been*
Future Perfect:	I/we/you/he/she/it *will have been*

Notice that different forms of the *verb* (*am, are, is, were, was, will be, have been, had been, will have been*) are used depending on point of view (called "case" in grammar) and whether the action is now, in the past, or in the future (called "tense" in grammar). In many dialects, the words *be* and *was* are used instead of the special forms given. For example, many speakers might say "They *be* going home" or "They *was* going home." But the ACT would require you to write "They *are* (or *were*) going home."

ERROR 16: *-ING* ENDINGS (UNIDIOMATIC VERB USE)

Don't use *-ing* endings where they aren't needed. They are used to indicate repeated or continuous action and shouldn't be used for a single action that occurs once.

Wrong: "When I left for the store, I was forgetting my list."

Problem: The *-ing* ending isn't necessary.

Correction: "When I left for the store, I forgot my list."

ERROR 17: *-ER* AND *-EST*, *MORE*, AND *MOST* (COMPARATIVES AND SUPERLATIVES)

Whenever you see the endings *-er* or *-est*, or the words *more* or *most*, double-check to make sure they're used logically. Words with *-er* or with *more* should be used to compare only two things. If there are more than two things involved, use *-est* or *most*.

Wrong: "Bob is the fastest of the two runners."

Problem: The comparison is between just two things, so *-est* is inappropriate.

Correction: "Bob is the faster of the two runners."

Don't use the words *more* or *most* if you can use the endings instead. Say "I think vanilla is tastier than chocolate," not "I think vanilla is more tasty than chocolate." Never use both *more* or *most and* an ending. Don't say "Of the five flavors of frozen yogurt I've eaten, strawberry delight is the most tastiest." Just say it's "the tastiest."

A note on *than* and *then*: *Than* is used in comparisons such as "Bob is faster than Jim." *Then* refers to time, as in "Bob ran and then stopped."

ERROR 18: *BETWEEN* OR *AMONG*

Make sure that you use the word *between* only when there are two things involved. When there are more than two things, or an unknown number of things, use *among*.

Wrong: "I will walk among the two halves of the class." "I will walk between the many students in class."

Problem: Use *between* for two things; *among* for more than two.

Correction: "I will walk between the two halves of the class." "I will walk among the many students in class."

ERROR 19: *LESS* OR *FEWER*

Make sure that you use the word *less* only for uncountable things. When things can be counted, they are *fewer*.

Wrong: "I have fewer water than I thought, so I can fill less buckets."

Problem: You can count buckets; you can't count water.

Correction: "I have less water than I thought, so I can fill fewer buckets."

Hint: People are **always** countable, so use *fewer* when writing about them.

CHAPTER 13: MATH WORKOUT 3: FIGURING IT OUT

Every ACT Math subject test has about 14 geometry questions and exactly 4 trigonometry questions. Depending on what kind of score you're aiming for, you don't need to spend too much time working on trigonometry problems, but you definitely want to spend some time brushing up on your geometry skills.

Fortunately, a good number of the geometry questions are straightforward. Nothing is distorted or disguised. With these questions, you know what to do—if you know your geometry—the instant you understand them.

TEN TEXTBOOK GEOMETRY QUESTIONS

Here's a set of ten such questions. When you take the ACT, you will see quite a few questions just like these—possibly reworded and certainly with different numbers and figures. Use these questions to find out how well you remember your geometry.

Example

1. In the figure below, line *t* crosses parallel lines *m* and *n*. What is the degree measure of ∠*x* ?

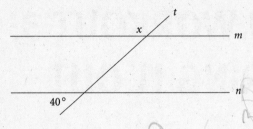

A. 40

B. 50

C. 60

D. 130

E. 140

2. What is the slope of the line perpendicular to the equation $4x + 3y = 9$?

F. $-\dfrac{4}{3}$

G. $-\dfrac{3}{4}$

H. $\dfrac{4}{3}$

J. $\dfrac{3}{4}$

K. 3

3. In the figure below, ∠*B* is a right angle and the lengths of $\overline{AB}$, $\overline{BC}$, and $\overline{CD}$ are given in units. What is the area of △*ACD*, in square units?

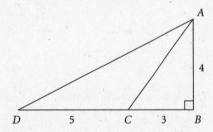

A. 10

B. 12

C. 16

D. 20

E. 32

4. In the figure below, △*ABC* is similar to △*DEF*. ∠*A* corresponds to ∠*D*, ∠*B* corresponds to ∠*E*, and ∠*C* corresponds to ∠*F*. If the given lengths are of the same unit of measure, what is the value of *x* ?

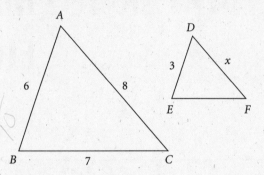

F. 3

G. 3.5

H. 4

J. 5

K. 6

5. In △*ABC* below, ∠*B* is a right angle. If $\overline{AB}$ is 1 unit long and $\overline{BC}$ is 2 units long, how many units long is $\overline{AC}$?

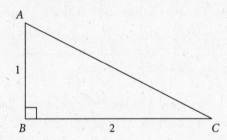

A. $\sqrt{2}$

B. $\sqrt{3}$

C. 2

D. $\sqrt{5}$

E. 3

6. Point P (−3, 5) and point Q (0, 1) are points on the x-y coordinate plane. What is the distance between points P and Q?

    F. 4
    G. 5
    H. 6
    J. 7
    K. 8

7. In the figure below, $\overline{BE}$ is perpendicular to $\overline{AD}$, and the lengths of $\overline{AB}$, $\overline{BC}$, $\overline{CD}$, and $\overline{BE}$ are given in inches. What is the area, in square inches, of trapezoid ABCD ?

    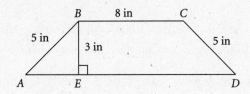

    A. 24
    B. 30
    C. 32
    D. 34
    E. 36

8. What is the area, in square inches, of a circle with a diameter of 8 inches?

    F. 4π
    G. 8π
    H. 16π
    J. 32π
    K. 64π

9. In the circle centered at O in the figure below, the measure of ∠AOB is 40°. If $\overline{OA}$ is 9 units long, how many units long is minor arc AB ?

    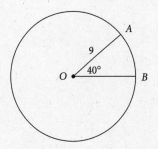

    A. π
    B. 2π
    C. 9
    D. 9π
    E. 40

10. In the figure below, ABCD is a square and $\overline{AB}$ is a diameter of the circle centered at O. If $\overline{AD}$ is 10 units long, what is the area, in square units, of the shaded region?

    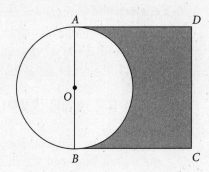

    F. $100 - 50\pi$
    G. $100 - 25\pi$
    H. $100 - \dfrac{25\pi}{2}$
    J. $100 - 10\pi$
    K. $100 - 5\pi$

ANSWERS

1. E
2. J
3. A
4. H
5. D
6. G
7. E
8. H
9. B
10. H

SCORING

10 correct: You have a solid grounding in geometry. Straightforward textbook geometry questions are no problem for you. Skip ahead to the section called Tackling More Complex Geometry Questions.

8–9 correct: You have a pretty good grasp of the geometry you need to know for the ACT. Before moving on to the discussion of more complex geometry, read the explanations below of the questions you got wrong, and study the appropriate pages of the 100 Key Math Concepts for the ACT section at the back of this book.

0–7 correct: You have gaps in your knowledge of geometry. Before you can hope to get much out of our discussion of more complex geometry, you had better solidify your geometry foundations. Look at the explanations below and study the corresponding pages of the 100 Key Math Concepts for the ACT section at the back of this book.

ANSWERS AND EXPLANATIONS

1. When a transversal crosses parallel lines, the four acute angles formed are all equal, the four obtuse angles formed are all equal, and any angles that are not equal are supplementary. The angle marked x is obtuse, so it's supplementary to the given 40° angle. $180 - 40 = 140$. The answer is E. (*100 Key Math Concepts for the ACT, #79*)

2. First you need to put the equation you are given into $y = mx + b$ form. When you do this, you can see that the slope of this line is $-\frac{4}{3}$. We are looking for the slope of the line perpendicular to this line. That means that we need the opposite reciprocal slope, which is $\frac{3}{4}$, J. (*100 Key Concepts for the ACT, #73*)

3. The formula for the area of a triangle is $A = \frac{1}{2}bh$. To apply this formula, you need the base and the height. Here you can use $\overline{CD}$ for the base and $\overline{AB}$ for the height. So: Area $= \frac{1}{2}(CD)(AB) = \frac{1}{2}(5)(4) = 10$. The answer is A. (*100 Key Math Concepts for the ACT, #83*)

4. In similar triangles, corresponding sides are proportional. $\overline{DE}$ corresponds to $\overline{AB}$, and $\overline{DF}$ corresponds to $\overline{AC}$, so we can set up this proportion:

$$\frac{AB}{DE} = \frac{AC}{DF}$$

$$\frac{6}{3} = \frac{8}{x}$$

$$6x = 3 \times 8$$

$$6x = 24$$

$$x = 4$$

The answer is H. (*100 Key Math Concepts for the ACT, #82*)

5. The Pythagorean theorem says: $(\text{leg}_1)^2 + (\text{leg}_2)^2 = (\text{hypotenuse})^2$. Here the legs have lengths of 1 and 2, so plug them into the formula:

$$(1)^2 + (2)^2 = (\text{hypotenuse})^2$$

$$1 + 4 = x^2$$

$$x^2 = 5$$

$$x = \sqrt{5}$$

The answer is D. (*100 Key Math Concepts for the ACT, #84*)

6. There are a couple of ways to solve a distance problem. If you can remember the formula, great! If you can't, you can still get this problem correct. Draw a quick graph and plot the two points that you are given. See if you can make a triangle once you draw the points, and then determine the lengths of the two legs. You will need to solve for the hypotenuse, but you know how to do this—the Pythagorean theorem! You might also recognize the Pythagorean triplet (3-4-5). Any way you solve it, you will get 5, G. (*100 Key Math Concepts for the ACT, #85*)

7. The formula for the area of a trapezoid is $A = \left(\dfrac{b_1 + b_2}{2}\right)h$, where b_1 and b_2 are the lengths of the parallel sides. You could think of it as the height times the average of the bases. You're given the height (3 inches), one base (8 inches), and enough information to figure out the other base. Notice that $\triangle ABE$ is a 3-4-5 triangle, so $\overline{AE} = 4$ inches. And if you were to drop an altitude down from point C, you'd get another 3-4-5 triangle on the right:

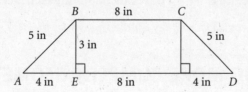

Now you can see that the bottom base is 16 inches. Plug these numbers into the formula:

$$A = \left(\frac{b_1 + b_2}{2}\right)h$$

$$= \left(\frac{8 + 16}{2}\right) \times 3$$

$$= 12 \times 3 = 36$$

The answer is E. (*100 Key Math Concepts for the ACT, #87*)

8. The formula for the area of a circle is $A = \pi r^2$, where r is the radius. If the diameter is 8 inches, then the radius is 4 inches, which we plug into the formula:

$$A = \pi r^2$$

$$= \pi(4)^2$$

$$= 16\pi$$

The answer is H. (*100 Key Math Concepts for the ACT, #91*)

9. The central angle of minor arc AB is $40°$, which is $\frac{1}{9}$ of the whole circle's $360°$. The length of minor arc AB, therefore, is $\frac{1}{9}$ of the whole circle's circumference.

$$C = 2\pi r = 2\pi(9) = 18\pi$$
$$\frac{1}{9}C = \frac{1}{9}(18\pi) = 2\pi$$

The answer is B. (*100 Key Math Concepts for the ACT, #90*)

10. The shaded region is equal to the area of the square minus the area of the semicircle. The area of the square is $10 \times 10 = 100$. The radius of the circle is half of 10, or 5, so the area of the whole circle is $\pi(5)^2 = 25\pi$, and the area of the semicircle is $\frac{25\pi}{2}$. The square minus the semicircle, then, is: $100 - \frac{25\pi}{2}$. The answer is H. (*100 Key Math Concepts for the ACT, #87, #91*)

TACKLING MORE COMPLEX GEOMETRY QUESTIONS

Not all ACT geometry questions are straightforward. The test writers have ways of further complicating them. It's not always obvious at first what the question is getting at. Sometimes you really have to think about the figure and the given information before that lightbulb goes on in your head. Often, the inspiration that brings illumination is finding the hidden information.

Example

1. In the figure below, $\triangle ABC$ is a right triangle and $\overline{AC}$ is perpendicular to $\overline{BD}$. If $\overline{AB}$ is 6 units long, and $\overline{AC}$ is 10 units long, how many units long is $\overline{AD}$?

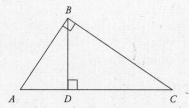

   A. 3
   B. $2\sqrt{3}$
   C. 3.6
   D. 4
   E. $3\sqrt{2}$

At first this looks like a Pythagorean theorem question. In fact, the two given sides of $\triangle ABC$ identify it as the 6-8-10 version of the 3-4-5 special right triangle. (*100 Key Math Concepts for the ACT, #85*) So we know that $\overline{BC} = 8$. So what? How's that going to help us find $\overline{AD}$?

The inspiration here is to realize that this is a "similar triangles" problem. We don't see the word *similar* anywhere in the question stem, but the stem and the figure combined actually tell us that all three triangles in the figure—$\triangle ABC$, $\triangle ADB$, and $\triangle BDC$—are similar. We know the triangles are similar because they all have the same three angles. Here are the three triangles separated and oriented to show the correspondences:

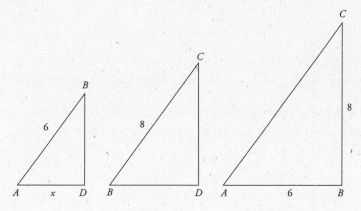

In this orientation it's easy to see the proportion setup that will solve the problem:

$$\frac{10}{6} = \frac{6}{x}$$

$$10x = 36$$

$$x = 3.6$$

The answer is C.

Example

2. In the figure below, the area of the circle centered at O is 25π, and $\overline{AC}$ is perpendicular to $\overline{OB}$. If $\overline{AC}$ is 8 units long, how many units long is $\overline{BD}$?

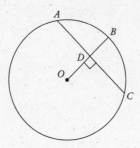

F.   2

G.   2.5

H.   3

J.   3.125

K.   4

This is a tough one. It's not easy to see how to get $\overline{BD}$ from the given information. You can use the area—25π—to figure out the radius, and then you'd know the length of $\overline{OB}$:

$$\text{Area} = \pi r^2$$

$$25\pi = \pi r^2$$

$$25 = r^2$$

$$r = 5$$

So you know $\overline{OB} = 5$, but what about $\overline{BD}$? If you knew $\overline{OD}$, you could subtract that from $\overline{OB}$ to get what you want. But do you know $\overline{OD}$? This is the place where most people get stuck.

The inspiration that will lead to a solution is that you can take advantage of the right angle at D. Look what happens when you take a pencil and physically add $\overline{OA}$ and $\overline{OC}$ to the figure:

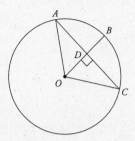

ΔOAD and ΔOCD are right triangles. And when we write in the lengths, we discover some special right triangles:

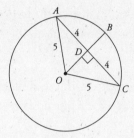

Now it's apparent that $\overline{OD} = 3$. Since $\overline{OB} = 5$, $\overline{BD}$ is $5 - 3 = 2$. The answer is F.

FIGURELESS PROBLEMS

Some ACT geometry problems present an extra challenge because they don't provide a figure. You have to "figure it out" for yourself. Try this one:

Example

3. If one side of a right triangle is 3 units long, and a second side is 4 units long, which of the following could be the length, in units, of the third side?

    A.   1

    B.   2

    C. $\sqrt{7}$

    D. $3\sqrt{2}$

    E. $3\sqrt{3}$

The key to solving most figureless problems is to sketch a diagram, but sometimes that's not so easy because the test makers deliberately give you less information than you might like. Question 3 is the perfect example. It gives you two sides of a right triangle and asks for the third. Sounds familiar. And the two sides it gives you—3 and 4—*really* sound familiar. It's a 3-4-5, right?

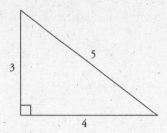

So the answer's 5 . . .

Whoops! There's no 5 among the answer choices! What's going on?!

Better check back. Notice that the question asks, "Which of the following *could* be the length . . ." That *could* is crucial. It suggests that there's more than one possibility. Our answer of 5 was too obvious. There's another one somewhere.

Can you think of another way of sketching the figure with the same given information? Who says that the 3 and 4 have to be the two legs? Look at what happens when you make one of them—the larger one, of course—the *hypotenuse*:

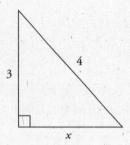

This is not a 3-4-5 triangle, because in a 3-4-5, the 3 and the 4 are the legs. This is no special right triangle; to figure out the length of the third side, resort to the Pythagorean theorem:

$$(\text{leg}_1)^2 + (\text{leg}_2)^2 = (\text{hypotenuse})^2$$
$$3^2 + x^2 = 4^2$$
$$9 + x^2 = 16$$
$$x^2 = 7$$
$$x = \sqrt{7}$$

The answer is C.

MANY STEPS AND MANY CONCEPTS

Some of the toughest ACT geometry questions are ones that take many steps to solve and combine many different geometry concepts. The following is an example:

Example

4. In the figure below, $\overline{AB}$ is tangent to the circle at A. If the circumference of the circle is 12π

units and $\overline{OB}$ is 12 units long, what is the area, in square units, of the shaded region?

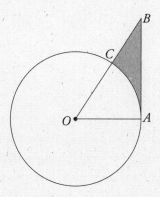

F. $18\sqrt{3} - 6\pi$

G. $24\sqrt{3} - 6\pi$

H. $18\sqrt{3} - 2\pi$

J. $12\pi - 12$

K. $243 - 2\pi$

This is about as hard as they come on the ACT. It is by no means clear how the given information—the circumference of the circle and the length of $\overline{OB}$—will lead you to the area of the shaded region.

So what do you do? Give up? No. *Don't* give up immediately unless you're really short on time or you know for sure you can't do the problem.

So then should you just plow ahead blindly and figure out every length, angle, and area you can and see where that leads you? *Well, not exactly*. It would be better to be more systematic.

The key to success with a circuitous problem like this is to focus on your destination—what you're looking for—and think about what you need to get there. Then go back to the given information and see what you can do to get you going in the right direction. Think about where you're headed before you take even one step; otherwise you may just have to backtrack.

Your destination in question 4 is "the area of the shaded region." That region is a shape that has no name, let alone an area formula. Like most shaded regions, this one is in fact the difference between two familiar shapes with names and area formulas. Think of the shaded region in question 4 as:

$$(\text{the area of } \triangle AOB) - (\text{the area of sector } AOC)$$

So now you know you need to figure out the area of the triangle and the area of the sector.

First, the triangle. You are explicitly given $\overline{OB} = 12$. You are also given that $\overline{AB}$ is tangent to the circle at A, which tells you that $\overline{OA}$ is a radius and that $\angle OAB$ is a right angle. So if you can figure out the radius of the circle, you'll have two sides of a right triangle, which will enable you to figure out the third side, and then figure out the area.

You can get the radius from the given circumference. Plug what you know into the formula and solve for r:

$$\text{Circumference} = 2\pi r$$

$$12\pi = 2\pi r$$

$$r = \frac{12\pi}{2\pi} = 6$$

$$OA = 6$$

Aha! So it turns out that $\triangle AOB$ is no ordinary right triangle. Since one leg—6—is exactly half the hypotenuse—12—you're looking at a 30°-60°-90° triangle. By applying the well-known side ratios $(1{:}\sqrt{3}{:}2)$ for a 30°-60°-90° triangle (*100 Key Math Concepts for the ACT, #85*), you determine that $\overline{AB} = 6\sqrt{3}$. Now plug the lengths of the legs in for the base and altitude in the formula for the area of a triangle, and you'll get:

$$\text{Area} = \frac{1}{2}bh$$

$$= \frac{1}{2}(6\sqrt{3})(6)$$

$$= 18\sqrt{3}$$

Already it looks like the answer is going to be F or H—they're the choices that begin with $18\sqrt{3}$. You could just guess F or H and move on, but if you've come this far, you might as well go all the way.

Next, you need to determine the area of the sector. Fortunately, while working on the triangle, you figured out the two things you need to get the area of the sector: the radius of the circle (6) and the measure of the central angle (60°). The radius tells you that the area of the whole circle (πr^2) is 36π. And the central angle tells you that the sector is $\frac{60}{360}$ or $\frac{1}{6}$ of the circle. One sixth of 36π is 6π. So the area of the shaded region is $18\sqrt{3} - 6\pi$, choice F.

CHAPTER 14: READING WORKOUT 3: SUBJECT MATTERS

IF YOU LEARN ONLY TWO THINGS IN THIS CHAPTER . . .

1. In the Prose Fiction passage, concentrate on who the characters are and what they are doing. What are the characters' attitudes toward each other? What is the author's attitude toward his characters?

2. For the Natural Sciences passage, ask yourself, "What's new?" in each paragraph. Don't get bogged down in details or terminology. All you need is the general idea of how the paragraphs fit together.

Now that you've learned the general approach to ACT Reading and the approach for each of the specific question-types, let's look more closely at the two passage types that give students the most trouble—the Prose Fiction passage and the Natural Sciences passage.

The passage breakdown for the ACT Reading test is as follows:

Prose Fiction—one passage per test

Nonfiction—three passages per test, one each in:

- Social Studies
- Natural Sciences
- Humanities

Your approach will be essentially the same for all three Nonfiction passages, since they're all well-organized essays. Your approach to the Prose Fiction passage, however, will be somewhat different.

GO ONLINE

The Diagnostic Quiz in your Online Companion includes a practice Prose Fiction passage and a practice Natural Sciences passage. Test your skills on these special passage types.

What follows are two full ACT Reading passages—one Prose Fiction passage and one Natural Sciences passage (which, for convenience, we'll call just Science)—complete with questions. We'll talk about specific strategies for each, but, just as important, we'll talk about how you can bring together everything you've learned so far and combine this knowledge into a plan of attack for *all* Reading passages. At the end of the workout, we'll also show you how to salvage a few extra points if you find yourself near the end of the test with not enough time to read the final passage.

THE PROSE FICTION PASSAGE

The Prose Fiction passage differs from the three Nonfiction passages in that it is not a well-structured essay designed to communicate ideas in a logical, orderly way. It is, usually, a story in which characters fully equipped with their own motivations and emotions interact with each other in revealing ways. For that reason, the Prose Fiction passage won't break down into an orderly outline or road map, so don't even try to characterize the function of each paragraph. Pay attention instead to the *story*.

In the Prose Fiction passage, almost all of the questions relate to the characters. Your job is to find the answers to the following questions:

- **Who are these people?** What are they like? How are they related to each other?

- **What is their state of mind?** Are they angry? Sad? Reflective? Excited?

- **What's going on?** What's happening on the surface? What's happening beneath the surface?

- **What's the author's attitude toward the characters?**

Most of the passages focus on one person or are written from the point of view of one of the characters. Figure out who this main character is and pay special attention to what he or she is like. **Read between the lines to determine unspoken emotions and attitudes. Little hints—a momentary frown, a pointed or sarcastic comment—are sometimes all you have to go on, so *pay attention*.** In fact, you'll probably want to spend more time prereading the Prose Fiction passage than you do any of the other three passages. It's important to get a good feel for the tone and style of the passage as a whole before going to the questions.

Fortunately, the questions that accompany these passages tend to go more quickly than those for the other passages, so you'll be able to make up some of that time you lose reading the passage.

> **EXPERT TUTOR TIP**
>
> " Fiction passages focus on the characters. Who are they? What are they like? What do they think about each other? So watch what they say and do in the passages. "

MAKE IT A MOVIE IN YOUR HEAD

Try to make the passage into a movie! Imagine the scenes, the characters, the events. In the Prose Fiction passage, it should be easy to imagine the story unfolding like a movie. Pay careful attention not only to what the characters say but how they say it as well.

And don't forget to read actively, as always. Don't just read and then react. Once you have an idea of the personality of the characters, you should be able to respond to the questions. What should you do if you are struggling to understand what's going on? Go to the questions and let the line and paragraph references guide you to important words, phrases, and sentences. One or two questions should help you discover the meaning of the passage. And don't forget to guess.

THE REAL THING: PRACTICE PASSAGE

What follows is a typical ACT Prose Fiction passage, complete with questions. Before trying it, you might want to glance back at the techniques discussed in our first Reading Workout. Review the Kaplan Reading Method. **Recall that you should probably plan to spend about three minutes prereading (a little more, actually, since this is the Prose Fiction passage). Then do whichever questions you can figure out quickly. Skip any hard or time-consuming problems and come back for them later.**

When you work on the questions, constantly refer to the passage. Plan to spend much more time with your eyeballs pointed at the passage than at the questions. And don't forget to answer the questions in your own words (based on what you've preread and reread in the passage) *before* you look at the answers.

> **TEST TIP**
>
> ❝ Once you've finished reading a passage and its questions, put it out of your mind. There's no connection at all between passages, so don't carry your stress or doubt to the next one. Approach each passage as if it were the only one. **Stay active and confident!** ❞

PASSAGE III

I recall a mist starting in as I crossed the lawn
that afternoon. I was making my way up to the
summer house for the purpose of clearing away the
Line remains of his lordship's taking tea there with
(5) some guest a little while earlier. I can recall spotting from some distance . . . Miss Kenton's figure
moving about inside the summerhouse. When I
entered she had seated herself on one of the wicker
chairs scattered around its interior, evidently
(10) engaged in some needlework. On closer inspection, I saw she was performing repairs to a cushion. I went about gathering up the various items
of crockery from amidst the plants and the cane
furniture, and as I did so, I believe we exchanged a
(15) few pleasantries, perhaps discussed one or two
professional matters. For the truth was, it was
extremely refreshing to be out in the summerhouse after many continuous days in the main
building and neither of us was inclined to hurry
(20) with our tasks . . . In fact, I was looking out over
the lawn to where the mist was thickening down
around the poplar trees planted along the cart-
track, when I finally introduced the topic of the
previous year's dismissals. Perhaps a little pre-
(25) dictably, I did so by saying:

"I was just thinking earlier, Miss Kenton. It's
rather funny to remember now, but you know,
only this time a year ago, you were still insisting
you were going to resign. It rather amused me to
(30) think of it." When I finally turned to look at her,
she was gazing through the glass at the great
expanse of fog outside.

"You probably have no idea, Mr. Stevens," she
said eventually, "how seriously I really thought of
(35) leaving this house. I felt so strongly about what
happened. Had I been anyone worthy of any
respect at all, I dare say I would have left
Darlington Hall long ago." She paused for a while,
and I turned my gaze back out to the poplar trees
(40) down in the distance. Then she continued in a
tired voice: "It was cowardice, Mr. Stevens. Simple
cowardice. Where could I have gone? I have no
family. Only my aunt. I love her dearly, but I can't
live with her for a day without feeling my whole
(45) life is wasting away. I did tell myself, of course, I
would soon find some situation.

"But I was so frightened, Mr. Stevens.
Whenever I thought of leaving, I just saw myself
going out there and finding nobody who knew or
(50) cared about me. There, that's all my high principles amount to. I feel so ashamed of myself. But I
just couldn't leave, Mr. Stevens. I just couldn't
bring myself to leave."

Miss Kenton paused again and seemed to be
(55) deep in thought. I thus thought it opportune to
relate at this point, as precisely as possible, what
had taken place earlier between myself and Lord
Darlington. I proceeded to do so and concluded
by saying:

(60) "What's done can hardly be undone. But it is at
least a great comfort to hear his lordship declare
so unequivocally that it was all a terrible misun-
derstanding. I just thought you'd like to know,
Miss Kenton, since I recall you were as distressed
(65) by the episode as I was."

"I'm sorry, Mr. Stevens," Miss Kenton said
behind me in an entirely new voice, as though she
had just been jolted from a dream, "I don't understand you." Then as I turned to her, she went on:
(70) "As I recall, you thought it was only right and
proper that Ruth and Sarah be sent packing. You
were positively cheerful about it."

"Now really, Miss Kenton, that is quite incorrect and unfair. The whole matter caused me great
(75) concern, great concern indeed. It is hardly the sort
of thing I like to see happen in this house."

"Then why, Mr. Stevens, did you not tell me so at
the time?"

I gave a laugh, but for a moment was rather at
(80) a loss for an answer. Before I could formulate one,
Miss Kenton put down her sewing and said:

"Do you realize, Mr. Stevens, how much it
would have meant to me if you had thought to
share your feelings last year? You knew how upset
(85) I was when my girls were dismissed. Do you realize how much it would have helped me? Why, Mr.
Stevens, why, why, why do you always have to
pretend?"

I gave another laugh at the ridiculous turn the
(90) conversation had suddenly taken. "Really, Miss
Kenton," I said, "I'm not sure I know what you
mean. Pretend? Why, really . . ."

"I suffered so much over Ruth and Sarah leaving us. And I suffered all the more because I
(95) believed I suffered alone."

1. According to the passage, the author thinks Mr. Stevens is:

   A. worthy of respect.

   B. not an admirable person.

   C. too formal in his demeanor.

   D. disloyal to his friends.

2. The statement "Had I been anyone worthy of any respect at all, I dare say I would have left Darlington Hall long ago" (lines 36–38) can be interpreted to mean:

   F. no one at Darlington Hall truly respects Miss Kenton.

   G. Miss Kenton has little respect for Mr. Stevens.

   H. Miss Kenton feels she betrayed her principles by staying.

   J. Miss Kenton senses that Mr. Stevens feels superior to her.

3. According to the passage, the intent of Mr. Stevens's recollection of Miss Kenton's desire to resign (lines 26–30) is most likely to:

   A. open up a discussion of an event that had upset Miss Kenton.

   B. turn the conversation to the professional topic of furniture repair.

   C. indulge in nostalgic reminiscences of happier days.

   D. irritate Miss Kenton by mocking the seriousness of that desire.

4. Mr. Stevens gives "a laugh" (line 79) because he is suddenly:

   F. amused.

   G. insecure.

   H. suspicious.

   J. sarcastic.

5. The main point of Miss Kenton's references to her own family (lines 42–45) is that:

   A. she would have nowhere to turn if she left her job.

   B. children often reject those they should love.

   C. she was afraid of discovering that she did not love her aunt.

   D. life becomes very tedious when one visits relatives.

6. What is it that Mr. Stevens describes as "done" (line 60)?

   F. Lord Darlington's earlier conversation with him

   G. Miss Kenton's talk of leaving Darlington Hall

   H. Ruth and Sarah's dismissal

   J. Any talk of Miss Kenton's dismissal

7. As he is revealed in the passage, Mr. Stevens is:

   A. bored with their conversation in the summer house.

   B. increasingly hostile to Miss Kenton's depiction of his actions.

   C. uncomfortable with expressing his deep affection for Miss Kenton.

   D. unaware of how his past behavior had affected Miss Kenton.

8. Which of the following would be out of character for the narrator?

    I. Pointing out to Miss Kenton why she was unfairly characterizing his actions

    II. Spending time thinking about Miss Kenton's accusations

    III. Ridiculing Miss Kenton for poorly repairing the cushion

    F. I only

    G. II only

    H. I and II only

    J. III only

9. Miss Kenton interacts with Mr. Stevens in a way that can best be described as:

    A. sincere but formal.

    B. indifferent but polite.

    C. timid but angry.

    D. patronizing but kindly.

10. At the end of the passage, Miss Kenton asks "Why, Mr. Stevens, why, why, why do you always have to pretend?" (lines 86–88) What specific action of Mr. Stevens does she have in mind?

    F. His apparent cheerfulness at Ruth and Sarah's dismissal

    G. His simulation of great affection for her

    H. His phony concern for her own future employment

    J. His empty expressions of sympathy for her own suffering

ANSWERS AND EXPLANATIONS

Paragraphs in the Prose Fiction passage move the story forward. Your prereading road map should center on answers to four main questions about character, actions, and attitudes. They are:

- **Who are these people?** The first paragraphs are peppered with hints about who these people are. Lines 3–4 discuss Mr. Stevens "clearing away the remains of his lordship's taking tea." Lines 11–12 describe Miss Kenton "performing repairs to a cushion." Lines 28–29 discuss her previous plans for resigning. Clearly, Mr. Stevens and Miss Kenton are servants (we later learn—in lines 57–58—that their employer is Lord Darlington). Notice how, by answering this basic question, you've already answered question 1.

- **What is their state of mind?** We read of "the previous year's dismissals" (line 23–24) and Miss Kenton's intentions to leave the house (lines 34–36) as a result of them. She "felt so strongly about what happened" (lines 35–36) but she was afraid to take the step of actually leaving in protest ("It was cowardice," she admits in line 41). It sounds like some other servants were dismissed unfairly last year, and that this upset Miss Kenton. Apparently, Mr. Stevens also found the incident distressing (lines 64–65), but Miss Kenton hadn't realized this at the time.

- **What's going on?** These are obviously very formal people, but there are strong emotions rumbling beneath the surface. It's clear that Miss Kenton is very upset because she didn't realize that Mr. Stevens disapproved of the dismissals, too ("Do you realize, Mr. Stevens, how much it would have meant to me if you had thought to share your feelings last year?"—lines 82–84. And later: "Why, Mr. Stevens, why, why, why do you always have to pretend?"—lines 86–88). We get the impression that Mr. Stevens is not a man who very readily shows his feelings and emotions—as Miss Kenton puts it, he always *pretends*.

- **What is the author's attitude toward the characters?** Often, there will be a question asking about the author's point of view. Be careful here—don't confused what the characters think about each other with what the author thinks. The two may not be the same.

Note: The first question here is about Writer's View. Your best bet is to skip the question and leave it to last.

Notice how many inference-type questions there are. This is typical of the Prose Fiction passage, where so much information is conveyed implicitly—"between the lines." In most cases, you have to read around the specific line references in order to find your answer. If you've done your preread properly, however, you should be able to knock off most of the questions quickly.

KEY TO PASSAGE III

(PROSE FICTION)

Answer	Refer to	Type	Comments
1. B	First 2 paragraphs	Inference	Stevens says he was "amused" and thought it "funny" that she wanted to resign her position. Miss Kenton replies very seriously to his words, saying she doesn't understand him and how he could be so cheerful, if he disapproved of the two firings. Miss Kenton has plainly suffered, and Mr. Stevens has not reacted kindly to her pain. The author's sympathy is with Miss Kenton, not Mr. Stevens.
2. H	Lines 36–38, 50–51	Inference	"There, that's all my high principles amount to," she says.
3. A	Lines 26–30, 55–58	Inference	Lines 55–58 show that Mr. Stevens has just been discussing this subject with Lord Darlington, and now wants to discuss it with Miss Kenton.
4. G	Lines 79–80	Inference	He is "at a loss for an answer," and clearly not laughing out of amusement.
5. A	Lines 42–45	Detail	"Where could I have gone? I have no family."
6. H	Lines 60–65	Detail	Refers to "the previous year's dismissals," first mentioned in lines 23–24.
7. D	Throughout	Big Picture	Mr. Stevens's nervous laughs hint that he had no idea how deeply Miss Kenton was affected.
8. J	Throughout	Inference	I—He does this in lines 73–76. II—He wishes to respond to the accusations in lines 70–72. III—This kind of blatant harshness would be uncharacteristic of so discreet and proper a man.
9. A	Throughout	Big Picture	Miss Kenton freely expresses her feelings to him throughout, so she is sincere. But she **never** loses her formal language and demeanor.
10. F	Lines 82–86, 66–72	Inference	She wishes that he "had thought to share [his] feelings"; she was under the impression that he was "positively cheerful about [the dismissals]."

THE NATURAL SCIENCES PASSAGE

The Science passage in the Reading subject test emphasizes reading. Here, it is more important to understand ideas than to analyze experiments and data.

Approaching the Science passage is really not any different from approaching the other Nonfiction passages, since all are well-organized essays that lay out ideas in a straightforward, logical way. But you may be more likely to find unfamiliar vocabulary in Science passages. ***Don't panic.* Any unfamiliar terms will usually be defined in the passage, or else will have definitions inferable from context.**

DON'T GET LOST!

In the Science passage, it's easy to lose yourself in complex details. Don't do it. **It's *especially* important not to get bogged down in the Science passage!** Many students try to understand and remember everything as they read. But that's not the right ACT mind-set. In your preread of the passage, just get the "gist" and the outline; don't sweat the details. As always, use line references in the questions when possible. They will lead you back to the details that are important. You'd be surprised how many questions you can answer on a passage you don't really understand.

THE REAL THING: PRACTICE PASSAGE

The next passage is a typical ACT-style Science passage with questions. Try to attack it with the same Kaplan Method you use for other passages. Don't worry if you don't understand everything. Your only goal is to get a sense of the passage and its outline.

PASSAGE IV

Atoms can be excited in many ways other than by absorbing a photon. The element phosphorous spontaneously combines with oxygen when
Line exposed to air. There is a transfer of energy to the
(5) phosphorous electrons during this chemical reaction which excites them to sufficiently high energy states that they can subsequently emit light when dropping into a lower state. This is an example of what is termed chemiluminescence, the emission
(10) of light as a result of chemical reaction.

A related effect is bioluminescence, when light is produced by chemical reactions associated with biological activity. Bioluminescence occurs in a variety of life forms and is more common in
(15) marine organisms than in terrestrial or freshwater life. Examples include certain bacteria, jellyfish, clams, fungi, worms, ants, and fireflies. There is considerable diversity in how light is produced. Most processes involve the reaction of a protein
(20) with oxygen, catalyzed by an enzyme. The protein varies from one organism to another, but all are grouped under the generic name luciferin. The enzymes are known as luciferase. Both words stem from the Latin lucifer meaning light-bearing. The
(25) various chemical steps leading to bioluminescence are yet to be explained in detail, but in some higher organisms the process is known to be activated by the nervous system.

The firefly is best understood. Its light organ is
(30) located near the end of the abdomen. Within it luciferin is combined with other atomic groups in a series of processes in which oxygen is converted into carbon dioxide. The sequence culminates when the luciferin is split off from the rest, leaving
(35) it in an excited state. The excess energy is released as a photon. The peak in the emission spectrum lies between 550 and 600 nm depending on the type of luciferase. This flash produced by the simultaneous emission of many photons serves to
(40) attract mates, and females also use it to attract males of other species, which they devour.

Certain bacteria also produce light when stimulated by motion. This is why the breaking sea or a passing boat generate the greenish light seen in
(45) some bodies of water such as Phosphorescent Bay

in Puerto Rico. Some fish have a symbiotic relationship with bacteria. The "flashlight fish" takes advantage of the light created by bacteria lodged beneath each eye. Certain other fish produce their
(50) own bioluminescence, which serves as identification. However, the biological advantage if any of bioluminescence in some other organisms such as fungi remains a mystery.

Triboluminescence is the emission of light
(55) when one hard object is sharply struck against another. This contact, when atom scrapes against atom, excites electrons and disrupts electrical bonds. Light is then created when the electrons find their way to lower states. Triboluminescence
(60) is not to be confused with the glow of small particles that may be broken off by the impact. Such "sparks" are seen as a result of their high temperature. Light given off by hot objects is known as thermoluminescence, or incandescence.

(65) Another form of thermoluminescence is the basis for dating ancient ceramic objects. Quartz and other constituents of clay are continually irradiated by naturally occurring radioactive elements (e.g., uranium and thorium) and by cosmic rays.
(70) This produces defects in the material where electrons may be trapped. Heating pottery to 500°C releases the trapped electrons, which can then migrate back to their original atoms, where on returning to an atomic orbit they then emit a pho-
(75) ton. The intensity of thermoluminescence is therefore a measure of the duration of irradiation since the time when the pottery had been previously fired.

Excitation is also possible by other means. The
(80) passage of an electrical current (electroluminescence) is one. The impact of high energy particles is another. The *aurora borealis* and its southern counterpart the *aurora australis* arise when a stream of high energy particles from the sun
(85) enters the earth's upper atmosphere and literally shatters some of the molecules of the air. This leaves their atoms in excited states, and the light subsequently given off is characteristic of the atoms. Although the oxygen molecule, a major
(90) constituent of our atmosphere, has no emission in the visible, the oxygen atom can emit photons in

either the red or green portions of the spectrum. Other atoms contribute to light at other wavelengths.

11. According to the information in the sixth paragraph (lines 65–78), the brighter the thermoluminescence of a heated piece of ancient pottery:

   A. the younger the piece is.

   B. the older the piece is.

   C. the less irradiation has occurred within the piece's clay.

   D. the fewer electrons have become trapped within the clay.

12. If an ancient ceramic bowl is heated to 500°C, light is emitted when certain electrons:

   F. release radioactive elements found in the clay.

   G. scrape against other electrons.

   H. become superheated.

   J. return to their former atoms.

13. Compared to bioluminescence, chemiluminescence is NOT produced by:

   A. organic proteins that have been catalyzed.

   B. a chemical reaction.

   C. any reaction involving oxygen.

   D. a change in energy states.

14. It can be inferred from the passage that the description of the firefly's production of light is a good example of the degree to which researchers understand:

   F. why light attracts fireflies.

   G. how a chemical process can trigger bioluminescence.

   H. how female fireflies attack male fireflies.

   J. how to measure the intensity of a firefly's bioluminescence.

15. In both chemiluminescence and bioluminescence, photons are emitted:

   A. as excess energy.

   B. only by certain marine organisms.

   C. only when luciferase is present.

   D. only when phosphorous is present.

16. Based on details in the passage, the word *excited* as used in line 1 means:

   F. split off from a molecule.

   G. agitated until glowing.

   H. raised to a higher energy level.

   J. heated to the point of disintegration.

17. In discussing the creation of the two kinds of aurora, the passage asserts that the oxygen molecule "has no emission in the visible [spectrum]" (lines 90–91) but also states that "the oxygen atom can emit photons in either the red or the green portions of the spectrum" (lines 91–92). Is the passage logically consistent?

   A. Yes, because visible light is emitted after the oxygen molecules have been broken apart into oxygen atoms.

   B. Yes, because the passage presents factual information and therefore cannot be illogical.

   C. No, because the oxygen molecule forms the largest part of the atmosphere and scientific theories must account for its invisible emissions.

   D. No, because the writer has failed to adequately differentiate between the oxygen molecule's behavior and that of the oxygen atom.

18. Assume that two meteors have collided and shattered. Astronomers see both a burst of light and then a subsequent glow. Such a visual phenomenon could best be explained as the result of:

   I. chemiluminescence

   II. triboluminescence

   III. thermoluminescence

   F. II only

   G. II and III only

   H. I and III only

   J. I, II, and III

19. Based on information presented in the passage, which of the following is a hypothesis, rather than a fact?

   A. Fireflies use bioluminescence to attract mates.

   B. Thermoluminescence and triboluminescence are two distinctly different kinds of light emission.

   C. A firefly's type of luciferase determines the peak of its light emission's intensity.

   D. All organisms that produce bioluminescence do so for some biological advantage.

20. According to the last paragraph (lines 79–94), both the *aurora borealis* and the *aurora australis*:

   F. demonstrate the effects on atoms of high energy particles.

   G. occur without the presence of oxygen.

   H. emit light due to the presence of electrical currents.

   J. are visible from the surface of the earth.

ANSWERS AND EXPLANATIONS

Feeling a little numb? Unless you're a real science buff, you probably found this passage a lot less exciting than the atoms did. And you may have found yourself adrift in a sea of bewildering terms—*chemiluminescence, luciferin, aurora australis*.

We hope, though, that you didn't panic. You could still get points—and lots of them—from this passage even if all that you took away from your preread was a sense that the passage was mainly about things in nature glowing when their atoms are excited. That, and a sense of a road map, was really all you needed. Most of the questions were answerable by referring to the appropriate lines in the passage and paraphrasing what you read there.

Here's a possible road map for the passage:

- **First paragraph:** Introduction of idea of excited atoms releasing photons (i.e., luminescence). Discusses *chemiluminescence* (resulting from a chemical reaction).

- **Second paragraph:** Discusses *bioluminescence* (associated with biological activity—that is, with things that are alive).

- **Third paragraph:** Example of *bioluminescence*—fireflies.

- **Fourth paragraph:** More examples of *bioluminescence*—sea life.

- **Fifth paragraph:** Discusses *triboluminescence* (things hitting each other) and *thermoluminescence* (hot objects).

- **Sixth paragraph:** Example of *thermoluminescence*—refired ceramic objects.

- **Seventh paragraph:** Concludes with discussion of *electroluminescence* (associated with electrical currents).

Basically, the author is giving us a rundown on the various kinds of luminescence in nature. When the questions ask about one kind or another, you simply refer to the appropriate paragraph and lines.

Following is a key to the answers for this passage. Notice how you could have gotten an answer to number 12, for instance, *even if you were totally confused*. If you found "500°" in the passage (line 71), the sentence more or less spelled out the answer for you, requiring a minimum of paraphrasing.

KEY TO PASSAGE IV

(NONFICTION—NATURAL SCIENCES)

Answer	Refer to	Type	Comments
11. B	Lines 65–78	Inference	More time since last (presumably the original) firing to trap more electrons, creating brighter glow.
12. J	Lines 65–75	Detail	"migrate back to their original atoms"
13. A	Paragraph 2	Detail	Be careful with the reversal word NOT in the question. Organic means "having to do with life."
14. G	Lines 19–28, 29–41	Inference	Remember, passage is about luminescence, not fireflies.
15. A	Lines 4–10, 38–40	Inference	B and C aren't chemi-; D isn't bio-. Only A is both.
16. H	Lines 2–10, 56–66	Detail	Lines 4–8 say it all.
17. A	Lines 79–93	Detail	Note difference between oxygen molecule and oxygen atom.
18. G	Lines 54–64	Inference	I—No, since no chemical reaction II—Yes, since impact reaction III—Yes, since "subsequent glow" (probably a heat reaction)
19. D	Throughout	Big Picture	Any statement about "all organisms" is probably a hypothesis, since no one can verify what's true of every organism in existence.
20. F	Lines 79–94	Detail	"a stream of high energy particles from the sun."

EMERGENCY STRATEGY FOR TEST DAY

If you have less than four minutes left and have an entire passage untouched, you need to shift to last-minute strategies. Don't try to preread the passage; you'll just run out of time before you answer any questions. Instead, scan the questions without reading the passage and look first for the ones that mention line numbers or specific paragraphs. You can often get quick points on these questions by referring back to the passage as the question stem directs, reading a few lines around the reference, and taking your best shot.

Of course, the most important thing is to make sure you have gridded in at least a random guess on every question. If some of your blind guesses are right (as some of them statistically *should* be), they'll boost your score just as much as well-reasoned, thought-out answers would!

CHAPTER 15: SCIENCE WORKOUT 3: KEEP YOUR VIEWPOINTS STRAIGHT

IF YOU LEARN ONLY THREE THINGS IN THIS CHAPTER . . .

1. Each ACT Science test has one Conflicting Viewpoints passage in which two scientists debate an issue.

2. Spend more time prereading Conflicting Viewpoints passages. Determine each scientist's view and identify the supporting and undermining evidence.

3. You can get many Science questions right even when you don't understand the entire passage. Don't panic when faced with a tough passage.

On the Science test, you'll find one Conflicting Viewpoints passage, in which two scientists propose different theories about a particular scientific phenomenon. Often, the two theories are just differing interpretations of the same data; other times, each scientist offers his own data to support his own opinion. In either case, it's essential that you know more or less what theory each scientist is proposing, and that you pay careful attention to how and where their theories differ.

In Science Workout 2, we talked about how scientists think, and you should bring all of that information to bear on the Conflicting Viewpoints passage. Since the scientists are disagreeing on interpretation, it's usually the case that they're engaging in specific-to-general thinking. They're each using specific data, sometimes the *same* specific data, but they're coming to very different general conclusions.

EXPERT TUTOR TIP

" This passage is usually the hardest passage for students. Don't worry! There is only one passage like this, and you can save it for last if it is easier for you. "

Your job is _not_ to figure out which scientist is right and which is wrong. Instead, you'll be tested on whether you _understand_ each scientist's position and the thinking behind it.

PREREADING THE CONFLICTING VIEWPOINTS PASSAGE

When tackling the Conflicting Viewpoints passage, you'll probably want to spend a little more time than usual on the prereading step of the Kaplan Reading Method. As we saw on other Science passages, your goal in prereading is to get a general idea of what's going on so that you can focus when you do the questions. But we find that **it pays to spend a little extra time with the Conflicting Viewpoints passage in order to get a clearer idea of the opposing theories and the data behind them.**

The passage will usually consist of a short introduction laying out the scientific issue in question, followed by the different viewpoints. Sometimes these viewpoints are presented under the headings Scientist 1 and Scientist 2, or Theory 1 and Theory 2, or Hypothesis 1 and Hypothesis 2.

A scientific viewpoint on the ACT will typically consist of two parts:

- A statement of the general theory
- A summary of the data behind the theory

Usually, the first line of each viewpoint expresses the general theory. Scientist 1's first sentence might be something like: _The universe will continue to expand indefinitely._ This is Scientist 1's viewpoint boiled down to a single statement. Scientist 2's first sentence might be: _The force of gravity will eventually force the universe to stop expanding and to begin contracting._ This is Scientist 2's viewpoint, and it clearly contradicts Scientist 1's opinion.

While it's important that you understand these basic statements of theory, it is just as important that you see how they oppose each other. In fact, you might want to circle the theory statement for each viewpoint, right there in the test booklet, to fix the two positions in your mind.

After each statement of theory will come the data that's behind it. As we said, sometimes the scientists are just drawing different interpretations from the same data. But usually, each will have different supporting data. There are two different kinds of data:

- Data that supports the scientist's own theory
- Data that weakens the opposing scientist's theory

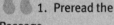

KAPLAN'S STRATEGY FOR ACT SCIENCE

1. Preread the Passage
2. Consider Each Question Stem
3. Refer to the Passage (before looking at the choices)
4. Answer the Question in Your Own Words
5. Match Your Answer with One of the Choices

It's normally a good idea to identify the major points of data for each theory. You might underline a phrase or sentence that crystallizes each, or even take note of whether it primarily supports the scientist's own theory or shoots holes in the opposing theory.

Once you understand each scientist's theory and the data behind it, you'll be ready to move on to the questions. Remember that some of the questions will refer to only one of the viewpoints. **Whatever you do, *don't mix up the two viewpoints*!** A question asking about the data supporting Theory 2 may have wrong answers that perfectly describe the data for Theory 1. If you're careless, you can easily fall for one of these wrong answers.

THE REAL THING: PRACTICE PASSAGE

What follows is a full-fledged, ACT-style Conflicting Viewpoints passage. Give yourself six minutes or so to read the passage and do all seven questions.

PASSAGE V

Tektites are natural, glassy objects that range in size from the diameter of a grain of sand to that of a human fist. They are found in only a few well-defined areas, called strewn fields. Two theories about the origin of tektites are presented below.

SCIENTIST 1

Tektites almost certainly are extraterrestrial, probably lunar, in origin. Their forms show the characteristics of air-friction melting. In one study, flanged, "flying saucer" shapes similar to those of australites (a common tektite form) were produced by ablating lenses of tektite glass in a heated airstream that simulated atmospheric entry.

Atmospheric forces also make terrestrial origin extremely improbable. Aerodynamic studies have shown that because of atmospheric density, tektite-like material ejected from the earth's surface would never attain a velocity much higher than that of the surrounding air, and therefore would not be shaped by atmospheric friction. Most likely, tektites were formed either from meteorites or from lunar material ejected in volcanic eruptions.

Analysis of specimen #14425 from the *Apollo* 12 lunar mission shows that the sample strongly resembles some of the tektites from the Australasian strewn field. Also, tektites contain only a small fraction of the water that is locked into the structure of terrestrial volcanic glass. And tektites never contain unmelted crystalline material; the otherwise similar terrestrial glass produced by some meteorite impacts always does.

EXPERT TUTOR TIP

Keep viewpoints straight:

1. Read the intro and Scientist 1 passage.
2. Answer questions that say "Scientist 1."
3. Read Scientist 2 paragraph.
4. Answer "Scientist 2" questions.
5. Answer any other questions.

EXPERT TUTOR TIP

Marking up the intro and the Scientist 1 and 2 paragraphs is critical. Bracket and circle key phrases and sentences as you go.

Scientist 2

Nonlocal origin is extremely unlikely, given the narrow distribution of tektite strewn fields. Even if a tightly focused jet of lunar matter were to strike the earth, whatever was deflected by the atmosphere would remain in a solar orbit. The next time its orbit coincided with that of the earth, some of the matter would be captured by earth's gravity and fall over a wide area.

There are striking similarities not only between the composition of the earth's crust and that of most tektites but between the proportions of various gases found in the earth's atmosphere and in the vesicles of certain tektites.

Tektites were probably formed by meteorite impacts. The shock wave produced by a major collision could temporarily displace the atmosphere above. Terrestrial material might then splatter to suborbital heights and undergo air-friction melting upon reentry. And tektite fields in the Ivory Coast and Ghana can be correlated with known impact craters.

1. The discovery that many tektites contain unmelted, crystalline material would:

   A. tend to weaken Scientist 1's argument.

   B. tend to weaken Scientist 2's argument.

   C. be incompatible with both scientists' views.

   D. be irrelevant to the controversy.

2. Which of the following is a reason given by Scientist 2 for believing that tektites originate on the earth?

   F. The density of the earth's atmosphere would prevent any similar lunar or extraterrestrial material from reaching the earth's surface.

   G. Tektites have a composition totally unlike that of any material ever brought back from the moon.

   H. Extraterrestrial material could not have been as widely dispersed as tektites are.

   J. Material ejected from the moon or beyond would eventually have been much more widely distributed on earth.

3. Scientist 1 could best answer the point that some tektites have vesicles filled with gases in the same proportion as the earth's atmosphere by:

   A. countering that not all tektites have such gas-filled vesicles.

   B. demonstrating that molten material would be likely to trap some gases while falling through the terrestrial atmosphere.

   C. suggesting that those gases might occur in the same proportions in the moon's atmosphere.

   D. showing that similar vesicles, filled with these gases in the same proportions, are also found in some terrestrial volcanic glass.

4. How did Scientist 2 answer the argument that tektite-like material ejected from the earth could not reach a high enough velocity relative to the atmosphere to undergo air-friction melting?

   F. By asserting that a shock wave might cause a momentary change in atmosphere density, permitting subsequent aerodynamic heating

   G. By pointing out that periodic meteorite impacts have caused gradual changes in atmospheric density over the eons

   H. By attacking the validity of the aerodynamic studies cited by Scientist 1

   J. By referring to the correlation between tektite fields and known impact craters in the Ivory Coast and Ghana

5. The point of subjecting lenses of tektite glass to a heated airstream was to:

   A. determine their water content.

   B. see if gases became trapped in their vesicles.

   C. reproduce the effects of atmospheric entry.

   D. simulate the mechanism of meteorite formation.

6. Researchers could best counter the objections of Scientist 2 to Scientist 1's argument by:

   F. discovering some phenomenon that would quickly remove tektite-sized objects from orbit.

   G. proving that most common tektite shapes can be produced by aerodynamic heating.

   H. confirming that active volcanoes once existed on the moon.

   J. mapping the locations of all known tektite fields and impact craters.

7. Which of the following characteristics of tektites is LEAST consistent with the theory that tektites are of extraterrestrial origin?

   A. Low water content

   B. "Flying saucer" shapes

   C. Narrow distribution

   D. Absence of unmelted material

ANSWERS

1. A
2. J
3. B
4. F
5. C
6. F
7. C

ANSWERS AND EXPLANATIONS

Your preread of the introduction should have revealed the issue at hand—namely, tektites, which are small glassy objects found in certain areas known as strewn fields. The conflict is about the *origin* of these objects: in other words, where did they come from?

Scientist 1's theory is expressed in his first sentence: "Tektites almost certainly are extraterrestrial, probably lunar, in origin." Put that into a form you can understand: In other words, Scientist 1 believes that tektites come from space, probably the moon. Scientist 2, on the other hand, has an opposing theory, also expressed in her first sentence: "Nonlocal origin is extremely unlikely." In other words, it's unlikely that tektites came from a nonlocal source; instead, they probably came from a *local* source, i.e., right here on Earth. The conflict is clear. One says that tektites come from space; the other says they come from Earth. You might have even labeled the two positions: "space origin" and "Earth origin."

Scientist 1 presents three points of data:

1. Tektite shapes show characteristics of "air-friction melting" (supporting the theory of space origin).

2. "Atmospheric forces" wouldn't be great enough to shape tektite-like material ejected from Earth's surface (weakening the theory of Earth origin).

3. Tektites resemble moon rocks gathered by *Apollo 12* but not Earth rocks (strengthening the theory of space origin).

Scientist 2 also presents three points of data:

1. Any matter coming from space would "fall over a wide area" instead of being concentrated in strewn fields (weakening the theory of space origin).

2. There are "striking similarities" between tektites and the composition of the earth's crust (strengthening the theory of Earth origin).

> **EXPERT TUTOR TIP**
>
> " Active Reading in the Conflicting Viewpoints passage will make it easier to find the information you need to answer questions correctly. "

3. "Meteorite impacts" could create shock waves, explaining how terrestrial material could undergo air-friction melting (strengthening the theory of Earth origin by counteracting Scientist 1's first point).

Obviously, you don't have time to write out the supporting data for each theory the way we've done above. But it is important to circle or bracket the key phrases in the data descriptions ("air-friction melting," "*Apollo 12*," etc.) and number them. **What's important is that you have an idea of what data supports which theory.** The questions, once you get to them, will then force you to focus.

Question 1 asks how it would affect the scientists' arguments if it were discovered that many tektites contain unmelted crystalline material. Well, Scientist 1 says that tektites **never** contain unmelted crystalline material, and that the terrestrial glass produced by some meteorite impacts **always** does. Therefore, by showing a resemblance between tektites and Earth materials, this discovery would weaken Scientist 1's argument for extraterrestrial origin. Choice A is correct.

For **question 2**, you had to identify which answer choice was used by Scientist 2 to support the argument that tektites are terrestrial in origin. You should have been immediately drawn to choice J, which expresses what we've identified above as Scientist 2's first data point. Notice how choice F is a piece of evidence that Scientist 1 cites. (Remember not to confuse the viewpoints!) As for G, Scientist 2 says that tektites *do* resemble Earth materials, but **never** says that they *don't* resemble lunar materials. And choice H gets it backwards; Scientist 2 says that extraterrestrial material *would* be widely dispersed and that the tektites are *not* widely dispersed, rather than vice versa.

For **question 3,** you need to find the best way for Scientist 1 to counter the point that some tektites have vesicles filled with gases in the same proportion as the earth's atmosphere. First, make sure you understand the meaning of that point. The idea that these gases must have been trapped in the vesicles (little holes) while the rock was actually being formed is being used by Scientist 2 to suggest that tektites are of terrestrial origin. Scientist 1 *could* say that not all tektites have such gas-filled vesicles—choice A—but that's not a great argument. If any reasonable number of them *do*, Scientist 1 would have to come up with an alternative explanation (Scientist 2 **never** claimed that *all* tektites contained these vesicles). But if, as B suggests, Scientist 1 could demonstrate that molten material would be likely to trap some terrestrial gases while falling through the earth's atmosphere, this would explain how tektites might have come from beyond the earth and still contain vesicles filled with earthlike gases. Choice C is easy to eliminate if you know that the moon's atmosphere is extremely thin and totally different in composition from the earth's atmosphere, so it doesn't make

> **EXPERT TUTOR TIP**
>
> " Many Conflicting Viewpoints questions relate to evidence (or *data*). You may be asked:
>
> What was presented?
>
> Why?
>
> Would it help or hurt a scientist's claim? "

much sense to suggest that those gases might occur in the same proportions as in the moon's atmosphere. Finally, since it's Scientist 2 who claims that tektites are terrestrial in origin, choice D, showing that similar gas-filled vesicles occur in some terrestrial volcanic glass, wouldn't help Scientist 1 at all.

In **question 4,** you're asked how Scientist 2 answered the argument that tektite-like material ejected from the earth could not reach a high enough velocity to undergo air-friction melting. Well, that was Scientist 2's third data point. The shock wave produced by a major meteorite collision could momentarily displace the atmosphere right above the impact site (meaning the air moved out of the way for a brief time). So when the splattered material reentered the atmosphere, it would undergo air-friction melting. That's basically what choice F says, so F is correct.

In **question 5,** the concept of subjecting lenses of tektite glass to a heated airstream was mentioned toward the beginning of Scientist 1's argument. The point was to simulate the entry of extraterrestrial tektite material through Earth's atmosphere, and that's closest to choice C.

Question 6 shows again why it pays to keep each scientist's viewpoint straight. You can't counter the objections of Scientist 2 to Scientist 1's argument unless you know what Scientist 2 was objecting to. Scientist 2's first data point is the only one designed to shoot holes in the opposing viewpoint. There, Scientist 2 takes issue with the idea that lunar material could strike the earth without being dispersed over a far wider area than the known strewn fields. But if, as correct choice F says, researchers found some force capable of removing tektite-sized objects from orbit *quickly*, it would demolish the objection that Scientist 2 raises in her first paragraph. The tektite material would strike the earth or be pulled away quickly, instead of remaining in a solar orbit long enough to be captured by the earth's gravity and subsequently be distributed over a wide area of the earth.

Question 7 wasn't too tough if you read the question stem carefully. You want to find the tektite characteristic that is LEAST consistent with the theory that tektites came from the moon or beyond. This is Scientist 1's theory, so you want to pick the answer choice that doesn't go with his argument. Scientist 1's evidence *does* include tektites' low water content, "flying saucer" shapes, and absence of unmelted material. The only answer choice that she didn't mention was the narrow distribution of the strewn fields. And with good reason. That's part of Scientist 2's argument *against* an extraterrestrial origin. So the correct answer is choice C.

THE DEEP END: FACING TOUGH SCIENCE PASSAGES

Now we're going to do something very cruel. We're going to to throw you a Science passage of such technical difficulty that you will want to go screaming for the exit before you finish reading it.

We're doing this for a reason. Sometimes on the ACT Science test, you'll find yourself encountering a bear of a passage—one that seems entirely incomprehensible. **The secret to success with these passages is: *don't panic*.** As we'll show you, you can get points on even the most difficult Science passage in the entire history of the ACT—as long as you keep your cool and approach it in a savvy, practical way. Here's the passage:

> **EXPERT TUTOR TIP**
>
> " If a passage looks very difficult for you, skip it. Do the easy passages first then come back to the passages that look like they are harder. "

PASSAGE VI

Neutrinos (n) are subatomic particles that travel at approximately the speed of light. They can penetrate most matter, because they are electrically neutral and effectively massless.

Generally accepted theory holds that the nuclear reactions that power the Sun create vast quantities of neutrinos as byproducts. Three proposed stages (PPI, PPII, and PPIII) of the most important solar reaction are shown in Figure 1, along with their neutrino-producing subpaths. Equations for the subpaths are shown in Table 1, as are the predicted neutrino energies and fluxes.

Figure 1

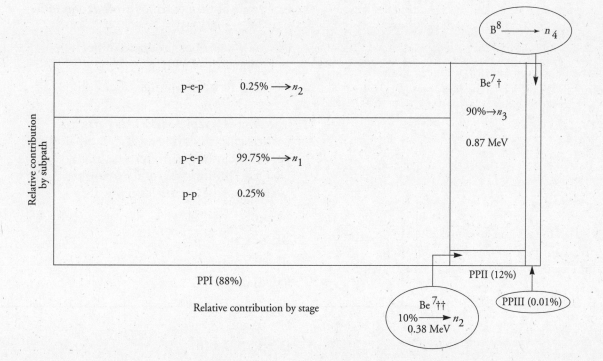

Table 1

Subpath name	Subpath equation	Neutrino energy (MeV)	Expected flux on Earth (10^{10}cm^{-2}sec^{-1})
p-p	$_1H^1 + _1H^1 \longrightarrow {_1H^2} + \beta^+ + n$	0.42	6.06781
p-e-p	$_1H^1 + \beta^- + _1H^1 \longrightarrow {_1H^2} + n$	1.44	0.01524
Be^7†	$_4Be^7 + \beta^- \longrightarrow {_3Li^7} + n$	0.87	0.43924
Be^7††	$_4Be^7 + \beta^- \longrightarrow {_3Li^7} + n$	0.38	0.04880
B^8	$_5B^8 \longrightarrow {_4Be^8} + \beta^+ + n$	14.05*	0.00054

†Be^7 subpath 1
††Be^7 subpath 2

*Maximum

8. According to the information presented in the passage, which of the following stages or subpaths should contribute the smallest portion of the total solar neutrino flux on Earth?

F. p-p
G. PPI
H. PPII
J. PPIII

9. Of the neutrinos that are produced in the subpaths described in the passage, which type can have the greatest energy?

A. n_1
B. n_2
C. n_3
D. n_4

10. Based on the information presented in the passage, the percentage of solar neutrinos produced by Be^7 subpath 2 is approximately:

F. 1.2%
G. 10%
H. 12%
J. 90%

11. Solar neutrinos are detected through a reaction with $_{37}Cl$ for which the minimum neutrino energy is approximately 0.8 MeV. Of the neutrinos discussed in the passage, this method would detect:

A. all of the neutrinos produced in PPI and PPII.

B. some of the neutrinos produced in PPI, PPII, and PPIII.

C. only neutrinos produced in Be^7 subpath 1 of PPII.

D. only neutrinos produced in PPIII.

12. The symbol β represents a beta particle, a particle emitted during nuclear decay. Beta particles may be positively or negatively charged. During which of the following subpaths are beta particles emitted?

I. p-p
II. p-e-p
III. B^8

F. II only
G. I and III only
H. II and III only
J. I, II, and III

ANSWERS

8. J
9. D
10. F
11. B
12. G

ANSWERS AND EXPLANATIONS

Confused? If you aren't, you should stick close to your phone, because the Nobel Prize committee will probably be calling sometime soon! On the other hand, if you are confused, don't sweat it. **As we said in ACT Basics, some ACT questions are so hard that even your teachers would have a hard time getting them correct.**

The good news is that you don't have to understand a passage to get a few questions right. Here's how you might have approached the passage above.

GETTING POINTS EVEN IF YOU DON'T GET THE POINT

Your preread of the introduction should have told you that the passage is about neutrinos coming from the sun. But that may be all you were able to get from this gibberish. You may have been in a total fog looking at Figure 1 and Table 1. But if you didn't panic, you might have noticed a few things: first, that whatever Figure 1 illustrates, there are some really big parts and some really small parts. If you look at the x-axis of the chart, you'll see that, whatever PPI, PPII, and PPIII are, the first is 88 percent, the second only 12 percent, and the third only .01 percent.

Is that tiny, vague insight enough to get a point? Yes! Look at **question 8**. It asks which stage or subpath contributes the *smallest* portion of flux. Well, look for a small portion. PPIII's figure of 0.01 percent is a very small number, whatever it's supposed to be referring to, so PPIII would be a good guess here. And indeed, choice J is correct for question 8.

What about Table 1? This is a little easier to understand, especially if you ignore the column about subpath equations. But "neutrino energy" sounds like something we can comprehend. Apparently, each subpath produces a different level of neutrino energy. Some have high energy (like B^8, with 14.06) and some have low energy (like B^{7++}, with only 0.38). Energy is mentioned in **question 9**. Which type of neutrinos can have the greatest energy? Well, if B^8 were a choice, we'd pick that. But the choices are ns, not Bs. Well, try to find B^8 somewhere in the other chart—Figure 1. There we find it somehow associated with n_4 neutrinos. So take a gamble; choose n_4—which is choice D—for this question. If you did that, you'd still have gotten another point, still without really understanding much more than before.

You're hot; keep it going. **Question 10** refers to Be^7 subpath 2. You may have noticed in the note under Table 1 that the Be^7 with two little dagger marks signifies subpath 2. So far, so good. Notice that the choices are all percentages. Where are percentages mentioned? In Figure 1. So find Be^7 with two dagger marks in Figure 1. You find it in the area of PPII, which is 12 percent of the x-axis in that chart. But notice that Be^7 with two dagger marks represents only *part* of that part of the figure—10 percent, to be exact. So 10 percent of 12 percent would be 1.2 percent. That's choice F. It's also the correct answer.

Things get a little harder with **question 11,** but you still might have gotten the answer if you used common sense. Here we get some mumbo jumbo about $_{37}Cl$, but the part of the question that should have caught your eye was the bit about a minimum neutrino energy of 0.8 MeV. Neutrino energy was represented in the third column of Table 1. According to that table, only three subpaths have an energy greater than 0.8—p-e-p (with 1.44), Be^7 with one dagger mark (with 0.87) and B^8 (the champion, with 14.06). Unfortunately, the answer choices aren't expressed in those terms; they're expressed in terms of PPI, II, and III, so we're going to have to translate from table to figure again, just as we did with question 9.

Take p-e-p first. That's part (but not all) of the PPI portion of Figure 1. Be^7 with one dagger mark, similarly, is part (but not all) of the PPII portion. And B^8 is all of the PPIII portion. So there are at least parts of PPI, PPII, and PPIII implicated here. That should have led you to choice B, which would have gotten you yet another point. Notice that choice A is inaccurate because it talks about *all* of something in PPI and PPII, and doesn't mention PPIII at all. Choices C and D, meanwhile, seem too limited, since they only mention one of the PP areas (whatever they are). So B was definitely the closest answer choice.

Finally, **question 12** talks about beta particles. Well, that little beta symbol appears only in the subpath column of Table 1. There we find beta symbols in the equations for *all* of the subpaths in the table. That may have led you to believe that all three Roman numerals should be included, and no one would have blamed you for choosing choice J (I, II, and III). You would have been wrong, but you can't win them all when you're winging questions you don't really understand.

Of course, if you noticed that the question was asking for beta particles *emitted*, and if you knew that in the subpath equations everything *before* the arrow is what you start with while everything *after* the arrow is what you finish with, you might have been able to make a better guess. You would have realized that those equations with a beta symbol *before* the arrow were ones in which a beta particle was *absorbed*, while those with a beta symbol *after* the arrow were ones in which a beta particle was *emitted*. In that case, then, you would have seen that the equations for p-p and B^8 do have beta particles emitted, while the equation for p-e-p does not. That might have led you to choice G—I and III only—which is the correct answer.

Six questions, six points—and all without understanding the passage in any deep or thorough way. Of course, if you understand the mysteries of neutrino flux and p-e-p subpaths, congratulations. You're probably enough of a science whiz to ace the subject test anyway. But if you're like most ACT test takers, you won't understand everything the passages talk about. Sometimes you'll even find yourself totally lost.

The moral of the story, of course, **is don't give up on a passage just because you don't understand it.** You may not be able to get *every* point associated with the passage, but you may be able to get at least one or two (or three or four). Remember: The test is designed in such a way that you can *figure out* many of the questions, even if you don't know the subject area.

Let's conclude now with another quick point about getting quick points. If you're nearly out of time and you've still got a whole Science passage left, you need to shift to last-minute strategies. As in Reading, don't try to preread the passage, or you'll just run out of time before you answer any questions. Instead, scan the questions without reading the passage and look first for the ones that require only reading data off of a graph or table. You can often get a couple of quick points just by knowing how to find data quickly.

Again, the most important thing is to make sure you have gridded in at least a random guess on every question.

> **EXPERT TUTOR TIP**
>
> " If you run out of time, guess the same letter on every problem. This will give you a higher chance of increasing your score purely by guessing. "

CHAPTER 16: WRITING WORKOUT: WRITE WHAT COUNTS

IF YOU LEARN ONLY FOUR THINGS IN THIS CHAPTER . . .

1. You should be familiar with Kaplan's Four-Step Method for the ACT Essay: pause to know the prompt, plan, produce, and proofread.

2. The Writing test asks you to take a position on the issue in the prompt. The best essays knock down the opposing arguments and positively support the side you take.

3. Support your view with relevant and clearly organized evidence. Examples will come from your own experiences.

4. Pacing is crucial to getting all your ideas on paper. Be sure to leave yourself two or three minutes to proofread.

A growing number of colleges want an assessment of your written communication skills. If you consider yourself a good writer and are accustomed to scoring well on essays, there may be a temptation to skip this chapter. Don't. Top scores are not given out easily, and writing a scored first draft in under a half hour is unlike most of your past writing experiences.

In addition, the ACT essay is not a typical essay that you are used to writing in school. For example:

- You are allowed (even encouraged) to use the first person "I" and "we" in your argument.

- Personal experiences are excellent ways to back up your position. If you need to embroider the facts a little to make your point, no one is going to fact-check your essay.

Let's start with the facts.

JUST THE FACTS

Writing has **always** been an essential skill for college success. An optional Writing test will be available when you take the ACT. Some colleges require it; others do not. **Before registering for the ACT, find out if the schools to which you're applying want applicants to take the Writing test.**

The ACT English test already measures knowledge of effective writing skills, including grammar, punctuation, organization, and style. The Writing test complements that evaluation of technical skill with an example of your simple, direct writing.

HOW THE ACT ESSAY IS SCORED

Your essay will be graded on a holistic scale of 1–6 (6 being the best). Graders will be looking for an overall sense of your essay, not assigning separate scores for specific elements like grammar or organization. Two readers read and score each essay; then those scores are added together to arrive at your Writing subscore (from 2–12). If there's a difference of more than a point between the two readers' scores, your essay will be read by a third reader.

Statistically speaking, there will be few essays that score 6. If each grader gives your essay a 4 or 5, that will place you at the upper range of those taking the exam.

WHAT SHOULD I DO?

The readers realize you're writing under time pressure and expect you to make some mistakes. **The facts in your essay are not important; readers are not checking them. Nor will they judge you on your opinions. What they want is to see how well you can communicate a relevant, coherent point of view.**

The test makers identify the following as the skills tested in the Writing test:

- **Answer the question in the prompt.** State a clear perspective on an issue.

- **Build an argument.** Assemble supporting evidence logically with relevant, specific points.

- **Maintain focus and organize your specific points logically.** Avoid digressions and be sure to draw everything together in a concluding paragraph.

- **Address the complexity of the issue.** Discuss BOTH sides of the argument. Don't ignore the opposite side.

- **Write clearly.** Make sure your argument is easy to follow. Grammar rules are not the point of the essay; however, many errors that interfere with the essay's argument will hurt your score.

CAN I PREPARE FOR THE ESSAY?

The underlying skill in the Writing test is speed. On the ACT you have only 30 minutes, and you must accomplish a lot in that time. It takes practice (and more practice) to read the prompt, organize your position with relevant ideas and facts, write a concluding paragraph—and proofread the whole.

DO YOU NEED TO PREPARE FOR THE ESSAY?

The ACT essay is not like other writing experiences. It's a first draft that will be graded. Not only must it be complete and well organized, but it must also be easy for a grader to see that it is complete and well organized (and the grader may spend as little as a minute reading your essay). That's a lot to do in 30 minutes, so preparation and practice are a good idea.

By the way, practicing the ACT essay also reinforces what you've learned for the English test and strengthens your Reading test skills: in Reading, you take an argument apart; in Writing, you put together an argument.

THE KAPLAN FOUR-STEP METHOD FOR THE ACT ESSAY

Step 1: Pause to Know the Prompt

Step 2: Plan

Step 3: Produce

Step 4: Proofread

If you plan your essay and adhere to your plan when you write, the result will be solidly organized. Between now and test day, you can't drastically change your overall writing skills—and you probably don't need to. **If your plan is good, all you need to do in the writing and proofreading steps is draw on your strengths and avoid your weaknesses.** Get to know what those are as you practice.

Write what counts. To maximize your score, use the Kaplan Method to help you focus on writing what the scorers will look for—*and nothing else.*

Step:	A high-scoring essay:	A low-scoring essay:
Prompt	clearly develops a position on the prompt	does not clearly state a position
Plan	supports with concrete, relevant examples	is general, repetitious, and/or overly simplistic in its ideas
Produce	maintains clear focus and organization	digresses or has weak organization
Proofread	shows competent use of language	contains errors that reduce clarity

EXPERT TUTOR TIP

Note that you can't earn a 5 or 6 if you haven't met the basic requirements for a 4, so think of the requirements as building blocks and be sure you have the foundation in place.

Kaplan has found this approach useful in its many years of experience with hundreds of sample essay statements on a wide range of tests. Let's look at what the test makers tell you about how the essays are scored.

To score Level 4, you must:

- **Answer the question.**
- **Support ideas with examples.**
- **Show logical thought and organization.**
- **Avoid major or frequent errors that make your writing unclear.**

> **EXPERT TUTOR TIP**
>
> " Note that you can't earn a 5 or 6 (10 or 12) if you haven't met the basic requirements for a 4 (8). Think of the requirements as building blocks to higher scores. "

Organization and clarity are key to an above-average essay. If the reader can't follow your train of thought—if ideas aren't clearly organized or if grammatical errors, misspellings, and incorrect word choices make your writing unclear—you can't do well.

To score Level 5, all you have to add to a 4 is:

- **Address the topic in depth.**

This means adding a discussion of the other side to your essay. If you successfully knock down the opposing side, you have automatically improved your own argument—and increased the complexity of the issue.

Another way to add depth to your essay is to take a third position (one that is slightly different from the two sides presented in the prompt). This position should be a slight variation, not a big departure. The graders will then easily see that you have given the prompt extra thought. Be aware, however, that you must be able to support this new position on the topic.

To score Level 6, all you have to add to a 5 is:

- **Make transitions smoother and show variety in syntax and vocabulary.**

Use words from the prompt to tie paragraphs together, rather than relying exclusively on connectors like *however* and *therefore*. Vary your sentence structure, sometimes using simple sentences and other times using compound and complex ones. Adding a few college-level vocabulary words will also boost your score.

Now let's apply the Kaplan Method to a practice prompt:

STEP 1: PAUSE TO KNOW THE PROMPT

The ACT Writing prompt usually relates to a topic that is familiar to high school students. It will outline an issue that teenagers are likely to have an opinion on, or on which they can devise one fairly easily.

If, by chance, the prompt describes a situation you feel strongly about, be sure to present your argument in a careful, thoughtful manner. Do NOT write an overly emotional response.

Spend less than a minute reading the prompt on test day.

Step 2: Plan

Take five or six minutes to build a plan before you write. This step is critical—a successful plan leads directly to a high-scoring essay. Focus on what kinds of reasoning and examples you can use to support your position.

Note: If you find you have more examples for a position different from the one you thought you would take originally, *change your position*.

There is no one way to plan an essay. One method is to draw a large "T" on the page and align examples and ideas on either side of the line. So you might have the following notes on the prompt we started with in Step 1:

NEWSPAPERS IN SCHOOL

Safe learning environment (more control)	• Freedom of speech • (less control)
	What? add coverage of state, local elections, & discussion of school issues imp't to students
A. Can have faculty advisor monitor coverage to make sure issues are clearly, fairly, and *tastefully* presented	*Why?* 1. help prepare students to be adults who know how to think and to vote
B. Administration can get its side heard too	2. air debates about student rights ex. dress code ex. off-campus lunch privileges
C. Promotes safe discussion, improves student morale, and avoids protests	3. students have rights and should be acknowledged.

CONCLUSION: Everyone benefits from freedom of speech in a school newspaper.

Information Banks. Don't wait until test day to think of examples you can use to support your ideas. Regardless of what question is raised in the prompt, you will draw your support from the things you know best and are most comfortable writing about—things that you know a fair amount of concrete detail about.

Refresh your memory about your favorite or most memorable books, school subjects, historical events, personal experiences, activities—anything. By doing so, you strengthen mental connections to those ideas and details—that will make it easier to connect to the right examples on test day.

Structure your essay. Plan a clear introduction, a distinct middle section, and a strong conclusion. **Choose your best examples, decide in what order you'll handle them, and plan your paragraphs.**

With that in mind, we suggest:

- **Use an effective *hook* to bring the reader in.**
- **Use regular *transitions* to provide the glue that holds your ideas together.**
- **End with a *bang* to make your essay memorable.**

A "hook" means avoiding an essay that opens (as thousands of other essays will): "In my opinion, …, because…." Try a more general statement that introduces one or more of the key words you will use from the prompt.

Using the "T" model presented earlier, you might use the following sentence: *A student newspaper should help students learn to think and express themselves.*

A "bang" means a closing that ties the three paragraphs together. Good choices can be a clear, succinct statement of your thesis in the essay or a vivid example that's right on point.

To conclude the planned "T" essay, you might finish with: *Both students and the administration would benefit from a school newspaper that covers a broad array of topics.* Plan for the prompt using a paragraph-by-paragraph method. The answer we've chosen is:

> I agree that restrictions on student newspapers violate free-dom of speech and I also believe restrictions impede student learning.

This position clearly responds to the assignment, and adding some reasoning *not* taken directly from the prompt immediately tells the reader "I have ideas of my own."

Next, working with our proposed response, comb your memory or your imagination for supporting reasons and examples to use. We'll use:

Point: Student newspapers should mimic real life newspapers.

Point: Not being in the school paper doesn't mean it's not discussed.

Point: Students can avoid "harming" others as well as adults.

Point: Censorship is anti-democratic.

Fill in the details. Jot down any notes you need to ensure that you use the details you've developed, but don't take the time to write full sentences. When you have

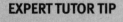

enough ideas for a few supporting paragraphs, decide what your introduction and conclusion will be and the order in which you'll discuss each supporting idea.

Here's our sample plan:

> Para 1: I agree with "free speech." Student newspapers should prepare for real life.
>
> Para 2: Press is treated specially in real life.
>
> Para 3: Potential harm not a good argument.
>
> Para 4: Censorship vs. democracy.
>
> Para 5: Better to have discussion out in the open.
>
> Para 6: Restate thesis.

If you take our advice and use examples that are very familiar to you, you won't have to write much in your plan in order to remember the point being made. **Learn how brief you can make your notes and still not lose sight of what you mean to say.**

A good plan:

- **Responds to the prompt**
- **Has an introduction**
- **Has strong examples, usually one per paragraph**
- **Has a strong conclusion**

In addition to writing practice essays, practice just making plans on your own whenever you have a few spare minutes, using ideas for changes in high school curriculum, events, lifestyle, and activities such as: longer vs. shorter class sessions; students should/should not be allowed off campus during the school day; study halls should/should not be eliminated; vocational options vs. all college prep. The more you do this, the easier it will become.

STEP 3: PRODUCE

Appearances count. In purely physical terms, your essay will make a better impression if you fill a significant portion of the space provided and if it is clearly divided into three to five reasonably equal paragraphs (except that the final paragraph can be shorter). **Use one paragraph for your introduction, one for each example or line of reasoning, and one for your conclusion so your essay will be easy for readers to follow.**

Write neatly: graders will give you a zero if your essay is very hard to read. If your handwriting is a problem, print.

EXPERT TUTOR TIP

" On test day use 6–7 minutes for planning and 23–24 minutes for writing and proofreading. Try writing practice essays in 20 minutes to make the "real" essay seem easier. "

Stick with the plan. You only have a short time for your essay. **Use the ideas and organization you established in your plan.** Resist any urge to introduce new ideas—no matter how good you think they are—or to digress from the central focus or organization of each paragraph.

Think twice, write once. Think carefully before you write it down. If your sentences are not varied (meaning singsong—"The newspaper should cover many topics. The students should learn about many issues…") or full of mistakes, your essay score will suffer.

Use topic sentences in each paragraph. Each paragraph should be organized around a topic, or summary, sentence.

Use topic sentences. Each paragraph should be organized around a topic sentence that you should finish in your mind before you start to write:

- *I believe…*
- *One example…*
- *Another example…*
- *Another example…*
- *Therefore we can conclude…*

You don't have to write it this way in the essay, but completing these sentences in your mind ensures that you focus on what idea organizes each paragraph.

Choose words carefully. Use vocabulary that you know well. Inserting new or fancy words that you have learned recently often stick out. The result of unfamiliar words in an essay is the opposite of what you want: awkward, confusing thoughts. Instead of impressing the graders, you have made a mess. Two more points here:

- Avoid using *I* excessively.
- Avoid slang.

Use transitions. Think about the relationship between ideas as you write, and spell them out clearly. This makes it easy for the readers to follow your reasoning, and they'll appreciate it. **Use key words from the prompt as well as the kinds of words you've learned about in Reading that indicate contrast, opinion, relative importance, and support.**

Essay length. While many poor essays can be quite long, there will be few 6 essays under about 300 words, so take this into consideration as you practice. The length of an essay is no assurance of its quality. However, it's hard to develop an argument in depth—something the graders look for—in one or two short paragraphs.

> **EXPERT TUTOR TIP**
>
> " The ACT essay isn't the place for creative writing. Make your writing direct, persuasive, and error-free. Give the graders what they are looking for. "

Don't ramble, digress, or write off topic just to make your essay longer. Practice writing organized essays with developed examples, and you'll find yourself writing more naturally.

Don't sweat the small stuff. Do not obsess over every little thing. If you cannot remember how to spell a word, do your best and just **keep going.** Even the top scoring essays can have minor errors. The essay readers understand that you are writing first drafts and have no time for research or revision.

Step 4: Proofread

Always leave yourself two or three minutes to review your work—the time spent will definitely pay off. Very few of us can avoid the occasional confused sentence or omitted word when writing under pressure. Quickly review your essay to be sure your ideas are on the page, not just in your head.

Don't hesitate to make corrections on your essay—these are timed first drafts, not term papers. But keep it clear: use a single line through deletions and an asterisk to mark where text should be inserted.

You don't have time to look for every minor error or to revise substantially. Learn the types of mistakes you tend to make and look for them. Some of the most common mistakes in students' essays are those found in the English test questions.

COMMON ERRORS

- Omitted words
- Sentence fragments
- Subject-verb agreement or verb tense errors
- Misplaced modifiers
- Pronoun agreement errors
- Misused words—especially homonyms like *their* for *there* or *they're*
- Spelling errors

COMMON STYLE PROBLEMS

- Choppy sentences (combine some)
- Too many long, complex sentences (break some up)
- Too many stuffy-sounding words (replace some with simple words)
- Too many simple words (add a few college-level words)

> **EXPERT TUTOR TIP**
>
> " Use a caret ∧ or an asterisk * to insert a word or words. Write a backward P to create a new paragraph, and cross words out with one line. Don't make a mess! "

KNOW THE SCORE: SAMPLE ESSAYS

The best way to be sure you've learned what the readers will look for is to try scoring some essays yourself.

The graders will be scoring holistically, not checking off "points"—but to learn what makes a good essay, it may help to consider these questions, based on the test makers' scoring criteria:

Does the author answer the question?

Is the author's position clearly stated?

Does the body of the essay support and develop the position taken?

Are there at least three supporting paragraphs?

Is the relevance of each supporting paragraph clear?

Does the writer address the other side of the argument?

Is the essay organized, with a clear introduction, middle, and end?

Did the author use one paragraph for each new idea?

Is each sentence in a paragraph relevant to the point made in that paragraph?

Are transitions clear?

Is the essay easy to read? Is it engaging?

Are sentences varied?

Is good vocabulary used effectively?

Don't just answer "yes" or "no"—locate specific text in the essay that answers the question.

Let's look at a sample essay based on the prompt and plan we've been looking at.

Here's the prompt:

In many high schools, the administration has provided guidelines for the publication of student newspapers. These guidelines often determine which topics can and cannot be discussed in the newspaper and prohibit what the administration deems inappropriate language. Many administrators and teachers feel that these restrictions enable them to provide a safe learning environment for students. Others feel that any restriction on the student newspaper is a violation of freedom of speech. In your opinion, should high schools place restrictions on student newspapers?

In your essay, take a position on this question. You may write about either one of the two points of view given, or you may present a different point of view on this question. Use specific reasons and examples to support your position.

SAMPLE ESSAY 1

In many high schools, the administration has provided guidelines for the publication of student newspapers. These guidelines often determine which topics can and cannot be discussed in the newspaper, and prohibit what the administration deems inappropriate language. Many administrators and teachers feel that these restrictions enable them to provide a safe, appropriate learning environment for students. Others feel that any restriction on the student newspaper is a violation of freedom of speech. In my opinion, students should be free to write on any topic.

Firstly, restrictions will not stop certain topics being talked about. Students will always discuss topics that they are interested in. Second, students are more aware of what is or is not appropriate than the administration might think. A newspaper is there to tell news and students will therefore write about the news.

Finally and most importantly, a right such as freedom of speech should not be checked at the school door. Students not being able to cognizant and value rights such as these if they are not taught their importance in school. So high schools should not place restrictions on student newspapers.

Score: _____/6

> **EXPERT TUTOR TIP**
>
> " This doesn't mean you shouldn't quote from the prompt. On the contrary, you should use as much language from the prompt as possible, but always tie language from the prompt to your own ideas. "

It should have been fairly easy to see that this isn't a strong essay. The author does state a clear opinion, but half of the essay is a direct copy of the prompt—something the graders will notice and, if anything, be annoyed by. The time and space spent just quoting the prompt was completely wasted—it earned the writer zero points.

The rest of the essay is organized and uses transition words (*firstly* and *finally*). The author states her thesis, follows with three supporting reasons, and then a conclusion. However, none of this is discussed fully enough—no concrete detail or examples are given. In the second paragraph, for instance, the author should have added an example demonstrating that students are aware of what is appropriate or an example of topics that students will discuss.

The language is understandable but there are significant errors affecting clarity. For instance, the second sentence of paragraph 3 is a fragment—there is no verb.

> **EXPERT TUTOR TIP**
>
> " Never spend more than seven minutes planning, no matter how much you wish you could think of "better" ideas. "

Some vocabulary words are clearly plugged in without a clear understanding of their meaning: in paragraph 3, "not being able to cognizant" is incorrect; perhaps the student meant "not being able to understand."

This essay looks like the writer couldn't think of "good" ideas, waited too long, and had to write in a hurry.

Let's try another, better essay. Read quickly and select a score before reading our evaluation.

SAMPLE ESSAY 2

Many high schools place restrictions on appropriate topics and language for student newspapers. Many people disagree with these restrictions. While arguments can be made for either side, I believe that newspapers, as part of the school, should be placed under guidelines of the school.

First, a high school necessarily has stricter rules than normal society. These rules are not in place to punish students. They protect them and providing a suitable learning environment. In this way, when students leave high school they will have grown from children to adults, ready to succeed in the larger world. For example, the strict time schedule, with exactly three or four minutes given between classes, prepares students for strict schedules in the broader world.

Second, students interested in journalism should have instruction in how to write and publish newspaper articles. A student newspaper, which for obvious reasons has limited scope, is a perfect laboratory for students to experiment with journalistic writing. The administration and faculty dedicated to the newspaper can guide students in choosing appropriate topics, such as student elections. Then they can write articles on politics in the future. Imagine a student whose high school teacher taught the proper techniques for reporting on the race for student council president, joining a major news organization and reporting on the United States Presidential election.

Lastly, students may not realize the harm which their writing may cause. In my school, a student discovered a teacher's affair and "reported" on it in a story on the student's TV network, before the school could interfere. The teacher's career was destroyed and his marriage fell apart. Perhaps he deserved it, but student television should not have been the vehicle that ruined his life. The student reporter felt terribly in the end, as she had not thought through the consequences of her story. The same consequences could occur in a student newspaper that was restricted by no guidelines from the school.

Therefore, while many people argue that freedom of speech is a right too precious to give up, it is more important to provide guidelines for young people.

Score: _____/6

Okay, now do you want to revise the score you gave this essay?

Actually, this sample exceeds the basic requirements for a 4; it's a 5.

This essay addresses the assignment. The writer's position is clear and the personal example in the fourth paragraph provides good support. The organization is good and the author uses transition words. Each paragraph discusses a different aspect of the writer's argument. Let's look at why it doesn't rate a 6.

Some of the support isn't explained enough. The second paragraph, for example, doesn't show the connection between strict schedules and restrictions on newspaper reporting—the subject of the essay. The idea, in paragraph 3, of a student growing up to be a presidential reporter is interesting, but it doesn't particularly address the idea of restrictions. The final paragraph doesn't tie back to the main argument about newspapers; it only generally mentions "guidelines for young people."

The author's writing is good, but unexceptional. There are a few examples of complex sentences. For example, in paragraph 2: "A student newspaper, which for obvious reasons has limited scope, is a perfect laboratory for students to experiment with journalistic writing." The essay includes grammar mistakes, however—such as in paragraph 2: "They protect them and providing a suitable learning environment."

In paragraph 3, the sentence "Then they can write articles on politics in the future" includes the ambiguous *they*, which could refer to the administration and teachers or the students.

Let's look at another essay. Read it quickly and decide how you would score it.

SAMPLE ESSAY 3

School administrations and teachers who support restrictions believe that these restrictions are needed to form an appropriate learning environment. But I agree with those who oppose such restrictions because they violate freedom of speech and these limits impede student progress and success after high school.

Despite the true need for rules in high schools, newspapers should be exempt. Students need discipline in the form of detention for misbehavior or demerits for poor study, but the student newspaper should not be a part of that system. Rather, it should mimic "real world" journalism.

EXPERT TUTOR TIP

" To get from a 4 to a 5, you need fully developed examples and logic.
To get to a 6, you need lively, mostly error-free writing. "

Student editors, usually seniors aged seventeen or eighteen, are well aware of the overall environment in which they publish, and understand what is or is not appropriate. High school should give students practice at being cognizant of the larger arena in which they act. The few negative incidents that free press will admittedly cause will teach students that in life, one must take responsibility for one's actions.

Therefore, the argument for freedom of speech in student newspapers advances substantial educational goals for students, as well as our unalienable right of freedom of speech. This right, however, is paramount. The American public school is an extension of the American government and community, and censorship is inconsistent with American democracy. Again, students need to be prepared for the world they will live in; depriving them of rights that are promoted in the greater community prepares students poorly for life after high school.

Finally, censoring information in the student newspaper will not remove the subject from student discussion. Rather, it will remove a balanced, informative viewpoint, and often make the "inappropriate" action more desirable and "cool." Placing restrictions on student newspapers would be a serious mistake that would hinder students from learning what it is to participate in a free society.

Score: _____/6

Did you recognize this as an essay similar to the plan we did earlier?

> Para 1: I agree with "free speech." Student newspapers should prepare for real life.
>
> Para 2: Press is treated specially in real life.
>
> Para 3: Potential harm not a good argument.
>
> Para 4: Censorship vs. democracy.
>
> Para 5: Not discussing in press doesn't mean not discussing in school.

This essay is pretty good—it would earn a 4. The position is clearly stated, and some supporting reasoning is given.

However, the reasoning is too general and the writing is too ordinary to earn the top score. Let's see how it could be improved.

TURNING A 4 INTO A 6

The essay plunges right into the two points of view offered in the prompt. It could be improved by introducing the issue with a general statement, like:

> Many students, parents, and school administrators are debating the proper role of student newspapers. Should their language and content be restricted?

In the last sentence of the first paragraph, the writer introduces some additional reasoning *not* included in the prompt. That's excellent, but it would be better to make it clear where the position from the prompt ends and the author's position begins, perhaps like this:

> But I agree with those who oppose such restrictions because they violate freedom of speech. I would further argue that these limits impede student progress and success after high school.

The second paragraph is relevant and organized—it covers one of the two positions offered in the prompt. But it would be better if the writer tied this argument more clearly to something specific in the prompt, perhaps with an opening sentence using language from the prompt, like:

> Some people claim that high school students need strict guidelines in order to prepare for life after school.

Moreover, at the end of the paragraph the reference to mimicking "real world" journalism would be improved by telling the reader what "real world" journalism is:

> Rather, it should mimic "real world" journalism, which strives to provide valid, balanced reporting on events important to the public, or in this case the student body.

The third paragraph addresses the view in the prompt that students can cause harm by printing inappropriate articles. But, again, it should be made clearer what part of the prompt this paragraph is responding to, with a first sentence like:

> Others believe that students may cause unintended harm with newspaper articles written on controversial subjects. I think that is laughable.

Paragraph four is pretty good, as is. It states clearly what the author considers the most important argument. The fifth paragraph raises good arguments, but leaves them undeveloped. It would be best to provide an example of what type of story would help promote "balanced, informative" discussion to counteract "inappropriate…cool" actions, like:

> For instance, a reporter for my high school paper researched and wrote an in-depth story on the increasing drug problem among students. The administration quickly intervened and stopped the story, declaring that drugs were an inappropriate topic for student discussion. This story, however, would have focused discus-

sion on a crucial issue for students, so that they can make the right choice when offered drugs or when they see friends using drugs. Unfortunately, this is a situation most students will face, and they need to be prepared. Suppressing the story made drugs seem even more rebellious and mysterious and most importantly did not give students facts with which they could prepare.

This makes it clear why the writer saved this argument for the last—an important, detailed example.

Finally, since this writer offers a fair number of supporting ideas, it would also be a good idea to add some transitions that establish the relative importance of those ideas. For example, in the third paragraph:

> First of all, student editors, usually seniors aged seventeen or eighteen, are well aware of the overall environment in which they publish, and understand what is or is not appropriate. But even more importantly, high school should give students practice at being cognizant of the larger arena in which they act.

Here's how this essay would look with the improvements we've suggested:

> Many students, parents, and school administrators are debating the proper role of student newspapers. Should their language and content be restricted? School administrations and teachers who support restrictions believe that these restrictions are needed to form an appropriate learning environment. But I agree with those who oppose such restrictions because they violate freedom of speech. I would further argue that these limits impede student progress and success after high school.
>
> Some people claim that high school students need strict guidelines in order to prepare for life after school. Despite the true need for rules in high schools, newspapers should be exempt. Students need discipline in the form of detention for misbehavior or demerits for poor study, but the student newspaper should not be a part of that system. Rather, it should mimic "real world" journalism, which strives to provide valid, balanced reporting on events important to the public, or in this case the student body.
>
> Others believe that students may cause unintended harm with newspaper articles written on controversial subjects. I think that is laughable. First of all, student editors, usually seniors aged seventeen or eighteen, are well aware of the overall environment in which they publish, and understand what is or is not appropriate. But even more importantly, high school should give students practice at being cognizant of the larger arena in which they act. The few negative incidents that free press will admittedly cause will teach students that in life, one must take responsibility for one's actions.

Therefore, the argument for freedom of speech in student newspapers advances substantial educational goals for students, as well as our unalienable right of freedom of speech. This right, however, is paramount. The American public school is an extension of the American government and community, and censorship is inconsistent with American democracy. Again, students need to be prepared for the world they will live in; depriving them of rights that are promoted in the greater community prepares students poorly for life after high school.

Finally, censoring information in the student newspaper will not remove the subject from student discussion. Rather, it will remove a balanced, informative viewpoint, and often make the "inappropriate" action more desirable and "cool." For instance, a reporter for my high school paper researched and wrote an in-depth story on the increasing drug problem among students. The administration quickly intervened and stopped the story, declaring that drugs were an inappropriate topic for student discussion. This story, however, would have focused discussion on a crucial issue for students, so that they can make the right choice when offered drugs or when they see friends using drugs. Unfortunately, this is a situation most students will face, and they need to be prepared. Suppressing the story made drugs seem even more rebellious and mysterious and most importantly did not give students facts with which they could prepare.

Placing restrictions on student newspapers would be a serious mistake that would hinder students from learning what it is to participate in a free society.

> **EXPERT TUTOR TIP**
>
> " There are no right or wrong opinions. You can earn a 6 with an essay for or against the issue raised in the prompt. "

This is now a 6 essay. It addresses the task both fully and concretely. It addresses both sides of the argument, refutes two opposing arguments, and then moves to the bulk of the author's own reasoning. The first paragraph introduces all the lines of reasoning that will be used, demonstrating to the reader that the writer knew right from the start where this essay was headed. The development of ideas is clear and logical and the paragraphs reflect this organization.

The author shows a high level of skill with language. The transitions between paragraphs are clear and guide the reader through the reasoning. The sentence structure varies throughout the passage and is at times complex.

So what did we do to our 4 to make it a 6?

- We added examples and detail.

- We varied sentence structure and added stronger vocabulary (*strives, laughable, intervened,* and *suppressing*).

- While length alone doesn't make a 6, we've added detail to our original essay.

- The conclusion, rather than being lost in the fifth paragraph, is now a strong, independent statement that concisely sums up the writer's point of view.

Remember that your graders will be reading *holistically*. They will not be grading you by assigning points to particular aspects of your writing. However, as you practice essay writing, you can build an otherwise humdrum essay into a 6 by working on specific elements, with the net effect of giving your essay that 6 glow.

PREPARING FOR THE ESSAY

INFORMATION BANKS

Don't wait until test day to think about what subjects you can draw on for your examples to create animated and engaging essays. Examples can be drawn from anywhere: your life experience, a story you saw on the news, etc. So prepare yourself by refreshing your memory about your favorite subjects—collect examples that can be used for a variety of topics.

READ OP-ED ESSAYS

Newspapers and blogs have op-ed (stands for opinion-editorial) articles. These present arguments and opinions, which present authors' opinions on a wide range of topics. Some will present their arguments well, others will not. Make a point of reading and evaluating them. Ask yourself:

- What is the author's point?

- How is it supported?

- Is the argument convincing? If not, why?

FOLLOW A PRACTICE REGIMEN

Don't try to cut corners. Learn the Kaplan Method and practice writing at least one essay a week; last minute cramming will not be effective. If you intend to maximize your score, you must establish and adhere to a practice schedule. And practice at the same time of day that you will be writing on test day.

Be hard on yourself. **Always** time yourself to internalize the necessary pacing. Don't allow yourself any extra minutes to complete an essay.

Never start to write until you have a complete plan, and then adhere to your plan.

Always reserve two minutes to look over the essay and make needed additions or corrections.

SELF-EVALUATION

After each practice essay, score yourself based on the guidelines provided. As part of your self-evaluation, determine which types of example are most useful to you and what types of error you make most often. Then analyze how well you followed the Kaplan Method in constructing your essay and what you might focus on to improve. Do you have a tendency to rush your plan, or do you find that you don't have two minutes to proofread at the end? **Practice to make your pacing reliable.**

GET A SECOND OPINION

Ask someone else to read and critique your practice essays. If you know someone else who's taking the ACT, you might agree to assist each other in this way. Knowing whether another person can follow your reasoning is the single most important learning aid you can have for the essay.

IF YOU'RE NOT A "WRITER"

While the essay is optional, many colleges require the ACT essay. Remember that the essay is set up so that *everyone* can do well on it. You don't have to be a writer to formulate a good argument and support it well. Plain, clear language will go a long way toward getting a good score.

IF ENGLISH IS YOUR SECOND LANGUAGE

The ACT essay can be a special challenge for the international student or ESL student here in the United States. On the ACT, you will be taking a position on the prompt, something that sometimes, but not always, happens on the TOEFL® (Test of English as a Foreign Language). However, plan your essay using all the tools in this chapter, and write according to your plan. Make a special point of spending time proofreading your practice essays when you finish them, and edit anything that makes your writing unclear. There's a strong connection between your English reading skills and your writing skills, so keep reading as well (and don't forget to look for material for your Information Banks as well).

> **EXPERT TUTOR TIP**
>
> " It's difficult to create a good essay in the last few minutes. If you're down to the wire, allow yourself a few minutes to plan and then write, based on that plan, no matter how much you wish you could think of other ideas. "

PRACTICE ESSAY

Try out the Kaplan Method on the following essay prompt. After you're finished, read over your essay and if possible, have someone else read it as well. You can compare it to the model essay that follows the lined pages. Good luck!

Many city councils have introduced proposals that would give them the power to ban certain books from the children's and young adult sections of local public libraries. Some citizens support such proposals because they hope to limit young people's exposure to inappropriate materials. However, other people believe that these measures are equivalent to censorship. In your opinion, should the government have the right to restrict the materials available to young people in libraries?

In your essay, take a position on this question. You may write about either one of the two points of view given, or you may present a different point of view on this question. Use specific reasons and examples to support your position.

_____

_____

_____

_____

_____

_____

_____

_____

_____

_____

_____

_____

_____

_____

_____

_____

_____

MODEL ESSAY

Here's one possible way to approach this essay prompt. Remember that the opinion you express is less important than the way you present it. Notice how this response includes a logically arranged argument with specific examples.

In some districts, city councils and other governing bodies have suggested that they be given the power to ban certain teen and children's books from public libraries. While some citizens believe that it would be beneficial for an outside party to screen the books that are available to young people, others are upset at what they see as censorship of the library's offerings.

Leaving the question of censorship aside, I believe that decisions about which books are appropriate for young people should be left to the young people themselves and their parents, not to city councils or librarians. Young people's reading levels and maturity levels can vary dramatically even within the same age group, and parents are the best judges of what kinds of books are suitable for their children. The proposal to have the city council make these decisions also fails to take into account the huge variations in parents' own preferences for their children; the idea of inappropriateness is a very subjective one. While some parents may agree with the city council's decisions, others may feel that the city council bans too many books, or even too few. In the end, parents must be responsible for knowing what books their children are reading and making their own decisions about those books' appropriateness within the context of their own values.

Additionally, whether certain books are appropriate or not, it's unrealistic to think that removing "objectionable" material from public libraries will keep young people from ever encountering that kind of material. Between television, the Internet, and interactions with friends and classmates, young people encounter all sorts of situations that may not necessarily be age appropriate. It's understandable that adults are concerned, but trying to keep potentially objectionable books away from young readers doesn't ensure that they won't encounter the language or situations used in those books elsewhere. To my mind, the best solution is for adults to encourage young people to analyze these situations thoughtfully, ask questions, and form their own opinions, rather than trying to shield them from the realities of the world.

Finally, although certain books contain elements that some people may find offensive or upsetting, those elements don't necessarily outweigh the literary merits of the books in question. One example of this is *Huckleberry Finn*, which all of the students at my school read as a requirement in English classes. It is widely recognized as a classic of American literature, even though it also includes portrayals of African-American characters that many people find offensive. The historical context that is necessary to understand *The Diary of Anne Frank* may be upsetting to younger readers, but the diary is still a significant historical document. Many books with controversial content are still worth reading, and a policy that screens out books based on their potential to offend may exclude important works of literature from libraries.

In conclusion, I believe that the power to make determinations about a book's appropriateness should lie not with a city council or a librarian, but with young readers and their parents. The role of a library is to make information available, not to make or enforce judgments about what its patrons should or should not be reading.

| Part Three |

READY, SET, GO

CHAPTER 17: STRATEGIC SUMMARIES

ENGLISH TEST

The English subject test:

- Is 45 minutes long.

- Includes five passages, representing a range of writing styles and levels of formality.

- Consists of 75 questions, divided among the five passages. They test many points of grammar, punctuation, writing mechanics, usage, and rhetorical skills, by proposing ways of expressing information underlined at various points in the passages. We divide the questions strategically into three groups:

  1. Economy Questions

  2. Sense Questions

  3. Technicality Questions

There are also a few Nonstandard-Format Questions that require different strategies, as outlined in Special Strategies below.

The questions **do *not* get harder** as you proceed through the section.

MIND-SET

- **When in doubt, take it out.** Make sure that everything is written as concisely as possible. If you think something doesn't belong in a sentence, it probably doesn't, so choose an answer that leaves it out.

- **Make it make sense.** Grammar allows language to communicate meaning clearly. Most grammatically faulty sentences on the ACT don't say what the author intended to say. If a sentence has more than one possible meaning, figure out what the author intended to say, and fix the sentence so it conveys that meaning properly.

- **Trust your eyes and ear.** Mistakes in grammar often look or sound bad. Don't choose the answer that "sounds fancy," choose the one that "sounds right." Review the Grammer Rules to know in English Workout 3.

THE KAPLAN METHOD

For each question, ask yourself three things. Note that you may actually have your answer before getting to all three questions:

1. **Ask: Do these words belong here?** Is it redundant? Is it relevant? Is this a long way to say a short idea? If so, choose an answer that gets rid of the stuff that doesn't belong.

2. **Ask: Do these words make sense?** The ACT test makers want short, simple, easy-to-understand prose. They expect everything to fit together logically. Choose the answer that turns nonsense into sense.

3. **Ask: Do I hear or see an eror?** If so, choose the answer that fixes the problem. Recognize the issues discussed in English Workout 3 and let them help out when your ear isn't sure. These errors appear again and again on ACT English subject tests.

SPECIAL STRATEGIES

A few questions will require you to rearrange the words in a sentence, the sentences in a paragraph, or even the paragraphs in a passage. Others may ask questions about the meaning of all or part of the passage, or about its structure. Your approach to these Nonstandard-Format Questions should be:

1. **Determine your task.** What are you being asked to do?

2. **Consider the passage as a whole.** Read the sentences without a numbered question. You need to know the various points made there. Most passages will have a well-defined theme, laid out in a logical way. Choose the answer that expresses this theme, or the arrangement of elements that best continues the logical "flow" of the passage.

3. **Predict your answer.** As in Reading, you should have an idea of what the answer is before looking at the choices.

Note: Grammer "fixes" cannot be predicted. There are many ways to make a sentence correct grammatically.

TIMING

We recommend that you *not* skip around in the English subject test. Although you can certainly use the usual Two-Pass Approach, you might prefer to go straight from beginning to end, answering all of the questions as you go. Unlike in other sections, in English you'll usually have at least a sense of what the right answer should be rather quickly. Remember, even the correct answer will start to sound wrong if you think about it too much!

Set your watch to 12:00 at the beginning of the subject test. Although you should go faster if you can, here's roughly where you should be at the following checkpoints:

12:09 . . . . . One passage finished and answers gridded in

12:18 . . . . . Two passages finished and answers gridded in

12:27 . . . . . Three passages finished and answers gridded in

12:36 . . . . . Four passages finished and answers gridded in

12:45 . . . . . Five passages finished and answers for the entire section gridded in

Note that you should do at least some work on all 75 English questions, and make sure you have at least one guess gridded in for every question when time is called.

WHEN YOU'RE RUNNING OUT OF TIME

If you have no time left even to read the last few questions, choose the shortest answer for each one. Remember that OMIT, when it appears, counts as the shortest answer.

SCORING

Your performance on the English subject test will be averaged into your ACT Composite Score, weighted equally with your scores on the other three major subject tests. You will also receive:

- English subject score—from 1 to 36—for the entire English subject test
- Usage/Mechanics subscore—from 1 to 18—based on your performance on the questions testing grammar, usage, punctuation, and sentence structure
- Rhetorical Skills subscore—from 1 to 18—based on your performance on the questions testing strategy, organization, and style
- Writing subscore—from 2 to 12—based on the optional Writing test
- Combined English-Writing score—from 1 to 36—if you take the optional Writing test

MATH TEST

The Math subject test:

- Is 60 minutes long.
- Consists of 60 questions, which test your grasp of pre-algebra, algebra, coordinate geometry, plane geometry, and trigonometry. We break down the questions into the following strategic categories:

  1. **Diagram Questions**

  2. **Story Questions**

  3. **Concept Questions**

The math concepts tested **do get harder** as you proceed through the section.

MIND-SET

- **The end justifies the means.** That means getting as many correct answers as quickly as possible. If that means doing straightforward questions in a straightforward way, that's fine. But many questions can be solved faster by unorthodox methods.

- **Take time to save time.** It sounds paradoxical, but to go your fastest on the Math test you've got to slow down. **Never** dive in headlong, wildly crunching numbers or manipulating equations without first giving the problem some thought.

- **When in doubt, shake it up.** ACT Math questions are not **always** what they seem at first glance. Sometimes all you need is a new perspective to break through the disguise.

THE KAPLAN METHOD

1. **Understand.** First focus on the question stem and make sure you understand the problem. Underlining what the question is asking might help you. If it is a word problem and you are completely lost, try taking notes. You will pull out the information that is necessary to solve the problem. Think to yourself: "What kind of problem is this? What am I looking for? What am I given?"

2. **Analyze.** Think for a moment and decide on a plan of attack.

   - **Math skills.** Do you know how to solve the problem using your math knowledge? Go for it!

   - **Picking numbers.** Are there variables in the answer choices? If so, is there a way to pick numbers for the variable to help you get to the right answer?

   - **Back-solving.** Are there numbers in the answer choices? What is the question asking for? That is what the numbers in the answer choices represent. Is there a way to use the answers to get to the right answer?

3. **Select.** Once you get an answer, does it match one of the answer choices? If so, circle the answer in your test book and fill in the appropriate bubble on your answer grid. If you are stuck, circle the problem in your test book and move on to get all your "easy" points first! Come back to this problem after you have gone through the entire test.

We offer several recommendations for what to do when you get stuck. If after a few moments of thought you find you still can't come up with a reasonable way of doing the problem, try one of these techniques:

1. **Restate.** When you get stuck, try looking at the problem from a different angle. Try rearranging the numbers, changing decimals to fractions, fractions to decimals, multiplying out numbers, factoring problems, redrawing a diagram, or anything that might help you to look at the problem a bit differently.

2. **Remove the disguise.** A problem might look like a different problem sometimes! Find out what the question is really asking, and it might not be what the problem looks like it would be asking. See Math Workout 2 for some examples!

3. **Try Eyeballing.** Even though the directions warn you that diagrams are "not necessarily" drawn to scale, eyeballing is a surprisingly effective guessing strategy. Unless a problem says "Note: Not drawn to scale," you can assume that it is drawn to scale! Use that to help you eliminate answer choices that you know are wrong!

TIMING

Remember the Two-Pass Approach. **Spend about 45 minutes on your first pass through the Math subject test: do the easier questions, guess on the questions you know you'll never get, and mark the tough ones that you'll want to come back to.** Spend the last 15 minutes picking up those questions that you skipped on the first pass.

We recommend that you grid your answers at the end of every page or two. In the last five minutes or so, start gridding your answers one by one. And make sure that you have an answer (even if it's a blind guess) gridded for every question by the time the test is over.

Don't worry if you have to guess on a lot of the Math questions. You can miss a lot of questions on the subject test and still get a great score. **Remember that the average ACT test taker gets less than half the Math questions right!**

WHEN YOU'RE RUNNING OUT OF TIME

If at some point you realize you have more questions left than you have time for, be willing to skip around, looking for questions you understand right away. Pick your spots. Concentrate on the questions you have the best chance of correctly answering. Just be sure to grid an answer—even if it's just a wild guess—for every question.

SCORING

Your performance on the Math subject test will be averaged into your ACT Composite Score, equally weighted with your scores on the other three major subject tests. You will also receive:

- Math subject score—from 1 to 36—for the entire Math subject test
- Pre-algebra/Elementary Algebra subscore—from 1 to 18
- Intermediate Algebra/Coordinate Geometry subscore—from 1 to 18
- Plane Geometry/Trigonometry subscore—from 1 to 18

READING TEST

The Reading subject test:

- Is 35 minutes long.

- Includes four passages:

  — Three Nonfiction passages (one each in Social Studies, Natural Sciences, and Humanities, though there is no significant difference among them except subject matter)

  — One Prose Fiction passage (an excerpt from a short story or novel)

- Consists of 40 questions, 10 on each passage. They include:

1. Specific Questions

   a. Detail

   b. Vocab-in-Context

   c. Function (Why)

2. Conclusion Questions

   a. Inference

   b. Writer's View

3. Generalization Questions

The questions **do *not* get harder** as you go through the section.

MIND-SET

- **Know where the passage is going.** Read the passages actively, and pay attention to structural clues and key words and sentences. The easiest way to do this is to create a road map using the ABCs of Active Reading:

  — **A**bbreviate margin notes.

  — **B**racket key sentences.

  — **C**ircle key words and phrases.

- **Conquer the questions.** Look up the answers; don't remember them.

THE KAPLAN METHOD

1. **Preread the passage.** Try to understand the "gist" of the passage. Get a sense of the overall structure of the passage. Create a road map to make referring back easier.

2. **Consider the question stem.** Understand the question first, without looking at the array of answer choices. Remember that many wrong choices are designed to mislead test takers who just jump past the question stem and start comparing choices to each other.

3. **Refer to the passage before looking at the choices. Always** refer to the passage before answering the question. If the question includes line references, read around them. Only then look at the choices. Make sure your answer matches the passage in meaning.

4. **Answer the question in your own words** before looking at the choices.

5. **Match your answer with one of the choices.** Having an answer in mind will keep you from getting bogged down.

SPECIAL STRATEGIES

THE PROSE FICTION PASSAGE

When you preread the passage, pay attention to the characters, especially the main character. Read between the lines to determine unspoken emotions and attitudes. Ask yourself:

- **Who are these people?** What are they like? **How do the characters relate to each other?**

- **What is their state of mind?** Are they angry, sad, reflective, excited?

- **What's going on?** What's happening on the surface? What's happening beneath the surface?

NONFICTION PASSAGES

Don't be thrown by unfamiliar vocabulary or topics. The Natural Science passage may enter strange territory. Everything you need to know will be covered in the passage. If you find a difficult term, odds are the definition will be given to you in context (or else it simply might not matter what the word means). You can still get lots of questions right, even if you don't fully understand the passage. **Remember, you can find all the answers in the passage.**

TIMING

You might want to take a few seconds at the beginning of the subject test to page through the passages, gauging the difficulty of each one. At first glance you may wish to skip an entire passage if it seems very difficult.

We recommend that you treat each passage and its questions as a block. Take two passes through each block before moving on to the next (skip around if you like, but watch your answer grid if you do!). Get the easy questions on the first pass through and save the tougher ones for the second pass. Just make sure to keep track of time.

Set your watch to 12:00 at the beginning of the subject test. Although you should go faster if you can, here's roughly where you should be at the following checkpoints:

12:09 . . . . . One passage finished and answers gridded in

12:18 . . . . . Two passages finished and answers gridded in

12:27 . . . . . Three passages finished and answers gridded in

12:35 . . . . . Four passages finished and answers for the entire section gridded in

Note: The last passage is the eight-minute one.

Don't spend time agonizing over specific questions. Avoid thinking long and hard about the answer choices. Make your best guess and keep moving on.

Three minutes to read; about 30 seconds (average) per question. Some questions take more time than others (ones with Roman numerals in them and ones that have EXCEPT are examples). If you feel the need to spend a lot of time to get the right answer, don't. Either guess or skip and come back. (Don't forget to do so.)

Do the best you can to finish all four passages, but don't panic if you don't. Develop a fallback position to use, if you fall short (see below). If, during practice, you often don't get to *many* of the questions, approach all the passages this way:

1. Learn to spot the easier questions and answer these quickly.
2. Address the ones you might be able to get with more research.
3. Guess randomly on the ones you would need lots of time for.

Note: If you are a slow reader and have trouble with the ABCs of Active Reading, this method may help.

WHEN YOU'RE RUNNING OUT OF TIME

If you have less than five minutes left for the last passage, do the following:

1. **Skip the prereading step.**
2. **Look for questions with specific line references and do them.**
3. **Refer to the cited location in the passage and answer the question as best you can, based on what you see there.**
4. **Make sure you have gridded in an answer for every question before time is called.**

SCORING

Your performance on the Reading subject test will be averaged into your ACT composite score, weighted equally with your scores on the other three major subject tests. You will also receive:

- Reading subject score—from 1 to 36—for the entire Reading subject test
- Social Science/Sciences subscore—from 1 to 18—based on your performance on the Nonfiction passages drawn from Social Studies and Natural Sciences
- Arts/Literature subscore—from 1 to 18—based on your performance on the Nonfiction passage (drawn from the Humanities) and on the Prose Fiction passage

SCIENCE TEST

The Science subject test:

- Is 35 minutes long.

- Includes seven passages, or sets of scientific information, involving graphs, tables, and research summaries. Typically, one of the passages involves two conflicting viewpoints on a single scientific issue.

- Consists of 40 questions, divided among the seven passages. We divide the questions strategically into three categories:

  1. Figure Interpretation Questions

  2. Patterns Questions

  3. Scientific Reasoning Questions

The questions **do *not* get harder** as you proceed through the section.

MIND-SET

- **Look for patterns.** Usually, the exact data contained in Science passages is not as important as are changes in the data. Look for extremes (maximums and minimums), critical points (points of change), and variation (direct and inverse).

- **Know your direction.** There are two kinds of scientific reasoning—general-to-specific and specific-to-general. **Always** be aware of when scientists are inferring a specific case from a general rule and when they are using specific data to form a (general) hypothesis.

- **Refer, don't remember.** Don't even think of trying to remember data. It's **always** there, right on the page, for you to refer to when needed.

THE KAPLAN METHOD

1. **Preread the passage.** Actively read the passage looking for and marking the purpose, method, and results. What is being researched? How are the scientists varying? What are the scientists keeping constant? Don't get bogged down in the details, and don't worry about understanding everything.

2. **Consider the question stem.** Make sure you understand exactly what the question is asking. Get a sense of what the answer should be without looking at the choices, many of which are designed to mislead you if you're indecisive.

3. **Refer to the passage before looking at the choices.** **Always** refer back to the passage before looking at the choices and selecting one. Make sure you read charts and graphs accurately and that you do not confuse different kinds of units.

4. **Answer the question in your own words.** Don't rely too much on your knowledge of science. Paraphrase the information in the passage.

5. Match your answer with one of the choices. Having an answer in mind will help you to avoid falling for a wrong answer.

SPECIAL STRATEGIES

READING TABLES AND GRAPHS

When reading tables and graphs, you should ask yourself:

- **What does the figure show?**
- **What are the units of measurement?**
- **What is the pattern in the data?**

EXPERIMENTS

Remember how experiments work. There is typically (though not **always**) a control group plus an experimental group or groups. In a well-designed experiment, the only difference between the groups will be a variation in the factor that's being tested. Ask yourself:

- **What's the factor that's being varied?**
- **What's the control group, if any?**
- **What do the results show? What differences exist between the results for one group and those for another?**

CONFLICTING VIEWPOINTS PASSAGE

Spend a little more time than usual on the prereading step of this passage. Focus on the two points of view. What are the scientists arguing about? What do they agree on, if anything? What do they differ on? Identify the following for each scientist:

- **Basic theory statement** (usually the first sentence of each scientist's presentation)
- **Major pieces of data behind the theory** (keeping in mind whether each supports the scientist's own theory or weakens the opposing scientist's theory)

TIMING

Some Science passages are a lot harder than others, and they're not arranged in order of difficulty, so you might want **to take a few seconds at the beginning of the subject test to page through the passages, gauging the difficulty of each one.** You may wish to skip an entire passage if it seems very difficult (but remember that a very difficult passage may have very easy questions).

As in Reading, treat each passage and its questions as a block, taking two passes through each block before moving on to the next. Get the easy questions on the first pass through and save the tougher ones for the second pass. Some questions will probably be impossible for you to answer; take an intuitive guess on these.

Set your watch to 12:00 at the beginning of the subject test. Although you should go faster if you can, here's where you should be at the following checkpoints:

12:05 . . . . . One passage finished and answers gridded in

12:10 . . . . . Two passages finished and answers gridded in

12:15 . . . . . Three passages finished and answers gridded in

12:20 . . . . . Four passages finished and answers gridded in

12:25 . . . . . Five passages finished and answers gridded in

12:30 . . . . . Six passages finished and answers gridded in

12:35 . . . . . Seven passages finished and answers for the entire section gridded in

Don't spend time agonizing over specific questions. Avoid thinking long and hard about the answer choices. If you've spent a minute or so on a question and don't seem to be making any headway, make your best guess and move on.

Don't panic if you can't finish all seven passages, but try to do a good job on at least five of them. And make sure you remember to grid answers (even if they're blind guesses) for all questions by the end.

WHEN YOU'RE RUNNING OUT OF TIME

If you have fewer than three minutes left for the last passage, do the following:

1. **Skip the prereading step.**

2. **Look for questions that refer to specific experiments or to specific graphs or tables.**

3. **Refer to the cited location in the passage and answer the question as best you can, based on what you see there.**

4. **Make sure you have gridded in an answer for every question before time is called.**

SCORING

Your performance on the Science subject test will be averaged into your ACT composite score, weighted equally with your scores on the other three major subject tests. You will also receive:

• Science subject score—from 1 to 36—for the entire Science subject test

Unlike the other three subject scores, the Science score is not divided into subscores.

WRITING TEST

The Writing test:

• Is optional (check with the schools to which you are applying and with your guidance counselor about whether you should take the test).

- Is 30 minutes long.

- Includes just one prompt about which you must write an essay. The essay must:

   1. State a point of view on the issue.

   2. Support the point of view with concrete, detailed examples.

   3. Provide a clear and coherent argument, which includes a discussion of the opposite point of view.

MIND-SET

Don't wait until test day to think of examples you can use to support your ideas. Regardless of what question is raised in the prompt, you will draw your support from the things you know best and are most comfortable writing about—things that you know a fair amount of concrete detail about.

Refresh your memory about school subjects, current events, personal experiences, and activities—anything. By doing so, you strengthen mental connections to those ideas and details—that will make it easier to connect to the right examples on test day.

THE KAPLAN METHOD

1. **Pause to know the prompt.** Read about the issue and take a position on it. There is no right or wrong answer, but make sure you address the issue. In other words, answer the question.

2. **Plan.** Take six or seven minutes or less to plan the essay before you write. Focus on what kinds of reasoning and examples you can use to support your position. If you find you have more examples for a position different from the one you thought you would take, *change your position*.

3. **Produce.** Write your draft, sticking closely to your plan. The essay should have three to five well-developed paragraphs with topic sentences and supporting details. Include an introductory paragraph stating your position and a concluding paragraph. Write neatly.

4. **Proofread. Always** leave yourself two minutes to review your work—the time spent will definitely pay off. Very few of us can avoid the occasional confused sentence or omitted word when writing under pressure. Quickly review your essay to be sure your ideas are on the page, not just in your head.

HELPFUL STRATEGIES

You must be very focused in order to write a complete, coherent essay in 30 minutes. During the planning stage, use one of the two following strategies:

1. **Draw a "T" and list your argument on either side** of it (your stance on one side, and your arguments addressing the other side on the other). See page 215. This method will help you decide if you have enough to back up your stance. You may find you need to take the opposite point of view!

   OR

2. **List the topic of each paragraph** you plan to write, noting the segments of the argument that you want to make.

Stick to the plan as you write the essay. Don't change the plan in midstream if another idea suddenly comes to you; it might derail the essay. Keep your focus on the issue and don't digress.

Make the structure of your essay very easy for the reader to see. Have an introductory paragraph, two or three middle paragraphs, each focused on one example or bit of evidence, and a concluding paragraph.

Write neatly. Graders will give you a poor grade if it's hard to decipher. If your handwriting is a problem, print.

TIMING

With only 30 minutes, efficient use of time is critical. Divide your time as follows:

6–7 minutes—Read the prompt and plan the essay.

20–21 minutes—Draft the essay, sticking to the plan.

3 minutes—Proofread and correct any errors.

WHEN YOU'RE RUNNING OUT OF TIME

Try not to. Running out of time doesn't just mean guessing the last few questions as it does on the other tests; it means your essay won't be as complete and coherent as it should be. If you do start running out of time, forget the proofreading stage. If absolutely necessary, leave out one of your example paragraphs and go on to the concluding paragraph.

SCORING

Your essay will be graded on a holistic scale of 1–6 or 2–12 (6/12 being the best). Graders will be looking for an overall sense of your essay, not assigning separate scores for specific elements like grammar or organization. Two readers read and score each essay; then those scores are added together to arrive at your Writing subscore (from 2–12), which is reported as part of your English score. If there's a difference of more than a point between the two readers' scores, your essay will be read by a third reader. A combined English-Writing score also will be recorded. Two-thirds of this score is based on your English score and one-third is based on your writing subscore. The combined English-Writing score does not count toward your composite score.

Statistically speaking, there will be few essays that score 6/12. If each grader gives your essay a 4 or 5 (8 or 10), that will place you at the upper range of those taking the exam.

CHAPTER 18: LAST-MINUTE TIPS

Is it starting to feel like your whole life is a buildup to the ACT? You've known about it for years, you've worried about it for months, and now you've spent at least a few hours in solid preparation for it. As the test gets closer, you may find your anxiety is on the rise. But you really shouldn't worry. After the preparation you've received from this book, you're in good shape for test day.

To calm any pretest jitters you may have (and assuming you've left yourself at least some breathing time before your ACT), let's go over a few last-minute strategies for the couple of days before and after the test.

THREE DAYS BEFORE THE TEST

- If you haven't already done so, take one of the full-length Practice Tests in this book under timed conditions. If you have already worked through all the tests in the book, try an actual published ACT (your guidance counselor might have one).

- Try to use all of the techniques and tips you've learned in this book. Take control. Approach the test strategically and creatively.

WARNING: Don't take a full practice ACT unless you have at least 48 hours left before the test! Doing so will probably exhaust you, hurting your scoring potential on the actual test! You wouldn't run a marathon the day before the real thing, would you?

TWO DAYS BEFORE THE TEST

- Go over the results of your Practice Test. Don't worry too much about your score or whether you got a specific question right or wrong. Remember the Practice Test doesn't count. But do examine your performance on specific questions with an eye to how you might get through each one faster and with greater accuracy on the actual test to come.

> **EXPERT TUTOR TIP**
>
> " If you have two weeks or fewer to prep for the ACT, read this chapter. It tells you how to use your time wisely before, during, and after the test. "

- After reviewing your test, look over the Strategic Summaries. If you feel a little shaky about any of the areas mentioned, quickly read the relevant workouts.

- This is the day to do your last studying—review a couple of the more difficult principles we've covered, do a few more practice problems, and call it quits. It doesn't pay to make yourself crazy right before the test. Besides, you've prepared. You'll do well.

THE DAY BEFORE THE TEST

EXPERT TUTOR TIP

" Guard against being easily distracted during the test—by traffic outside or a sniffling neighbor. Try practicing in a coffee shop or with the door to your room open. "

- **Don't study.**

- **Get together an "ACT survival kit" containing the following items:**
  - Digital Watch
  - At least three sharpened No. 2 pencils
  - Pencil sharpener
  - Two erasers
  - Photo ID card (if you're not taking the test at your high school, make sure your ID is official)
  - An approved calculator
  - Your admission ticket
  - Snack and a bottle of water—there's a break, and you'll probably get hungry
  - Confidence

- **Know exactly where you're going and how you're getting there.** It's probably a good idea to visit your test center sometime before test day, so that you know what expect on the big day.

- **Relax!** Read a good book, take a bubble bath, watch TV. Exercise can be a good idea early in the afternoon. Working out makes it easier to sleep when you're nervous, and it also makes many people feel better. Of course, don't work so hard that you can't get up the next day!

- **Get a good night's sleep.** Go to bed early and allow for some extra time to get ready in the morning.

THE MORNING OF THE TEST

- **Eat breakfast.** Protein is brain food, but don't eat anything too heavy or greasy. Don't drink a lot of coffee if you're not used to it; bathroom breaks cut into your time, and too much caffeine—or any other kind of drug—is a bad idea.

- **Dress in layers** so that you can adjust to the temperature of the test room.

- **Read something.** Warm up your brain with a newspaper or a magazine. Don't let the ACT be the first thing you read that day.

- **Be sure to get there early.** Allow yourself extra time for traffic, mass-transit delays, and any other possible problems.

- **If you can, go to the test with a friend** (even if he or she isn't taking the test). It's nice to have somebody supporting you right up to the last minute.

DURING THE TEST

- **Don't get rattled.** If you find your confidence slipping, remind yourself how well you've prepared. You've followed the Four Commandments of ACT Success and you have practiced. You know the test; you know the strategies; you know the material tested. You're in great shape, as long as you relax!

- **Even if something goes really wrong, don't panic.** If the test booklet is defective—two pages are stuck together or the ink has run—try to stay calm. Raise your hand, and tell the proctor you need a new book. If you accidentally misgrid your answer page or put the answers in the wrong section, again don't panic. Raise your hand, and tell the proctor. He or she might be able to arrange for you to regrid your test after it's over, when it won't cost you any time.

AFTER THE TEST

Once the test is over, put it out of your mind. If you don't plan to take the ACT again, shelve this book and start thinking about more interesting things.

You might walk out of the ACT thinking that you blew it. This is a normal reaction. Lots of people—even the highest scorers—feel that way. You tend to remember the questions that stumped you, not the many that you knew. If you're really concerned, call us for advice. Also call us if you had any problems with your test experience—a proctor who called time early, a testing room whose temperature hovered just below freezing. We'll do everything we can to make sure that your rights as a test taker are preserved!

However, we're positive that you performed well and scored your best on the exam because you followed our ACT Strategies, Practices, and Review program. Be confident that you were prepared, and celebrate in the fact that the ACT is a distant memory.

If you want more help or just want to know more about the ACT, college admissions, or Kaplan prep courses for the ACT, give us a call at 800-KAP-TEST or visit us at www.kaptest.com. We're here to answer your questions and to help you in any way we can. Also, be sure to return one last time to your online syllabus and complete our survey. We're only as good as our successful students.

| Part Four |

PRACTICE TESTS AND EXPLANATIONS

PRACTICE TEST ONE

HOW TO TAKE THESE PRACTICE TESTS

Practice Tests One and Two are Kaplan-created tests, similar to the actual ACT test booklet. Before taking a Practice Test, find a quiet room where you can work uninterrupted for three hours. Make sure you have a comfortable desk, your calculator, and several No. 2 pencils. Use the answer sheet to record your answers. Once you start a Practice Test, don't stop until you've finished. Remember: You can review any questions within a section, but you may not jump from one section to another.

You'll find the answers and explanations to the test questions immediately following each test.

ACT Practice Test One
Answer Sheet

English Test

10. Ⓕ Ⓖ Ⓗ Ⓙ	20. Ⓕ Ⓖ Ⓗ Ⓙ	30. Ⓕ Ⓖ Ⓗ Ⓙ	40. Ⓕ Ⓖ Ⓗ Ⓙ	50. Ⓕ Ⓖ Ⓗ Ⓙ	60. Ⓕ Ⓖ Ⓗ Ⓙ	70. Ⓕ Ⓖ Ⓗ Ⓙ
1. Ⓐ Ⓑ Ⓒ Ⓓ	11. Ⓐ Ⓑ Ⓒ Ⓓ	21. Ⓐ Ⓑ Ⓒ Ⓓ	31. Ⓐ Ⓑ Ⓒ Ⓓ	41. Ⓐ Ⓑ Ⓒ Ⓓ	51. Ⓐ Ⓑ Ⓒ Ⓓ	61. Ⓐ Ⓑ Ⓒ Ⓓ	71. Ⓐ Ⓑ Ⓒ Ⓓ
2. Ⓕ Ⓖ Ⓗ Ⓙ	12. Ⓕ Ⓖ Ⓗ Ⓙ	22. Ⓕ Ⓖ Ⓗ Ⓙ	32. Ⓕ Ⓖ Ⓗ Ⓙ	42. Ⓕ Ⓖ Ⓗ Ⓙ	52. Ⓕ Ⓖ Ⓗ Ⓙ	62. Ⓕ Ⓖ Ⓗ Ⓙ	72. Ⓕ Ⓖ Ⓗ Ⓙ
3. Ⓐ Ⓑ Ⓒ Ⓓ	13. Ⓐ Ⓑ Ⓒ Ⓓ	23. Ⓐ Ⓑ Ⓒ Ⓓ	33. Ⓐ Ⓑ Ⓒ Ⓓ	43. Ⓐ Ⓑ Ⓒ Ⓓ	53. Ⓐ Ⓑ Ⓒ Ⓓ	63. Ⓐ Ⓑ Ⓒ Ⓓ	73. Ⓐ Ⓑ Ⓒ Ⓓ
4. Ⓕ Ⓖ Ⓗ Ⓙ	14. Ⓕ Ⓖ Ⓗ Ⓙ	24. Ⓕ Ⓖ Ⓗ Ⓙ	34. Ⓕ Ⓖ Ⓗ Ⓙ	44. Ⓕ Ⓖ Ⓗ Ⓙ	54. Ⓕ Ⓖ Ⓗ Ⓙ	64. Ⓕ Ⓖ Ⓗ Ⓙ	74. Ⓕ Ⓖ Ⓗ Ⓙ
5. Ⓐ Ⓑ Ⓒ Ⓓ	15. Ⓐ Ⓑ Ⓒ Ⓓ	25. Ⓐ Ⓑ Ⓒ Ⓓ	35. Ⓐ Ⓑ Ⓒ Ⓓ	45. Ⓐ Ⓑ Ⓒ Ⓓ	55. Ⓐ Ⓑ Ⓒ Ⓓ	65. Ⓐ Ⓑ Ⓒ Ⓓ	75. Ⓐ Ⓑ Ⓒ Ⓓ
6. Ⓕ Ⓖ Ⓗ Ⓙ	16. Ⓕ Ⓖ Ⓗ Ⓙ	26. Ⓕ Ⓖ Ⓗ Ⓙ	36. Ⓕ Ⓖ Ⓗ Ⓙ	46. Ⓕ Ⓖ Ⓗ Ⓙ	56. Ⓕ Ⓖ Ⓗ Ⓙ	66. Ⓕ Ⓖ Ⓗ Ⓙ	
7. Ⓐ Ⓑ Ⓒ Ⓓ	17. Ⓐ Ⓑ Ⓒ Ⓓ	27. Ⓐ Ⓑ Ⓒ Ⓓ	37. Ⓐ Ⓑ Ⓒ Ⓓ	47. Ⓐ Ⓑ Ⓒ Ⓓ	57. Ⓐ Ⓑ Ⓒ Ⓓ	67. Ⓐ Ⓑ Ⓒ Ⓓ	
8. Ⓕ Ⓖ Ⓗ Ⓙ	18. Ⓕ Ⓖ Ⓗ Ⓙ	28. Ⓕ Ⓖ Ⓗ Ⓙ	38. Ⓕ Ⓖ Ⓗ Ⓙ	48. Ⓕ Ⓖ Ⓗ Ⓙ	58. Ⓕ Ⓖ Ⓗ Ⓙ	68. Ⓕ Ⓖ Ⓗ Ⓙ	
9. Ⓐ Ⓑ Ⓒ Ⓓ	19. Ⓐ Ⓑ Ⓒ Ⓓ	29. Ⓐ Ⓑ Ⓒ Ⓓ	39. Ⓐ Ⓑ Ⓒ Ⓓ	49. Ⓐ Ⓑ Ⓒ Ⓓ	59. Ⓐ Ⓑ Ⓒ Ⓓ	69. Ⓐ Ⓑ Ⓒ Ⓓ	

Math Test

9. Ⓐ Ⓑ Ⓒ Ⓓ Ⓔ	18. Ⓕ Ⓖ Ⓗ Ⓙ Ⓚ	27. Ⓐ Ⓑ Ⓒ Ⓓ Ⓔ	36. Ⓕ Ⓖ Ⓗ Ⓙ Ⓚ	45. Ⓐ Ⓑ Ⓒ Ⓓ Ⓔ	54. Ⓕ Ⓖ Ⓗ Ⓙ Ⓚ
1. Ⓐ Ⓑ Ⓒ Ⓓ Ⓔ	10. Ⓕ Ⓖ Ⓗ Ⓙ Ⓚ	19. Ⓐ Ⓑ Ⓒ Ⓓ Ⓔ	28. Ⓕ Ⓖ Ⓗ Ⓙ Ⓚ	37. Ⓐ Ⓑ Ⓒ Ⓓ Ⓔ	46. Ⓕ Ⓖ Ⓗ Ⓙ Ⓚ	55. Ⓐ Ⓑ Ⓒ Ⓓ Ⓔ
2. Ⓕ Ⓖ Ⓗ Ⓙ Ⓚ	11. Ⓐ Ⓑ Ⓒ Ⓓ Ⓔ	20. Ⓕ Ⓖ Ⓗ Ⓙ Ⓚ	29. Ⓐ Ⓑ Ⓒ Ⓓ Ⓔ	38. Ⓕ Ⓖ Ⓗ Ⓙ Ⓚ	47. Ⓐ Ⓑ Ⓒ Ⓓ Ⓔ	56. Ⓕ Ⓖ Ⓗ Ⓙ Ⓚ
3. Ⓐ Ⓑ Ⓒ Ⓓ Ⓔ	12. Ⓕ Ⓖ Ⓗ Ⓙ Ⓚ	21. Ⓐ Ⓑ Ⓒ Ⓓ Ⓔ	30. Ⓕ Ⓖ Ⓗ Ⓙ Ⓚ	39. Ⓐ Ⓑ Ⓒ Ⓓ Ⓔ	48. Ⓕ Ⓖ Ⓗ Ⓙ Ⓚ	57. Ⓐ Ⓑ Ⓒ Ⓓ Ⓔ
4. Ⓕ Ⓖ Ⓗ Ⓙ Ⓚ	13. Ⓐ Ⓑ Ⓒ Ⓓ Ⓔ	22. Ⓕ Ⓖ Ⓗ Ⓙ Ⓚ	31. Ⓐ Ⓑ Ⓒ Ⓓ Ⓔ	40. Ⓕ Ⓖ Ⓗ Ⓙ Ⓚ	49. Ⓐ Ⓑ Ⓒ Ⓓ Ⓔ	58. Ⓕ Ⓖ Ⓗ Ⓙ Ⓚ
5. Ⓐ Ⓑ Ⓒ Ⓓ Ⓔ	14. Ⓕ Ⓖ Ⓗ Ⓙ Ⓚ	23. Ⓐ Ⓑ Ⓒ Ⓓ Ⓔ	32. Ⓕ Ⓖ Ⓗ Ⓙ Ⓚ	41. Ⓐ Ⓑ Ⓒ Ⓓ Ⓔ	50. Ⓕ Ⓖ Ⓗ Ⓙ Ⓚ	59. Ⓐ Ⓑ Ⓒ Ⓓ Ⓔ
6. Ⓕ Ⓖ Ⓗ Ⓙ Ⓚ	15. Ⓐ Ⓑ Ⓒ Ⓓ Ⓔ	24. Ⓕ Ⓖ Ⓗ Ⓙ Ⓚ	33. Ⓐ Ⓑ Ⓒ Ⓓ Ⓔ	42. Ⓕ Ⓖ Ⓗ Ⓙ Ⓚ	51. Ⓐ Ⓑ Ⓒ Ⓓ Ⓔ	60. Ⓕ Ⓖ Ⓗ Ⓙ Ⓚ
7. Ⓐ Ⓑ Ⓒ Ⓓ Ⓔ	16. Ⓕ Ⓖ Ⓗ Ⓙ Ⓚ	25. Ⓐ Ⓑ Ⓒ Ⓓ Ⓔ	34. Ⓕ Ⓖ Ⓗ Ⓙ Ⓚ	43. Ⓐ Ⓑ Ⓒ Ⓓ Ⓔ	52. Ⓕ Ⓖ Ⓗ Ⓙ Ⓚ	
8. Ⓕ Ⓖ Ⓗ Ⓙ Ⓚ	17. Ⓐ Ⓑ Ⓒ Ⓓ Ⓔ	26. Ⓕ Ⓖ Ⓗ Ⓙ Ⓚ	35. Ⓐ Ⓑ Ⓒ Ⓓ Ⓔ	44. Ⓕ Ⓖ Ⓗ Ⓙ Ⓚ	53. Ⓐ Ⓑ Ⓒ Ⓓ Ⓔ	

Reading Test

6. Ⓕ Ⓖ Ⓗ Ⓙ	12. Ⓕ Ⓖ Ⓗ Ⓙ	18. Ⓕ Ⓖ Ⓗ Ⓙ	24. Ⓕ Ⓖ Ⓗ Ⓙ	30. Ⓕ Ⓖ Ⓗ Ⓙ	36 Ⓕ Ⓖ Ⓗ Ⓙ
1. Ⓐ Ⓑ Ⓒ Ⓓ	7. Ⓐ Ⓑ Ⓒ Ⓓ	13. Ⓐ Ⓑ Ⓒ Ⓓ	19. Ⓐ Ⓑ Ⓒ Ⓓ	25. Ⓐ Ⓑ Ⓒ Ⓓ	31. Ⓐ Ⓑ Ⓒ Ⓓ	37. Ⓐ Ⓑ Ⓒ Ⓓ
2. Ⓕ Ⓖ Ⓗ Ⓙ	8. Ⓕ Ⓖ Ⓗ Ⓙ	14. Ⓕ Ⓖ Ⓗ Ⓙ	20. Ⓕ Ⓖ Ⓗ Ⓙ	26. Ⓕ Ⓖ Ⓗ Ⓙ	32. Ⓕ Ⓖ Ⓗ Ⓙ	38. Ⓕ Ⓖ Ⓗ Ⓙ
3. Ⓐ Ⓑ Ⓒ Ⓓ	9. Ⓐ Ⓑ Ⓒ Ⓓ	15. Ⓐ Ⓑ Ⓒ Ⓓ	21. Ⓐ Ⓑ Ⓒ Ⓓ	27. Ⓐ Ⓑ Ⓒ Ⓓ	33. Ⓐ Ⓑ Ⓒ Ⓓ	39 Ⓐ Ⓑ Ⓒ Ⓓ
4. Ⓕ Ⓖ Ⓗ Ⓙ	10. Ⓕ Ⓖ Ⓗ Ⓙ	16. Ⓕ Ⓖ Ⓗ Ⓙ	22. Ⓕ Ⓖ Ⓗ Ⓙ	28. Ⓕ Ⓖ Ⓗ Ⓙ	34. Ⓕ Ⓖ Ⓗ Ⓙ	40. Ⓕ Ⓖ Ⓗ Ⓙ
5. Ⓐ Ⓑ Ⓒ Ⓓ	11. Ⓐ Ⓑ Ⓒ Ⓓ	17. Ⓐ Ⓑ Ⓒ Ⓓ	23. Ⓐ Ⓑ Ⓒ Ⓓ	29. Ⓐ Ⓑ Ⓒ Ⓓ	35. Ⓐ Ⓑ Ⓒ Ⓓ	

Science Test

6. Ⓕ Ⓖ Ⓗ Ⓙ	12. Ⓕ Ⓖ Ⓗ Ⓙ	18. Ⓕ Ⓖ Ⓗ Ⓙ	24. Ⓕ Ⓖ Ⓗ Ⓙ	30. Ⓕ Ⓖ Ⓗ Ⓙ	36. Ⓕ Ⓖ Ⓗ Ⓙ
1. Ⓐ Ⓑ Ⓒ Ⓓ	7. Ⓐ Ⓑ Ⓒ Ⓓ	13. Ⓐ Ⓑ Ⓒ Ⓓ	19. Ⓐ Ⓑ Ⓒ Ⓓ	25. Ⓐ Ⓑ Ⓒ Ⓓ	31. Ⓐ Ⓑ Ⓒ Ⓓ	37. Ⓐ Ⓑ Ⓒ Ⓓ
2. Ⓕ Ⓖ Ⓗ Ⓙ	8. Ⓕ Ⓖ Ⓗ Ⓙ	14. Ⓕ Ⓖ Ⓗ Ⓙ	20. Ⓕ Ⓖ Ⓗ Ⓙ	26. Ⓕ Ⓖ Ⓗ Ⓙ	32. Ⓕ Ⓖ Ⓗ Ⓙ	38. Ⓕ Ⓖ Ⓗ Ⓙ
3. Ⓐ Ⓑ Ⓒ Ⓓ	9. Ⓐ Ⓑ Ⓒ Ⓓ	15. Ⓐ Ⓑ Ⓒ Ⓓ	21. Ⓐ Ⓑ Ⓒ Ⓓ	27. Ⓐ Ⓑ Ⓒ Ⓓ	33. Ⓐ Ⓑ Ⓒ Ⓓ	39 Ⓐ Ⓑ Ⓒ Ⓓ
4. Ⓕ Ⓖ Ⓗ Ⓙ	10. Ⓕ Ⓖ Ⓗ Ⓙ	16. Ⓕ Ⓖ Ⓗ Ⓙ	22. Ⓕ Ⓖ Ⓗ Ⓙ	28. Ⓕ Ⓖ Ⓗ Ⓙ	34. Ⓕ Ⓖ Ⓗ Ⓙ	40. Ⓕ Ⓖ Ⓗ Ⓙ
5. Ⓐ Ⓑ Ⓒ Ⓓ	11. Ⓐ Ⓑ Ⓒ Ⓓ	17. Ⓐ Ⓑ Ⓒ Ⓓ	23. Ⓐ Ⓑ Ⓒ Ⓓ	29. Ⓐ Ⓑ Ⓒ Ⓓ	35. Ⓐ Ⓑ Ⓒ Ⓓ	

ENGLISH TEST

45 Minutes—75 Questions

Directions: In the following five passages, certain words and phrases have been underlined and numbered. You will find alternatives for each underlined portion in the right-hand column. Select the one that best expresses the idea, that makes the statement acceptable in standard written English, or that is phrased most consistently with the style and tone of the entire passage. If you feel that the original version is best, select "NO CHANGE." You will also find questions asking about a section of the passage or about the entire passage. For these questions, decide which choice gives the most appropriate response to the given question. For each question in the test, select the best choice, and fill in the corresponding space on the answer folder. You may wish to read each passage through before you begin to answer the questions associated with it. Most answers cannot be determined without reading several sentences around the phrases in question. Make sure to read far enough ahead each time you choose an alternative.

PASSAGE I

Many people enjoy the hobby of aquarium keeping.

It has several advantages. As pets they are very quiet,not
                                          1
worrying too much about pats on the head or 4:00 A.M.
                                              1
walks. Yet even many avid aquarists are unaware of the
  1
fact that their hobby has a fascinating history.

Fish keeping actually has ancient origins, who
                                             2
beginning with the Sumerians over 4,500 years
      2
ago. They kept fish in artificial ponds. The ancient

Assyrians and Egyptians also kept fish. In addition to

keeping and having fish as pets, the Chinese used them
        3
for practical purposes, raising carp for food as early as

100 B.C. They were probably the first people to breeds
                                                    4
fish with any degree of success. Their selective

breeding of ornamental goldfish was introduced in Japan,

where the breeding of ornamental carp was perfected.

1. A. NO CHANGE
   B. Fish make quiet pets; they do not need to be patted on the head or walked at 4:00 A.M.
   C. Their owner who did not pat them on the head is not worried about walking these quiet pets at 4:00 A.M.
   D. These quiet pets without a pat on the head from their owners are not to be walked at 4:00 A.M. by necessity.

2. F. NO CHANGE
   G. which begins with
   H. beginning with
   J. who, beginning at

3. A. NO CHANGE
   B. keeping and possessing
   C. keep and have
   D. keeping

4. F. NO CHANGE
   G. breeded
   H. breed
   J. bred

GO ON TO THE NEXT PAGE

The ancient Romans kept fish for food and
5

entertainment. They were the first known seawater

aquarists, constructing ponds supplied with fresh ocean

water. The Romans were also the first to use open-air

tanks to preserve and fatten fish for market.

In seventeenth-century England, goldfish were

being kept in glass containers, but aquarium keeping
6

did not become well established until the relationship

among animals, oxygen, and plants became known a
7

century later. In the eighteenth century, France's

importation of goldfish from the Orient created a need

for small aquariums. Ceramic bowls, occasionally fitted

with transparent panels, were produced. 8

By 1850, the keeping of fish, reptiles, and

amphibians had become a useful method of study for

naturalists. Philip Gosse, a British ornithologist, first

coined the term "aquarium." The first display aquariums

opened in 1853 at Regent's Park in London aquariums
9

soon appeared in Naples, Berlin, and Paris. The first

aquarium to serve as a financial enterprise was opened

by the circus entrepreneur P. T. Barnum at the American

Museum in New York City. By 1928, 45 public or

5. A. NO CHANGE
    B. These are the ancient Romans
    C. Yes, one can find ancient Romans which
    D. The ancient Romans, nevertheless,

6. F. NO CHANGE
    G. to have been
    H. sometimes being
    J. OMIT the underlined portion.

7. A. NO CHANGE
    B. which became known
    C. becoming known
    D. were known almost

8. The purpose of the preceding sentence is to:
    F. emphasize the inappropriateness of the aquariums produced at that time.
    G. illustrate the fact that the importation of goldfish produced a corresponding need for small containers.
    H. contradict the assertion made earlier in the paragraph that the English kept gold-fish in glass containers.
    J. explain why goldfish could not live for long in small containers.

9. A. NO CHANGE
    B. London, which
    C. London, where it
    D. London, and

GO ON TO THE NEXT PAGE

commercial aquariums were opened. <u>Then it slowed</u>
                                        10
<u>and few new large aquariums appeared until after</u>
                        10
<u>World War II.</u> Marineland of Florida, built in 1956, was
    10

the first oceanarium. <u>*Flipper* was a popular television</u>
                                    11
<u>show about a dolphin.</u> So next time you meet an aquarist
    11

you might share some of this <u>"fish trivia." For</u> fish
                                    12
keeping is not only an entertaining hobby; it also has a

rich and long history, <u>have playing</u> a role in many
                            13
diverse cultures since ancient times.

10. F. NO CHANGE
    G. Then its growth having slowed; few
        new large ones appeared until after
        World War II.
    H. Then having slowed, few new large ones
        appeared until after World War II was over.
    J. Then growth slowed, and few new
        large aquariums appeared until after
        World War II.

11. A. NO CHANGE
    B. A popular television show about a
        dolphin was *Flipper*.
    C. (A popular television show, *Flipper*, was
        about a dolphin.)
    D. OMIT the underlined portion.

12. F. NO CHANGE
    G. —fish trivia. For
    H. "fish trivia," and
    J. "fish trivia! For

13. A. NO CHANGE
    B. having played
    C. has
    D. had played

Items 14–15 ask about the passage as a whole.

14. What conclusion does the essay make?

    F. The study of history is a valuable task.
    G. People who keep aquariums must learn
        "fish trivia."
    H. The hobby of keeping aquariums has an
        intriguing past.
    J. Maintaining an aquarium is a big
        responsibility.

15. The essay is made up of five paragraphs.
    Which of the following is the best description
    of how the paragraphs are organized?

    A. First example, second example, third
        example, definition, argument.
    B. Introduction, earliest examples, later exam-
        ples, most recent examples, conclusion.
    C. Historical survey, first example, second
        example, third example, fourth example.
    D. Introduction, background information,
        argument, counterargument, personal
        account.

GO ON TO THE NEXT PAGE

PASSAGE II

The late twentieth and early twenty-first centuries may well be remembered as the Age of the "Yuppie" (young urban professional). Our society seems obsessed with the notion of social mobility. There are two different types of social mobility: horizontal and vertical. If there is a change in occupation, but no change in social class, it is called "horizontal mobility." One example of this would be a lawyer who changes law firms that are comparable in pay salary and prestige. A change in role involving a change in social standing is called "vertical mobility" and can be either upward or downward.

The extent of change can vary greatly. At one pole, social mobility may affect only one member of a society. At the other extreme, it may change the entire social system. The Russian Revolution of 1917, therefore, altered an entire class structure.

[1] In addition to involving degrees of change, social mobility occurs at a variety of rates. [2] The "American dream" is based in part on the notion of rapid social mobility, in which an unknown individual becomes an "overnight success." [3] One example of rapid social mobility would be the young guitar player who

16. F. NO CHANGE
    G. mobility horizontal, and vertical.
    H. mobility; horizontal and vertical.
    J. mobility: being horizontal and vertical.

17. A. NO CHANGE
    B. in pay and prestige
    C. with pay, salary and prestige
    D. pay in terms of salary and prestige

18. F. NO CHANGE
    G. it's called "vertical mobility"
    H. they're called "vertical mobility"
    J. it is called "vertical mobility"

19. A. NO CHANGE
    B. nonetheless
    C. for instance
    D. consequently

20. F. NO CHANGE
    G. In addition, it involved differing degrees of change,
    H. In addition to the fact that it involved change's differing degrees,
    J. It involves degrees of change,

GO ON TO THE NEXT PAGE →

becomes an instant rock star. [4] The athlete who wins

an Olympic gold medal too. [5] For instance, each
                          21
generation in a family may be a little better off than the

generation before it. [6] Social mobility may also be

accomplished by more gradual changes. 22

The results of mobility are difficult to measure in that.
                                                    23
Some view large-scale mobility in a negative light,

claiming that it disintegrates class structure and puts an

end to meaningful traditions. Accordingly others claim
                            24

that they're attempting to rise validate and therefore
        25
reinforce the class system. They see mobility as a

positive thing, enabling individuals to improve their

own lives and the lives of their families. 26

Still others see social mobility as destroying, rather

21. A. NO CHANGE
    B. is another example
    C. is too
    D. OMIT the underlined portion and end
       with a period.

22. For the sake of unity and coherence,
    sentence 6 should be placed:
    F. where it is now.
    G. after sentence 2.
    H. after sentence 4.
    J. at the beginning of the next paragraph.

23. A. NO CHANGE
    B. in.
    C. on.
    D. OMIT the underlined portion and end
       the sentence with a period.

24. F. NO CHANGE
    G. (Begin new paragraph) Similarly,
    H. (Begin new paragraph) Likewise,
    J. (Do NOT begin new paragraph) On the
       other hand,

25. A. NO CHANGE
    B. they
    C. those who are
    D. their

26. Suppose that at this point in the passage the
    writer wanted to add more information.
    Which of the following additions would be
    most relevant to the paragraph?
    F. A discussion of the problems of the edu-
       cational system in America
    G. A listing of average salaries for different
       occupations
    H. Some examples of the benefits of social
       mobility
    J. A discussion of a rock star's new video

GO ON TO THE NEXT PAGE

than reinforced—the class system yet they feel this is a
27

positive change. According to them, society will benefit

from the breakdown like a flat tire of a social system in
28

which material wealth is given so much importance.

Whether we view it positively or negatively, social

mobility is a basic fact of modern industrial society. The

crowd of yuppies hitting the shopping malls, credit cards

in hand, show that vertical mobility is very much with us
29

and so will a lot of other things be.
30

27. A.   NO CHANGE
    B.   reinforcing, the class system; yet
    C.   reinforced. The class system; and
    D.   that it reinforces the class system

28. F.   NO CHANGE
    G.   (such as a flat tire)
    H.   (like the kind a flat tire gets)
    J.   OMIT the underlined portion.

29. A.   NO CHANGE
    B.   shows
    C.   showing
    D.   to show

30. F.   NO CHANGE
    G.   and there they will be for some time to come.
    H.   and will be for some time to come.
    J.   OMIT the underlined portion and end the sentence with a period.

GO ON TO THE NEXT PAGE

Passage III

The following paragraphs may or may not be in the most logical order. Each paragraph is numbered in brackets, and item 45 will ask you to choose the sequence of paragraph numbers that is in the most logical order.

[1]

The critic George Moore once said of this artist that
<u>31</u>
is "her pictures are the only pictures painted by a woman
31
that could not be destroyed without creating a blank, a

hiatus in the history of art." In part a tribute to Morisot,

Moore's <u>statement are also one</u> that shows the prejudices
32
Morisot faced as a woman in a male-dominated

discipline.

[2]

The Impressionist painter Berthe Morisot was

born in 1841 to a wealthy family that had connections

to the French government. Yet it was no surprise to

anyone when Morisot <u>showed little interest in it, and</u>
33
<u>instead took after her grandfather</u> the painter Jean
33

Honoré Fragonard. <u>Being her earliest childhood,</u> she
34
had the desire to be an artist. At the age of twenty-one,

she began seven years of study with Corot. She had her

first work accepted at the Paris Salon in 1864. In 1868

31. A. NO CHANGE
    B. that being that
    C. is
    D. that

32. F. NO CHANGE
    G. statement's is also one
    H. statement is also one
    J. statements are also among those

33. A. NO CHANGE
    B. showed little interest in politics and instead took after her grandfather,
    C. with little interest in it—politics—took up after her grandfather instead
    D. was little interested in it, taking after her grandfather

34. F. NO CHANGE
    G. From, her being in earliest
    H. Being in early
    J. From her earliest

GO ON TO THE NEXT PAGE

she met the Impressionist painter Edouard <u>Manet and</u>
35

served as his model for several portraits. She was

actively involved with the Impressionist exhibiting

society of the 1870s and 1880s.

[3]

<u>Either Morisot's subject matter nor her style is</u>
36

distinctive. As a woman, she lacked the freedom

enjoyed by her male <u>colleagues, who face</u> no threat of
37

social disapproval in their journeys through Parisian

cafes, theaters, and parks. <u>Therefore,</u> Morisot turned
38

her limitations to her advantage, creating a unique

vantage point. Unlike her fellow Impressionists, who

painted scenes of Parisian night life, Morisot

35. A. NO CHANGE
    B. Manet (who was neither Belgian nor Dutch) and
    C. Manet (a man not Belgian and not Dutch) and
    D. Manet—a man of neither Belgian nor Dutch extraction, and

36. F. NO CHANGE
    G. Neither Morisot's subject matter nor her style is
    H. Neither Morisot's subject matter or her style are
    J. Neither Morisot's subject matter nor her style

37. A. NO CHANGE
    B. colleagues, whom faced
    C. colleagues, who faced
    D. colleagues, and faced

38. F. NO CHANGE
    G. Similarly,
    H. Likewise,
    J. However,

GO ON TO THE NEXT PAGE

concentrated on her own private sphere. Portraying
                                                    39
women performing domestic and social activities. 40

[4]

Morisot's paintings frequently feature female

members of her family, especially her daughter. She

often captures her models at thoughtful moments in

their chores. In contrast to the vast landscapes of her

male colleagues, Morisot's figures are generally

enclosed by some device: such as a balustrade, balcony,
                   41
veranda, or embankment. The sense of confinement

conveyed by many of her paintings may be in part a

reflection of the barriers Morisot faced as a woman

artist. But despite the obstacles, Morisot managed to

achieve the recognition she deserved, helping to ease

the way for her successors the people who followed
                                42
after her.
   42

39. A. NO CHANGE
     B. sphere. She began to portray
     C. sphere insofar portraying
     D. sphere, which were

40. Paragraph 3 makes the point that Morisot's
     painting did not include subject matter
     available to her male colleagues. The author
     wants to revise the whole paragraph to
     emphasize a more positive judgment of her
     work's value and a less negative view of its
     limitations. Which revision of the paragraph's
     first sentence would best allow her to express
     this changed perspective?

     F. While Morisot's subject matter lacks
         originality, her style, in fact, is quite suited
         to expressing her distinctive interests.
     G. Morisot's subject matter and style are
         somewhat limited by her society's con-
         fining standards, but her work takes on a
         greater meaning in its social context.
     H. Morisot's subject matter may not appear
         particularly distinctive, but her work has
         great meaning in its social context.
     J. Few can say that Morisot is one of the
         great Impressionists, but there are not
         many great Impressionists in any case.

41. A. NO CHANGE
     B. some device—
     C. some device:
     D. some such device such as,

42. F. NO CHANGE
     G. those who came after.
     H. which followed her.
     J. OMIT the underlined portion and end
         the sentence with a period.

GO ON TO THE NEXT PAGE ▷

Items 43–45 ask about the passage as a whole.

---

43. The writer could best continue this essay by:

   A. discussing how Morisot's success influenced social attitudes toward later women artists.

   B. comparing several Impressionist landscape paintings by various artists.

   C. providing background information on the art critic George Moore.

   D. listing, by title and author, a series of articles on important Impressionists.

44. In the second paragraph, is the writer's reference to specific dates appropriate?

   F. No, because the information interferes with the biographical purpose of this essay.

   G. No, because the information, while it does not interfere with the biographical purpose of the essay, is out of place, since the rest of the essay does not cite dates.

   H. Yes, because the information helps to make the story of Morisot believable.

   J. Yes, because the information helps to carry out the biographical purpose of this essay.

45. Choose the sequence of paragraph numbers that will make the passage's structure most logical.

   A. NO CHANGE

   B. 2, 1, 3, 4

   C. 2, 3, 1, 4

   D. 3, 2, 4, 1

GO ON TO THE NEXT PAGE

PASSAGE IV

It used to be that when people wanted to see a

scary movie they could choose from films such as

Dracula and *Frankenstein*. But these classic monster

movies, with some exceptions, has been replaced
                                46

by a different breed of horror film the slasher movie. It
                                 47
is interesting and perhaps somewhat disturbing to

examine what such changes in taste may indicate about

some of the values at work in our nation.

First: commercially successful low-budget chiller
48
was *Halloween*, and in its wake psycho-slasher films

have the movie market glutted. The formula for these
                        49
movies consists of the serial murder of teenagers by a

ruthless psychotic, with some humor thrown in. The fact
                                                    50
of the matter being that the popularity of the series of
                        50
Friday the Thirteenth movies and their hundreds of silly

imitators indicates that there is a huge market for such

portrayals of random violence. Indeed, filmgoers

appear to cast their votes for more and more graphic

46. F. NO CHANGE
     G. have been replaced
     H. were being replaced
     J. replaced

47. A. NO CHANGE
     B. film, which is the
     C. film: the
     D. film known, as the

48. F. NO CHANGE
     G. First;
     H. The first
     J. First—

49. A. NO CHANGE
     B. (Place after *have*)
     C. (Place after *movie*)
     D. (Place after *wake*)

50. F. NO CHANGE
     G. The fact of the matter being
     H. The popularity
     J. Factually speaking, in terms of
         popularity,

GO ON TO THE NEXT PAGE

forms of violence. As a result, filmmakers—those who
                                                    51

actually made films—generate increasing gory
          51   52

productions.

As a result of this trend, slasher films now represent
                        53

mainstream Hollywood movies. Once limited only to the

periphery (fringe) of the movie industry, the exploitation
        54

of gore has become a major box office attraction. Older

slasher films such as *Psycho* actually seem like classics

in comparison. Now they're many high grossing
                        55

franchises that produce countless sequels like

Halloween 20: H₂0. These movies have made a big

wad of cash! [56]

Although the popularity of such films has declined

somewhat as their novelty has worn off. However, they
                                      57

remain a standard feature of the yearly production

schedule. Even many high-budget films have adopted

the slasher formula of chills and violence. More recent

films, such *Scream*, examine the slasher movie's

formulaic conventions, while the *Scary Movie* series

plays them for laughs.

51. A. NO CHANGE
     B. —those making the films, actually
     C. (which are the people making the films)
     D. OMIT the underlined portion.

52. F. NO CHANGE
     G. increasing, gory,
     H. increasingly full of gore,
     J. increasingly gory

53. A. NO CHANGE
     B. trend:
     C. trend—
     D. —trend—

54. F. NO CHANGE
     G. periphery
     H. periphery (that is, the fringe)
     J. periphery, fringe,

55. A. NO CHANGE
     B. they are
     C. there's
     D. there are

56. Is the final sentence of this paragraph
     appropriate?

     F. No, because it is irrelevant to the topic.
     G. No, because its reference to money, while
         relevant to the topic, is inappropriate
         in tone.
     H. Yes, because the exclamation with which
         the sentence ends heightens the drama.
     J. Yes, because it clarifies the preceding
         sentence.

57. A. NO CHANGE
     B. off, and they
     C. off, so they
     D. off, they

GO ON TO THE NEXT PAGE

Are these movies a means of harmless fun? Are they a

reflection of an <u>increasingly and ever more violent</u>
                                    58
society? Or do such movies encourage violence?

Considering the great changes both within the

movie industry and in <u>public (human)</u> taste, these
                                    59
are questions that we must begin to consider. 60

58. F.   NO CHANGE
    G.   more, and more, and more violent
         society
    H.   increasingly violent society
    J.   increasingly violent society, with anger
         and blood

59. A.   NO CHANGE
    B.   public, and human
    C.   public
    D.   human's

60. How can this essay best be described?

    F.   The tone is serious; the purpose is
         to point out a significant change in
         entertainment.
    G.   The tone is lighthearted; the pur-
         pose is to recommend a new form of
         entertainment.
    H.   The tone is sarcastic; the purpose is
         to show how contemporary movies
         lack value.
    J.   The tone is harsh; the purpose is to urge
         people not to attend slasher films.

GO ON TO THE NEXT PAGE

PASSAGE V

> The following paragraphs may or may not
> be in the most logical order. Each paragraph
> is numbered in brackets, and item 75 will
> ask you to choose the sequence of paragraph
> numbers that is in the most logical order.

[1]

The strangest of these events all involve <u>unexplained</u>
                                            61
<u>disappearances—the kind that haven't been fully</u>
                        61
<u>explained.</u> Ships have been found <u>abandoned and</u>
    61   62
<u>deserted</u> for no apparent reason. <u>Without transmitting</u>
    62   63
<u>distress signals, some ships having vanished forever.</u>
                        63
Planes have reported their position and then

disappeared. Even rescue missions are said to have

vanished while flying in the area. Theories accounting for

such occurrences <u>ranging towards</u> the interference of
                        64
UFOs to the existence of powerful fields of some

unknown force. So far, no conclusions <u>have been reached.</u>
                                            65

61. A. NO CHANGE
    B. unexplained disappearances, which
       haven't been explained, fully.
    C. unexplained disappearances.
    D. unexplained disappearances that have
       not been explained.

62. F. NO CHANGE
    G. abandoned
    H. abandoned, including left
    J. abandoned (deserted)

63. A. NO CHANGE
    B. They've not transmitted distress signals,
       and they've vanished forever, never to
       return.
    C. Transmitting no distress signals, having
       vanished forever, have been some ships.
    D. Some ships have vanished forever with-
       out transmitting any distress signal.

64. F. NO CHANGE
    G. range to
    H. ranging from
    J. range from

65. A. NO CHANGE
    B. have (yet) been reached.
    C. having yet been reached.
    D. yet reached.

GO ON TO THE NEXT PAGE

[2]

In the North Atlantic Ocean, the Bermuda Islands—a

jumble of 300 islets, rocks, and islands—form part of a

roughly triangular region (England is roughly triangular,
                    66

too) whose other boundaries are the southern U.S. coast
66   67

and the Greater Antilles. Perhaps the first European to
67

explore this area was Juan de Bermudez in 1515. They
                                              68

wonder who whether he ever experienced anything
    68

strange back then, for this is the region known today as

the Bermuda Triangle. Extremely strange events had been
                                                     69

frequently reported from this area. [70]

66. F.   NO CHANGE
    G.   region (like England)
    H.   region
    J.   England-like region

67. A.   NO CHANGE
    B.   coast (but not rivers) and
    C.   coast, but not rivers, and
    D.   coast—but not rivers—and

68. F.   NO CHANGE
    G.   We are those who wonder
    H.   Some wonder
    J.   Some of them are wondering

69. A.   NO CHANGE
    B.   has been
    C.   is
    D.   have been

70. Is the mention of Juan de Bermudez
    appropriate?

    F.   No, because it connects two dissimilar
         things, exploration and the Bermuda
         Triangle.

    G.   Yes, because it provides background
         information while introducing the main
         subject of the passage.

    H.   Yes, because the passage suggests that
         exploration is more significant than the
         supernatural.

    J.   Yes, because Juan de Bermudez is the
         only person named in the passage.

GO ON TO THE NEXT PAGE

[3]

Others are critical of the claims posed about the

Bermuda Triangle. They point out that wreckage has not

been found and that scientific searches have uncovered

nothing to substantiate the strange events attributed to the

region. Also, they question <u>so it can be</u> that boaters and
                                71
fliers continue to travel through the region unharmed. 72

71. A.   NO CHANGE
     B.   which
     C.   how
     D.   OMIT the underlined portion.

72. Suppose that at this point the writer wanted to
     add more information. Which of the following
     additions would be most relevant?

     F.   A geographical description of the
          Bermuda Triangle
     G.   A brief allusion to other well-known
          supernatural phenomena
     H.   More evidence disputing the occurrence
          of supernatural forces
     J.   A discussion of Bermuda's tourist trade

GO ON TO THE NEXT PAGE

[4]

We may never be certain in the way a judge is of the
                                    73

truth about the Bermuda Triangle. Yet people will

continue to be intrigued by the supernatural and the

strange. One thing we can be sure of is that this enigmatic

place will continue to fascinate the public and stir up

controversy for years to come.

73. A. NO CHANGE
    B. absolutely certain
    C. certain like a judge
    D. certain as a judge is

Items 74–75 ask about the passage as a whole.

---

74. Suppose the editor of a travel magazine had
    requested that the writer give an account of
    one specific disappearance that has occurred
    in the Bermuda region. Does this essay
    successfully fulfill that request?

    F. Yes, because the disappearances
        described are actual events.

    G. Yes, because the essay focuses on mys-
        terious disappearances in the Bermuda
        Triangle.

    H. No, because the writer has relied on
        generalities in discussing the nature of
        disappearances in the region.

    J. No, because the essay lacks factual infor-
        mation of any sort.

75. For the sake of unity and coherence,
    Paragraph 1 should be placed:

    A. where it is now.
    B. after Paragraph 2.
    C. after Paragraph 3.
    D. after Paragraph 4.

IF YOU FINISH BEFORE TIME IS CALLED, YOU MAY CHECK YOUR WORK ON
THIS SECTION ONLY. DO NOT TURN TO ANY OTHER SECTION IN THE TEST.

STOP

MATH TEST

60 Minutes—60 Questions

Directions: Solve each of the following problems, select the correct answer, and then fill in the corresponding space on your answer sheet.

Don't linger over problems that are too time-consuming. Do as many as you can, then come back to the others in the time you have remaining.

Calculator use is permitted, but some problems can best be solved without a calculator.

Note: Unless otherwise noted, all of the following should be assumed.

1. Illustrative figures are *not* necessarily drawn to scale.
2. All geometric figures lie in a plane.
3. The term *line* indicates a straight line.
4. The term *average* indicates arithmetic mean.

1. If $5x + 3 = -17$, then $x = ?$

   A. -25
   B. $-7\dfrac{1}{3}$
   C. -4
   D. 4
   E. $6\dfrac{1}{3}$

2. John wants to make fruit salad. He has a recipe that serves 6 people and uses 4 oranges, 5 pears, 10 apples, and 2 dozen strawberries. If he wants to serve 18 people, how many pears will John need?

   F. 5
   G. 10
   H. 15
   J. 20
   K. 25

DO YOUR FIGURING HERE.

GO ON TO THE NEXT PAGE ⟹

3. What is the greatest integer that is a factor of both 8×10^9 and 6×10^3?

A. 1×10^9

B. 2×10^6

C. 6×10^3

D. 2×10^3

E. 1×10^3

DO YOUR FIGURING HERE.

4. What is the area of the rectangle in the standard (x, y) coordinate plane shown in the figure below?

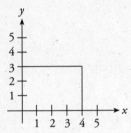

F. 4

G. 7

H. 10

J. 12

K. 14

5. A costume designer wants to put a white silk band around a cylindrical top hat. If the radius of the cylindrical part of the top hat is 4 inches, how long, in inches, should the white silk band be to just fit around the top hat?

A. 8π

B. 25π

C. 50π

D. 100π

E. 200π

GO ON TO THE NEXT PAGE

6. A large jar holds 48 olives while a small jar holds only 32 olives. Which of the following expressions represents the number of olives needed to fill x large jars and y small jars?

F. $48x + 32y$

G. $\dfrac{x}{48} + \dfrac{y}{32}$

H. $\dfrac{xy}{80}$

J. $80xy$

K. $\dfrac{1,536}{xy}$

7. If $f(x) = 3x^2 + 4, f(x + 1) = ?$

A. $3x^2 + 5$

B. $3x^2 + x + 4$

C. $3x^2 + 4$

D. $3x^2 + 2x + 5$

E. $3x^2 + 6x + 7$

8. $5\dfrac{5}{6} + 3\dfrac{5}{8} + 1\dfrac{1}{3} = ?$

F. $9\dfrac{11}{17}$

G. $9\dfrac{19}{24}$

H. $10\dfrac{9}{24}$

J. $10\dfrac{4}{5}$

K. $10\dfrac{19}{24}$

DO YOUR FIGURING HERE.

GO ON TO THE NEXT PAGE

9. Jimmy's school is 10 miles from his house, on the same street. If he walks down his street directly from the school to his house he passes a candy store and a grocery store. The candy store is 2.35 miles from the school and the grocery store is 3.4 miles from the candy store. How many miles is it from the grocery store to Jimmy's house?

A. 3.75

B. 4.25

C. 4.75

D. 5.25

E. 5.75

10. Harry is a piano student who can learn 2 new pieces in a week. If his piano teacher gives him 3 new pieces every week for 4 weeks, how many weeks will it take Harry to learn all these pieces?

F. 6

G. 7.5

H. 8

J. 12

K. 15

11. In △DEF below, the measure of ∠EDF is 35° and the measure of ∠DFE is 65°. What is the measure of ∠DEF?

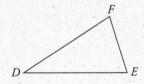

A. 35°

B. 45°

C. 75°

D. 80°

E. 100°

DO YOUR FIGURING HERE.

GO ON TO THE NEXT PAGE

12. Randy scored 150, 195, and 160 in 3 bowling games. What should she score on her next bowling game if she wants to have an average score of exactly 175 for the 4 games?

F.   205
G.   195
H.   185
J.   175
K.   165

13. Which of the following best describes a triangle in the standard (x, y) coordinate plane with vertices having coordinates $(0, 0)$, $(3, 5)$, and $(0, 2)$?

A.   All three angles measure less than 90°.
B.   All three sides are the same length.
C.   Exactly two sides are the same length.
D.   One angle measures 90°.
E.   One angle measures more than 90°.

14. What is the sum of the solutions of the equation $2y^2 - 4y - 6 = 0$?

F.   −4
G.   −2
H.   −1
J.   2
K.   4

15. Which of the following is the decimal equivalent of $\frac{7}{8}$?

A.   1.125
B.   1.120
C.   0.875
D.   0.870
E.   0.625

DO YOUR FIGURING HERE.

GO ON TO THE NEXT PAGE

16. June, Maria, and Billy each have a collection of marbles. June has 20 more marbles than Billy, and Maria has 3 times as many marbles as Billy. If altogether they have 100 marbles, how many marbles does Billy have?

    F.   16
    G.   20
    H.   25
    J.   30
    K.   32

DO YOUR FIGURING HERE.

17. The equation $3x - 2y = 4$ can be graphed in the standard (x, y) coordinate plane. What is the y-coordinate of a point on the graph whose x-coordinate is 6?

    A.   11
    B.   7
    C.   5
    D.   3
    E.   −11

18. In the figure below, parallel lines r and s are cut by transversal t. The measure of $\angle p$ is 20° less than three times the measure of $\angle q$. What is the value of $p - q$?

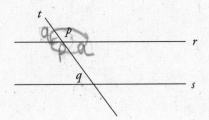

    F.   80°
    G.   90°
    H.   100°
    J.   130°
    K.   160°

GO ON TO THE NEXT PAGE

19. Which of the following systems of equations does NOT have a solution?

   A. $x + 3y = 19$
       $3x + y = 6$

   B. $x + 3y = 19$
       $x - 3y = 13$

   C. $x - 3y = 6$
       $3x - y = 7$

   D. $x - 3y = 19$
       $3x + y = 6$

   E. $x + 3y = 6$
       $3x + 9y = 7$

20. In the figure below, $L, M, R,$ and S are collinear. $\overline{LS}$ is 50 units long; $\overline{MS}$ is 38 units long; and $\overline{MR}$ is 13 units long. How many units long is $\overline{LR}$?

   F. 13

   G. 20

   H. 23

   J. 25

   K. 37

21. If $33\frac{1}{2}\%$ of t is 9, what is $133\frac{1}{3}\%$ of t?

   A. 12

   B. 18

   C. 27

   D. 36

   E. 42

DO YOUR FIGURING HERE.

GO ON TO THE NEXT PAGE →

22. In $\triangle DEF$ below, $\overline{DE} = 1$ and $\overline{DF} = \sqrt{2}$ What is the value of tan x ?

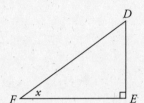

F. $\dfrac{\sqrt{2}}{2}$

G. 1

H. $\sqrt{2}$

J. $\sqrt{3}$

K. 2

23. A circle with center at the origin and radius 7 is graphed in the standard (x, y) coordinate plane. Which of the following is NOT a point on the circumference of the circle?

A. $(7, 0)$

B. $(-3, 2\sqrt{10})$

C. $(\sqrt{7}, 3)$

D. $(0, -7)$

E. $(-\sqrt{26}, -\sqrt{23})$

DO YOUR FIGURING HERE.

GO ON TO THE NEXT PAGE

24. Points A and B have integral coordinates in the standard (x, y) coordinate plane below. What is the product of the y-coordinates of A and B?

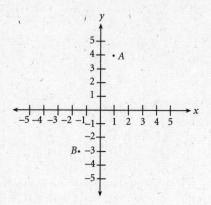

DO YOUR FIGURING HERE.

F. 12

G. 6

H. −2

J. −6

K. −12

25. In the figure below, line m is parallel to line n, point A lies on line m, and points B and C lie on line n. If $\angle BAC$ is a right angle, what is the measure of $\angle y$?

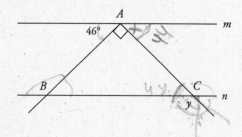

A. 54°

B. 90°

C. 124°

D. 136°

E. 154°

GO ON TO THE NEXT PAGE

26. If $s = -3$, then $s^3 + 2s^2 + 2s = ?$

    F. -15

    G. -10

    H. -5

    J.   5

    K.   33

27. For all $r, s, t,$ and $u, r(t + u) - s(t + u) = ?$

    A. $(r + s)(t + u)$

    B. $(r - s)(t - u)$

    C. $(r + s)(t - u)$

    D. $(r - s)(t + u)$

    E.   0

28. In the figure below, $\angle ABC$ is a right angle and $\overline{DF}$ is parallel to $\overline{AC}$. If $\overline{AB}$ is 8 units long, $\overline{BC}$ is 6 units long and $\overline{DB}$ is 4 units long, what is the area in square units of $\triangle DBF$?

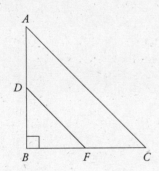

    F.   6

    G.   12

    H.   16

    J.   24

    K.   48

DO YOUR FIGURING HERE.

GO ON TO THE NEXT PAGE

29. What is the value of cos 225°?

    A. $-\dfrac{\sqrt{2}}{2}$

    B. $-\dfrac{\sqrt{3}}{3}$

    C. $-\dfrac{1}{2}$

    D. $\dfrac{1}{2}$

    E. $\dfrac{\sqrt{2}}{2}$

30. In triangle $\triangle XYZ$ below, $\overline{XS}$ and $\overline{SZ}$ are 3 and 12 units long, respectively. If the area of $\triangle XYZ$ is 45 square units, how many units long is altitude $\overline{YS}$?

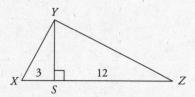

    F.   3

    G.   6

    H.   9

    J.   12

    K.   15

DO YOUR FIGURING HERE.

GO ON TO THE NEXT PAGE

31. In the figure below, O is the center of the circle, C and D are points on the circle, and C, O, and D are collinear. If the length of $\overline{CD}$ is 10 units, what is the circumference, in units, of the circle?

A. 10π

B. 20π

C. 25π

D. 40π

E. 100π

32. The formula for the surface area of a right circular cone, including the base, is $A = \pi rs + \pi r^2$, where A is the surface area, r is the radius, and s is the length from the vertex to the edge of the cone. Which of the following represents an equivalent formula for A ?

F. $A = 2\pi rs$

G. $A = 2\pi r^2 s$

H. $A = \pi r(1 + s)$

J. $A = \pi r^2(1 + s)$

K. $A = \pi r(r + s)$

33. What is the slope of the line determined by the equation $5x + 3y = 13$?

A. -15

B. $-\dfrac{5}{3}$

C. $-\dfrac{3}{5}$

D. $\dfrac{3}{5}$

E. $\dfrac{5}{3}$

DO YOUR FIGURING HERE.

GO ON TO THE NEXT PAGE

34. Given any two real numbers a and b, which of the following is true about the quantity $|a - b| + \sqrt{b - a}$?

    F.   It is always equal to an integer.

    G.   It is positive if $b > a$.

    H.   It is always positive.

    J.   It is negative if $a = b$.

    K.   It is always real.

35. One of the solutions of the equation $x^2 - 7x + 8 = 0$ is $x = \dfrac{7 - \sqrt{17}}{2}$. What is the other solution?

    A. $-\dfrac{7}{2} - \sqrt{17}$

    B. $\dfrac{-7 - \sqrt{17}}{2}$

    C. $\dfrac{-7 + \sqrt{17}}{2}$

    D. $7 - \dfrac{\sqrt{17}}{2}$

    E. $\dfrac{7 + \sqrt{17}}{2}$

36. How many units long is one of the sides of a square that has a diagonal of 20 units long?

    F.   10

    G. $10\sqrt{2}$

    H.   15

    J.   20

    K. $15\sqrt{2}$

37. For all a, $(3a - 4)(a + 2) = ?$

    A. $3a^2 - 8$

    B. $3a^2 + 7a - 8$

    C. $3a^2 + 2a - 8$

    D. $3a^2 - 2a - 8$

    E. $3a^2 + 5a - 8$

DO YOUR FIGURING HERE.

GO ON TO THE NEXT PAGE

38. The midpoint of line segment $\overline{AC}$ in the standard (x, y) coordinate plane has coordinates $(4, 8)$. The (x, y) coordinates of A and C are $(4, 2)$ and $(4, s)$, respectively. What is the value of s?

F.   4
G.   5
H.   10
J.   12
K.   14

39. In a group of 3 numbers, the second number is 3 less than 4 times the first number, and the third number is 5 more than twice the first. If s represents the first number, which of the following expressions represents the sum of the three numbers in terms of s?

A. $5s$
B. $5s + 2$
C. $6s + 8$
D. $7s - 1$
E. $7s + 2$

40. In the figure below, line $\overline{PQ}$ intersects ABC at points E and D. $\angle B$ measures $80°$, $\angle SAB$ measures $130°$, and $\angle CDQ$ measures $110°$. What is the measure of $\angle DEC$?

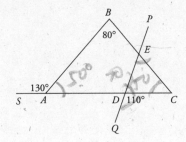

F.   40°
G.   50°
H.   60°
J.   70°
K.   80°

GO ON TO THE NEXT PAGE

41. Jack bought a painting for $200. A year later a friend bought it from him for $170. What percent of the original price did Jack lose in the overall transaction?

    A. 10%
    B. 12%
    C. 15%
    D. 22%
    E. 25%

42. Which of the following is the set of all values of x such that $0 \le x \le 2\pi$ and $\cos x = -\dfrac{1}{2}$?

    F. $\left\{ \dfrac{\pi}{6}, \dfrac{5\pi}{6} \right\}$

    G. $\left\{ \dfrac{\pi}{3}, \dfrac{5\pi}{6} \right\}$

    H. $\left\{ \dfrac{\pi}{2}, \dfrac{3\pi}{2} \right\}$

    J. $\left\{ \dfrac{2\pi}{3}, \dfrac{4\pi}{3} \right\}$

    K. $\left\{ \dfrac{2\pi}{3}, \dfrac{5\pi}{3} \right\}$

43. The roots of the equation $5x^2 + 2x - 7 = 0$ are $x = 1$ and $x = ?$

    A. -7
    B. $-\dfrac{7}{5}$
    C. -1
    D. 0
    E. $\dfrac{7}{5}$

DO YOUR FIGURING HERE.

GO ON TO THE NEXT PAGE

44. In the figure below, $\overline{PS}$ is parallel to $\overline{QR}$, and $\overline{PR}$ intersects $\overline{SQ}$ at T. If the measure of $\angle PST$ is 65° and the measure of $\angle QRT$ is 35°, then what is the measure of $\angle PTQ$?

DO YOUR FIGURING HERE.

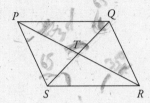

F.   55°

G.   75°

H.   90°

J.   100°

K.   115°

45. Ms. Rodriguez leaves her office and drives east. At the same time, Ms. Green leaves the same office and drives west at a rate of speed that is 15 miles per hour faster than Ms. Rodriguez. At the end of 5 hours, the two cars are 475 miles apart. How many miles were traveled by the faster car?

A.   200

B.   250

C.   275

D.   300

E.   350

GO ON TO THE NEXT PAGE

46. Line ℓ is graphed in the standard (x, y) coordinate plane as shown below. If the equation for line ℓ is written in the form $y = mx + b$, which of the following is true about m and b?

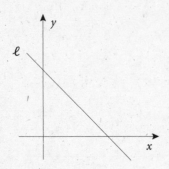

F. m and b are both positive.

G. m is negative and b is positive.

H. m is positive and b is negative.

J.   Either m or b must equal 0.

K. m and b are both negative.

47. Which of the following must be true of the fraction $\dfrac{x^2}{y^2}$ if $|y| < |x|$, and $xy \neq 0$?

A. $\dfrac{x^2}{y^2}$ must be greater than or equal to 2.

B. $\dfrac{x^2}{y^2}$ must be greater than 1.

C. $\dfrac{x^2}{y^2}$ could equal 1.

D. $\dfrac{x^2}{y^2}$ must be less than 1.

E. $\dfrac{x^2}{y^2}$ cannot equal $\dfrac{3}{2}$.

DO YOUR FIGURING HERE.

GO ON TO THE NEXT PAGE

48. What is the value of $a^2 - 2ab + b^2$ if $a - b = 12$?

    F. 0
    G. 24
    H. 48
    J. 144
    K. 288

49. In $\triangle DEF$, x represents the measure of $\angle EDF$. The measure of $\angle DEF$ is 30° greater than the measure of $\angle EDF$, and the measure of $\angle EFD$ is 15° less than the sum of the measures of $\angle EDF$ and $\angle DEF$. Which of the following expressions represents the measure of $\angle EFD$?

    A. $-2x + 15°$
    B. $-x + 15°$
    C. $x + 15°$
    D. $2x - 15°$
    E. $2x + 15°$

50. In the figure below, $\overline{CD}$ is parallel to $\overline{AB}$, and $\overline{PQ}$ intersects $\overline{CD}$ at R and $\overline{AB}$ at T. If the measure of $\angle CRP = 110°$, then what is the measure of $\angle ATQ$?

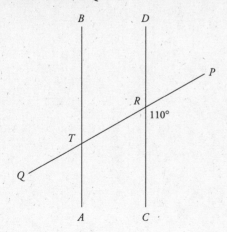

    F. 30°
    G. 50°
    H. 70°
    J. 90°
    K. 110°

DO YOUR FIGURING HERE.

GO ON TO THE NEXT PAGE

51. If $x = \sin\theta$, $y = \cos\theta$, and $z = \tan\theta$, then $x^2 + y^2 = ?$

    A. z^2

    B. $(x + y)^2$

    C. $2y$

    D. 0

    E. 1

DO YOUR FIGURING HERE.

52. Line T in the standard (x, y) coordinate plane has y-intercept -3 and is parallel to the line determined by the equation $3x - 5y = 4$. Which of the following is an equation for line T?

    F. $y = -\dfrac{3}{5}x + 3$

    G. $y = -\dfrac{5}{3}x - 3$

    H. $y = \dfrac{3}{5}x + 3$

    J. $y = \dfrac{5}{3}x + 3$

    K. $y = \dfrac{3}{5}x - 3$

53. On the number line below, what is the distance from A to B?

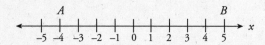

    A. 1

    B. 4

    C. 5

    D. 9

    E. 18

GO ON TO THE NEXT PAGE

54. In the standard (x, y) coordinate plane shown in the figure below, points A and B lie on line m, and point C lies below it. The coordinates of points A, B, and C are $(0, 5)$, $(5, 5)$, and $(3, 3)$, respectively. What is the shortest distance from point C to line m?

DO YOUR FIGURING HERE.

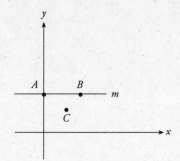

F.   2

G. $2\sqrt{2}$

H.   3

J. $\sqrt{13}$

K.   5

55. Which of the following inequalities is equivalent to $-2 - 4x \leq -6x$?

A. $x \geq -2$

B. $x \geq 1$

C. $x \geq 2$

D. $x \leq -1$

E. $x \leq 1$

GO ON TO THE NEXT PAGE

56. In the figure below, each corner of the polygon is a right angle. What is the area of the polygon?

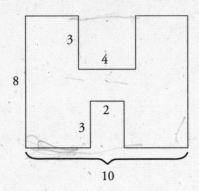

DO YOUR FIGURING HERE.

   F.   50

   G. 56

   H. 62

   J.   72

   K. 80

57. In the standard (x, y) coordinate plane shown below, two circles of the same radius r are enclosed by rectangle $ABCD$. Which of the following expressions is equal to $a - b$?

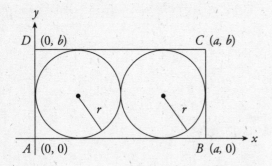

   A. $-r$

   B. 0

   C. r

   D. $2r$

   E. $4r$

GO ON TO THE NEXT PAGE ▷

58. Each one of the 60 teenagers in an after-school club is 14, 15, 16, 17 or 18 years old. 20 teenagers are 15 years old, 8 are 18 years old, and 20% are 14 years old. There are twice as many 16-year-olds as there are 18-year-olds. What percent of the teenagers are either 17 or 18 years old?

   F.   10%

   G.   15%

   H.   20%

   J.   25%

   K.   30%

59. Darryl has 5 blue T-shirts and 7 orange T-shirts. If he picks one T-shirt at random, what is the probability that it will NOT be blue?

   A.   1

   B. $\dfrac{7}{12}$

   C. $\dfrac{1}{2}$

   D. $\dfrac{5}{12}$

   E. $\dfrac{1}{6}$

DO YOUR FIGURING HERE.

GO ON TO THE NEXT PAGE

60. What is the equation of the ellipse graphed in the standard (x, y) coordinate plane below?

DO YOUR FIGURING HERE.

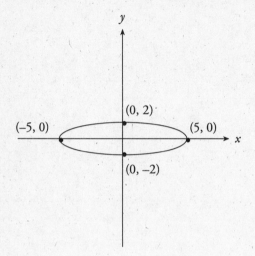

F. $\dfrac{x^2}{25} + \dfrac{y^2}{4} = 1$

G. $\dfrac{x^2}{25} - \dfrac{y^2}{9} = 1$

H. $\dfrac{x^2}{25} - \dfrac{y^2}{4} = 1$

J. $\dfrac{x^2}{25} + \dfrac{y^2}{9} = 1$

K. $\dfrac{x^2}{20} + \dfrac{y^2}{4} = 1$

IF YOU FINISH BEFORE TIME IS CALLED, YOU MAY CHECK YOUR WORK ON THIS SECTION ONLY. DO NOT TURN TO ANY OTHER SECTION IN THE TEST.

STOP

READING TEST

35 Minutes—40 Questions

Directions: This test contains four passages, each followed by several questions. After reading a passage, select the best answer to each question and fill in the corresponding oval on your answer sheet. You are allowed to refer to the passages while answering the questions.

PASSAGE I

It was late afternoon and the shadows were slanting swiftly eastward when George Webber came to his senses somewhere in the wilds of the
Line upper Bronx. How he got there he never knew. All
(5) he could remember was that suddenly he felt hungry and stopped and looked about him and realized where he was. His dazed look gave way to one of amazement and incredulity, and his mouth began to stretch into a broad grin. In his hand he
(10) still held the rectangular slip of crisp yellow paper, and slowly he smoothed out the wrinkles and examined it carefully.

It was a check for five hundred dollars. His book had been accepted, and this was an advance
(15) against his royalties.

So he was happier than he had ever been in all his life. Fame, at last, was knocking at his door and wooing him with her sweet blandishments, and he lived in a kind of glorious delirium. The
(20) next weeks and months were filled with the excitement of the impending event. The book would not be published till the fall, but meanwhile there was much work to do. Foxhall Edwards had made some suggestions for cutting and revising the
(25) manuscript, and, although George at first objected, he surprised himself in the end by agreeing with Edwards, and he undertook to do what Edwards wanted.

George had called his novel *Home to Our*
(30) *Mountains*, and in it he had packed everything he knew about his home town in Old Catawba and the people there. He had distilled every line of it

out of his own experience of life. And, now that the issue was decided, he sometimes trembled
(35) when he thought that it would only be a matter of months before the whole world knew what he had written. He loathed the thought of giving pain to anyone, and that he might do so had never occurred to him until now. But now it was out of
(40) his hands, and he began to feel uneasy. Of course it was fiction, but it was made as all honest fiction must be, from the stuff of human life. Some people might recognize themselves and be offended, and then what would he do? Would he have to go
(45) around in smoked glasses and false whiskers? He comforted himself with the hope that his characterizations were not so true as, in another mood, he liked to think they were, and he thought that perhaps no one would notice anything.
(50)   *Rodney's Magazine*, too, had become interested in the young author and was going to publish a story, a chapter from the book, in their next number. This news added immensely to his excitement. He was eager to see his name in print, and
(55) in the happy interval of expectancy he felt like a kind of universal Don Juan, for he literally loved everybody—his fellow instructors at the school, his drab students, the little shopkeepers in all the stores, even the nameless hordes that thronged the
(60) streets. Rodney's, of course, was the greatest and finest publishing house in all the world, and Foxhall Edwards was the greatest editor and the finest man that ever was. George had liked him instinctively from the first, and now, like an old
(65) and intimate friend, he was calling him Fox. George knew that Fox believed in him, and the

GO ON TO THE NEXT PAGE

editor's faith and confidence, coming as it had
come at a time when George had given up all
hope, restored his self-respect and charged him
(70) with energy for new work.

Already his next novel was begun and was
beginning to take shape within him. He would
soon have to get it out of him. He dreaded the
prospect of buckling down in earnest to write it,
(75) for he knew the agony of it. It was like a demoniacal possession, driving him with alien force much
greater than his own. While the fury of creation
was upon him, it meant sixty cigarettes a day,
twenty cups of coffee, meals snatched anyhow and
(80) anywhere and at whatever time of day or night he
happened to remember he was hungry. It meant
sleeplessness, and miles of walking to bring on the
physical fatigue without which he could not sleep,
then nightmares, nerves, and exhaustion in the
(85) morning. As he said to Fox:

"There are better ways to write a book, but this,
God help me, is mine, and you'll have to learn to
put up with it."

When *Rodney's Magazine* came out with the
(90) story, George fully expected convulsions of the
earth, falling meteors, suspension of traffic in the
streets, and a general strike. But nothing happened. A few of his friends mentioned it, but that
was all. For several days he felt let down, but then
(95) his common sense reassured him that people
couldn't really tell much about a new author from
a short piece in a magazine. The book would show
them who he was and what he could do. It would
be different then. He could afford to wait a little
(100) longer for the fame which he was certain would
soon be his.

1. Why does George think he would "have to
   go around in smoked glasses and false
   whiskers" (lines 44–45)?

   A. Famous authors have to protect their
       privacy from admiring strangers.

   B. A disguise would help him gather infor-
       mation for a new book.

   C. If he were going to be a famous writer he
       had better look the part.

   D. People he had offended might otherwise
       confront him.

2. According to George's description, the process
   of writing a novel:

   F. was similar to being overwhelmed by an
       alien spirit.

   G. was a time filled with unspoken rage.

   H. was best carried out during times when
       other people were asleep.

   J. could only be performed when he was
       physically exhausted.

3. By saying to Foxhall Edwards that "There are
   better ways to write a book, but this, God help
   me, is mine, and you'll have to learn to put up
   with it," (lines 86–88) George sought to:

   A. reassure Foxhall that the next book
       would, in fact, be completed.

   B. emphasize that the process, though dif-
       ficult, could not be avoided.

   C. rebuke Foxhall for not having enough
       faith in his new project.

   D. suggest that his own approach to writing
       was really superior to other approaches.

GO ON TO THE NEXT PAGE ⟹

4. Given George's expectations concerning the publication of his story in *Rodney's Magazine*, the public's response to the story can best be described as:

    F. sour.

    G. appropriate.

    H. ironic.

    J. enthusiastic.

5. According to the passage, Foxhall Edwards's belief in George's ability was important primarily because:

    A. George needed a friend he could confide in.

    B. *Home to Our Mountains* required extensive revision.

    C. George needed a friend he could look up to.

    D. Foxhall restored George's faith in his own work.

6. What was George's ultimate response to his story's publication in *Rodney's Magazine*?

    F. He refused to accept that the story had few readers.

    G. He expected that fame would come eventually anyway.

    H. He convinced himself that he had never wished for fame.

    J. He lost confidence in himself as a writer.

7. As it is used in the passage, the word *wooing* (line 18) means:

    A. courting.

    B. confusing.

    C. admiring.

    D. bothering.

8. The fact that George "sometimes trembled" (line 34) when he thought of his novel's publication indicates that he:

    F. secretly disliked Foxhall's suggestions.

    G. was eager to meet the people back in his home town.

    H. worried that some people would be hurt by his novel.

    J. feared that critics would denounce his novel.

9. George's estimation of his novel's achievement can best described as:

    A. vain but bitter.

    B. proud but concerned.

    C. modest but hopeful.

    D. angry but resigned.

10. The first paragraph suggests that, just prior to the moment at which this passage begins, George has most likely been:

    F. wandering in dazed excitement after learning that his book would be published.

    G. walking off nervous tension brought on by working on his second novel.

    H. trying to find his way home from his book publisher's office.

    J. in a joyous dream state as a result of being relieved of his financial difficulties.

GO ON TO THE NEXT PAGE

Passage II

In the 500 years since Leonardo, two ideas about
man have been especially important. The first is
the emphasis on the full development of the
Line human personality. The individual is prized for
(5) himself. His creative powers are seen as the core of
his being. The unfettered development of individual personality is praised as the ideal, from the
Renaissance artists through the Elizabethans, and
through Locke and Voltaire and Rousseau. This
(10) vision of the freely developing man, happy in the
unfolding of his own gifts, is shared by men as different in their conceptions as Thomas Jefferson
and Edmund Burke . . .

Thus the fulfillment of man has been one of the
(15) two most formative grand ideas . . . Men have seen
themselves entering the world with a potential of
many gifts, and they have hoped to fulfill these
gifts in the development of their own lives. This
has come to be the unexpressed purpose of the life
(20) of individuals: fulfilling the special gifts with
which a man is endowed.

The self-fulfillment of the individual has itself
become part of a larger, more embracing idea, the
self-fulfillment of man. We think of man as a
(25) species with special gifts, which are the human
gifts. Some of these gifts, the physical and mental
gifts, are elucidated for us explicitly by science;
some of them, the aesthetic and ethical gifts, we
feel and struggle to express in our own minds; and
(30) some of them, the cultural gifts, are unfolded for
us by the study of history. The total of these gifts
is man as a type or species, and the aspiration of
man as a species has become the fulfillment of
what is most human in these gifts.

(35) This idea of human self-fulfillment has also
inspired scientific and technical progress. We
sometimes think that progress is illusory, and that
the devices and gadgets which have become indispensable to civilized men in the last 500 years are
(40) only a self-propagating accumulation of idle

luxuries. But this has not been the purpose in the
minds of scientists and technicians, nor has it
been the true effect of these inventions on human
society. The purpose and the effect has been to
(45) liberate men from the exhausting drudgeries of
earning their living, in order to give them the
opportunity to live. From Leonardo to Franklin,
the inventor has wanted to give, and has succeeded
in giving, more and more people the ease and
(50) leisure to find the best in themselves which was
once the monopoly of princes.

Only rarely has a thinker in the last 500 years
gone back from the ideal of human potential and
fulfillment. Calvin was perhaps such a thinker
(55) who went back, and believed as the Middle Ages
did, that man comes into this world as a complete
entity, incapable of any worthwhile development.
And it is characteristic that the state which Calvin
organized was, as a result, a totalitarian state. For
(60) if men cannot develop, and have nothing in them
which is personal and creative, there is no point in
giving them freedom.

The second of the two grand formative ideas is
the idea of freedom. We see in fact that human ful-
(65) fillment is unattainable without freedom, so that
these two main ideas are linked together. There
could be no development of the personality of
individuals, no fulfillment of those gifts in which
one man differs from another, without the free-
(70) dom for each man to grow in his own direction.

What is true of individuals is true of human
groups. A state or a society cannot change unless
its members are given freedom to judge, to criticize, and to search for a new status for themselves.
(75) Therefore the pressure of ideas has been toward
freedom as an expression of individuality.
Sometimes men have tried to find freedom along
quiet paths of change, as the humanists did on the
eve of the Reformation, and as the dissenting
(80) manufacturers of the eighteenth century did. At
other times, the drive for freedom has been explosive: intellectually explosive in the Elizabethan age

GO ON TO THE NEXT PAGE ▷

and the Scientific Revolution, economically explosive in the Industrial Revolution, and politically
(85) explosive in the other great revolutions of our
period, from Puritan times to the age of
Napoleon.

. . . Freedom is a supple and elusive idea, whose
advocates can at times delude themselves that obe-
(90) dience to tyranny is a form of freedom. Such a
delusion ensnared men as diverse as Luther and
Rousseau, and Hegel and Marx. Philosophically,
there is indeed no unlimited freedom. But we have
seen that there is one freedom which can be
(95) defined without contradiction, and which can
therefore be an end in itself. This is freedom of
thought and speech: the right to dissent.

Excerpt from *The Western Intellectual Tradition: From
Leonardo to Hegel*, copyright © 1960 by Jacob Bronowski and
Bruce Mazlish. Reprinted by permission of HarperCollins
Publishers.

11. The authors mention Calvin in the fifth
    paragraph (lines 52–62) in order to:

    A. introduce the topic of the Middle Ages.
    B. praise an unusual thinker.
    C. present a counterexample.
    D. illustrate a point made in the previous
        paragraph.

12. As it is used in line 27, the word *elucidated*
    means:

    F. decided.
    G. revealed.
    H. invented.
    J. judged.

13. The passage implies that, in the past 500 years,
    history has revealed two intellectual traditions
    that are:

    A. equally important, even though mutually
        exclusive.
    B. similarly important and closely tied
        together.
    C. only now being seen as particularly
        important.
    D. less important than freedom of thought
        and speech.

14. In the fourth paragraph (lines 35–51) the
    authors' point about "devices and gadgets"
    is that:

    F. all technological progress is an illusion.
    G. all inventors attain self-fulfillment.
    H. these inventions have allowed people to
        work less.
    J. these inventions are a necessary evil.

15. What do the authors suggest was "once the
    monopoly of princes" (line 51)?

    A. Political power to create totalitarian states
    B. Vast amounts of wealth for personal use
    C. Leisure time for self-fulfillment
    D. Brilliant inventions to spur human
        progress

16. In the final paragraph, the authors indicate
    that the idea of freedom:

    F. always involves some element of political
        dissent.
    G. is actually a delusion.
    H. has, at times, been defined as obedience
        to tyranny.
    J. is sometimes seriously flawed.

GO ON TO THE NEXT PAGE

17. Which of the following opinions concerning "the self-fulfillment of the individual" (line 22) would the authors most likely reject?

    A. Self-fulfillment requires a degree of leisure.

    B. Self-fulfillment is a praiseworthy but unreachable goal.

    C. Self-fulfillment is an ideal shared by diverse thinkers.

    D. Self-fulfillment means pursuing one's creative potential.

18. The authors clearly indicate that they believe freedom is:

    F. essential if societies are to progress.

    G. the product of stable societies only.

    H. a prerequisite for world peace.

    J. only attainable through revolution.

19. According to the passage, Luther, Rousseau, Hegel, and Marx have in common that they were:

    A. misled by a false idea of freedom.

    B. believers in unlimited freedom.

    C. supporters of the right to dissent.

    D. opponents of tyranny.

20. The authors' attitude toward intellectual, economic, and political revolutions is best characterized as:

    F. detached.

    G. concerned.

    H. suspicious.

    J. approving.

GO ON TO THE NEXT PAGE

PASSAGE III

Italy emerged from World War I battered and
humiliated. Although it was one of the victorious
Allies, Italy's armies had made a poor showing,
Line and Italy had realized few of the grandiose ambi-
(5) tions for which it had entered the war. In the Paris
peace settlements Italy had been awarded the adjacent Italian-speaking areas of Austria-Hungary
but had been denied further acquisitions east of
the Adriatic and in Asia and Africa, some of which
(10) it ardently desired. These frustrations were severe
blows to Italian national pride.

Italy's weak economy emerged from the war
acutely maladjusted. The national debt was huge
and the treasury empty. The inflated currency,
(15) together with a shortage of goods, raised prices
ruinously. Hundreds of thousands of demobilized
veterans could find no jobs. In the summer of
1919, there was widespread disorder. Veterans
began seizing and squatting on idle, and some-
(20) times on cultivated, lands. Sit-down strikes developed in the factories. During the winter of
1920–1921, several factories were seized by the
workers, and Marxism seemed to be gaining
strength. The Italian government, torn by factions,
(25) seemed too weak to prevent the disorder and protect private property. Although the strife diminished and the Marxist threat waned before the end
of 1921, the landlords and the factory owners were
thoroughly frightened. Many of them, and indeed
(30) many small-business and professional people,
longed for vigorous leadership and a strong
government. The vigorous leader who stepped forward was Benito Mussolini. The strong government was his Fascist dictatorship.

(35) Mussolini was a dynamic organizer and leader.
The son of a blacksmith, he became first a teacher
and later a radical journalist and agitator. Before
World War I he was a pacifistic socialist, but during the war he became a violent nationalist. After
(40) the war he began organizing unemployed veterans
into a political action group with a socialistic and

extremely nationalistic program. During the labor
disturbances of 1919–1921, Mussolini stood aside
until it became apparent that the radical workers'
(45) cause would lose; then he threw his support to the
capitalists and the landlords. Crying that he was
saving Italy from communism and waving the flag
of nationalism, Mussolini organized his veterans
into terror squads of black-shirted "Fascisti," who
(50) beat up the leaderless radical workers and their
liberal supporters. He thereby gained the support
of the frightened capitalists and landed aristocracy.
By 1922 Mussolini's Fascist party was strong
enough to "march on Rome" and seize control of
(55) the faction-paralyzed government. Appointed premier by the weak and distraught King Victor
Emmanuel III, Mussolini acquired extraordinary
powers. Between 1924 and 1926 Mussolini turned
his premiership into a dictatorship. All opposition
(60) was silenced. Only the Fascist party could engage
in organized political activity. The press and the
schools were turned into propaganda agencies.
The secret police were everywhere. Eventually, the
Chamber of Deputies itself was replaced by
(65) Mussolini's handpicked Fascist political and economic councils.

Italy's economic life was strictly regimented but
in such a way as to favor the capitalistic classes.
Private property and profits were carefully pro-
(70) tected. All labor unions were abolished except
those controlled by the Fascist party. Strikes and
lockouts were forbidden. Wages, working conditions, and labor-management disputes were settled
by compulsory arbitration under party direc-
(75) tion. An elaborate system of planned economy
was set up to modernize, coordinate, and increase
Italy's production of both industrial and agricultural goods. The very complicated economic and
political machinery that Mussolini created for
(80) these purposes was called the corporate state. On
the whole there was probably a small decline in
per capita income under Italian fascism despite
some superficial gains. The budget was balanced

GO ON TO THE NEXT PAGE ▷

and the currency stabilized. But Italy's taxes were
(85) the highest in the world, and labor's share of economic production was small.

    Fascism, however, was primarily political in
character, not economic. The essence of its ideol-
ogy was nationalism run wild. Although Italy
(90) never became such a full-blown, viciously anti-
Semitic police state as Germany, Mussolini understood the dynamic, energizing quality of militant
nationalism. His writings and speeches rang with
such words as *will, discipline, sacrifice, decision,*
(95) *and conquest.* "The goal," he cried, "is always—
mpire! To build a city, to found a colony, to
establish an empire, these are the prodigies of the
human spirit…We must resolutely abandon the
whole liberal phraseology and way of thinking.
(100) . . . Discipline. Discipline at home in order that we
may present the granite block of a single national
will. War alone brings up the highest tension, all
human energy and puts the stamp of nobility
upon the people who have the courage to meet it."

    Excerpt from *A Short History of Western Civilization, Volume 1*
by John B. Harrison, Richard E. Sullivan, and Dennis Sherman.
Copyright © 1990 by McGraw-Hill, Inc. Reprinted by permission of McGraw-Hill, Inc.

21. According to information presented in the
passage, "grandiose ambitions" (line 4–5)
refers to Italy's desire for:

    A. territorial expansion.

    B. complete victory at the end of
        World War I.

    C. peacetime employment for all its
        veterans.

    D. a supremely powerful army.

22. The passage suggests that Mussolini came to
power in 1922 largely as a result of:

    I. a desire for stability among property-
       owning middle classes.

    II. a lack of strong opposition from the gov-
        ernment in Rome.

    III. his violent opposition to radical workers.

    F. I and II only

    G. I and III only

    H. II and III only

    J. I, II, and III

23. In which of the following ways does the
passage support the theory that fascism arises
after periods of diminished national pride?

    A. It attributes the fascists' seizure of power
        from the King to Mussolini's abilities as a
        leader.

    B. It demonstrates that Mussolini achieved
        national fame largely because of his
        eagerness to fight communism.

    C. It shows a connection between the
        growth of the corporate state and
        Mussolini's rise to power.

    D. It links Mussolini's ascendancy to the
        fact that Italy gained less than it hoped
        for after World War I.

24. The author suggests that, during the disturbances of 1919–1921, "Mussolini stood aside
until it became apparent that the radical workers'
cause would lose" (lines 43–45) because he was:

    F. secretly hoping the radical workers
        would win.

    G. an opportunist, waiting for his chance to
        seize power.

    H. unaware of the importance of the radi-
        cals' challenge.

    J. basically a pacifist at that time in his life.

GO ON TO THE NEXT PAGE

25. A dictatorship is commonly defined as a form of government that has absolute authority over its citizens. Which of the following statements from the passage supports the view that Mussolini's government was a dictatorship?

   A. "Mussolini was a dynamic organizer and leader."

   B. "All labor unions were abolished except those controlled by the Fascist party."

   C. "Veterans began seizing and squatting on idle, and sometimes on cultivated, lands."

   D. "The budget was balanced and the currency stabilized."

26. It can be inferred from the passage that, to Mussolini, nationalism was a:

   F. way to protect Italy from German aggression.

   G. method to bring economic prosperity to war-ravaged Italy.

   H. powerful political tool.

   J. threat to his rise to power.

27. The passage suggests that if the rights of factory workers in 1920 were compared to their rights in 1926, one could accurately say that:

   A. while workers' per capita income rose, workers lost their rights to collective bargaining.

   B. labor's share of economic production grew.

   C. workers' collective action was increasingly disallowed.

   D. workers' collective action was completely suppressed.

28. The passage suggests that under the Italian fascists, economic rebuilding was:

   F. undermined by labor disturbances.

   G. resisted by the corporate state.

   H. marred by excessively high taxation.

   J. slowed by a failure to balance the budget.

29. Based on information in the passage, the "corporate state" can best be defined as a:

   A. system of structuring government according to business practices.

   B. series of economic programs aimed at ending an inflated currency.

   C. negotiating team that arbitrated worker-management disputes.

   D. complex, planned economy designed to maximize the production of goods.

30. It can be inferred that the author quotes Mussolini's words in the last paragraph (lines 87–104) for the purpose of:

   F. illustrating the nationalistic element in his words.

   G. praising his abilities as a public speaker.

   H. condemning the ideas that Mussolini advances.

   J. demonstrating the difference between Italian and German fascism.

GO ON TO THE NEXT PAGE

PASSAGE IV

Tornadoes have long been an enigma, striking sporadically and violently, generating the strongest of all surface winds, and causing more deaths
Line annually in the United States than any other natu-
(5) ral phenomenon other than lightning. It is esti- mated that tornadoes can generate a maximum wind speed of 300 miles per hour, based on analy- sis of motion pictures and damage to structures.

Tornadoes are formed in the updrafts of a
(10) thunderstorm or are associated with hurricanes when they pass over land. They are tightly wound vortexes of air, rarely more than several hundred feet across. They rotate in a counterclockwise direction in the Northern Hemisphere and a
(15) clockwise direction in the Southern Hemisphere. Drawn by the greatly reduced atmospheric pressure in the central core, air streams into the base of the vortex from all directions. The air then turns abruptly to spiral upward around the core, and
(20) finally merges with the airflow in the parent cloud at the upper end of the tornado. The pres- sure within the core might be as little as 10 per- cent lower than the surrounding atmosphere, which would be equivalent to a sudden drop in
(25) pressure from that at sea level to an altitude of 3000 feet.

The vortex frequently becomes visible as a wide, dark funnel cloud hanging partway or all the way to the ground. A funnel cloud can only
(30) form if the pressure drop in the core reaches a critical value, which depends on the temperature and humidity of the inflowing air. As air flows into the area of lower pressure, it expands and cools, causing water vapor to condense and form
(35) water droplets.

Sometimes, no condensation cloud forms, and the only way a tornado can reveal itself is by the dust and debris it carries aloft over land or water spray over the ocean. In that case, it becomes a
(40) waterspout, which often frequent the Florida coast and the Bahamas.

The funnel is usually cone shaped, but short, broad, cylindrical pillars up to a mile wide are formed by very strong tornadoes, and often, long,
(45) ropelike tubes dangle from the storm cloud. Over the tornado's brief lifetime, usually no more than a few hours, the size, shape, and color of the fun- nel might change markedly, depending on the intensity of the winds, the properties of the
(50) inflowing air, and the type of ground over which it hovers. The color varies from a dirty white to a blue gray when it consists mostly of water droplets, but if the core fills with dust, it takes on the color of the soil and other debris. Tornadoes
(55) are also noisy, often roaring, like a laboring freight train or a jet plane taking off. The sound results from the interaction of the concentrated high winds with the ground.

The world's tornado hot spot, with about 700
(60) tornadoes yearly, is the United States, particularly the central and southeastern portions of the coun- try, known as tornado alley. The states most fre- quently visited by tornadoes are Texas, Arkansas, Oklahoma, Kansas, Nebraska, and Missouri, with
(65) a high occurrence of tornadoes continuing on up into Canada.

Tornadoes develop in the spring and to a lesser extent in the fall, when conditions are ripe for the formation of tornado-generating thunderstorms.
(70) These conditions include a highly unstable distri- bution of temperature and humidity in the atmo- sphere, strong cold fronts that provide the lift needed to start convection, and winds in the upper atmosphere favorable for the formation of
(75) strong updrafts.

For a tornado to form, the air in the updraft must begin to rotate. This is accomplished by a wind shear where the wind speed increases with height and veers from southeast to west. Once
(80) rotation begins, the tornado builds down toward the ground, although not all tornadoes actually reach the ground. When on the ground, the torna- do funnel sucks up air at its lower end, like the hose of a vacuum cleaner.

GO ON TO THE NEXT PAGE ⟶

(85)   Tornadoes are steered by the jet stream, and
generally travel in a northeasterly direction for
about 5 to 15 miles. Their forward ground speed
is normally slow enough (30 to 60 miles per hour)
for them to be outrun by an automobile, although
(90) this is not always a recommended practice because
of the unpredictable nature of tornadoes, which
often hop about from place to place. Members of
NOAA's National Severe Storms Laboratory at the
University of Oklahoma actually chase tornadoes
(95) in vehicles carrying an instrument package known
as TOTO which stands for Totable Tornado
Observatory. This package is placed in the path of
the tornado. TOTO is equipped to measure a tornado's behavior such as wind speed, wind direc-
(100) tion, atmospheric temperature and pressure, and
electric field strength.

Excerpt from Book #2942 *Violent Storms* by Jon Erickson,
copyright © 1988 by TAB Books, a division of McGraw-Hill,
Inc. Reprinted by permission of McGraw-Hill, Inc.

31. The author refers to tornadoes as "vortexes
of air" (line 12) to emphasize the fact that the
air is:

A.   moving downward.

B.   expanding.

C.   dispersing.

D.   whirling.

32. The inspection of films showing the action of
tornadoes allowed researchers to determine
that tornadoes:

F.   are often accompanied by lightning.

G.   gain maximum size when they pass
over land.

H.   are caused by the updrafts of thunderstorms.

J.   reach wind speeds of up to 300 miles
per hour.

33. The passage suggests that the direction of a
tornado's rotation is influenced chiefly by:

A.   whether a hurricane or a thunderstorm
has caused it to form.

B.   the difference in pressure between air
in the core and air in the surrounding
atmosphere.

C.   the direction of the airflow in its
parent cloud.

D.   where the tornado is located on the
earth's surface.

GO ON TO THE NEXT PAGE

34. Researchers often have difficulty getting TOTO to record the information they need. Based on the information in the last paragraph, this is most likely true because:

   F. no scientific instruments can withstand a tornado's force.

   G. it is difficult to predict precisely the path a tornado will take.

   H. tornadoes' characteristics vary too much to measure accurately.

   J. the majority of tornadoes occur over water and are thus unapproachable.

35. If a tornado is to form, which of the following must occur first?

   A. Powerful updrafts and wind shear

   B. Movement of the funnel toward the ground

   C. Movement of air up the funnel from the ground

   D. Uniform distribution of temperature and humidity in the atmosphere

36. The expression "wind shear" (line 78) means that, while gaining altitude, wind:

   F. direction changes, while wind speed stays the same.

   G. speed changes, while wind direction stays the same.

   H. speed and wind direction both change.

   J. is sucked up the lower end of a funnel.

37. The passage suggests that it should be possible to predict when tornadoes are likely to form if:

   A. certain key atmospheric conditions are known.

   B. "tornado alley" can be accurately identified.

   C. the movement of warm fronts can be predicted.

   D. TOTO's readings are accurate.

38. According to the passage, a condensation cloud is created when:

   F. water vapor entering the funnel is affected by changes in air pressure.

   G. the funnel passes over a body of water.

   H. cool air rushes into the funnel and immediately forms droplets.

   J. dust and debris are sucked into the funnel.

39. The main purpose of the third and fourth paragraphs (lines 27–41) is to describe:

   A. how funnels are formed.

   B. how a condensation cloud is formed.

   C. the main factors that make tornadoes visible.

   D. how funnel clouds can vary in color, shape, and size.

40. Based on information presented in the passage, it is a fact that all tornadoes:

   F. are colored by the dust and debris they carry.

   G. touch the earth's surface.

   H. occur in the spring.

   J. are steered by the jet stream.

IF YOU FINISH BEFORE TIME IS CALLED, YOU MAY CHECK YOUR WORK ON THIS SECTION ONLY. DO NOT TURN TO ANY OTHER SECTION IN THE TEST.

SCIENCE TEST

35 Minutes—40 Questions

Directions: Each of the following seven passages is followed by several questions. After reading each passage, decide on the best answer to each question and fill in the corresponding oval on your answer sheet. You are allowed to refer to the passages while answering the questions. Calculator use is not allowed on this test.

PASSAGE I

Medical researchers and technicians can track the characteristic radiation patterns emitted by certain inherently unstable isotopes as they spontaneously decay into other elements. The half-life of a radio-active isotope is the amount of time necessary for one-half of the initial amount of its nuclei to decay. The decay curves of isotopes $^{90}_{39}Y$ and $^{91}_{39}Y$ are graphed below as functions of the ratio of N, the number of nuclei remaining after a given period, to N_0, the initial number of nuclei.

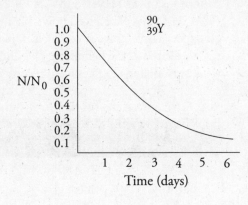

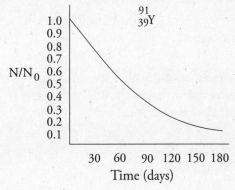

1. The half-life of $^{90}_{39}Y$ is approximately:

   A.   2.3 days.

   B.   5.4 days.

   C.   27 days.

   D.   58 days.

2. What will the approximate ratio of $^{90}_{39}Y$ to $^{91}_{39}Y$ be after 2.3 days if the initial samples of the two isotopes contain equal numbers of nuclei?

   F.   1:1

   G.   1:2

   H.   2:1

   J.   10:1

GO ON TO THE NEXT PAGE

3. When inhaled by humans, $^{90}_{39}Y$ accumulates in the gastrointestinal tract, whereas $^{91}_{39}Y$ accumulates in the bones. If the total amount of each isotope inhaled goes to the specified area, which of the following situations will exist three days after a patient inhales these substances, assuming none of the isotopes leave the specified areas due to physiological factors?

   A. The amount of $^{91}_{39}Y$ in the gastrointestinal tract will be approximately equal to the total amount inhaled.

   B. The amount of $^{91}_{39}Y$ in the bones will be approximately one-half of the total amount inhaled.

   C. The amount of $^{91}_{39}Y$ in the gastrointestinal tract will be approximately one-half of the total amount inhaled.

   D. None of the $^{91}_{39}Y$ inhaled will be left in the bones.

4. Approximately how many $^{91}_{39}Y$ nuclei will exist after three half-lives have passed, if there are 1,000 nuclei to begin with?

   F. 50
   G. 125
   H. 250
   J. 500

5. Which of the following conclusions is/are supported by the information given in the passage?

   I. $^{90}_{39}Y$ is less stable than $^{91}_{39}Y$
   II. Only one-quarter of the original amount of $^{90}_{39}Y$ will remain after 116 days.
   III. $^{90}_{39}Y$ and $^{91}_{39}Y$ are both radioactive.

   A. I only
   B. III only
   C. I and II only
   D. I and III only

PASSAGE II

Recently, college teams from all over the country sent tennis players to participate in a series of experiments conducted by the Physical Education Department of a major university. A variety of coaching methods was used to improve the players' serves, as described below.

EXPERIMENT 1

Two groups of 50 tennis players worked on the speed of their basic serves for two weeks. One group consisted solely of right-handed players; the other consisted solely of left-handed players. Half of each group watched videos of a right-handed tennis coach, while the other half watched videos of a left-handed coach. Each player was told to pattern his or her serve on that of the coach in the video. The players received no verbal or physical guidance. The average speed of each player's serve was measured at the beginning and end of the two-week period, and changes were recorded in Table 1.

Table 1

Players' handedness	Coach's handedness	Average change in speed (mph)
Right	Right	+5
Right	Left	+2
Left	Right	−1
Left	Left	+8

EXPERIMENT 2

For two weeks, a second group of 100 right-handed tennis players watched the same videos of the right-handed tennis coach. The coach also physically guided 50 of those players through the motions of the serve. Again, no verbal instruction was given during the experiment. The average speed and accuracy of each player's serves were recorded at the beginning and end of this two-week period. The results are recorded in Table 2.

GO ON TO THE NEXT PAGE →

Table 2

Guided	Average Change in Speed (mph)	Average Change in Accuracy
No	+5	+15%
Yes	+9	+25%

EXPERIMENT 3

For two weeks, a third group of 100 right-handed tennis players worked on their basic serves. 50 players received no verbal instruction; they watched the same video of the right-handed tennis coach, who also physically guided them through the motions of the serve. The other 50 players did not observe the video but received verbal instruction from the coach, who then physically guided them through the motions of the serve. The results are shown in Table 3.

Table 3

Guidance Plus	Average Change in Speed (mph)
Video	+7
Verbal Coaching	+10

6. Which of the following results would be expected if Experiment 3 were repeated using left-handed tennis players and a left-handed coach?

   F. The average service accuracy of all the players would increase by at least 30%.

   G. The average service speed of all the players would decrease slightly.

   H. Verbal coaching would improve average service speed less than would watching the video.

   J. The average service speed of the players who watched the video would increase by at least 8 mph.

7. Which of the following conclusions could NOT be supported by the results of Experiment 1?

   A. Imitating someone whose handedness is the opposite of one's own will cause one's skills to deteriorate.

   B. Left-handed people are better than right-handed people at imitating the movement of someone with similar handedness.

   C. People learn more easily by observing someone with similar handedness than by observing someone with handedness opposite their own.

   D. Right-handed people are better than left-handed people at imitating the movement of someone whose handedness is opposite their own.

8. Which of the following hypotheses is best supported by the results of Experiment 2?

   F. Instructional videos are more helpful for right-handed tennis players than is verbal instruction.

   G. Instructional videos are more helpful for left-handed tennis players than for right-handed tennis players.

   H. Physical guidance by a coach improves both speed and accuracy of service for right-handed tennis players.

   J. Physical guidance by a coach improves service accuracy for right-handed tennis players more than for left-handed players.

GO ON TO THE NEXT PAGE

9. Suppose 50 left-handed tennis players watch a video of a left-handed coach and are also physically guided by that coach. The results of the experiments suggest that the players' average change in service speed will most closely approximate:

   A. –1 mph.

   B. +5 mph.

   C. +8 mph.

   D. +12 mph.

10. Which of the following hypotheses is best supported by the results of Experiment 1 alone?

    F. Tennis players improve less by observing coaches whose handedness is the opposite of their own than by observing those with similar handedness.

    G. Right-handed tennis players are coached by left-handed coaches more frequently than left-handed players are coached by right-handed coaches.

    H. Right-handed coaches are better models for all tennis players than are left-handed coaches.

    J. People learn much better from physical contact plus a visual stimulus than from the visual stimulus alone.

11. What change in procedure would allow a researcher to best determine the effects of verbal instruction on the average service speed of tennis players?

    A. Repeating Experiment 3 with left-handed players

    B. Repeating Experiment 2 with an instructional audio tape instead of a video

    C. Measuring the service speed of 100 tennis players before and after they listened to an instructional audio tape

    D. Verbally coaching 50 left-handed and 50 right-handed tennis players and then measuring their service speed

Passage III

The temperature of any stellar body causes it to emit a characteristic spectrum of radiation. The apparent color of the star corresponds to the wavelength at which most of its radiation is emitted. Stars are assigned to spectral classes according to these characteristic wavelengths, with O as the bluest/warmest and M as the reddest/coolest. The Hertzsprung-Russell (H-R) diagram below plots each known star within 5 parsecs of the Sun by spectral class and absolute magnitude. Absolute magnitude is a measure of luminosity as viewed from a distance of 10 parsecs. An absolute magnitude of +1.0 indicates maximum brightness. (1 parsec = 3.23 light years.)

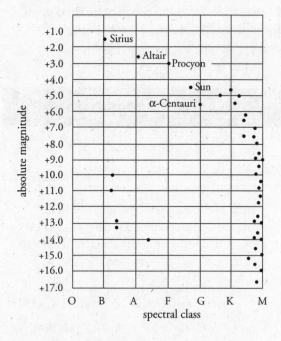

12. According to the data shown, most stars within 5 parsecs of the Sun have:

    F. a spectral class of M.

    G. an absolute magnitude of +11.0.

    H. a mass similar to that of the Sun.

    J. a bluish color.

GO ON TO THE NEXT PAGE ▷

13. According to the information given, which of the following stars—Sirius, Altair, α-Centauri—are likely to be hotter than the Sun?

    A. Sirius, Altair, and α-Centauri

    B. Sirius and Altair

    C. Sirius

    D. α-Centauri

14. The faintest stars that are visible to the naked eye are of the 6th magnitude. On the basis of this information and the data given, which of the following conclusions is most likely to be valid?

    F. The majority of stars within 5 parsecs of the Sun are visible from a distance of 10 parsecs.

    G. The majority of stars within 5 parsecs of the Sun are not visible from a distance of 10 parsecs.

    H. Stars in spectral classes K and M are visible from a distance of 10 parsecs.

    J. Stars in spectral class B are visible from a distance of 10 parsecs.

15. The data given in the passage support which of the following conclusions?

    I. α-Centauri is redder in color than Sirius.

    II. The Sun has a higher surface temperature than does Altair.

    III. If both the Sun and Procyon were viewed at a distance of 10 parsecs, the Sun would appear brighter.

    A. I only

    B. III only

    C. I and II only

    D. II and III only

16. In which of the following ways would a Hertzsprung-Russell diagram that included all of the known stars within 10 parsecs of the Sun differ from the one shown here?

    F. The number of points on the graph would approximately double, while the shape would remain the same.

    G. Most of the additional stars would fall in the portion of the graph between Sirius and α-Centauri.

    H. Most of the additional stars would be in spectral class M with an absolute magnitude of less than +16.0.

    J. It cannot be determined from the information given.

GO ON TO THE NEXT PAGE

PASSAGE IV

The reaction of a certain cobalt complex with sodium nitrite ($NaNO_2$) can yield two different products. Product A is a light orange solid with a melting point measured at approximately 90.5° C; Product B is a dark pink solid with a melting point of 68° C. A series of experiments was performed to determine the reaction conditions that favor each product.

EXPERIMENT 1

Two separate solutions of the cobalt complex were prepared as follows. Solution 1 was acidified to pH 5.5; Solution 2 was made basic to pH 8.5. All other conditions were identical for the two solutions. When $NaNO_2$ was added to Solution 1, a dark pink solid with a melting point of 68° C was formed. Adding $NaNO_2$ to Solution 2 produced a white solid with a melting point of 81° C.

EXPERIMENT 2

Two separate solutions of the cobalt complex were prepared as above. After addition of $NaNO_2$, the solutions were heated to 110° C for 20 minutes. Solution 1 produced a dark pink solid with a melting point of 68° C. Solution 2 produced a light orange solid which melted at 91° C.

EXPERIMENT 3

Two separate solutions were prepared as in the previous experiments. After the addition of $NaNO_2$, each solution was treated with a small amount of citrate ion and then heated as in Experiment 2. Solution 1 remained a clear purple liquid. Solution 2 produced a light orange solid which melted at 90° C.

17. The experimental results indicate that Product B is most likely to form when one heats:

A. a basic solution with added citrate ion.

B. an acidic solution with added citrate ion.

C. an acidic solution with no added citrate ion.

D. a basic solution with no added citrate ion.

18. Which of the following conclusions is NOT supported by the experimental results?

F. The formation of Product B is not affected by the presence of citrate ion.

G. The formation of Product B is not affected by the heating of the solution.

H. Products A and B form under different conditions.

J. The formation of Product A is affected by the heating of the solution.

19. Which of the following additional experiments would yield the most useful data concerning the reaction conditions that favor each product?

A. Varying the concentration of the solutions

B. Testing with pH levels of 7.0

C. Heating the solutions to 175° C

D. Freezing the solutions

GO ON TO THE NEXT PAGE

20. Which of the following hypotheses is supported by the results of Experiment 2 only?

  F. Products A and B can both be formed in solutions heated to 110° C.

  G. Solution 1 must be heated to yield any product.

  H. Citrate ion prevents the formation of Product A.

  J. Product B forms more readily at lower temperatures.

21. Which of the following conditions remain(s) constant in all three experiments?

  A. The temperature of the solutions during the experiments

  B. The initial amount of cobalt complex present

  C. The amount of citrate ion present

  D. The amount of cobalt complex and the amount of citrate ion present

22. It is suggested that Product B may react to form other, more readily dissolved compounds in the presence of certain ions. Such a hypothesis is best supported by the fact that:

  F. Product A forms at a different pH than Product B.

  G. Solution 2 yields a different color solid when heated.

  H. Product B is unstable in the presence of Product A.

  J. no solid forms in Solution 1 when citrate ion is added prior to heating.

PASSAGE V

Two scientists present various grounds for classifying the giant panda (*Ailuropoda melanoleuca*) as a raccoon or as a bear.

SCIENTIST 1

Although the giant panda superficially resembles a bear (*Ursidae*), many of its anatomical, behavioral, and genetic characteristics are closer to those of raccoons (*Procyonidae*). The bones and teeth of *Ailuropoda melanoleuca*, for example, are very similar in structure to those of the raccoon. While male bears can be up to 100% larger than females of the same species, male giant pandas and raccoons differ very little in size from females of their species. Like the raccoon, the giant panda has a friendly greeting which consists of bleating and barking. When intimidated, both animals cover their eyes with their front paws. Most bears do not exhibit these behaviors. Finally, *Ailuropoda melanoleuca* and the *Procyonidae* have 21 and 19 pairs of chromosomes, respectively, while the *Ursidae* have 36 pairs.

SCIENTIST 2

Giant pandas should be classified as *Ursidae*. Research studies have shown that the ancestors of *Ailuropoda melanoleuca* had about 40 chromosomal pairs, and geneticists theorize that the reduction occurred when the chromosomes underwent head-to-head fusion. Other research has shown that the DNA of the giant panda is far more similar to that of the *Ursidae* than to that of any other family. Furthermore, giant pandas and other bears are not only of similar size, but also have very similar body proportions and walk with the same pigeon-toed gait. Giant pandas display aggressive behavior in the same manner as do other bears, by swatting and trying to grab adversaries with their forepaws.

GO ON TO THE NEXT PAGE

23. Which of the following, if true, would provide additional support for the hypothesis of Scientist 2?

    A. The blood proteins of giant pandas are very similar to those of several bear species.

    B. Giant pandas and raccoons have similar markings, including dark rings around their eyes.

    C. Giant pandas have 21 pairs of chromosomes while raccoons have only 19 pairs.

    D. There is little difference in size between male and female giant pandas.

24. Scientist 1 and Scientist 2 would agree on which of the following points?

    F. Giant pandas should be classified in a separate family.

    G. The giant panda should not be classified as a raccoon.

    H. Raccoons and bears are physically and behaviorally very similar.

    J. Animals should be classified into families based on their physical, behavioral, and genetic characteristics.

25. Which of the following characteristics would support the classification of a mammal as a member of the *Ursidae*?

    I. 36 pairs of chromosomes and DNA similar to that of many bear species

    II. Raccoonlike markings and 19 pairs of chromosomes

    III. 62% greater average size among males than among females

    A. I only

    B. II only

    C. I and III only

    D. II and III only

26. According to Scientist 1, which of the following is the giant panda most likely to do when frightened?

    F. Bleat and bark

    G. Cover its eyes with its paws

    H. Swat and grab with its forepaws

    J. Walk away pigeon-toed

27. According to Scientist 2, the giant panda should be classified as a bear because:

    A. there is little disparity in the size of male and female giant pandas.

    B. the greeting rituals of the giant panda resemble those of bears.

    C. both bears and giant pandas are herbivorous.

    D. the DNA of giant pandas is similar to that of bears.

28. Suppose that giant pandas have glandular scent areas. This fact could be used to support the viewpoint of:

    F. Scientist 1, if it were also shown that raccoons also have glandular scent areas.

    G. Scientist 2, if it were also shown that bears do not have glandular scent areas.

    H. Scientist 1, if it were also shown that raccoons have a very poor sense of smell.

    J. Scientist 2, if it were also shown that bears urinate to lay down their scent.

GO ON TO THE NEXT PAGE

29. Which of the following arguments could Scientist 1 use to counter Scientist 2's claim about the behavior of giant pandas and bears?

    A. The giant panda walks with a pigeon-toed gait.

    B. Unlike most bears, but like raccoons, an aggressive giant panda bobs its head up and down.

    C. The giant panda swats and grabs at its adversaries.

    D. Unlike most bears, the giant panda has only 19 pairs of chromosomes.

PASSAGE VI

The graph below shows different primary energy sources as percentages of energy consumption in the United States during selected years from 1850 to 1985.

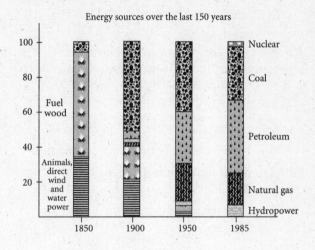

Energy sources over the last 150 years

30. As the relative importance of petroleum as a primary energy source increased, the use of coal:

    F. also increased.

    G. decreased.

    H. remained constant.

    J. stopped completely.

31. The data shown support the hypothesis that the ability to utilize coal as an energy source:

    A. was developed during the 1900s.

    B. was dependent on the development of mechanized mining techniques.

    C. predated the ability to utilize natural gas.

    D. was predated by the ability to utilize natural gas.

GO ON TO THE NEXT PAGE ⇨

32. As the consumption of alternate energy sources increased, the use of farm animals:

    F.   decreased to below 1% of the total.

    G.   increased to over 30% of the total.

    H.   increased, then decreased.

    J.   remained the same.

33. Which of the following conclusions concerning energy consumption from 1900 to 1950 is supported by the information given in the graph?

    A.   Energy sources became more diverse.

    B.   Work animals became more important.

    C.   Natural gas became the major energy source.

    D.   Coal remained the largest single source of energy.

34. The data on the graph support which of the following conclusions?

    I.   Energy consumption in 1985 relied in part on technologies that did not exist in 1850.

    II.   The largest source of energy in the United States has always been coal.

    III.   The short supply of available petroleum will lead to a decrease in its use.

    F.   I only

    G.   III only

    H.   I and II only

    J.   II and III only

PASSAGE VII

The regenerative powers of *Asterias rubens*, a common starfish, were investigated in the following experiments.

EXPERIMENT 1

Randomly selected starfish were divided into five groups of 25 each. The individuals in one group were left intact. Members of the other four groups were subjected to selective amputation, as indicated in the table below. The starfish were kept in laboratory tanks simulating the natural environment of *Asterias rubens* for nine months. The results of periodic observations are recorded in Table 1.

Table 1

Removed Portion	# fully regenerated after[†]:			# of starfish dead after 9 mos.
	3 mos.	6 mos.	9 mos.	
None	—	—	—	3
Outer arm	20	23	23	2
Whole arm	15	22	22	3
Arm & 1/5 body	6	21	23	2
2 arms & 1/3 body	5	12	24	1

[†]cumulative total

EXPERIMENT 2

The regenerative powers of portions of *Asterias rubens* were investigated next. Three groups of 25 pieces of *Asterias rubens* were selected at random, placed in separate laboratory tanks under the same conditions as in Experiment 1, and observed for one year. The combined results from all three tanks are presented in Table 2.

GO ON TO THE NEXT PAGE

Table 2

| # of starfish fully regenerated after[†]: | | | | | |
Remaining Body Portion	3 mos.	6 mos.	9 mos.	1 yr.	# dead after 1 yr.
Lower arm	0	0	0	0	25
Arm & 1/5 body	0	0	8	20	2
2 arms & 1/3 body	0	2	13	22	2

[†]cumulative total

35. According to the experimental results, approximately what percentage of *Asterias rubens* specimens can regenerate two entire arms and part of the central body within six months?

    A.   25%

    B.   50%

    C.   75%

    D.   100%

36. Which of the following conclusions is supported by the results of Experiment 2 only?

    F.   Starfish are only capable of regenerating arms.

    G.   Starfish with larger portions removed regenerate at faster rates.

    H.   Some starfish die as a result of confinement in laboratory tanks.

    J.   Regeneration is dependent upon the existence of a portion of the central body.

37. The information given supports which of the following conclusions?

    I.   *Asterias rubens* are often found in very deep water.

    II. *Asterias rubens* can regenerate limbs lost due to attack by other marine animals.

    III. The population of *Asterias rubens* would probably increase if body parts were broken off.

    A.   I only

    B.   III only

    C.   II and III only

    D.   I, II, and III

38. The first group of starfish was used in Experiment 1:

    F.   as a control to see how many starfish were likely to die under the conditions of the experiment.

    G.   as a control for the second experiment.

    H.   to test the natural recuperative powers of *Asterias rubens*.

    J.   to determine the effect of a freshwater environment on *Asterias rubens*.

GO ON TO THE NEXT PAGE ▷

39. In Experiment 2, the sum of fully regrown and dead starfish after one year did not always equal 25. The hypothesis which best explains this is that:

A. some of the starfish were lost during the experiment.

B. the researchers miscalculated somewhere during the course of the experiment.

C. some body parts fused together to form single starfish.

D. some of the starfish were alive but not fully regenerated.

40. Starfish prey on abalone. At one time it was common practice for abalone fishermen to chop starfish into pieces and throw them back into the ocean. What was the most probable result of this practice?

F. The starfish population immediately skyrocketed.

G. The starfish population increased over a period of time as some pieces underwent regeneration.

H. The starfish population decreased drastically.

J. Every piece that was returned to the ocean eventually became a complete starfish again.

IF YOU FINISH BEFORE TIME IS CALLED, YOU MAY CHECK YOUR WORK ON THIS SECTION ONLY. DO NOT TURN TO ANY OTHER SECTION IN THE TEST.

STOP

WRITING TEST

30 Minutes—1 Question

Directions: This section will test your writing ability. You will have thirty (30) minutes to compose an essay in English. Prior to planning your essay, pay close attention to the essay prompt so that you understand exactly what you are supposed to do. Your essay's grade will be based on how well it expresses an opinion on the question in the prompt, as well as its logical construction, supporting evidence, and clarity of expression based on the standards of written English.

You may use the unlined space on the next page to plan your essay. Anything written in this space will not be scored by the graders. Your essay must be written on the lined pages. While you may not need all the space to finish, you should not skip lines. Corrections and additions may be written neatly in between lines but not in the margins. Be sure to write clearly. Illegible work will not receive credit.

If you finish in under thirty minutes, you may review your essay. When time is called, lay your pencil down immediately.

DO NOT CONTINUE UNTIL TOLD TO DO SO.

While some high schools offer art and music courses to their students, these courses are not always mandatory. Some teachers, students, and parents think that schools should emphasize traditional academic subjects like math and science, as those skills will help the students more in the future when they join the workforce. Others feel that requiring all high school students to take classes in music or the visual arts would teach equally valuable skills that the students may not learn otherwise, and would also help them do better in traditional academic subject areas. In your opinion, should art or music classes be mandatory for all high school students?

In your essay, take a position on this question. You may write about either one of the two points of view given, or you may present a different point of view on this question. Use specific reasons and examples to support your position.

Use this space to *plan* your essay. Your work here will not be graded.

Practice Test One: **Answer Key**

ENGLISH TEST

1. B	26. H	51. D
2. H	27. B	52. J
3. D	28. J	53. A
4. H	29. B	54. G
5. A	30. J	55. D
6. J	31. D	56. G
7. A	32. H	57. D
8. G	33. B	58. H
9. D	34. J	59. C
10. J	35. A	60. F
11. D	36. G	61. C
12. F	37. C	62. G
13. B	38. J	63. D
14. H	39. B	64. J
15. B	40. H	65. A
16. F	41. C	66. H
17. B	42. J	67. A
18. F	43. A	68. H
19. C	44. J	69. D
20. F	45. B	70. G
21. B	46. G	71. C
22. H	47. C	72. H
23. D	48. H	73. B
24. J	49. B	74. H
25. C	50. H	75. B

MATH TEST

1. C	31. A
2. H	32. K
3. D	33. B
4. J	34. G
5. A	35. E
6. F	36. G
7. E	37. C
8. K	38. K
9. B	39. E
10. F	40. H
11. D	41. C
12. G	42. J
13. E	43. B
14. J	44. J
15. C	45. C
16. F	46. G
17. B	47. B
18. F	48. J
19. E	49. E
20. J	50. H
21. D	51. E
22. G	52. K
23. C	53. D
24. K	54. F
25. D	55. E
26. F	56. H
27. D	57. D
28. F	58. H
29. A	59. B
30. G	60. F

READING TEST

1. D	21. A
2. F	22. J
3. B	23. D
4. H	24. G
5. D	25. B
6. G	26. H
7. A	27. D
8. H	28. H
9. B	29. D
10. F	30. F
11. C	31. D
12. G	32. J
13. B	33. D
14. H	34. G
15. C	35. A
16. H	36. H
17. B	37. A
18. F	38. F
19. A	39. C
20. J	40. J

SCIENCE TEST

1. A	21. B
2. G	22. J
3. C	23. A
4. G	24. J
5. D	25. C
6. J	26. G
7. A	27. D
8. H	28. F
9. D	29. B
10. F	30. G
11. C	31. C
12. F	32. F
13. B	33. D
14. G	34. F
15. A	35. B
16. J	36. J
17. C	37. C
18. F	38. F
19. B	39. D
20. F	40. G

ANSWERS AND EXPLANATIONS

ENGLISH TEST

The questions fall into the following categories, according to the skills they test. If you notice that you're having trouble with particular categories, review the following:

1. REDUNDANCY—English Workout 1

2. RELEVANCE—English Workout 1

3. VERBOSITY—English Workout 1

4. JUDGING THE PASSAGE—English Workout 2

5. LOGIC—English Workout 2

6. READING-TYPE QUESTIONS—English Workout 2

7. STRUCTURE AND PURPOSE—English Workout 2

8. TONE—English Workout 2

9. VERB USAGE—English Workout 2

10. COMPLETENESS—English Workouts 2 and 3

11. IDIOM—English Workouts 2 and 3

12. PRONOUNS—English Workouts 2 and 3

13. SENTENCE STRUCTURE—English Workouts 2 and 3

14. PUNCTUATION—English Workout 3

PASSAGE I

1. (B)—Pronouns

A plural pronoun must logically refer to the closest plural noun that came before it. Choice (A) is incorrect because the word *they* can't logically stand for *people* here. It must mean *fish*, but *fish* hasn't been used yet in the sentence. Choices (C) and (D) make the same error but use *these* and *them*. They also suffer from wordiness.

2. (H)—Pronouns

Trust your ear. In original version (F), you wouldn't say "origins who." *Who* can refer only to people. Choice (G) correctly uses *which,* but its singular verb, *begins,* can't go with the plural *origins.* Along with the faulty pronoun *who,* (J) contains the unidiomatic *beginning at.*

3. (D)—Redundancy

The words *keep(ing), possess(ing), having* and *have* all essentially mean the same thing. Using two of them together (choices A, B, and C) adds redundancy, not meaning, to the sentence.

4. (H)—Verb Usage

Trust your ear. The infinitive form of the verb is *to breed,* so the correct choice is (H). The other options produce the incorrect verb forms *to breeds* (choice (F)), *to breeded* (choice G), and *to bred* (choice (J)).

5. (A)—Logic

Trust your ear, and make it make sense. Choices (B), (C), and (D) don't add anything to the sentence that isn't already expressed in correct choice (A). In fact, the sentence makes no sense when (B) or (C) is plugged into it. The "nevertheless" in choice (D) suggests some sort of contrast, but there is none; the Romans are just another example of fish keepers.

6. (J)—Verb Usage

What happened in seventeenth-century England? Goldfish "were kept" in glass containers. The verb tense is wrong in choices (F), (G), and (H).

7. (A)—Verb Usage

Ask yourself how the underlined verb is being used. It's the main verb for the subject *relationship*. (A) is the only choice that works. In choice (B), the sentence won't make sense if we insert *which*. (C) is wrong because a main verb can never have an *-ing* form unless there is some form of the verb *to be* in front of it. You can say "I am running," but not "I running."

8. (G)—Reading-Type Question

The preceding sentence tells you how the need for small aquariums was met. It does not indicate that the container was inappropriate (choice (F)), contradict a statement about English containers (choice (H)), or talk about goldfish life spans (choice (J)).

9. (D)—Sentence Structure

The full sentence from which this question is taken is actually two short but complete sentences: "The first display aquariums opened . . . in London" and "aquariums soon appeared in Naples, Berlin, and Paris." When two short sentences are joined into one, and linked by a comma, the comma must be followed by a conjunction—a word like *and, but,* or *or*. In this case, the word is *and*.

10. (J)—Pronouns

Choices (F) and (G) are incorrect because they use *it* or *its* to refer to *the growth in aquariums* without having first used the longer phrase. Choice (H) is incorrect because it does not say what has been slowed.

11. (D)—Relevance

It is irrelevant to mention a television show about dolphins (choices (A), (B), and (C)) in a passage that discusses aquariums, even though dolphins are sometimes found in aquariums.

12. (F)—Logic

The two ideas here are *causally* related: You would share fish trivia *because* fish keeping has an interesting history. "For" (choice (F)) illustrates this connection. Choice (G) illogically sets "fish trivia" apart from the rest of the sentence. Choice (J) uses one set of quotation marks, but quotation marks always come in pairs.

13. (B)—Verb Usage

Trust your ear. *Have playing* sounds weird, and it doesn't mean anything. Choices (C) and (D) also sound odd. Whenever a sentence has more than one verb, there must be a conjunction between them. ("Fish keeping is [verb] . . . but [conjunction] . . . it also has [verb] . . . .") There is no conjunction before the underlined phrase, so it cannot be a verb (choices (C) and (D)). It's really a descriptive phrase (choice (B)).

14. (H)—Reading-Type Question

This passage is about the history of aquariums. It doesn't discuss the study of history in general (choice F) or the responsibility involved in maintaining an aquarium (choice (J)). It mentions that an aquarist might enjoy "fish trivia," but doesn't state that such trivia must be learned (choice (G)).

15. (B)—Structure and Purpose

Look at the first and last paragraphs. The first paragraph of the passage leads into, or introduces, the discussion of the history of aquariums. It's not an example (choice (A)) or a historical survey (choice (C)). The last paragraph is a wrap-up for the passage, not a personal account (choice (D)).

PASSAGE II

16. (F)—Punctuation

The sentence is correct as it stands. There is clearly a pause between *mobility* and *horizontal,* so we need some form of punctuation between the two words. Choice (H) uses a semicolon, but semicolons connect two phrases that could be sentences by themselves. The phrase *horizontal and vertical* could not be a sentence. (F) and (J) correctly use a colon, which introduces a list or definition. However, (J) unnecessarily inserts the word *being.* Don't add what you don't need.

17. (B)—Redundancy

The words *pay* and *salary* have approximately the same meaning. It is redundant to use both (choices A and C). Choice (D) produces the phrase *firms that are comparable pay in terms of salary and prestige,* which makes no sense.

18. (F)—Pronouns

Think about what the sentence is saying. (G), (H), and (J) add unnecessary pronouns to the sentence. The subject, *change,* is right there, so it's wrong to throw in the pronoun *they* or *it.*

19. (C)—Logic

The mention of the Russian Revolution illustrates the point made in the preceding sentence, that social mobility "may change the entire social system." *For instance* (choice (C)) correctly indicates this. (A) and (D) are wrong because this sentence does not offer a conclusion based on the preceding sentence. It does not contradict the preceding sentence, so (B) is also wrong.

20. (F)—Completeness

We hope your ear told you that (G) and (J) sound funny. Since choices (G) and (J) are complete sentences inthemselves, you can't connect them to another complete sentence, "social mobility occurs at a variety of rates," with a comma. We also hope you steered clear of choice (H), with its incorrect and confusing phrase *change's differing degrees.*

21. (B)—Completeness

The underlined word occurs in an incomplete sentence that lacks a verb. Choices (A), (C), and (D) are incorrect because they do not create complete sentences. (C) adds the verb *is,* but doesn't tell us *what* the athlete is. Choice (B), however, adds a verb and completes the meaning.

22. (H)—Structure and Purpose

Sentence 6 says that gradual changes can accomplish social mobility, so it makes most sense before sentence 5, which gives an example of a gradual change. Choice (H) is correct.

23. (D)—Completeness

The phrase *in that* (choice (A)) sounds funny and makes the sentence incomplete. Changing the phrase to *in* (choice (B)) or *on* (choice (C)) still doesn't complete the sentence. Omitting the phrase, however, leaves a complete sentence.

24. (J)—Logic

The preceding sentence stated that some people view large-scale mobility negatively. This sentence offers a contrasting opinion. The words *accordingly* (choice (F)), *similarly* (choice (G)), and *likewise* (choice (H)) are incorrect because they imply agreement. The phrase *on the other hand* (choice (J)) correctly introduces a differing thought.

25. (C)—Pronouns

Your ear can help on this one. You might say *they attempt*, but not *they attempting* (choice (B)). In choice (A), *they are attempting* sounds okay until you keep reading. Ask yourself what *they are attempting to rise validate* means.

26. (H)—Relevance

The main theme of the passage is social mobility. The American educational system (choice (F)), salary ranges (choice (G)), or a rock video (choice (J)) have nothing to do with this. The correct choice is (H), since it talks about some benefits of social mobility.

27. (B)—Verb Usage

The sentence compares two verbs: *destroy* and *reinforce*. Things that are compared need to be in the same form. *Destroying* ends in *-ing*, so we need the *-ing* form of *reinforce*. Only choice (B) uses this form.

28. (J)—Relevance

OMIT the underlined portion (choice (J)). The comparison to a flat tire doesn't add information and doesn't match the tone of the passage. (G) and (H) don't help.

29. (B)—Verb Usage

The subject of the sentence is *crowd*, not *yuppies*. A crowd is singular, no matter how many yuppies are in it, so we need the singular *shows* instead of *show*.

30. (J)—Verbosity

The point of the sentence is that vertical mobility is not a passing phenomenon. The underlined portion is not necessary and only distracts from this point.

PASSAGE III

31. (D)—Sentence Structure

(D) is the simplest version, and it's right. Use your ear, or ask yourself what the subject of *is* or *being* is in choices (A), (B), and (C). It can't be *that* because *that* isn't a pronoun here; so *is* or *being* doesn't refer to anything here. Rather, *that* is a conjunction, a word that combines one phrase, *The critic George Moore once said of this artist*, with another, *her pictures are the only pictures . . .*

32. (H)—Verb Usage

Use your ear: *statement are* sounds funny. That's because a singular noun must have a singular verb. *Statement* is singular, but *are* is plural. Choice (H) corrects the problem by making the verb singular. Choice (J) corrects it by making the noun plural, but *statement* also has to agree with *shows*, so we need the singular form in choice (H).

33. (B)—Pronouns

A pronoun must refer to something. In (A) and (D), we can guess that *it* refers to politics, but this isn't made clear in the sentence. Choice (C) adds the word *politics*, but the construction is clumsy. Correct choice (B) is simplest and clearest.

34. (J)—Logic

Trust your ear. *Being her earliest childhood* (choice (F)) sounds odd, and it is. It means that she *was* her earliest childhood. Choice (G) starts with the word *from* set off with a comma. The only time this construction is used is when someone is signing a letter.

35. (A)—Relevance

The passage is talking about the painters Morisot studied with, not about their nationalities. Manet's heritage, no matter how it is phrased, is not relevant. Choice (A) is correct.

36. (G)—Idiom

Make it all match. *Either* goes with *or. Neither* goes with *nor.* The two *n* words go together. Choices (G) and (J) use a correct pair, but (J) leaves out the verb. Choice (G) correctly uses a singular verb form. (Although *either/or* and *neither/nor* compare two things, they treat each thing separately, as a singular subject.)

37. (C)—Pronouns

Who is doing the facing? Morisot's male colleagues are, so they should be referred to by the pronoun *who.* The passage is talking about Morisot's lifetime, which was in the *past.* So we use the past tense, *faced.*

38. (J)—Logic

The previous sentence talks about Morisot's setbacks. This sentence talks about the way she overcame them. We are looking for a connecting word that implies *contrast:* Morisot did well *in spite of* her hardships. *However* (choice (J)) provides the contrast we are looking for.

39. (B)—Completeness

In choice (A), *Portraying women performing domestic and social activities* is not a complete sentence. It has no subject. Choice (C) uses the word *insofar* incorrectly. Choice (D) says "her sphere *were.*" Since *sphere* is singular, we would have to say "her sphere *was.*" Correct choice (B) makes the fragment into a sentence by giving it the subject *she* and using an appropriate form of the verb (*began to portray*).

40. (H)—Structure and Purpose

We're looking for a statement that will present Morisot in a more positive light. Choice (H) suggests

that while her subject matter may *appear* limited, it could *actually* be considered quite meaningful, given the social context in which it was produced. Choices (F), (G), and (J), in contrast, are all somewhat negative in tone.

41. (C)—Punctuation

We can introduce a list of examples with a colon or with the words *such as,* but not with both, so choice (A) is wrong. A dash doesn't introduce a list of examples, so choice (B) is wrong. Choice (D) is wrong because it uses a comma after the phrase *such as.* If you read the sentence with a pause after *such as,* it sounds awkward.

42. (J)—Redundancy

Choices (F), (G), and (H) are redundant. By definition, successors are the people who follow in order or sequence someone else.

43. (A)—Structure and Purpose/Relevance

Ask yourself: What is the main point of the passage? The passage is about Morisot's experience as a female artist. Only choice (A) is relevant to that topic. Choice (C) refers to George Moore, who is mentioned in the passage in relation to Morisot. To devote a section of the passage to him, however, would change its focus. Likewise, a discussion of Impressionism would divert the focus of the passage away from Morisot.

44. (J)—Judging the Passage/Relevance

Does the inclusion of dates seem appropriate? Well, the passage is a biography, and dates are generally appropriate in a biography, so the correct answer is (J). The story of Morisot isn't unbelievable, so the author would have no reason to introduce something just to make us believe it (choice (H)).

45. (B)—Structure and Purpose

First, try to find an appropriate beginning. Paragraph 1 is especially easy to eliminate, since it refers to "this artist" without ever telling us her name. Paragraph 3 is less obvious, but it talks about Morisot's subject matter and style without telling us who she is. The passage can't start with paragraph 4, because none of the answer choices does. Paragraph 2 provides general background information on Morisot, so it should be first. That leaves choices (B) and (C). Paragraph 3 introduces Morisot's subject matter, which paragraph 4 talks about in greater detail. So it makes sense to put paragraph 3 immediately before 4.

PASSAGE IV

46. (G)—Verb Usage

Make sure everything matches. Ask, *what is the subject?* Even though *exception* occurs right before the verb, the subject is *movies*. *Movies* is plural, so we need a plural verb. *Were being replaced* (choice H) is plural, but it illogically changes the tense. We're talking about a change in movies right now, not in the distant past. Use your ear. You should be able to tell that choice (H) sounds funny.

47. (C)—Punctuation

"The slasher movie" is the "new breed of horror film." We need something to connect a thing and its definition: either punctuation or a connecting phrase. Choice (D) inserts an unnecessary comma, and both (B) and (D) are wordy. A colon, in choice (C), works just fine.

48. (H)—Completeness

The subject of the sentence is *the first commercially successful low-budget chiller.* Choices (F), (G), and (J)

separate *first* from *commercially successful low-budget chiller.* The sentence doesn't make sense this way. *The first* tells us *which* "commercially successfully low budget film" we are talking about, so it must be connected to that phrase.

49. (B)—Verb Usage

Plug the choices in. Choices (A), (C), and (D) don't make sense. That's because the verb is *have glutted*, and the whole verb has to go in one place.

50. (H)—Verbosity

Choices (F) and (J) sound funny. That's because they use complicated expressions. Not only does (G) use an awkward construction, it also eliminates the subject (popularity). Simpler is better. Choice (H) is the right answer.

51. (D)—Redundancy

The word *filmmakers* is all that's needed.

52. (J)—Verbosity

Trust your ear. *Increasing gory* sounds a bit off. Choice (J) adds an *-ly* which makes it correct. Notice that *increasingly* describes *gory. Gory* is an adjective, and if you want to describe anything that's not a noun, you need an adverb. Most adverbs (like *increasingly*) are formed by adding *ly* to an adjective (like *increasing*).

53. (A)—Punctuation

Ask yourself what job the punctuation is doing. In this sentence, the punctuation indicates a slight pause. Since commas do that, the comma (choice (A)) is correct.

54. (G)—Redundancy

When in doubt, take it out. *Periphery* means *fringe,* so using both words is unnecessary.

55. (D)—Verb Usage

They're may sound like *there are* but it means *they are*, which doesn't make sense here. Also, *they're* is the same as *they are* in choice (B). There can't be two correct answers, so whenever two answers mean the same thing they must both be wrong.

56. (G)—Tone

Try to decide on appropriateness first: "a big wad of cash!" sounds out of place because it is very informal, while the passage is relatively formal. So we can decide that the statement is not appropriate, and look for an answer that gives us this reason. The correct choice (G) refers to the passage's tone.

57. (D)—Sentence Structure

Conjunctions are words that combine one phrase with another. Using two conjunctions, like *although* and *however* in choice (A), is redundant, illogical, and wrong. Choices (B) and (C) make this same mistake. You should be able to hear these errors, but be careful! You have to read the entire sentence in order to notice the *although*.

58. (H)—Redundancy

Increasingly, evermore, and *more, and more, and more* all mean the same thing, just as *violent* and *with anger and blood* mean the same thing. Say each once.

59. (C)—Redundancy

The public is, by definition, made up of human beings, so choices (A) and (B) are redundant. In choice (D), *human's* refers to one specific being, but the passage is talking about the general taste.

60. (F)—Tone

Answer one part of the question first. Look at the tone. People who make sarcastic remarks are being

harsh, derisive, and often ironic—that is, they mean the opposite of what they say. The passage does not do this, nor is it lighthearted, so we can eliminate choices (G) and (H). The author is serious, and does discuss a change in entertainment, so (F) is correct.

PASSAGE V

61. (C)—Redundancy

"Unexplained" things *are* things that haven't been explained yet. When in doubt, take it out.

62. (G)—Redundancy

Abandoned means "deserted," so don't say both.

63. (D)—Verb Usage

Listen to the sentence as it stands. It sounds odd, because *having* can't be the main verb of a sentence. You can say "I am going," or "I go," but not, "I going." Choice (D) is simple and it has a subject (*some ships*) and an acceptable verb (*have vanished*).

64. (J)—Idiom

Trust your ear. English speakers use certain idioms or expressions, just because that's the way we say things. Something ranges "from the interference of UFOs to the existence of powerful fields," *not* "to" or "toward the interference of UFOs to the existence of powerful fields," as in choices (F) and (G).

65. (A)—Redundancy

So far means the same as *yet,* so (B), (C), and (D) are all redundant. Also, if you read choice (D) back into the sentence, you'll hear that it leaves out the verb (*have been*). Choice (A) is correct.

66. (H)—Relevance

It's not important to the passage that England is also triangular. When in doubt, take it out.

67. (A)—Logic

Think about it: if a country's coast is a boundary, why bring rivers into the discussion?

68. (H)—Verbosity

Say it simply. Choices (F), (G), and (J) are all wordy and awkward. Those qualities are not admired by the ACT test makers.

69. (D)—Verb Usage

The first problem here is verb tense. The meaning of the sentence as it stands is that strange events were reported in the *past*, but people are wondering about the region *now*. If the events "had" been reported (choice (A)) the author would be talking about a *past* conception of the Bermuda Triangle. The second problem is number. *Events* is plural. *Is* (choice (C)) and *has* (choice (B)) are singular.

70. (G)—Relevance

Inappropriate statements usually stick out. You stop reading and wonder why you were told something. That doesn't happen here, so the mention of Juan de Bermudez is probably appropriate. Now consider *why* it is appropriate. Choice (H) is incorrect and choice (J) has nothing to do with why the mention of Bermudez is appropriate. Choice (G) is correct. (If you're not sure the statement is relevant, look at the reason given for saying it's not: exploration and the Bermuda Triangle are not dissimilar, since we are talking about the exploration of Bermuda.)

71. (C)—Sentence Structure

Trust your ear. What are they questioning?

72. (H)—Relevance

What new information would be a continuation of the topic? The passage at this point isn't talking about geography (choice (F)), the tourist trade (choice (J)), or other supernatural phenomena (choice (G)). It is discussing doubts about whether there have been supernatural occurrences in the Bermuda Triangle.

73. (B)—Redundancy

We know what *certain* means. Adding a definition is redundant.

74. (H)—Structure and Purpose

Answer the question first. The passage talks about many events, not just one, so the answer to the question is "no." Now look at the reasons. The passage does contain factual information, so choice (J) is wrong. Choice (H) is correct because the writer does not focus on one specific disappearance.

75. (B)—Structure and Purpose

Paragraph 1 is a discussion of the types of strange events that have been reported. It should logically come after the introduction of the fact that strange events have been reported. Choice (B) is correct since paragraph 2 introduces the fact that strange events have been reported.

MATH TEST

1. (C)—Solving a Linear Equation

100 Key Math Concepts for the ACT, #63. Find x by getting it by itself on one side of the equation:

$$5x + 3 = -17$$

Subtract 3 from both sides. $5x = -20$

Divide both sides by 5. $x = \dfrac{-20}{5}$

Simplify. $x = -4$

Alternatively, use back-solving. $5x + 3 = -17$ will be true for the correct value of x only. Since the answer choices are in numerical order, try (C) first.

$$x = -4, \text{ then } 5(-4) + 3 = -17$$
$$-20 + 3 = -17$$
$$-17 = -17$$

This is true, so (C) must be correct.

2. (H)—Solving a Proportion

100 Key Math Concepts for the ACT, #38. Six people are served by 4 oranges, 5 pears, 10 apples, and 24 strawberries. Eighteen people—that is, 3×6 people—will need 3 times as much, that is, 3 times as many of each ingredient. So John needs $3 \times 5 = 15$ pears.

3. (D)—Greatest Common Factor

100 Key Math Concepts for the ACT, #15. Factor both numbers:

$$8 \times 10^9 = 2 \times 2 \times 2 \times 10 \times 10 \times 10 \times 10 \times 10 \times$$
$$10 \times 10 \times 10 \times 10$$
$$6 \times 10^3 = 2 \times 3 \times 10 \times 10 \times 10$$

Since both numbers have a factor of 2 and three factors of 10, the greatest integer that is a factor of both will be $2 \times 10 \times 10 \times 10 = 2 \times 10^3$.

4. (J)—Areas of Special Quadrilaterals

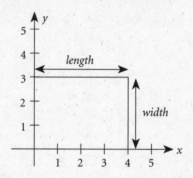

100 Key Math Concepts for the ACT, #87. Area of a rectangle = length × width. From the diagram, length = 4 and width = 3. Therefore area = $4 \times 3 = 12$.

5. (A)—Circumference of a Circle

100 Key Math Concepts for the ACT, #89. Draw a diagram to help visualize the situation:

As can be seen from the diagram, the length of the band is the same as the circumference of the cylinder. The circumference of a cylinder and the circumference of a circle are determined in the same way:

$$\text{Circumference} = 2\pi r = 2 \times \pi \times 4 = 8\pi$$

6. (F)—Translating from English into Algebra

100 Key Math Concepts for the ACT, #65. For every large jar there are 48 olives, so x large jars hold $48x$ olives. For every small jar there are 32 olives, so y small jars hold $32y$ olives. The total number of olives needed is $48x + 32y$.

This problem could also be attacked by picking numbers. Let $x = 1$ and $y = 2$. Then there is one large jar needing 48 olives, and two small jars needing $2 \times 32 = 64$ olives, for a total of $48 + 64 = 112$ olives. Any answer choice which does not result in 112 when $x = 1$ and $y = 2$ may be eliminated.

(F) $48x + 32y = 48 \times 1 + 32 \times 2 = 112$ —This may be correct.

(G) $\dfrac{x}{48} + \dfrac{y}{32} = \dfrac{1}{48} + \dfrac{2}{32} \neq 112$ —Discard.

(H) $\dfrac{xy}{80} = \dfrac{1 \times 2}{80} = \dfrac{2}{80} \neq 112$ —Discard.

(J) $80xy = 80 \times 1 \times 2 \neq 112$ —Discard.

(K) $\dfrac{1,536}{xy} = \dfrac{1,536}{1 \times 2} = 768 \neq 112$ —Discard.

Since answer choice (F) was the only one to give the appropriate number, it is correct.

7. (E)—Evaluating an Algebraic Expression

100 Key Math Concepts for the ACT, #52.
Substitute $x + 1$ for x in the expression $3x^2 + 4$:

$$3(x + 1)^2 + 4$$

Expand $(x + 1)^2$. $= 3(x^2 + 2x + 1) + 4$

Multiply out parentheses. $= 3x^2 + 6x + 3 + 4$

Gather like terms. $= 3x^2 + 6x + 7$

8. (K)—Converting a Mixed Number to an Improper Fraction, Adding/Subtracting Fractions

100 Key Math Concepts for the ACT, #25, 22.

$$5\frac{5}{6} + 3\frac{5}{8} + 1\frac{1}{3} = 5 + 3 + 1 + \frac{5}{6} + \frac{5}{8} + \frac{1}{3}$$

$$= 9 + \frac{5}{6} + \frac{5}{8} + \frac{1}{3}$$

$$= 9 + \frac{20}{24} + \frac{15}{24} + \frac{8}{24}$$

$$= 9 + \frac{43}{24}$$

$$= 9 + 1\frac{19}{24}$$

$$= 10\frac{19}{24}$$

9. (B)—Miscellaneous Line Segments

Draw a diagram:

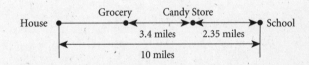

It is $2.35 + 3.4 = 5.75$ miles from the school to the grocery store. The distance from the grocery store to home is the remaining portion of the 10 miles between school and home. That is, (10 miles) − (5.75 miles) = 4.25 miles.

10. (F)—Rate

100 Key Math Concepts for the ACT, #39. Harry is given 3 pieces every week for 4 weeks, for a total of $3 \times 4 = 12$ pieces. He can learn 2 new pieces per week. To learn 12 pieces will take him $12 \div 2 = 6$ weeks.

11. (D)—Interior Angles of a Triangle

100 Key Math Concepts for the ACT, #80. The sum of the interior angles of any triangle is 180°. So:

$$\angle EDF + \angle DFE + \angle DEF = 180°$$
$$35° + 65° + \angle DEF = 180°$$
$$\angle DEF = 180° - 35° - 65°$$
$$\angle DEF = 80°$$

12. (G)—Averages—Finding the Missing Number

100 Key Math Concepts for the ACT, #44.

$$\text{Average} = \frac{\text{Sum of terms}}{\text{Number of terms}}$$

In this case she needs an average of 175. Let the score on the next game be x.

$$\text{Then } 175 = \frac{150 + 195 + 160 + x}{4}$$
$$175 \times 4 = 150 + 195 + 160 + x$$
$$700 = 505 + x$$
$$700 - 505 = x$$
$$195 = x$$

So she must score 195 on the next game for an average of 175.

13. (E)—Miscellaneous Coordinate Geometry and Triangles

Draw a diagram:

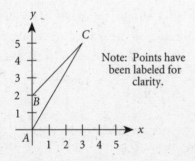

Note: Points have been labeled for clarity.

Run through the answer choices to see which one works.

(A) $\angle ABC$ is *greater* than 90°—Discard.

(B) All three sides are *not* the same length—Discard.

(C) *No* sides are the same length—Discard.

(D) *No* angle measures 90°—Discard.

(E) One angle, $\angle ABC$, is greater than 90°—This is correct.

14. (J)—Solving a Quadratic Equation

100 Key Math Concepts for the ACT, #66.

$2y^2 - 4y - 6 = 0$ is of the form $ax^2 + bx + c = 0$, and so its roots can be found by the quadratic formula.

$$x = \frac{-b \pm \sqrt{b^2 - 4ac}}{2a}$$
$$= \frac{-(-4) \pm \sqrt{(-4)^2 - 4 \times 2 \times (-6)}}{4}$$
$$= \frac{4 \pm \sqrt{16 + 48}}{4} = 1 \pm 2, \text{ which is 3 or } -1. \text{ The}$$

sum of 3 and −1 is 2.

15. (C)—Converting Fractions to Decimals

100 Key Math Concepts for the ACT, #29.
Eliminate answer choices (A) and (B) straight off; since the numerator is less than the denominator, $\frac{7}{8}$ must be less than 1.

$$\frac{1}{8} = 0.125, \text{ so } \frac{7}{8} = 7 \times 0.125 = 0.875$$

16. (F)—Translating from English into Algebra, Solving a System of Equations

100 Key Math Concepts for the ACT, #65, 67.
Translate:

"June has 20 marbles more than Billy."　　　　$J = B + 20$

"Maria has 3 times as many marbles as Billy." $M = 3B$

"Altogether they have 100 marbles." $J + M + B = 100$

We need B, the number of marbles Billy has.

Substitute the expressions in terms of B for J and M. $B + 20 + 3B + B = 100$

Gather like terms. $5B + 20 = 100$

Subtract 20. $5B = 80$

Divide by 5. $B = 16$

So Billy has 16 marbles.

17. (B)—Solving a Linear Equation

100 Key Math Concepts for the ACT, #63: Rather than graphing the equation, the quickest way to solve this is to substitute 6 for x in the equation, and to solve for y.

$$3x - 2y = 4$$

Substitute $x = 6$. $3(6) - 2y = 4$

Multiply out parentheses. $18 - 2y = 4$

Subtract 18 from both sides. $-2y = -14$

Divide both sides by −2. $y = \dfrac{-14}{-2}$

Simplify. $y = 7$

18. (F)—Parallel Lines and Transversals

100 Key Math Concepts for the ACT, #79. When a transversal cuts parallel lines, all acute angles formed are equal and all obtuse angles formed are equal. So here all obtuse angles measure p and all acute angles measure q. The question says that "the measure of

$\angle p$ is 20° less than three times the measure of $\angle q$." That is, $p = 3q - 20$. Also $p + q = 180$, since p and q are supplementary angles; that is, they form a straight line.

Solve for q:

$$p + q = 180$$

Substitute $3q - 20$ for p. $3q - 20 + q = 180$

Gather like terms. $4q - 20 = 180$

Add 20 to both sides. $4q = 200$

Divide both sides by 4. $q = 50$

So: $p = 3q - 20 = 3(50) - 20 = 150 - 20 = 130$

$p - q = 130 - 50 = 80$

(**Note:** By eyeballing you could have eliminated answer choices (J) and (K) as too large.)

19. (E)—Solving a System of Equations

100 Key Math Concepts for the ACT, #67. Do not solve all the systems of equations—this would be too time consuming. Think about the problem first. The solution of a system of equations is the point these equations intersect—if the lines are parallel, they will not intersect, and there will be no solution. The lines that are parallel will have the same slope. The answer choices are all in the form $Ax + By = C$. You could find the slopes if the equations were in the slope-intercept form. This can be done by subtracting Ax from both sides, and dividing by B to get $y = -\dfrac{A}{B}x + \dfrac{C}{B}$, so here slope $= \dfrac{\text{coefficient of } x}{\text{coefficient of } y} = -\dfrac{A}{B}$.

(A) Slope of 1st equation $= -\dfrac{1}{3}$

   Slope of 2nd equation $= -\dfrac{3}{1} = -3$

   The slopes are different—Discard.

(B) Slope of 1st equation $= -\dfrac{1}{3}$

   Slope of 2nd equation $= -\dfrac{1}{-3}$

   The slopes are different—Discard.

(C) Slope of 1st equation $= -\dfrac{1}{-3} = \dfrac{1}{3}$

   Slope of 2nd equation $= -\dfrac{3}{-1} = 3$

   The slopes are different—Discard.

(D) Slope of 1st equation $= -\dfrac{1}{-3} = \dfrac{1}{3}$

   Slope of 2nd equation $= -\dfrac{3}{1} = -3$

   The slopes are different—Discard.

(E) Slope of 1st equation $= -\dfrac{1}{3}$

   Slope of 2nd equation $= -\dfrac{3}{9} = -\dfrac{1}{3}$

20. (J)—Miscellaneous Line Segments

Mark in the lengths:

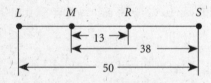

The distance LR is the distance LM plus the distance MR.

The distance MR is 13.

The distance LM is the distance LS minus the distance MS. That is $50 - 38 = 12$.

Therefore, $LR = 12 + 13 = 25$.

(**Note:** You could have discarded answer choice F straight away—LR must be longer than MR.)

21. (D)—Percent Formula

100 Key Math Concepts for the ACT, #32.

$133\dfrac{1}{3}\%$ is 4 times $33\dfrac{1}{3}\%$.

So, if $33\dfrac{1}{3}\%$ of $t = 9$, then $133\dfrac{1}{3}\% = 4 \times 9 = 36$.

22. (G)—Sine, Cosine, and Tangent of Acute Angles—SOHCAHTOA

100 Key Math Concepts for the ACT, #96. Since $\tan = \dfrac{\text{opposite}}{\text{adjacent}}$, you need to know the lengths of the side opposite x, $\overline{DE}$, and the side adjacent to x, $\overline{FE}$.

Since $DE = 1$ and $DF = \sqrt{2}$, this must be an isosceles right triangle with sides in the ratio $1{:}1{:}\sqrt{2}$. (You could also show this by using the Pythagorean theorem.) So $DE = FE = 1$.

$$\tan x = \frac{\text{opposite}}{\text{adjacent}} = \frac{DE}{FE} = \frac{1}{1} = 1$$

23. (C)—Equation for a Circle

100 Key Math Concepts for the ACT, #75.

Draw a diagram:

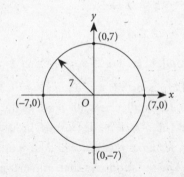

Obviously, A and D lie on the circle—Eliminate these answer choices.

The formula for a circle is $(x - a)^2 + (y - b)^2 = r^2$, where a and b are the x- and y-coordinates of the center, and r is the radius. In this case the center is $(0, 0)$ and r is 7. Therefore, the equation of this circle is $x^2 + y^2 = 49$, and any point that is not on the circle will not satisfy this equation.

(B) $(-3, 2\sqrt{10})$: $(-3)^2 + (2\sqrt{10})^2 = 9 + 40 = 49$—Discard.

(C) $(\sqrt{7}, 3)$: $(\sqrt{7})^2 + 3^2 = 7 + 9 = 16 \neq 49$—This point is not on the circle, and so C is correct.

24. (K)—Miscellaneous Coordinate Geometry

Point A is 4 units above the x-axis, so its y-coordinate is 4.

Point B is 3 units below the x-axis, so its y-coordinate is -3.

The product of the y-coordinates is $4 \times (-3) = -12$.

25. (D)—Intersecting Lines, Parallel Lines and Transversals

100 Key Math Concepts for the ACT, #78, #79. Since y is greater than 90°, answer choices A and B can be eliminated by eyeballing.

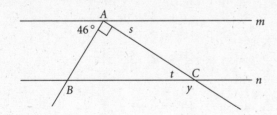

Since the angle marked 46°, the right angle, and angle s make up a straight line, they sum to 180°. So $46 + 90 + s = 180$, or $s = 44$. Both s and t are acute

angles formed by the same transversal, $\overline{AC}$, so t also has a measure of 44°.

Since y and t are supplementary, $y + t = 180$. That is $y = 180 - 44 = 136$.

26. (F)—Evaluating an Algebraic Expression

100 Key Math Concepts for the ACT, #52. Plug in -3 for s:

$$s^3 + 2s^2 + 2s = (-3)^3 + 2(-3)^2 + 2(-3)$$
$$= -27 + 2(9) + (-6)$$
$$= -27 + 18 - 6$$
$$= -15$$

27. (D)—Factoring Out a Common Divisor

100 Key Math Concepts for the ACT, #58. Notice that in the expression $r(t + u) - s(t + u)$ both r and s are being multiplied by $t + u$. Factor this out to get $(r - s)(t + u)$. If you didn't see this, you could try picking numbers.

Let $r = 2$, $s = 3$, $t = 4$, and $u = 5$.

Then $r(t + u) - s(t + u) = 2(4 + 5) - 3(4 + 5) = 18 - 27 = -9$.

Any of the answer choices that does not give a value of -9 for these values of r, s, t, and u may be discarded.

(A) $(r + s)(t + u) = (2 + 3)(4 + 5) = (5)(9) = 45$—Discard.

(B) $(r - s)(t - u) = (2 - 3)(4 - 5) = (-1)(-1) = 1$—Discard.

(C) $(r + s)(t - u) = (2 + 3)(4 - 5) = (5)(-1) = -5$—Discard.

(D) $(r - s)(t + u) = (2 - 3)(4 + 5) = (-1)(9) = -9$—This may be correct.

(E) 0—Discard.

So answer choice (D) is the only one that gives a value of −9 for the chosen values, and so it must be correct.

28. (F)—Similar Triangles, Area of a Triangle

100 Key Math Concepts for the ACT, #82, 83. $\triangle ABC$ and $\triangle DBF$ are similar, since corresponding angles are of the same measure. Therefore their sides are proportional.

That is $\dfrac{AB}{BC} = \dfrac{DB}{BF}$, or $\dfrac{8}{6} = \dfrac{4}{BF}$, so $BF = 3$.

The area of a triangle is $\dfrac{1}{2}$(base × height)= $\dfrac{1}{2}(3 \times 4) = 6$.

Note: You could have discarded answer choices (J) and (K) by logic—the area of the smaller triangle must be less than the area of the larger triangle, which is $\dfrac{1}{2}(6 \times 8) = 24$.

29. (A)—Trigonometric Functions of Other Angles

100 Key Math Concepts for the ACT, #98. Consider the unit circle:

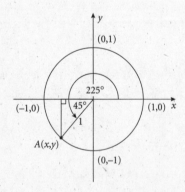

The cosine of any value is the x-coordinate when plotted on the unit circle, so cos 225° is the x-coordinate of A. Note that this point is below the x-axis, so the x-coordinate must be negative— eliminate answer choices (D) and (E). Also notice that x is the length of the leg of the right triangle

formed by dropping a line perpendicular to the x-axis from A.

This is an isosceles right triangle, since it has interior angles of 45° and 90°. The ratio of side lengths in such a triangle is $1:1:\sqrt{2}$. Since the hypotenuse has a length of 1, the legs must have lengths of $\dfrac{1}{\sqrt{2}} = \dfrac{1}{\sqrt{2}} \times \dfrac{\sqrt{2}}{\sqrt{2}} = \dfrac{\sqrt{2}}{2}$. So cos 225° = $-\dfrac{\sqrt{2}}{2}$.

30. (G)—Area of a Triangle

100 Key Math Concepts for the ACT, #83. The area of a triangle is $\dfrac{1}{2}$ (base × height). In this case the area is 45 square units, and the base is XZ, which is $3 + 12 = 15$. The height is YS.

So $45 = \dfrac{1}{2}(15 \times YS)$

$45 \times 2 = 15 \times YS$

$90 \div 15 = YS$

$6 = YS$

31. (A)—Circumference of a Circle

100 Key Math Concepts for the ACT, #89. The circumference of a circle is πd, where d is the diameter. Here the diameter is 10, so the circumference is 10π.

32. (K)—Factoring Out a Common Divisor

100 Key Math Concepts for the ACT, #58. Rearrange the formula:

$$A = \pi rs + \pi r^2$$

Factor out π. $A = \pi(rs + r^2)$

$$A = \pi(rs + rr)$$

Factor out an r. $A = \pi r(s + r)$

Alternatively, pick numbers. Let $r = 2$ and $s = 3$. Then $A = \pi rs + \pi r^2 = \pi(2)(3) + \pi(2)^2 = 10\pi$. Any answer choice which does not give a result of 10π can be eliminated.

(F) $A = 2\pi rs = 2\pi(2)(3) = 12\pi$—Discard.

(G) $A = 2\pi r^2 s = 2\pi(2)^2(3) = 24\pi$—Discard.

(H) $A = \pi r(1 + s) = \pi(2)(1 + 3) = 8\pi$—Discard.

(J) $A = \pi r^2(1 + s) = \pi(2)^2(1 + 3) = 16\pi$—Discard.

(K) $A = \pi r(r + s) = \pi(2)(2 + 3) = 10\pi$—This must be correct.

33. (B)—Using an Equation to Find the Slope

100 Key Math Concepts for the ACT, #73. Get $5x + 3y = 13$ into the slope-intercept form, $y = mx + b$. Then m will be the slope.

$$5x + 3y = 13$$

Subtract $5x$. $3y = -5x + 13$

Divide by 3. $y = -\dfrac{5}{3}x + \dfrac{13}{3}$

So: $m = \text{slope} = -\dfrac{5}{3}$

34. (G)—Miscellaneous Number Properties

Try to disprove the statements by picking numbers. Let $a = b = 1$. Then:

$|a - b| + \sqrt{b - a} = |1 - 1| + \sqrt{1 - 1} = 0 + 0 = 0$. So if $a = b$, the answer is not always negative, so discard answer choice (J). Since 0 is neither positive nor negative, also discard (H).

Try fractions. Let $a = \dfrac{1}{2}$ and $b = \dfrac{3}{4}$. Then $|a - b| +$

$\sqrt{b - a} = |\dfrac{1}{2} - \dfrac{3}{4}| + \sqrt{\dfrac{3}{4} - \dfrac{1}{2}} = |-\dfrac{1}{4}| + \sqrt{\dfrac{1}{4}} = \dfrac{1}{4} +$

$\dfrac{1}{2} = \dfrac{3}{4}$.

Now this is not equal to an integer, so discard answer choice (F).

What if $a = -1$ and $b = -2$? Then $|a - b| + \sqrt{b - a} =$

$|(-1) - (-2)| + \sqrt{(-2) - (-1)} = |1| + \sqrt{-1}$.

Now the square root of -1 is not real, so discard answer choice (K). That leaves only answer choice (G), which must then be correct.

35. (E)—Solving a Quadratic Equation

100 Key Math Concepts for the ACT, #66. The quadratic formula states that the roots of an equation in the form $ax^2 + bx + c = 0$ are $\dfrac{-b \pm \sqrt{b^2 - 4ac}}{2a}$.

In this case a = 1, b = −7 and c = 8, so the roots are:

$$\dfrac{-(-7) \pm \sqrt{(-7)^2 - 4 \times 1 \times 8}}{2 \times 1} =$$

$$\dfrac{7 \pm \sqrt{17}}{2} = \dfrac{7 + \sqrt{17}}{2} \text{ or } \dfrac{7 - \sqrt{17}}{2}$$

36. (G)—Special Right Triangles

100 Key Math Concepts for the ACT, #85. Draw a diagram:

The sides of the square are the legs of a right triangle. By the Pythagorean theorem:

$$\text{leg}_1^2 + \text{leg}_2^2 = \text{hypotenuse}^2$$
$$x^2 + x^2 = 20^2$$
$$2x^2 = 400$$
$$x^2 = 200$$
$$x = \sqrt{200}$$

Get the radical into the form of the answer choices:

$$x = \sqrt{200} = \sqrt{100} \times \sqrt{2} = 10\sqrt{2}$$

37. (C)—Multiplying Binomials—FOIL

100 Key Math Concepts for the ACT, #56.

$(3a - 4)(a + 2)$:

First	$3a \times a = 3a^2$
Outer	$3a \times 2 = 6a$
Inner	$-4 \times a = -4a$
Last	$-4 \times 2 = -8$

Combine: $3a^2 + 6a - 4a - 8 = 3a^2 + 2a - 8$

38. (K)—Finding the Distance between Two Points

100 Key Math Concepts for the ACT, #71. Draw a diagram:

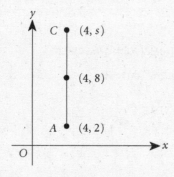

The midpoint must be the same distance from A as from C. Since it is 6 units above point A it must be 6 units below point C; i.e., C must have a y-coordinate of 14.

39. (E)—Translating from English into Algebra

100 Key Math Concepts for the ACT, #65. Translate into math.

The question says s represents the first number.

"The second number is 3 less than 4 times the first number," i.e., $4s - 3$.

"The third number is 5 more than twice the first," i.e., $2s + 5$.

The sum of all three numbers is then:

$$s + 4s - 3 + 2s + 5 = 7s + 2$$

40. (H)—Intersecting Lines, Angles of a Triangle

100 Key Math Concepts for the ACT, #78, 80, 81. Since $\angle SAB$ and $\angle BAC$ are supplementary, $\angle SAB + \angle BAC = 180°$. Since $\angle SAB = 130°$, $\angle BAC = 50°$. We now have two of the interior angles of $\triangle ABC$. Since the sum of the interior angles in a triangle is $180°$, $\angle BAC + \angle ABC + \angle ACB = 180°$. That is $50° + 80° + \angle ACB = 180°$. Therefore, $\angle ACB = 50°$. $\angle EDC$ is supplementary to $\angle QDC$. Since $\angle QDC = 110°$, $\angle EDC = 70°$. We now have two interior angles of $\triangle DEC$. The third is $\angle DEC$. Since the sum of the interior angles in a triangle is $180°$, $\angle DEC + \angle DCE + \angle EDC = 180°$. That is $\angle DEC + 50° + 70° = 180°$. Therefore, $\angle DEC = 60°$.

41. (C)—Percent Increase and Decrease

100 Key Math Concepts for the ACT, #33. Jack lost $\$200 - \$170 = \$30$.

$$\text{Percent} = \frac{\text{Part}}{\text{Whole}} \times 100\%$$

$$= \frac{\$30}{\$200} \times 100\% = 15\%$$

42. (J) Trigonometric Functions of Other Angles

100 Key Math Concepts for the ACT, #98. Consider the unit circle:

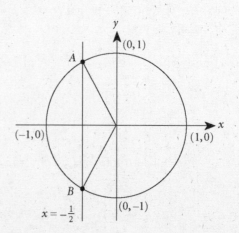

Cosine $x = -\dfrac{1}{2}$ for those values where $x = -\dfrac{1}{2}$ on the unit circle, in this case A and B. From the diagram, it can be seen that this occurs at $\dfrac{2\pi}{3}$ and $\dfrac{4\pi}{3}$.

43. (B)—Solving a Quadratic Equation

100 Key Math Concepts for the ACT, #66. The fastest way to solve is by back-solving. Plug the answer choices into $5x^2 + 2x - 7$ and see which one equals 0:

(A) $5(-7)^2 + 2(-7) - 7 = 245 - 14 - 7 =$
224—Discard.

(B) $\left(\dfrac{7}{5}\right)^2 + 2\left(-\dfrac{7}{5}\right) - 7 = 5\left(\dfrac{49}{25}\right) - \dfrac{14}{5} - 7$

$$= \dfrac{49}{5} - \dfrac{14}{5} - 7$$

$$= \dfrac{35}{5} - 7$$

$$= 0 \text{ — Correct.}$$

44. (J)—Intersecting Lines, Parallel Lines and Transversals, Angles of a Triangle

100 Key Math Concepts for the ACT, #78–81. It might help to redraw the diagram, extending lines:

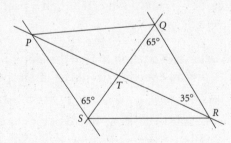

What you have is two parallel lines and two transversals. Since all acute angles that are formed by a transversal are the same size, $\angle PST = \angle TQR$. So $\triangle QRT$ has an interior angle of $65°(\angle TQR)$, and another of $35°(\angle QRT)$. Since the sum of

interior angles in a triangle is 180°, $\angle QTR = 180° - 65° - 35° = 80°$. Since $\angle QTR$ and $\angle PTQ$ are supplementary, that is, form a straight line, $\angle PTQ = 180° - \angle QTR = 180° - 80° = 100°$.

45. (C)—Rate

100 Key Math Concepts for the ACT, #39. Let the rate that Ms. Rodriguez travels at be x mph.

West		Starting Point		East
←	$x + 15$ mph	●	x mph	→

The speed at which the cars were traveling is needed to find how far either car traveled.

Use the distance formula to find x:

$$\text{Distance} = \text{Rate} \times \text{Time}$$

In this case:

Distance = (Ms. Rodriguez's speed $\times$ 5 hours)
$+$ (Ms. Green's speed $\times$ 5 hours)

475 miles = (x mph $\times$ 5 hours) $+$ [$(x + 15)$mph $\times$ 5 hours]

475 miles = $5x$ miles $+ 5x$ miles $+ 75$ miles

400 miles = $10x$ miles

$40 = x$

So Ms. Rodriguez drives at 40 mph, and Ms. Green at 55 mph.

In 5 hours the faster car will travel 55 mph $\times$ 5 hours = 275 miles.

46. (G)—Using an Equation to Find the Slope, Using an Equation to Find an Intercept

100 Key Math Concepts for the ACT, #73, 74. If the equation of a line is expressed in the form $y = mx + b$, then m is the slope and b is the y-intercept. From the graph it can be seen that the slope is negative,

since y decreases as x increases (any line that rises as you move right has a positive slope; any that falls off as you go right has a negative slope). So m is negative. Also from the graph, it can be seen that the line crosses the y-axis above the x-axis—that is, the y-intercept is positive—so b, the y-intercept, is positive. The only answer choice that agrees with this is answer choice (G).

47. (B)—Solving an Equation That Includes Absolute Value Signs

100 Key Math Concepts for the ACT, #68. If $xy \neq 0$ then $x \neq 0$ and $y \neq 0$.

The square of any nonzero number is positive, so x^2 and y^2 are positive.

The larger the magnitude of any number, the larger the square of that number.

So if $|y| < |x|$, that means $y^2 < x^2$.

Since x^2 and y^2 are also both positive, and $x^2 > y^2$, the numerator of the fraction $\dfrac{x^2}{y^2}$ will be greater than the denominator; i.e., the entire fraction must be greater than 1.

48. (J)—Evaluating an Algebraic Expression, Factoring the Square of a Binomial

100 Key Math Concepts for the ACT, #52, 60. If you did not recognize the common quadratic $a^2 - 2ab + b^2 = (a - b)^2$, you could factor the expression $a^2 - 2ab + b^2$ using FOIL in reverse.

$$a^2 - 2ab + b^2 = (a - b)(a - b) = (12)(12) = 144$$

49. (E)—Translating from English into Algebra, Interior Angles of a Triangle

100 Key Math Concepts for the ACT, #65, 80. $\angle EDF = x$.

"$\angle DEF$ has a measure of 30° more than $\angle EDF$" means that $\angle DEF = x + 30$.

"$\angle EFD$ is 15° less than the sum of the measures of $\angle EDF$ and $\angle DEF$" means that $\angle EFD = (x + x + 30) - 15 = 2x + 15$.

50. (H)—Parallel Lines and Transversals

100 Key Math Concepts for the ACT, #79. When a transversal cuts parallel lines, all acute angles formed are equal and all obtuse angles formed are equal.

So $\angle ATR = \angle CRP = 110°$

Since $\angle ATQ$ and $\angle ATR$ form a straight line, their sum is 180°.

So $\angle ATQ + 110° = 180°$

$\angle ATQ = 70°$

51. (E)—Simplifying Trigonometric Expressions

100 Key Math Concepts for the ACT, #99. Since $\sin^2 \theta + \cos^2 \theta = 1$, for all values of θ, and $x = \sin \theta$ and $y = \cos \theta$, then $x^2 + y^2 = 1$.

52. (K)—Using an Equation to Find the Slope, Using an Equation to Find an Intercept

100 Key Math Concepts for the ACT, #73, 74. All answer choices are in the slope-intercept form, $y = mx + b$, where m is the slope and b is the y-intercept.

Line T has a y-intercept of −3, so in this case $b = -3$. Discard answer choices (F), (H), and (J).

Since T is parallel to $3x - 5y = 4$, they have the same slope. Find the slope of $3x - 5y = 4$:

$$3x - 5y = 4$$
$$-5y = -3x + 4$$
$$y = \frac{3}{5}x - \frac{4}{5}$$

So the slope is $\frac{3}{5}$ and line T has equation $y = \frac{3}{5}x - 3$.

53. (D)—Adding/Subtracting Signed Numbers

100 Key Math Concepts for the ACT, #5. Simply count the number of spaces between A and B on the number line. If the distance is too great to count, in general the distance between any two points, A and B, is $|A - B|$.

54. (F)—Finding the Distance between Two Points

100 Key Math Concepts for the ACT, #71.

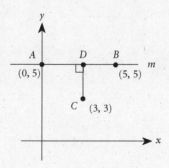

As can be seen from the diagram above, the shortest distance between C and line m is segment $\overline{CD}$. Since $\overline{CD}$ is parallel to the y-axis, the length of $\overline{CD}$ is the difference between the y-coordinates of D and C. Since line m is parallel to the x-axis, and passes through point $(0, 5)$, all points on line m have a y-coordinate of 5. Since C has a y-coordinate of 3, the distance CD is $5 - 3$, or 2.

55. (E)—Solving an Inequality

100 Key Math Concepts for the ACT, #69. Rearrange the inequality:

$$-2 - 4x \le -6x$$

Add 2 to both sides. $\qquad -4x \le -6x + 2$

Add $6x$ to both sides. $\qquad 2x \le 2$

Divide both sides by 2. $\qquad x \le 1$

56. (H)—Areas of Special Quadrilaterals

100 Key Math Concepts for the ACT, #87. The figure is a rectangle with two smaller rectangles cut out of it. The total area is the area of the large rectangle minus the area of the cutouts.

The area of any rectangle is length × width.

The area of the large rectangle = $8 \times 10 = 80$.

The area of the top cutout rectangle = $3 \times 4 = 12$.

The area of the bottom cutout rectangle = $3 \times 2 = 6$.

Total area = $80 - 12 - 6 = 62$.

57. (D)—Miscellaneous Quadrilaterals and Circles

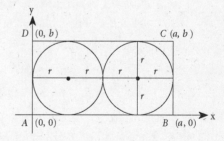

As can be seen from the above diagram, a is the distance between A and B, that is, the length of the rectangle $ABCD$. This is equal to $4r$. Similarly, b is the distance between A and D, that is, $2r$. So $a - b = 4r - 2r = 2r$.

58. (H)—Percent Formula

100 Key Math Concepts for the ACT, #32. Find the number of teenagers in each age group:

"20 teenagers are 15 years old"—20, 15-year-olds

"8 teenagers are 18 years old"—8, 18-year-olds

"20% are 14 years old"—20% of $60 = \dfrac{1}{5} \times 60 = 12$—12, 14-year-olds

"There are twice as many 16-year-olds as 18-year-olds"—There are 8, 18-year-olds, so there are $2 \times 8 = 16$, 16-year-olds.

Since there are 60 teenagers total, the remainder are 17 years old.

$60 - 20 - 8 - 12 - 16 = 4$, 17-year-olds.

There is a total of $4 + 8 = 12$, 17- and 18-year-olds.

Since Percent $= \dfrac{\text{Part}}{\text{Whole}} \times 100\%$, in this case Percent $= \dfrac{12}{60} \times 100\% = 20\%$.

59. (B)—Probability

100 Key Math Concepts for the ACT, #46. Probability of an event occurring $= \dfrac{\text{Number of favorable outcomes}}{\text{Number of possible outcomes}}$.

In this case, a favorable outcome is not picking a blue T-shirt. Since 7 T-shirts are not blue, the number of favorable outcomes is 7.

The number of possible outcomes is the total number of T-shirts that could be picked, that is, $5 + 7$, or 12.

So the probability of not picking a blue T-shirt $= \dfrac{7}{12}$.

60. (F)—Equation for an Ellipse

100 Key Math Concepts for the ACT, #77. The correct equation will be true for all the points on the ellipse. Four points are given in the diagram. Run them through the equations in the answer choices; if the equation is not true for any one of these points, it may be discarded.

(F) Try (0, 2): $\dfrac{x^2}{25} + \dfrac{y^2}{4} = \dfrac{0^2}{25} + \dfrac{2^2}{4} = \dfrac{4}{4} = 1$

Now try (5, 0): $\dfrac{x^2}{25} + \dfrac{y^2}{4} = \dfrac{5^2}{25} + \dfrac{0^2}{4} = \dfrac{25}{25} = 1$

Now try (−5, 0): $\dfrac{x^2}{25} + \dfrac{y^2}{4} = \dfrac{(-5)^2}{25} + \dfrac{0^2}{4} = \dfrac{25}{25} = 1$

Now try (0, −2): $\dfrac{x^2}{25} + \dfrac{y^2}{4} = \dfrac{0^2}{25} + \dfrac{(-2)^2}{4} = \dfrac{4}{4} = 1$

Since the equation is true for all 4 points, this is the correct answer.

READING TEST

PASSAGE I—PROSE FICTION

This is a Prose Fiction passage, so remember to ask yourself the three important questions:

1. *Who are these people?*
   George Webber is a young writer who has just heard that his novel has been accepted for publication.

2. *What is their state of mind?*
   George is feeling many things at once: happiness about having a novel accepted for publication; fear that parts of the novel might offend some people; eagerness to see a chapter of his novel published in a magazine; dread at the prospect of writing a second novel; and disappointment when people did not react to his writing in the way he had expected.

3. *What's going on?*
   George is going through some very mixed feelings. Although he is extremely excited about realizing his dream of becoming a writer, at the same time he's realizing that what is so momentous to him—the publication of his novel—is not really all that important to the rest of the world.

1. (D)—Inference Question

Remember to check back to the passage to make sure that your answer works in context. Lines 42–43 explain that George was concerned that "some people might recognize themselves and be offended." This is what made him think he might have "to go around in smoked glasses and false whiskers."

2. (F)—Detail Question

The sixth paragraph (lines 71–85) discusses George's feelings about writing his next novel. Lines 75–77 state that writing for him is "like a demoniacal

possession, driving him with alien force much greater than his own." This idea is paraphrased by choice (F).

3. (B)—Inference Question

The paragraph (lines 71–85) preceding the quote by George Webber to Foxhall Edwards explains the difficult, tortuous process that George goes through in writing. George probably sensed that his agony and fatigue would be obvious to Fox and others, but he knew that without this agony he would not be able to do good work. Line 73 especially shows that George knew that the act of writing would be painful—he would "get it out of him." Therefore, choice (B) best describes George's reason for offering the quote in question.

4. (H)—Inference Question

George "expected convulsions of the earth" lines 90–91) when his story was published. He had worried that "people might recognize themselves and be offended" (lines 42–43). Instead, "nothing happened. A few of his friends mentioned it, but that was all" (lines 92–94). No one was offended. For all the worrying and wondering that George did, the contrast between this calm public response and the anticipated response could be best characterized as "ironic."

5. (D)—Detail Question

Lines 66–70 discuss the very positive impact that Fox had on George. The text says that "the editor's faith and confidence, coming as it had come at a time when George had given up all hope, restored his self-respect and charged him with energy for new work." This idea is best summarized by choice (D).

6. (G)—Detail Question

The last paragraph (lines 89–102) describes what happened when *Rodney's Magazine* came out with

George's story. After an initial letdown (line 94), George decided that "people couldn't really tell much about a new author from a short piece in a magazine . . . He could afford to wait a little longer for the fame which he was certain would soon be his" (lines 95–102). Therefore, choice (G) best answers the question.

7. (A)—Detail Question

"Fame, at last, was knocking at his door and wooing him with her sweet blandishments" (lines 17–18). Typically, a suitor *woos* the object of his desire with gifts. In the previous paragraph we learned that George had just received a check for $500 as "an advance against his royalties" (lines 14–15) on a book he had written. This money could be considered fame's gift. The word *courting* in choice A best captures this concept of *wooing*.

8. (H)—Inference Question

The source of George's trembling (line 34) is explained in subsequent sentences. "He loathed the thought of giving pain to anyone . . . But . . . some people might recognize themselves and be offended" (lines 37–43).

9. (B)—Inference Question

To select the correct choice for this difficult question, you must analyze George's behavior. George is very proud of his work. This can be inferred from several parts of the passage. Lines 32–33 are worded to convey his pride of authorship when they say, "He had distilled every line of it out of his own experiences of life." His extremely high (and unrealistic) expectations about the effect of having his story published in *Rodney's Magazine* (lines 89–92) also convey George's belief that his work was very important. George does have concerns, though. The fourth paragraph discusses his worry that his fictional characterizations might

offend the real people on which they were based. This pride mixed with concern is expressed in choice (B).

10. (F)—Inference Question

When George is described early in this passage, the word *dazed* is used (in line 7). In lines 3–4 the reader learns that George has come "to his senses somewhere in the wilds of the Upper Bronx." In lines 13–15 the reader learns that the paper George was happily looking at earlier is a $500 royalty check. Therefore, you can infer that George has been wandering around dazed after learning that his book has been accepted for publication—choice (F). Choice (J) might have been tempting, but it's the fact that his book will be published, not the money he'll earn from it, that makes George dazed and happy.

PASSAGE II—HUMANITIES

This rather confusing passage deals with the connection between two "grand ideas": human self-fulfillment and freedom. Here's a road map to the passage:

- The **first and second paragraphs** provide some historical perspective on the ideal of human self-fulfillment.

- The **third paragraph** explains what the authors have in mind when they speak of human self-fulfillment.

- The **fourth paragraph** mentions that self-fulfillment has led to scientific and technical progress, which, in turn, has made individual self-fulfillment easier.

- The **fifth paragraph** discusses one thinker, Calvin, who did not believe in human self-fulfillment, and the consequences of this attitude.

- The **sixth and seventh paragraphs** tie together the ideals of human self-fulfillment and freedom, saying that the former is not possible without the latter, and introduces some historical examples to support this thesis.

- Finally, the **eighth paragraph** mentions some thinkers who distorted the idea of freedom, and the importance of freedom of thought and speech.

11. (C)—Big Picture Question

The passage talks about self-fulfillment and freedom and what these great ideas have inspired. Paragraph five begins with the sentence: "Only rarely has a thinker . . . gone back from the ideal of human potential and fulfillment." The next sentence, which introduces Calvin, says "Calvin was perhaps such a thinker who went back and believed. . . that man [is]. . . incapable of any worthwhile development" (lines 54–57). Calvin, therefore, is a counterexample offered to show that not everyone over the past five hundred years has believed in the ideals of self-fulfillment and human potential.

12. (G)—Detail Question

Reread the lines surrounding the word *elucidated* in line 26 to get its meaning. Lines 28–29 say "aesthetic and ethical gifts, we feel and struggle to express in our own minds." Lines 30–31 say "cultural gifts, are unfolded for us by the study of history." Considering this, "revealed," choice (G), best captures this idea of unfolding and struggling to express gifts.

13. (B)—Big Picture Question

Lines 64–66 explain that "human fulfillment is unattainable without freedom, so that these two main ideas are linked together." The sixth paragraph begins talking about freedom by describing it as "the second of the two grand formative ideas." This follows the first five paragraphs which discuss

fulfillment. This information supports (B) as the correct answer.

14. (H)—Detail Question

Lines 44–46 explain that, "The purpose and the effect [of devices and gadgets] has been to liberate men from the exhausting drudgeries of earning their living." Choice (H) best paraphrases these ideas.

15. (C)—Inference Question

Lines 50–51 indicate that, before the development of all sorts of work-saving devices and gadgets, princes alone had the "leisure to find the best in themselves."

16. (H)—Inference Question

In lines 88–90 the authors explain that "freedom . . . advocates can at times delude themselves that obedience to tyranny is a form of freedom." Therefore, the author's ideas are best expressed by choice (H).

17. (B)—Big Picture Question

You can find the answer to this question by a process of elimination (remember, you're looking for the choice that the authors would *reject*). Choice (A) is supported by the discussion in paragraph four (lines 35–51): People are able to find the best in themselves when they have more leisure time. Choice (C) is supported by paragraph one (lines 1–13): The authors mention various people in diverse professions in various eras who have all praised the development of the individual. Choice (D) is sup-ported in line 61, where the authors contend that men develop by having something in them "which is personal and creative." This leaves choice (B)—nowhere in the text do the authors say or imply that "self-fulfillment is a praiseworthy but unreachable goal." Indeed the authors seem to believe that self-fulfillment is possible.

18. (F)—Big Picture Question

Lines 64–65 say that freedom is necessary for human fulfillment. Lines 35–36 talk about self-fulfillment inspiring progress. The final paragraph talks about the importance of freedom of thought and speech. Thus, the authors would undoubtedly contend that freedom is necessary for a society to make progress.

19. (A)—Detail Question

Lines 88–92 talk about the delusion that "ensnared" Luther, Rousseau, Hegel, and Marx. According to the authors, all of them confused freedom with obedience to tyranny. Choice (A), therefore, is the answer.

20. (J)—Big Picture Question

The authors make it clear throughout the passage that they feel freedom is a valuable ideal. In the seventh paragraph, they suggest that revolutions have often made societies more free. Considering this, choice (J) is the best answer.

PASSAGE III—SOCIAL STUDIES

This well-organized passage is about Mussolini's rise to power in postwar Italy. A road map:

- The **first two paragraphs** discuss the territorial and economic problems that set the stage for Mussolini's rise to power.

- The **third paragraph** outlines the events that resulted in Mussolini's dictatorship.

- The **fourth and fifth** paragraphs explore Mussolini's economic and political philosophy.

21. (A)—Detail Question

Lines 5–10 talk about the lands that Italy obtained and hoped to obtain as it emerged from World War I. The author explains that in spite of being given land

in Austria-Hungary, the Italians were disappointed not to be awarded "further acquisitions east of the Adriatic and in Asia and Africa." "Grandiose ambitions," therefore, refers to the desire for more land.

22. (J)—Big Picture Question

There is evidence in this passage to support all three of the statements. Lines 28–32 explain the reaction of landlords, factory owners, small businesses and professional people to the economic unrest in Italy following the war—they "longed for vigorous leadership and a strong government." In other words, they desired the stability that Mussolini's regime seemed to offer, as statement I suggests. Statement II also contributed to Mussolini's rise to power. Lines 54–55 explain that he seized "control of the faction-paralyzed government" in Rome. Statement III also was important. Lines 48–52 explain that Mussolini's veterans terrorized "the leaderless radical workers and their liberal supporters." The answer is choice (J), which states that Statements I, II, and III were all important factors in Mussolini's rise to power.

23. (D)—Big Picture Question

The authors describe the rise of fascism in paragraphs 1 through 3. Paragraph 1 explains how the peace settlements following World War I resulted in "severe blows to Italian national pride" because Italy was awarded less land than it hoped for. This is discussed as the first of many problems that laid the groundwork for a new nationalistic, fascist leader like Mussolini to rise to power. So the way that the passage supports the theory (that fascism arises after periods of diminished national pride) is best stated by choice (D).

24. (G)—Inference Question

From the text it seems that Mussolini had organized unemployed veterans into a political action group (lines 41–43) before the end of the labor disturbances in 1921. Mussolini eventually sent his veterans to beat up the radical workers and their supporters (lines 48–52) in an effort to get the support of the capitalists and the landlords (lines 45–46). However, he waited to do so until it became clear that the workers would lose (lines 43–45). The reason he waited to commit his group of veterans was that he wanted to join up with the side that would ultimately be victorious. This certainly sounds opportunistic to us.

25. (B)—Inference Question

The correct answer should convey the idea that Mussolini had absolute power over the citizens of Italy. Choice (B)—abolishing all non-Fascist unions—is the only choice that conveys Mussolini's control over the lives of individuals.

26. (H)—Inference Question

Lines 87–95 describe the role of nationalism in Mussolini's Italy. The authors explain that Mussolini used the "energizing quality" of militant nationalism for political purposes—to attract support for his new regime. Choice (H) paraphrases this idea best.

27. (D)—Inference Question

One aspect of Mussolini's rise that comes across in paragraphs 2 through 4 is his hard-line policy towards labor. Lines 20–21 indicate that Italian workers were conducting sit-down factory strikes in 1920. By 1926 these workers were forbidden to strike and were subject to compulsory arbitration (lines 71–75). Choice (D) best states this crackdown on workers' rights.

28. (H)—Inference Question

The fourth paragraph talks about Italy's economic life under Mussolini's corporate state. Lines 81–86 describe the economic effects of Mussolini's

policies—even though he balanced Italy's budget and stabilized its currency, taxes reached record levels, leading to a decline in per capita income. Choice (H) is the correct answer here—excessively high taxation disrupted economic rebuilding.

29. (D)—Detail Question

Lines 75–78 describe the corporate state as a "planned economy [that] was set up to modernize, coordinate, and increase Italy's production of both industrial and agricultural goods." Choice (D) best paraphrases this information.

30. (F)—Inference Question

In the final paragraph in lines 88–89 the authors contend that fascism was nationalism "run wild." The subsequent quotes are intended to provide an illustration of those nationalistic ideas.

PASSAGE IV—NATURAL SCIENCES

The title of this wide-ranging passage could be "Everything You Ever Wanted to Know about Tornadoes." Or perhaps "Everything You Never Wanted to Know about Tornadoes." In any case, it's all here:

- The **first paragraph** mentions the destructive power of tornado winds.

- The **second, third, fourth, and fifth paragraphs** talk about the formation, structure, and physical appearance of tornadoes.

- The **sixth paragraph** discusses where tornadoes are most likely to form, in a place called (appropriately enough) "tornado alley."

- The **seventh and eighth paragraphs** explain when and under what conditions tornadoes are likely to emerge.

- The **ninth paragraph** talks about the unpredictable movements of tornadoes and why this makes them difficult to track and study.

31. (D)—Detail Question

The term *vortexes of air* appears in line 12. The text immediately following the use of this term discusses the rotation of tornadoes, mentioning that air streams into the base and then spirals upward (lines 13–21).

32. (J)—Detail Question

Lines 5–8 explain that the wind speeds of tornadoes have been determined "based [in part] on analysis of motion pictures."

33. (D)—Inference Question

Tornado rotation is discussed in lines 13–15. The direction of rotation is based on the hemisphere in which the tornado occurs.

34. (G)—Inference Question

Lines 91–92 in the last paragraph describe "the unpredictable nature of tornadoes, which often hop about from place to place." Since scientists operate the TOTO device by placing it "in the path of the tornado," you can infer that the unpredictable movements of tornadoes might make TOTO hard to use.

35. (A)—Detail Question

Paragraphs seven and eight (lines 67–84) discuss the conditions required for tornadoes to form. Lines 73–75 explain the need for strong updrafts. Lines 76–79 explain the effect of wind shear on the initiation of tornado rotation. These two factors are listed in choice (A).

36. (H)—Detail Question

Lines 78–79 explain what happens during wind shear—"wind speed increases with height and veers

from southeast to west." Choice (H) accurately rewords this information.

37. (A)—Inference Question

Paragraphs seven and eight (lines 67–84) discuss the factors that determine the formation of tornadoes. These factors are based on weather conditions in the sky. You can infer from this information that it would be possible to predict the formation of tornadoes if these atmospheric conditions were known.

38. (F)—Detail Question

This question requires a careful reading of the text. At the end of paragraph three, the author describes the formation of funnel clouds—we're told that a pressure drop in the core of the cloud causes air to flow in, where it hits an area of lower pressure, and causes water vapor to condense into droplets. The term *condensation cloud* is never used to describe a funnel cloud in paragraph three. However, the terms are synonymous. This becomes clear when you read the beginning of paragraph four: "Sometimes, no condensation cloud forms" (line 36). So correct choice (F) accurately describes the formation of condensation clouds.

39. (C)—Big Picture Question

Paragraph three (lines 27–35) begins "The vortex frequently becomes visible" (line 27). Paragraph four begins "Sometimes . . . the only way a tornado can reveal itself" (lines 36–37). So both paragraphs address what makes a tornado visible. The answer is choice (C).

40. (J)—Big Picture Question

Line 85 states that tornadoes "are steered by the jet stream." Choice (J) is the answer. Based on information in the passage choices (F), (G), and (H) are not true of *all* tornadoes.

SCIENCE TEST

PASSAGE I

The first passage mostly requires an ability to read the two given graphs, each of which traces the rate of decay in a different radioactive isotope. The y-axis of each graph represents the proportion of remaining (undecayed) nuclei to original nuclei, while the x-axis of each represents time. Notice, though, that the first graph runs from 0 days to just 6 days, while the second graph runs from 0 days to 180 days. That's a big difference, indicating that the second isotope—$^{91}_{39}Y$—decays at a much slower rate.

1. (A)

In the introduction to the passage, the "half-life" of an isotope is defined as the amount of time needed for one-half of the initial number of nuclei to decay. To figure out the half-life of $^{90}_{39}Y$, look at the first graph. When half of the nuclei have decayed, the N/N_0 ratio would be .5 (since there'd be half as many nuclei after the half-life as there were originally). Draw a horizontal line across the graph at the level of .5. The horizontal line will intersect the curve at a specific point; from this point, draw a vertical line down to the x-axis. The vertical line intersects the x-axis somewhere between 2 and 2.5 days, which means that the amount of time it takes for half of the nuclei to decay is between 2 and 2.5 days. Choice (A) is the only answer that falls in this range.

2. (G)

Since N_0 is the same for both samples, you can use the two graphs to figure out the ratio of $^{90}_{39}Y$ to $^{91}_{39}Y$ after 2.3 days. You know from having done the previous question that after 2.3 days about .5 of $^{90}_{39}Y$ still remains. Take a look at the graph for $^{91}_{39}Y$: after 2.3 days, hardly any will have decayed at all.

Therefore, the ratio of $^{90}_{39}Y$ to $^{91}_{39}Y$ will be .5 to 1, or 1 to 2 (G).

3. (C)

This is a rather strange, convoluted question, but what it means is that one isotope ($^{90}_{39}Y$) will accumulate in the gastrointestinal tract while the other ($^{91}_{39}Y$) will accumulate in the bones. Since none of the isotopes leave the bones or the gastrointestinal tract as a result of processes that normally occur in the human body, you can use the values for the half-lives given in the graphs. So after three days, a little over half of the original $^{90}_{39}Y$ will be left (in the gastrointestinal tract), but just about all of the $^{91}_{39}Y$ will be left (in the bones). With this information in hand, you just have to examine the choices. Choice (A) is incorrect because $^{91}_{39}Y$ accumulates in the bones, not the gastrointestinal tract. Choice (B) is incorrect since $^{90}_{39}Y$ accumulates in the gastrointestinal tract, not in the bones. Choice (C) is correct because, as we said, about half of the nuclei of $^{90}_{39}Y$ decay after 3 days, so about half of the inhaled amount will be in the gastrointestinal tract after 3 days. Choice (D) is out because after 3 days, almost all of the $^{91}_{39}Y$ will be left in the bones.

4. (G)

After one half-life has passed, half of the original 1,000 nuclei will have decayed, leaving 500. After the second half-life has passed, half of the 500 will be gone, leaving 250. When the third half-life has passed, half of the 250 will have decayed, leaving 125, choice (G).

5. (D)

Statement I is true: $^{90}_{39}Y$ is less stable than $^{91}_{39}Y$ because $^{90}_{39}Y$ decays more rapidly (remember that the x-axes are scaled differently). This rules out choice B.

Statement II is wrong because a very small fraction (much less than a quarter) of $^{90}_{39}Y$ would remain after 116 days. Choice (C) can thus also be eliminated. Statement III is obviously true, given the fact that they decay in this manner, making (D) the correct answer.

PASSAGE II

This passage involves three tennis-training experiments, the results of each being summarized in a table. Remember to look for patterns in the data. Notice, for instance, that in Table 1 the greatest increases in serving speed were obtained when right-handed players watched a right-handed coach and when left-handed players watched a left-handed coach. Similarly, in Table 2, coach guidance caused higher increases in *both* serving speed and serving accuracy. This kind of observation about the data should help you to formulate theories (e.g., that training is more effective when the coach uses the same hand as the player).

6. (J)

In Experiment 1, left-handed video watchers watching a left-handed coach improved their service speed by 8 mph. Since right-handed players in Experiment 3 (the one asked about here) improved even more with a combination of videos and physical instruction than with videos alone, lefties will probably improve at least as much in Experiment 3 as they did in Experiment 1, making choice (J) the right answer.

7. (A)

Choice (A) is the only conclusion that cannot be supported by the data of Experiment 1. Imitating someone with opposite handedness does not always cause a deterioration of skills: right-handed players

actually improved somewhat when they watched videos of left-handed coaches.

8. (H)

Experiment 2 was designed to determine whether right-handed players improve more with videos alone or with videos and physical guidance combined. The players given a combination of videos and guidance clearly showed greater improvement in both service speed and service accuracy as compared to those who just used videos. This supports the hypothesis (choice H) that physical guidance by a coach improves both speed and accuracy of service for right-handed players. (Note: There is nothing in Experiment 2 to support any conclusion whatsoever about left-handed players, since none was involved in the experiment.)

9. (D)

In Experiments 1 and 2, right-handed players who watched a right-handed coach on video improved 5 mph in speed. According to Experiment 2, right-handed players who watched videos and received physical guidance improved by 9 mph (4 mph more than with videos alone). Guidance appears to further improve service speed. Since left-handers improve by 8 mph with videos alone (Experiment 1), adding physical guidance to their training should make their overall improvement in service speed greater than 8 mph. The only choice greater than 8 mph is (D).

10. (F)

Experiment 1 investigated the effect of watching videos of left- or right-handed coaches on the service speed of left- or right-handed players. The results support the conclusion in choice (F). Players watching videos of coaches with the same handedness improved their speeds by 5 mph (righties) and 8 mph (lefties), whereas players watching videos of coaches with the opposite handedness improved their speed only a little (2 mph for righties) or not at all (for lefties). Tennis players seem to improve less when observing coaches whose handedness is opposite to their own.

11. (C)

Choice (C) is the best procedure to determine the effects of verbal instruction on average service speed because it measures the amount of improvement that is due solely to verbal instruction. In addition, all of the players receive the exact same verbal instruction, since the instructions have been recorded (personal verbal instruction may vary considerably). Choice (A)'s procedure is not optimal because Experiment 3 involves the factors of videos and physical guidance as well as verbal instruction. Choice (B)'s procedure involves physical guidance so it is also not ideal. Choice (D)'s procedure does not measure the players' service speed before instruction, so there is no way to gauge improvement.

PASSAGE III

This passage hinges on the Hertzsprung-Russell diagram, which plots individual stars in terms of their absolute magnitude (brightness, in other words) on the *y*-axis, and their spectral class (which is a measure of color/temperature) on the *x*-axis. What does this mean? It means that stars that are high on the chart are brighter than those that are low on the chart (because the greater the number for absolute magnitude, the dimmer the star). It also means that stars that are on the right side of the chart (which most of them are) are M class (i.e., the reddest and coolest), while those toward the left side of the chart are the bluest and warmest.

12. (F)

Nearly all of the stars on the diagram fall in the spectral class M, so choice (F) is correct.

13. (B)

The text explains that the spectral classes of stars on the diagram go from warmest on the left (O) to coolest on the right (M). Therefore, any stars in a spectral class to the left of G, the Sun's spectral class, are warmer than the Sun. Of the three named stars, only two are in a spectral class to the left of G: Sirius and Altair.

14. (G)

Most of the stars on the diagram fall below the absolute magnitude of 6; that is, they would not be visible to the naked eye from a distance of 10 parsecs. (Remember that 1.0 is the maximum brightness and that stars with absolute magnitudes of 15.0 to 17.0 are very dim.)

15. (A)

A quick review: Moving across the spectral classes from left to right, the stars go from warm to cool and from blue to red. Statement I is correct because α-Centauri is in a spectral class to the right of Sirius' spectral class. This means that you can eliminate choices (B) and (D), which do not contain Statement I. Statement II is incorrect because the Sun is to the right of Altair on the diagram, indicating that the Sun is cooler. This eliminates choice (C). Choice (A) is the correct answer, and you don't even have to look at Statement III (though if you do, you'll find that it's incorrect, since the Sun is lower on the diagram than is Procyon).

16. (J)

It's impossible to know what the diagram of stars within 10 parsecs of the Sun would look like, even though you have the graph of the stars within 5 parsecs of the sun in front of you. It may be tempting to assume that by doubling the distance the number of stars would be doubled as well (F). However, when you double the distance from the Sun, you more than double the volume of space; there may be, for all you know, many more than double the original number of stars on the new diagram. There is similarly no basis on which to judge the absolute magnitude or the spectral class of the additional stars (G and H).

PASSAGE IV

This passage is based around three different experiments, all designed to determine what conditions favor Product A and what conditions favor Product B when a particular cobalt complex reacts with sodium nitrite. Remember to note the differences in the procedures of the three experiments. Experiment 2 differs from Experiment 1 in that the solutions were heated after $NaNO_2$ was added. Experiment 3 differs from Experiment 1 in that after $NaNO_2$ was added, citrate ion was added and the solutions were heated.

17. (C)

To answer this question, look at the conditions in which Product B was formed. Solution 1 in Experiment 1 and Solution 1 in Experiment 2 both yielded Product B. These solutions were both acidic, so the correct answer must be either choice (B) or choice (C). The next step is to determine whether Product B was formed when citrate ion was added. The results of Experiment 3 show that there is no yield of Product B with added citrate ion, so choice (C) is the correct answer.

18. (F)

Choice (F) is the conclusion that is not supported by the experimental results. As you know from the previous question, Product B is not formed when citrate ion is added to the solution. Since it does form in the same solution if no citrate ion is added (Experiment 2), the presence of citrate ion does indeed affect the formation of Product B. All of the other choices are legitimate conclusions based on the experimental data.

19. (B)

Varying the pH (choice (B)) may well show that different degrees of acidity or basicity will have a marked impact on product formation. Heating the solutions has been tried already, and freezing the solutions should stop the reactions altogether. Varying the concentration, meanwhile, won't alter the ability of the known compound to react.

20. (F)

When you're answering a question that's based on only part of the data, make sure that the answer you choose is based only on the relevant data. In Experiment 2, it was found that when the solutions were heated to 110° C, both Product A and Product B were formed. Therefore, choice (F) is supported by the results of Experiment 2. All of the other choices are hypotheses that could only be supported or refuted using the results of Experiments 1 and 3 along with the results of Experiment 2.

21. (B)

This question asks you to identify the condition or conditions that are held constant through all three experiments. The temperature was varied, ruling out choice (A), and the amount of citrate ion was not the same in all three experiments, so you can eliminate choices (C) and (D). Only choice (B) remains. You are never told the specific quantity of cobalt complex used, but you can assume it was the same in all three experiments since the solutions of Experiments 2 and 3 were prepared just as they were in Experiment 1.

22. (J)

The fact that Product B is formed in Solution 1 when heated but is not formed when citrate ion is added prior to heating (J) is evidence to support the hypothesis that Product B may react to form other more readily dissolved compounds in the presence of certain ions. None of the other choices involves the presence of any type of ion.

PASSAGE V

This is the conflicting viewpoints passage; the viewpoints that are in question are different suggested classifications for the giant panda—as a raccoon or as a bear. Examine the scientists' positions carefully. Scientist 1 votes for a raccoon classification, citing as evidence anatomical similarities, comparable size among males and females, similar noises and eye-covering behavior, and certain chromosomal similarities. Scientist 2 votes for a bear classification, citing evidence such as DNA similarities, similar body proportions, and aggressive behavior.

23. (A)

In this question you are asked to determine which of the four choices would provide additional support for the viewpoint expressed by Scientist 2. Similarities between the blood proteins of giant pandas and several bear species (A) would certainly indicate that pandas should be classified as bears, which is Scientist 2's viewpoint. Watch out for choices that

support the other position in questions like this: Choices (B) and (D), for instance, are wrong because they support Scientist 1's argument that pandas should be classified as raccoons, not bears. Choice (C), meanwhile, is inconclusive.

24. (J)

Both scientists make their arguments by comparing the physical, behavioral, and genetic characteristics of the giant panda to the characteristics of either the bear or the raccoon family. They would definitely agree that animals should be classified into families based on these criteria.

25. (C)

Let's take a look at the statements. You know from Scientist 1's statement that *Ursidae* (bears) have 36 pairs of chromosomes, so Statement I would support the classification of the mammal as a bear. This narrows the possible choices down to (A) and (C). You also know from Scientist 1 that male bears can be twice the size of female bears, whereas male and female raccoons are the same size. Statement III, therefore, also supports the classification of the mammal as a bear. Choice (C) is the right choice, and you don't even have to look at Statement II (which would would argue *against* a classification as a bear).

26. (G)

Scientist 1 explains that both raccoons and pandas cover their eyes with their front paws whenever intimidated.

27. (D)

Scientist 2 mentions that research has shown that the giant panda's DNA is far more similar to a bear's DNA than to that of any other family. Choice (D) paraphrases this idea.

28. (F)

If giant pandas and raccoons both had glandular scent areas, this would be evidence to support the viewpoint of Scientist 1, who thinks that giant pandas should be classified as raccoons.

29. (B)

Scientist 2 contends that giant pandas display the same aggressive behavior as bears do: they swat and try to grab adversaries with their forepaws. The only choice that is a counter argument to this claim is (B): an aggressive panda's behavior is like a raccoon's behavior, not a bear's, in that the panda bobs its head up and down like a raccoon.

Passage VI

This passage consists almost exclusively of a complex bar graph recording primary energy sources at various times in history—namely, 1850, 1900, 1950, and 1985. Notice the changing proportions. Fuel wood, which was an extremely important source of energy in 1850, virtually disappeared by 1950 and 1985. Petroleum, on the other hand, which barely registers on the 1900 graph (and not at all on the 1850 graph) has by 1985 become the dominant source of energy. One reasonable conclusion to be drawn from these data trends? As technology changes over time, the fuels of choice seem to change as well.

30. (G)

Petroleum first appears on the graph as an energy source in 1900 and accounts for an increasingly greater percentage of total energy consumption in 1950 and 1985, judging by the increasing size of the petroleum portion of the bar. The portion of the bar representing coal, on the other hand, decreases from 1900 to 1950 and again from 1950 to 1985.

31. (C)

Focus on the coal portion of each bar. Coal was an energy source in 1850, so the ability to utilize it was developed well before the 1900s—choice (A) is wrong. The graph tells you nothing about mechanized mining techniques, so choice (B) is out, too. To choose between choices (C) and (D) you have to determine if the use of coal predated natural gas or vice versa. The first time coal appears on the graph is 1850, while the first time natural gas appears on the graph is 1900. Therefore, the use of coal must have predated the use of natural gas, making (C) the correct choice.

32. (F)

The portion of the bar that includes farm animals as an energy source is over 30 percent of the total in 1850, but it gets smaller in 1900 and 1950 until it disappears altogether by 1985. Choice (F) is the correct answer.

33. (D)

Compare the bars for 1900 and 1950. Choice (A) is wrong because the number of major energy sources was the same (six) in 1900 as in 1950. Choice (B) is out for reasons discussed in the previous question. Since coal, not natural gas, has the largest portion of the bar for 1950 (as it did for 1900), choice (D) is the correct answer.

34. (F)

Statement I is supported by the graph because nuclear power, natural gas, and petroleum were all energy sources in 1985 that did not exist in 1850. The graph does not support Statements II or III, however. Coal was not the largest source of energy in 1850 or 1985, which rules out II, and there is no way to know from the graph whether there is indeed a short supply of petroleum, so III is out. This makes choice (F) the correct answer.

PASSAGE VII

The scientists conducting the two experiments in this last passage might have a little trouble with animal-rights advocates if they're not careful. They apparently spend their days chopping body parts off of starfish and watching what happens. The results are recorded in two tables. Basically, the data in Table 1 seem to indicate that the bigger the chunk of a starfish you cut off, the longer it takes for the remaining starfish to regenerate the missing part (nothing surprising there). But starfish are strange creatures, and sometimes their missing parts themselves can regenerate into full starfish. That's what Table 2 records. Here, the data indicate that the smaller the chopped-off body part, the less likely it is to regenerate into a full starfish (and the more likely it is to be dead after a year). The general lesson to be learned here is that the bigger the chunk of starfish you have left, the more likely it is that it will eventually regenerate into a whole, live starfish. Now aren't you glad to know that?

35. (B)

According to the bottom row of Table 1, 12 of the starfish that had two arms and 1/3 of their body removed were fully regenerated after six months. Since each group started out with 25 starfish, 12 out of 25 starfish, or roughly 50 percent, regenerated two entire arms and part of the central body after six months. Choice (B) is correct.

36. (J)

In Experiment 2 certain body portions of *Asterias rubens* were allowed to regenerate. The number of whole starfish was recorded at 3-month intervals over the course of a year. According to the table of the results, no starfish was regenerated when only the lower arm was present. This would support the conclusion in choice (J)—that regeneration is dependent upon the existence of a portion of the central body. The results of Experiment 1 are not relevant to this conclusion, so choice (J) is the correct answer. The conclusion in choice (H), that some starfish die from confinement in lab tanks, is not supported by the results of Experiment 2, since no healthy starfish were studied. In order to conclude that starfish die from confinement in lab tanks and not as a result of amputating portions of their bodies, the scientists would have to study starfish with intact bodies as they did in Experiment 1. You are supposed to consider only the results of Experiment 2 here, so choice (H) is not correct.

37. (C)

There is no mention of water depth in the passage, the experiments, or the results, so Statement I is out. This means that you can eliminate choices (A) and (D) since both of them include Statement I. Statement II is supported by the experimental results that show starfish can regenerate limbs they have lost (how they lose them doesn't matter). Since Statement II is true, choice (C) must be the answer. Although it would not be necessary at this point to verify that Statement III is true, the data indicate that if a body part that includes some of the central body is broken off from a starfish, the part will regenerate to become an entirely new, separate starfish. This would increase the population of starfish, so Statement III is correct.

38. (F)

Look back quickly at Table 1. The starfish in the first group were whole throughout the experiment—nothing was chopped off, in other words. The group acted as a control for the experiment in that the effect of the artificial environment could be measured apart from the effect of amputation. Three intact starfish in Group 1 died solely from being kept in lab tanks. If this group had not been included in the experiment, the deaths of starfish in other groups would have been attributed solely to the effect of amputation. Choice (F) is the correct answer.

39. (D)

As the question indicates, the sum of fully regenerated starfish plus dead starfish does not equal 25 for the last two rows of Table 2. Partially regenerated, iving starfish would be omitted from this count, which makes choice (D) the correct explanation.

40. (G)

You know from Experiment 2 that starfish body parts can regenerate into whole starfish over time as long as there is a portion of the central body present. Immediate skyrocketing of the population (F) is not possible due to the amount of time it takes for starfish to regenerate. Choice (J) is wrong because some pieces will not contain portions of the central body and therefore will not regenerate. Choice (G) takes the time factor into account as well as the evidence from Experiment 2 that some pieces do not undergo regeneration, so choice (G) is the correct answer.

WRITING TEST

MODEL ESSAY

Below is an example of what a high-scoring essay might look like. Notice the author states her position clearly in the introductory paragraph and supports that position with evidence in the following paragraphs. This essay also uses transitions, some advanced vocabulary, and an effective "hook" to draw in the reader.

When people think about what students should learn in high school, they often focus on "the three Rs": reading, writing, and arithmetic. It's true that in an increasingly competitive global economy, those skills are more important than ever. However, in our society's rush to make sure students are keeping up through required standardized testing and increased computer education, are we forgetting another important aspect of education? Are we forgetting to teach our students how to think creatively and express themselves artistically? I think that requiring all high school students to take music or visual arts classes would benefit our country's students in several ways.

Learning about art and music actually helps students do better in other subjects. People often forget that studying art or music isn't just about putting paint to canvas or lips to trumpet. There is a lot of background information that students learn as well. When students study music they also have to learn a lot of history: who was the composer, where was he or she from, what was happening politically and socially during the time the music was composed, and how does the work compare historically to music by other composers. The same holds true for the visual arts; students can learn a lot from art history, not just about the artist but also about different cultures and time periods. Studies have shown that students who take music classes do better at math, maybe because these classes emphasize dividing up measures of music and counting out times.

With so much focus on standardized test scores and grade point averages, schools today emphasize individual academic performance and overlook the teaching of teamwork skills. Through playing in my high school's band, I have learned that even though it is important for me to practice so that I can play my best (and maybe move up a chair), what really matters is how we sound as a group. My bandmates and I push each other to succeed, and we get together outside of school to practice for big games and competitions. Band is also where I have made most of my friends. Participation in the arts is a great way for students to build social skills and create school spirit. It teaches students to help one another so that going to school isn't just about getting good grades for one's own benefit.

Learning about art or music is also helpful to students because it teaches them how to think creatively. When you take a photograph or paint a portrait you have to look at things in a new way, and you must try to synthesize your perception into a medium that other people can relate to. Between all the pressure to do well academically and all the social pressure teenagers face to fit in, being a teenager can be really stressful. Art and music can allow students to express their feelings in a positive, constructive way. Such classes can give students who aren't good at traditional academic subjects like math or science a chance to shine.

In conclusion, I think requiring all high school students to take music or visual arts classes would help students not only academically but socially and emotionally as well. Studying the arts actually helps students succeed in traditional subject areas, builds their confidence and social skills, and gives them the opportunity to learn to think creatively, all skills that will help them once they reach the workforce.

You can evaluate your essay and the model essay based on the following criteria, covered in chapter 16.

- Does the author answer the question?
- Is the author's position clearly stated?
- Does the body of the essay support and develop the position taken?
- Are there at least three supporting paragraphs?
- Is the relevance of each supporting paragraph clear?
- Is the essay a reasonable length?
- Is the essay organized, with a clear introduction, middle, and end?
- Did the author use one paragraph for each new idea?
- Is each sentence in a paragraph relevant to the point made in that paragraph?
- Are transitions clear?
- Is the essay easy to read? Is it engaging?
- Are sentences varied?
- Is vocabulary used effectively? Is college-level vocabulary used?

PRACTICE TEST TWO

ACT Practice Test Two
Answer Sheet

English Test

10. Ⓕ Ⓖ Ⓗ Ⓙ   20. Ⓕ Ⓖ Ⓗ Ⓙ   30. Ⓕ Ⓖ Ⓗ Ⓙ   40. Ⓕ Ⓖ Ⓗ Ⓙ   50. Ⓕ Ⓖ Ⓗ Ⓙ   60. Ⓕ Ⓖ Ⓗ Ⓙ   70. Ⓕ Ⓖ Ⓗ Ⓙ
1. Ⓐ Ⓑ Ⓒ Ⓓ   11. Ⓐ Ⓑ Ⓒ Ⓓ   21. Ⓐ Ⓑ Ⓒ Ⓓ   31. Ⓐ Ⓑ Ⓒ Ⓓ   41. Ⓐ Ⓑ Ⓒ Ⓓ   51. Ⓐ Ⓑ Ⓒ Ⓓ   61. Ⓐ Ⓑ Ⓒ Ⓓ   71. Ⓐ Ⓑ Ⓒ Ⓓ
2. Ⓕ Ⓖ Ⓗ Ⓙ   12. Ⓕ Ⓖ Ⓗ Ⓙ   22. Ⓕ Ⓖ Ⓗ Ⓙ   32. Ⓕ Ⓖ Ⓗ Ⓙ   42. Ⓕ Ⓖ Ⓗ Ⓙ   52. Ⓕ Ⓖ Ⓗ Ⓙ   62. Ⓕ Ⓖ Ⓗ Ⓙ   72. Ⓕ Ⓖ Ⓗ Ⓙ
3. Ⓐ Ⓑ Ⓒ Ⓓ   13. Ⓐ Ⓑ Ⓒ Ⓓ   23. Ⓐ Ⓑ Ⓒ Ⓓ   33. Ⓐ Ⓑ Ⓒ Ⓓ   43. Ⓐ Ⓑ Ⓒ Ⓓ   53. Ⓐ Ⓑ Ⓒ Ⓓ   63. Ⓐ Ⓑ Ⓒ Ⓓ   73. Ⓐ Ⓑ Ⓒ Ⓓ
4. Ⓕ Ⓖ Ⓗ Ⓙ   14. Ⓕ Ⓖ Ⓗ Ⓙ   24. Ⓕ Ⓖ Ⓗ Ⓙ   34. Ⓕ Ⓖ Ⓗ Ⓙ   44. Ⓕ Ⓖ Ⓗ Ⓙ   54. Ⓕ Ⓖ Ⓗ Ⓙ   64. Ⓕ Ⓖ Ⓗ Ⓙ   74. Ⓕ Ⓖ Ⓗ Ⓙ
5. Ⓐ Ⓑ Ⓒ Ⓓ   15. Ⓐ Ⓑ Ⓒ Ⓓ   25. Ⓐ Ⓑ Ⓒ Ⓓ   35. Ⓐ Ⓑ Ⓒ Ⓓ   45. Ⓐ Ⓑ Ⓒ Ⓓ   55. Ⓐ Ⓑ Ⓒ Ⓓ   65. Ⓐ Ⓑ Ⓒ Ⓓ   75. Ⓐ Ⓑ Ⓒ Ⓓ
6. Ⓕ Ⓖ Ⓗ Ⓙ   16. Ⓕ Ⓖ Ⓗ Ⓙ   26. Ⓕ Ⓖ Ⓗ Ⓙ   36. Ⓕ Ⓖ Ⓗ Ⓙ   46. Ⓕ Ⓖ Ⓗ Ⓙ   56. Ⓕ Ⓖ Ⓗ Ⓙ   66. Ⓕ Ⓖ Ⓗ Ⓙ
7. Ⓐ Ⓑ Ⓒ Ⓓ   17. Ⓐ Ⓑ Ⓒ Ⓓ   27. Ⓐ Ⓑ Ⓒ Ⓓ   37. Ⓐ Ⓑ Ⓒ Ⓓ   47. Ⓐ Ⓑ Ⓒ Ⓓ   57. Ⓐ Ⓑ Ⓒ Ⓓ   67. Ⓐ Ⓑ Ⓒ Ⓓ
8. Ⓕ Ⓖ Ⓗ Ⓙ   18. Ⓕ Ⓖ Ⓗ Ⓙ   28. Ⓕ Ⓖ Ⓗ Ⓙ   38. Ⓕ Ⓖ Ⓗ Ⓙ   48. Ⓕ Ⓖ Ⓗ Ⓙ   58. Ⓕ Ⓖ Ⓗ Ⓙ   68. Ⓕ Ⓖ Ⓗ Ⓙ
9. Ⓐ Ⓑ Ⓒ Ⓓ   19. Ⓐ Ⓑ Ⓒ Ⓓ   29. Ⓐ Ⓑ Ⓒ Ⓓ   39. Ⓐ Ⓑ Ⓒ Ⓓ   49. Ⓐ Ⓑ Ⓒ Ⓓ   59. Ⓐ Ⓑ Ⓒ Ⓓ   69. Ⓐ Ⓑ Ⓒ Ⓓ

Math Test

9. Ⓐ Ⓑ Ⓒ Ⓓ Ⓔ   18. Ⓕ Ⓖ Ⓗ Ⓙ Ⓚ   27. Ⓐ Ⓑ Ⓒ Ⓓ Ⓔ   36. Ⓕ Ⓖ Ⓗ Ⓙ Ⓚ   45. Ⓐ Ⓑ Ⓒ Ⓓ Ⓔ   54. Ⓕ Ⓖ Ⓗ Ⓙ Ⓚ
1. Ⓐ Ⓑ Ⓒ Ⓓ Ⓔ   10. Ⓕ Ⓖ Ⓗ Ⓙ Ⓚ   19. Ⓐ Ⓑ Ⓒ Ⓓ Ⓔ   28. Ⓕ Ⓖ Ⓗ Ⓙ Ⓚ   37. Ⓐ Ⓑ Ⓒ Ⓓ Ⓔ   46. Ⓕ Ⓖ Ⓗ Ⓙ Ⓚ   55. Ⓐ Ⓑ Ⓒ Ⓓ Ⓔ
2. Ⓕ Ⓖ Ⓗ Ⓙ Ⓚ   11. Ⓐ Ⓑ Ⓒ Ⓓ Ⓔ   20. Ⓕ Ⓖ Ⓗ Ⓙ Ⓚ   29. Ⓐ Ⓑ Ⓒ Ⓓ Ⓔ   38. Ⓕ Ⓖ Ⓗ Ⓙ Ⓚ   47. Ⓐ Ⓑ Ⓒ Ⓓ Ⓔ   56. Ⓕ Ⓖ Ⓗ Ⓙ Ⓚ
3. Ⓐ Ⓑ Ⓒ Ⓓ Ⓔ   12. Ⓕ Ⓖ Ⓗ Ⓙ Ⓚ   21. Ⓐ Ⓑ Ⓒ Ⓓ Ⓔ   30. Ⓕ Ⓖ Ⓗ Ⓙ Ⓚ   39. Ⓐ Ⓑ Ⓒ Ⓓ Ⓔ   48. Ⓕ Ⓖ Ⓗ Ⓙ Ⓚ   57. Ⓐ Ⓑ Ⓒ Ⓓ Ⓔ
4. Ⓕ Ⓖ Ⓗ Ⓙ Ⓚ   13. Ⓐ Ⓑ Ⓒ Ⓓ Ⓔ   22. Ⓕ Ⓖ Ⓗ Ⓙ Ⓚ   31. Ⓐ Ⓑ Ⓒ Ⓓ Ⓔ   40. Ⓕ Ⓖ Ⓗ Ⓙ Ⓚ   49. Ⓐ Ⓑ Ⓒ Ⓓ Ⓔ   58. Ⓕ Ⓖ Ⓗ Ⓙ Ⓚ
5. Ⓐ Ⓑ Ⓒ Ⓓ Ⓔ   14. Ⓕ Ⓖ Ⓗ Ⓙ Ⓚ   23. Ⓐ Ⓑ Ⓒ Ⓓ Ⓔ   32. Ⓕ Ⓖ Ⓗ Ⓙ Ⓚ   41. Ⓐ Ⓑ Ⓒ Ⓓ Ⓔ   50. Ⓕ Ⓖ Ⓗ Ⓙ Ⓚ   59. Ⓐ Ⓑ Ⓒ Ⓓ Ⓔ
6. Ⓕ Ⓖ Ⓗ Ⓙ Ⓚ   15. Ⓐ Ⓑ Ⓒ Ⓓ Ⓔ   24. Ⓕ Ⓖ Ⓗ Ⓙ Ⓚ   33. Ⓐ Ⓑ Ⓒ Ⓓ Ⓔ   42. Ⓕ Ⓖ Ⓗ Ⓙ Ⓚ   51. Ⓐ Ⓑ Ⓒ Ⓓ Ⓔ   60. Ⓕ Ⓖ Ⓗ Ⓙ Ⓚ
7. Ⓐ Ⓑ Ⓒ Ⓓ Ⓔ   16. Ⓕ Ⓖ Ⓗ Ⓙ Ⓚ   25. Ⓐ Ⓑ Ⓒ Ⓓ Ⓔ   34. Ⓕ Ⓖ Ⓗ Ⓙ Ⓚ   43. Ⓐ Ⓑ Ⓒ Ⓓ Ⓔ   52. Ⓕ Ⓖ Ⓗ Ⓙ Ⓚ
8. Ⓕ Ⓖ Ⓗ Ⓙ Ⓚ   17. Ⓐ Ⓑ Ⓒ Ⓓ Ⓔ   26. Ⓕ Ⓖ Ⓗ Ⓙ Ⓚ   35. Ⓐ Ⓑ Ⓒ Ⓓ Ⓔ   44. Ⓕ Ⓖ Ⓗ Ⓙ Ⓚ   53. Ⓐ Ⓑ Ⓒ Ⓓ Ⓔ

Reading Test

6. Ⓕ Ⓖ Ⓗ Ⓙ   12. Ⓕ Ⓖ Ⓗ Ⓙ   18. Ⓕ Ⓖ Ⓗ Ⓙ   24. Ⓕ Ⓖ Ⓗ Ⓙ   30. Ⓕ Ⓖ Ⓗ Ⓙ   36. Ⓕ Ⓖ Ⓗ Ⓙ
1. Ⓐ Ⓑ Ⓒ Ⓓ   7. Ⓐ Ⓑ Ⓒ Ⓓ   13. Ⓐ Ⓑ Ⓒ Ⓓ   19. Ⓐ Ⓑ Ⓒ Ⓓ   25. Ⓐ Ⓑ Ⓒ Ⓓ   31. Ⓐ Ⓑ Ⓒ Ⓓ   37. Ⓐ Ⓑ Ⓒ Ⓓ
2. Ⓕ Ⓖ Ⓗ Ⓙ   8. Ⓕ Ⓖ Ⓗ Ⓙ   14. Ⓕ Ⓖ Ⓗ Ⓙ   20. Ⓕ Ⓖ Ⓗ Ⓙ   26. Ⓕ Ⓖ Ⓗ Ⓙ   32. Ⓕ Ⓖ Ⓗ Ⓙ   38. Ⓕ Ⓖ Ⓗ Ⓙ
3. Ⓐ Ⓑ Ⓒ Ⓓ   9. Ⓐ Ⓑ Ⓒ Ⓓ   15. Ⓐ Ⓑ Ⓒ Ⓓ   21. Ⓐ Ⓑ Ⓒ Ⓓ   27. Ⓐ Ⓑ Ⓒ Ⓓ   33. Ⓐ Ⓑ Ⓒ Ⓓ   39. Ⓐ Ⓑ Ⓒ Ⓓ
4. Ⓕ Ⓖ Ⓗ Ⓙ   10. Ⓕ Ⓖ Ⓗ Ⓙ   16. Ⓕ Ⓖ Ⓗ Ⓙ   22. Ⓕ Ⓖ Ⓗ Ⓙ   28. Ⓕ Ⓖ Ⓗ Ⓙ   34. Ⓕ Ⓖ Ⓗ Ⓙ   40. Ⓕ Ⓖ Ⓗ Ⓙ
5. Ⓐ Ⓑ Ⓒ Ⓓ   11. Ⓐ Ⓑ Ⓒ Ⓓ   17. Ⓐ Ⓑ Ⓒ Ⓓ   23. Ⓐ Ⓑ Ⓒ Ⓓ   29. Ⓐ Ⓑ Ⓒ Ⓓ   35. Ⓐ Ⓑ Ⓒ Ⓓ

Science Test

6. Ⓕ Ⓖ Ⓗ Ⓙ   12. Ⓕ Ⓖ Ⓗ Ⓙ   18. Ⓕ Ⓖ Ⓗ Ⓙ   24. Ⓕ Ⓖ Ⓗ Ⓙ   30. Ⓕ Ⓖ Ⓗ Ⓙ   36. Ⓕ Ⓖ Ⓗ Ⓙ
1. Ⓐ Ⓑ Ⓒ Ⓓ   7. Ⓐ Ⓑ Ⓒ Ⓓ   13. Ⓐ Ⓑ Ⓒ Ⓓ   19. Ⓐ Ⓑ Ⓒ Ⓓ   25. Ⓐ Ⓑ Ⓒ Ⓓ   31. Ⓐ Ⓑ Ⓒ Ⓓ   37. Ⓐ Ⓑ Ⓒ Ⓓ
2. Ⓕ Ⓖ Ⓗ Ⓙ   8. Ⓕ Ⓖ Ⓗ Ⓙ   14. Ⓕ Ⓖ Ⓗ Ⓙ   20. Ⓕ Ⓖ Ⓗ Ⓙ   26. Ⓕ Ⓖ Ⓗ Ⓙ   32. Ⓕ Ⓖ Ⓗ Ⓙ   38. Ⓕ Ⓖ Ⓗ Ⓙ
3. Ⓐ Ⓑ Ⓒ Ⓓ   9. Ⓐ Ⓑ Ⓒ Ⓓ   15. Ⓐ Ⓑ Ⓒ Ⓓ   21. Ⓐ Ⓑ Ⓒ Ⓓ   27. Ⓐ Ⓑ Ⓒ Ⓓ   33. Ⓐ Ⓑ Ⓒ Ⓓ   39. Ⓐ Ⓑ Ⓒ Ⓓ
4. Ⓕ Ⓖ Ⓗ Ⓙ   10. Ⓕ Ⓖ Ⓗ Ⓙ   16. Ⓕ Ⓖ Ⓗ Ⓙ   22. Ⓕ Ⓖ Ⓗ Ⓙ   28. Ⓕ Ⓖ Ⓗ Ⓙ   34. Ⓕ Ⓖ Ⓗ Ⓙ   40. Ⓕ Ⓖ Ⓗ Ⓙ
5. Ⓐ Ⓑ Ⓒ Ⓓ   11. Ⓐ Ⓑ Ⓒ Ⓓ   17. Ⓐ Ⓑ Ⓒ Ⓓ   23. Ⓐ Ⓑ Ⓒ Ⓓ   29. Ⓐ Ⓑ Ⓒ Ⓓ   35. Ⓐ Ⓑ Ⓒ Ⓓ

ENGLISH TEST

45 Minutes—75 Questions

Directions: In the following passage, certain words and phrases have been underlined and numbered. You will find alternatives for each underlined portion in the corresponding questions and answer choices. Select the one that best expresses the idea, that makes the sentence acceptable in standard written English, or that is phrased most consistently with the style and tone of the entire passage. If you feel that the original version is best, select "NO CHANGE." You will also find questions asking about a section of the passage or the entire passage. For each question in the test, select the best choice. You may wish to read the passage through before you begin to answer questions associated with it. Most answers cannot be determined without reading several sentences around the phrases in question. Make sure to read far enough ahead each time you choose an alternative.

PASSAGE I

Until three years ago, I had never considered myself to be athletically talented. I have never been able to hit, catch, throw, or kick a ball with any degree of confidence or accuracy. For years, physical <u>education being</u> often the worst part of the school day

1

for me. Units on tennis, touch football, volleyball, and basketball were torturous. I not only dreaded fumbling a pass, <u>so</u> I also feared being hit in the face by a ball.

2

However, at the beginning of my freshman year of high school, my attitude toward sports changed.

Somehow, my good friend Gretchen convinced me to join <u>our schools</u> swim team. <u>Knowing that I enjoyed</u>

3   4

<u>swimming, over the course of two summers, it was</u>

4

<u>with Gretchen that I practically had lived at the pool.</u>

4

1. A. NO CHANGE
   B. education, was
   C. education was
   D. education,

2. F. NO CHANGE
   G. and
   H. but
   J. though

3. A. NO CHANGE
   B. our schools'
   C. our school's
   D. ours school

4. F. NO CHANGE
   G. Because we had spent two summers practically living at the pool, it was Gretchen who knew that swimming was enjoyed by me.
   H. Having practically lived at the pool over two summers, the two of us, Gretchen knew it was swimming that I enjoyed.
   J. Gretchen knew I enjoyed swimming, as we had spent two summers practically living at the pool.

GO ON TO THE NEXT PAGE →

My mother had <u>insisted</u> that I take swimming lessons
         5
every summer since I was seven, so I was entirely

comfortable in the water. I also was eager to start my

high school experience with a new challenge and a new

way to think of myself.

Of course, I had no idea what I was getting into when

Gretchen and I showed up for the first day of practice.

The team was made up of twenty young <u>women, most</u>
                                                 6
<u>of these swimmers</u> had been participating in the
       6
community swim team for years. I couldn't do a flip

turn at the end of the lane without getting water up my

nose. In contrast, most of the other swimmers, who

<u>had been swimming competitively, since elementary</u>
                        7
<u>school</u>, were able to gracefully somersault and begin
   7
the next lap. By the end of the first hour of practice, I

was exhausted and waterlogged.

However, I had no intention of <u>giving up, which</u>
                                           8
<u>would mean quitting</u>. I came back the next day and the
       8
next day for practice. Things <u>begun</u> to get serious in the
                              9
second week, when we started the regular schedule of

four early morning and five afternoon practices. Our

5. Of the four choices, which is the only one that
   does NOT indicate that the narrator's mother
   decided that the narrator must take swimming
   lessons?
   A. NO CHANGE
   B. suggested
   C. required
   D. demanded

6. F. NO CHANGE
   G. women, the majority of them
   H. women most of them
   J. women, most of whom

7. A. NO CHANGE
   B. had been swimming competitively since
       elementary school,
   C. had been swimming, competitively since
       elementary school,
   D. had been swimming competitively since
       elementary school

8. F. NO CHANGE
   G. giving up and resigning myself to failure.
   H. giving up and quitting what I had set out
       to do.
   J. giving up.

9. A. NO CHANGE
   B. had been begun
   C. had began
   D. began

GO ON TO THE NEXT PAGE ⇒

coach, whom had led the team to several state
         10
championships, demanded dedication from everyone

on the team. The hard work eventually paid off. By
                               11
the end of the first month, I had discovered that I was

good at the butterfly, a relatively new stroke that was
                        12
first introduced in the 1930s. I rarely won individual
         12
races, but I made a solid member of our team's medley
                                          13
relay.

  13

After that intimidating first season, I continued

swimming. I even will have earned a varsity letter last
                   14
year. Now I'm hoping to earn a spot in the state

competition my senior year. 15

10. F.   NO CHANGE
     G.   for whom
     H.   who
     J.   which

11. A.   NO CHANGE
     B.   eventually paid off, so, as a result
     C.   paid off eventually, however, by
     D.   paid off, eventually, by

12. Assuming each of the following creates a true
     statement, which provides the information
     most relevant to the narrator's experience on
     the swim team?
     F.   NO CHANGE
     G.   a difficult stroke that interested few other
          members of our team.
     H.   which is faster than the backstroke but
          somewhat slower than the crawl.
     J.   which is still sometimes called the dol-
          phin because it incorporates a two-stroke
          dolphin kick.

13. A.   NO CHANGE
     B.   team's medley relay (it consists of four
          swimmers).
     C.   team's medley relay, which the person
          swimming backstroke always begins.
     D.   team.

14. F.   NO CHANGE
     G.   would have earned
     H.   earned
     J.   earn

15. If inserted here, which of the following would
     be the most appropriate sentence to conclude
     the essay?
     A.   My coach continues to schedule
          demanding practices, but I have come to
          enjoy the early morning swims.
     B.   For someone who thought she didn't
          have any athletic talent, I have come a
          long way.
     C.   Gretchen is also still on the team, but she
          does not swim the medley relay.
     D.   I've always enjoyed swimming, so I'm
          not all that surprised by my success as an
          athlete.

GO ON TO THE NEXT PAGE →

PASSAGE II

[1]

One lazy day last summer, my parents decided that my younger sister and I needed a break from our vacation from academics. They took us to the National Mississippi River Museum and Aquarium in Dubuque, Iowa. I was prepared to be bored by this family educational trip. However, from the first moment I walked through the museum's doors, I was captivated; by
16
all that there was to learn about life in the Mississippi.

[2]

[1] A large tank stocked with fish and turtles was there to greet us as we walked into the main hall.
17
[2] There were also animals I had never before glimpsed, such as a fish called the long-nosed gar. [3] I was amazed by this fish in particular. [4] Its long, tubular shape and distinctive rod-shaped nose that made it
18
appear like something that lived in the dark depths of the ocean. [5] This first of five freshwater aquariums offered a close-up view of familiar animals that I had
19
seen before, such as ducks. [20]
19

16. F. NO CHANGE
    G. captivated, by
    H. captivated by,
    J. captivated by

17. A. NO CHANGE
    B. is there
    C. are there
    D. were there

18. F. NO CHANGE
    G. nose, which
    H. nose, and this
    J. nose

19. A. NO CHANGE
    B. animals that were familiar sights to me,
    C. familiar animals to which I was no stranger,
    D. familiar animals,

20. To make Paragraph 2 coherent and logical, the best placement of Sentence 5 is:
    F. where it is now.
    G. before Sentence 1.
    H. after Sentence 1.
    J. after Sentence 2.

GO ON TO THE NEXT PAGE ⇒

[3]

In the next aquarium, I see a catfish bigger than I had
                                        21
ever imagined this species could be. According to the

posted information, this specimen weighed more than

100 pounds. With its long whiskers and slow, lazy

movements, this catfish looked like the grandfather of

all the other fish in the tank.

[4]

I couldn't decide which I liked better, the catfish or the
                                                        22
long-nosed gar. The next floor-to-ceiling tank, which
      22
represented the ecosystem of the Mississippi bayou,

held an animal I had never seen: an alligator. At first, I

had a hard time spotting the creature—it blended in

almost completely with a half-submerged log. 23

Suddenly, though, it slides into the water and aims
                                        24
itself right at the glass separating me from its ferocious

claws and skin-tearing teeth. I had a slightly moment
                                               25
of panic before I remembered that, try as it might, this

alligator would never successfully hunt tourists like me.

As much of the onlookers squealed in delight as the
      26
alligator moved through the tank, I noticed his

companion. Far off in a corner slept an enormous

snapping turtle. I could imagine no better roommate

for the alligator than this hook-beaked turtle with

rough ridges running along its shell.

21. A. NO CHANGE
    B. had been seeing
    C. saw
    D. spot

22. Which sentence most effectively connects this
    paragraph to the preceding paragraph?
    F. NO CHANGE
    G. Although the catfish was impressive, it
       was not the biggest animal on display in
       the museum.
    H. After seeing the catfish, I was interested in
       exhibits that were a bit more hands-on.
    J. Until my visit to the museum, I had never
       really considered what the Mississippi
       River was like south of my home.

23. At this point, the writer is considering
    removing the following phrase:
    —it blended in almost completely with a half-
      submerged log.
    The primary effect of removing this phrase
    would be:
    A. a smoother transition between sentences.
    B. a greater contrast between images.
    C. the loss of descriptive information.
    D. an increased level of suspense.

24. F. NO CHANGE
    G. slides into the water to aim
    H. slid into the water and aiming
    J. slid into the water and aimed

25. A. NO CHANGE
    B. momentarily slight
    C. slight moment
    D. slight momentarily

26. F. NO CHANGE
    G. a large amount
    H. the many
    J. many

GO ON TO THE NEXT PAGE ⟩

[5]

Despite my initial expectations, I happily spent the entire day soaking up information about creatures that live in the Mississippi River. In one section of the museum, I held a crayfish. [27] Later, I had the opportunity to touch the cool, sleek skin of a stingray, which can be found where the Mississippi empties into the Gulf of Mexico.

[6]

After seeing all, I could inside the museum, I
                    28
wandered outside, only to find even more exhibits.

Having just enough time, it was that I was able to see
                    29
the otters and watch a riverboat launching, but it was closing time before I was able to see the most impressive thing the museum had to offer. A football-field-sized steamboat from the 1930s is open to tourists. And operates as a "Boat and Breakfast" that
        30
hosts overnight guests. I'm hoping that my family will plan another educational trip to Dubuque soon so I can experience life on a steamboat.

27. The writer would like to insert a sentence describing the appearance of the crayfish at this point. Which sentence would best accomplish the writer's goal?
   A. Also know as crawdads, crayfish are close relatives of the lobsters that live in "freshwater" one word.
   B. At an average length of about three inches, the crayfish looks like a miniature lobster, complete with small but effective front pincers.
   C. Although they are found throughout the United States, crayfish populations are densest in Kentucky and Mississippi.
   D. At first I was a bit nervous to touch the small creature, but then I relaxed and enjoyed the opportunity to look at it so closely.

28. F. NO CHANGE
   G. all I could inside the museum,
   H. all, I could inside the museum
   J. all I could inside the museum

29. A. NO CHANGE
   B. It was that I had just enough time, so I was able
   C. Having just enough time, it was possible
   D. I had just enough time

30. F. NO CHANGE
   G. tourists and that operates
   H. tourists, it operates
   J. tourists and

GO ON TO THE NEXT PAGE

PASSAGE III

> The paragraphs in this essay may or may not follow the most logical order. Each paragraph is numbered, and question 45 will ask you to determine the best placement of Paragraph 6.

[1]

Although secret identities and elaborate disguises are typically associated with the world of spies and villains, it has other uses. For six years Ruth Reichl the
                                                31   32
restaurant critic for *The New York Times*, used aliases
                                        32
and costumes as a regular part of her job.

[2]

Dining is big business in New York City, from the neighborhood noodle shops and diners to the upscale steak houses and four-star French restaurants. [33]

Many of the more than one million people who read *The Times* each day look to it for advice on where to
                                           34

31. A. NO CHANGE
    B. it does have
    C. they do have
    D. and they have

32. F. NO CHANGE
    G. Reichl, the restaurant critic, for
       The New York Times,
    H. Reichl, the restaurant critic for
       The New York Times,
    J. Reichl the restaurant critic for
       The New York Times

33. Should the following sentence be inserted into the passage at this point?
    The legendary French restaurant Le Bernardin received a four-star rating from *The Times* shortly after opening in 1986, an honor it has maintained ever since.
    A. Yes, because the added sentence emphasizes how important a positive review from *The Times* can be.
    B. Yes, because the specific information helps the reader develop a clearer picture of the type of restaurant reviewed by *The Times*.
    C. No, because it is unclear whether Reichl was responsible for reviewing this specific restaurant.
    D. No, because the specific information about one restaurant leads the reader away from the main topic of the essay.

34. F. NO CHANGE
    G. look with
    H. look by
    J. looking to

GO ON TO THE NEXT PAGE

eat. A positive review from *The Times* could have
                                          35

brought a restaurant unimagined success and
  35

month-long waiting lists for reservations. A negative

review, on the other hand, can undermine a

restaurant's popularity and seriously cut into its profits.

Obviously, restaurant owners and workers have a lot at
                    36

stake when the restaurant critic for *The Times* walks in

the door. Waiters and chefs often pull out all of the

stops to impress the writer that the meal can make or
                              37

break a restaurant.

[3]

Reichl was acutely aware that she received special
                                          38

treatment once restaurant staff recognized her. She
  38

would be graciously greeted and led to the best table in

the restaurant, offered dishes prepared specially by the

head chef, and given multiple courses of amazing

desserts. In other words, the dining experience of the

restaurant critic was nothing like that of the commonly
                                                39

ordinary person walking in from the street.
  39

35. A.   NO CHANGE
    B.   can bring
    C.   will have brought
    D.   will be bringing

36. F.   NO CHANGE
    G.   restaurant owners and workers;
    H.   restaurant, owners and workers
    J.   restaurant owners, and workers

37. A.   NO CHANGE
    B.   who's
    C.   whose
    D.   which

38. F.   NO CHANGE
    G.   special treatment was received by her
    H.   she was the recipient of special treatment
    J.   she was in the position of receiving spe-
         cial treatment

39. A.   NO CHANGE
    B.   common, representative, and average
    C.   typical
    D.   extravagant

GO ON TO THE NEXT PAGE

[4]

To remedy this, <u>Reichl decided a solution would be</u>
<u>40</u>
to become, for short periods of time, someone else.

<u>Transforming herself into different personas, Reichl</u>
<u>41</u>
<u>used wigs, special makeup, and carefully selected</u>
<u>41</u>
<u>clothing,</u> such as an attractive blonde named Chloe, a
41
redhead named Brenda, and an older woman named

Betty. 42

40. F. NO CHANGE
   G. she created a solution to the problem by becoming
   H. Reichl decided to become
   J. Reichl found a way to fix the problem, which involved becoming

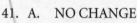

41. A. NO CHANGE
   B. With wigs, special makeup, and carefully selected clothing, Reichl transformed herself into different personas,
   C. Transformed with wigs, special makeup, and carefully selected clothing, Reichl's different personas,
   D. Reichl used wigs, special makeup, and carefully selected clothing, that transformed herself into different personas,

42. Which of the following true statements would make the most effective and logical conclusion for Paragraph 4?
   F. Reichl found that she could quickly disguise herself as Betty, but it took more time to become Chloe.
   G. Her true identity hidden, Reichl would then dine at a restaurant she was currently evaluating.
   H. After six years at *The Times*, Reichl moved on to become the editor of *Gourmet* magazine.
   J. The former restaurant critic for *The Times* did not always agree with Reichl's methods or her selection of restaurants to review.

GO ON TO THE NEXT PAGE ⟩

[5]

Sometimes, Reichl developed a different view about

the quality when she was not treated like a very important

person <u>of a restaurant</u>. Indeed, the difference between
        43

the treatment she received as herself and as one of her

characters was occasionally so great that Reichl would

revise her initial impression of a restaurant and write a

more negative review. 44

[6]

By becoming an average customer, Reichl encouraged

even the most expensive and popular restaurants to

improve how they treated all of their customers. After

all, waiters could never be certain when they were

serving the powerful restaurant critic for *The New York*

Times.

43. For the sake of logic and coherence, the underlined portion should be placed:
    A. where it is now.
    B. after the word *developed*.
    C. after the word *view*.
    D. after the word *quality*.

44. Would deleting the word *occasionally* from the previous sentence change the meaning of the sentence?
    F. Yes, because without this word the reader would not understand that Reichl had different experiences when she dined in disguise.
    G. Yes, because without this word the reader would think that Reichl always changed her impression of restaurants when she received different treatment because she was not recognized.
    H. No, because this word repeats an idea that is already presented in the sentence.
    J. No, because this word is used only to show emphasis, and it does not contribute to the meaning of the sentence.

Question 45 asks about the passage as a whole.

45. To make the passage flow logically and smoothly, the best place for Paragraph 6 is:
    A. where it is now.
    B. after Paragraph 1.
    C. after Paragraph 3.
    D. after Paragraph 4.

GO ON TO THE NEXT PAGE

PASSAGE IV

[1]

[1] I used to start every spring with great hopes for my backyard vegetable garden. [2] After the last freeze in late March or early April, I devoted an entire weekend to preparing the soil in the garden. [3] I thinned out the rows that had too many plants and spent hours tugging out each weed that threatened to rob my little plants of the nutrients they needed to thrive. [4] Once spring truly arrived, I marked out my rows and scattered the packets of seeds that I hoped, would
46
develop into prize-winning vegetables. [5] In the first few weeks of the season, I was almost always in the garden. 47

[2]

Despite my best intentions, my garden never lived up to the vision I had for it. After I had devoted several weekends to watering and weeding, the garden always started to become more of a burden less of a hobby. By
48
July, the garden was usually in disarray, and I didn't have the energy or time to save it. July and August are
49
always the hottest parts of the year.
49

46. F.   NO CHANGE
    G.   hoped, would,
    H.   hoped would,
    J.   hoped would

47. To make Paragraph 1 more logical and coherent, Sentence 3 should be placed:

    A.   where it is now.
    B.   before Sentence 1.
    C.   after Sentence 1.
    D.   after Sentence 4.

48. F.   NO CHANGE
    G.   burden:
    H.   burden and
    J.   burden, but,

49. A.   NO CHANGE
    B.   The hottest months are July and August.
    C.   (July, along with August, provides the hottest temperatures of the year.)
    D.   OMIT the underlined portion.

GO ON TO THE NEXT PAGE

[3]

This past year, <u>however</u>, my garden was finally the
            50
success I had imagined it could be. Instead of planning

the traditional garden of closely planted <u>rows that is</u>
                                                51
<u>modeled after large-scale farming</u>, I tried a new
            51
technique. My new approach is called square foot

gardening.

[4]

<u>A square foot garden is designed for efficiency.</u> In a
            52
<u>traditionally</u> garden, you scatter a packet of seeds down
    53
a row. When the plants emerge, <u>they spend</u> hours
                                        54
thinning each row by pulling out at least half of what

was planted. In a square foot garden, you plant each

seed individually, so there is never a need for thinning

50. Of the following choices, which would be
    the LEAST acceptable substitution for the
    underlined word?

F. on the other hand
G. indeed
H. though
J. in contrast

51. A. NO CHANGE
    B. rows, which is modeled after large-scale
        farming,
    C. rows, which is based on the techniques
        for large-scale farming,
    D. rows,

52. Which sentence most effectively links the topic
    of Paragraph 3 to the topic of Paragraph 4?

F. NO CHANGE
G. The technique of square foot gardening
    was pioneered by Mel Bartholomew.
H. One of the benefits of a square foot
    garden is that it is less expensive to
    maintain than a traditional garden.
J. My neighbor, who always has a beautiful
    garden, introduced me to the concept of
    square foot gardening, and I have been
    grateful ever since.

53. A. NO CHANGE
    B. conventionally
    C. traditional
    D. tradition

54. F. NO CHANGE
    G. he spends
    H. people spend
    J. you spend

GO ON TO THE NEXT PAGE

<u>in the garden</u>. You create the garden plan one square
   55

foot at a time, until you have a block of sixteen squares.

Sturdy pieces of lumber <u>which could make</u> effective
                56

borders for each square. Walking paths that are at least

two feet wide separate each sixteen-square-foot garden.

The design is clean and simple, and it eliminates the

problem of getting to the rows in the middle of a large

garden. In fact, <u>you can do</u> all the weeding, watering,
        57

and harvesting from the walking paths.

[5]

    In addition to being easier to weed and water, a

square foot garden takes up much less space than a regular

garden. I was able to grow <u>an increased number of more</u>
                        58

vegetables in two square foot gardens, which took up a

total of 32 square feet, than I ever had grown in my

traditional garden, which took up 84 square feet.

Preparing the soil for the smaller space only required a

few hours instead of a whole weekend. There was so

much less weeding to do that the task never felt

overwhelming. One season of using the square garden

techniques <u>were all</u> it took for me to convert to a
          59

completely new outlook on backyard gardening.

55. A. NO CHANGE
    B. out the garden
    C. in that garden
    D. OMIT the underlined portion.

56. F. NO CHANGE
    G. that make
    H. make
    J. OMIT the underlined portion.

57. A. NO CHANGE
    B. you could have done
    C. one can do
    D. one is able to do

58. F. NO CHANGE
    G. a larger quantity of more
    H. an increased, bigger quantity
    J. more

59. A. NO CHANGE
    B. were just what
    C. was all
    D. could be

> The following question asks about the passage in its entirety.

60. If the writer had intended to write an essay detailing how to plan, prepare, and care for a square garden, would this essay meet the writer's goal?
    F. No, because the writer relies on generalities rather than specifics when describing her square garden.
    G. No, because the writer focuses on comparing two different types of gardens instead of explaining how to begin and care for one type of garden.
    H. Yes, because the writer states specific measurements for her square garden.
    J. Yes, because the writer maintains that square gardens are superior to traditional gardens.

GO ON TO THE NEXT PAGE

Passage V

[1]

Most new car owners glance briefly at the owner's manual before depositing it in the glove compartment of their new automobile. Owners may dig out their manuals when something goes <u>wrong, such as a flat tire or a flashing engine light</u> but few car owners take the
61

time to learn the basics about maintaining their new purchase. This is truly unfortunate, as a few simple and routine steps <u>improves the long-term performance of an automobile and decreases</u> the possibility of a traffic
62

accident.

[2]

One of the easiest and most overlooked maintenance steps is caring for a car's wiper blades. Most people don't <u>notice a problem</u> until the blades fail to clear the
63

windshield during a rainstorm or heavy snowfall. When a driver's <u>vision being</u> obscured, an accident is
64

more likely to happen. Replacing the <u>set</u> blades at a
65

time each year greatly reduces this risk. In addition, frequently refilling the windshield washer fluid reservoir guarantees that there will be always be enough fluid to wash away grime that accumulates on the windshield.

61. A. NO CHANGE
   B. wrong; such as a flat tire or a flashing engine light
   C. wrong, such as a flat tire, or a flashing engine light
   D. wrong, such as a flat tire or a flashing engine light,

62. F. NO CHANGE
   G. improve the long-term performance of an automobile and decreases
   H. improve the long-term performance of an automobile and decrease
   J. improves the long-term performance of an automobile and decrease

63. A. NO CHANGE
   B. notice a problem that causes trouble
   C. recognize that their wiper blades are the source of a problem
   D. realize that their blades are failing and will become a problem

64. F. NO CHANGE
   G. vision, has been
   H. vision is
   J. vision,

65. The underlined word would be most logically placed:
   A. where it is now.
   B. before the word *time*.
   C. before the word *year*.
   D. before the word *risk*.

GO ON TO THE NEXT PAGE

[3]

Much of car maintenance focuses on preventing

problems before they occur. For example, checking the

levels of coolant, oil, brake fluid, and transmission fluid

can avert serious malfunctions. <u>In general,</u> these fluids
          66

should be checked monthly and refilled whenever the

need is indicated.

66. F. NO CHANGE
    G. For generally,
    H. With usual
    J. By typically,

[4]

<u>Cars are becoming more sophisticated every year, but</u>
                    67

<u>car owners without any expertise in mechanics can still</u>
                    67

<u>perform much of the basic upkeep of their vehicle.</u>
                    67

You should change the oil in most cars every 3,000 to

7,000 miles. This task requires a willingness to get a bit

dirty, <u>so</u> you don't have to be a mechanic to change a
      68

car's oil. Before you get started, read the oil change

<u>section, in your owner's manual</u> and collect all of the
                    69

67. Which sentence is the most effective way to
    begin Paragraph 4?

    A. NO CHANGE
    B. Changing the oil and oil filter regularly is
        another key to keeping your car's engine
        performing at its best.
    C. An entire industry now focuses on pro-
        viding regular car maintenance, such as
        changing the oil and rotating the tires.
    D. Even if you haven't read your car owner's
        manual, you probably know that your
        car needs a tune-up every so often.

68. F. NO CHANGE
    G. but
    H. for
    J. because

69. A. NO CHANGE
    B. section, in your owner's manual,
    C. section in your owner's manual;
    D. section in your owner's manual

GO ON TO THE NEXT PAGE ⟶

tools you will need. You won't need many tools, but
70
you will definitely need a car jack. Never get under
70
a car that is supported only by car jacks: you do not
71
want to risk being crushed by a car. After you've secured

the car, changing the oil is as straightforward as sliding

under the car with a drain pan to catch the oil and a

wrench to loosen the oil drain plug. Then follow the

instructions for changing the oil filter and fill the oil

pan to the recommended level with fresh oil. 72

[5]

These simple steps to maintaining the health of a car

can be done by just about anyone. However,

successfully changing a car's oil does not turn a car

owner into a repair expert. More complicated tasks,

such as adjusting a carburetor or installing new brake

pads, should be performed by a qualified auto
73
mechanic.

70. In Paragraph 4, the writer wants to provide an explanation of how to change the oil in an automobile. Which of the following would most logically fit the writer's intention for this paragraph?

F. NO CHANGE

G. need to get under the car to open the oil drain, so use car jacks to raise the car and sturdy car jack stands to support it.

H. may find it helpful to watch someone else change the oil before you try to perform the job on your own.

J. only need to follow a few basic steps in order to successfully change your car's oil.

71. A. NO CHANGE

B. jacks, you

C. jacks you

D. jacks you,

72. Paragraph 4 of the essay uses the second person (*you, your*). Revising this paragraph to remove the second-person pronouns would have the primary effect of:

F. disrupting the logical flow of the essay.

G. making Paragraph 4 more consistent with the voice used in the rest of the essay.

H. underscoring the direct advice given to the reader.

J. lightening the essay's formal tone

73. A. NO CHANGE

B. professionally completed by a qualified

C. performed by a certifiably qualified

D. undertaken by qualifying

GO ON TO THE NEXT PAGE

Questions 74–75 ask about the passage in
its entirety.

74. After reading back through the essay, the
writer decided that the following sentence
contains important information:

The owner's manual provides instructions on
how to test the levels of these different fluids
used to lubricate and cool the engine.

Logically, this sentence should be placed:

F. after the last sentence of Paragraph 2.

G. before the first sentence of Paragraph 3.

H. after the last sentence of Paragraph 3.

J. after the last sentence of Paragraph 4.

75. If the writer had intended to write an essay
persuading readers to familiarize themselves
with the basic safety features and maintenance
needs of their cars, would this essay meet the
writer's goal?

A. Yes, because the essay repeatedly encourages readers to refer to the owner's manual for their car.

B. Yes, because the essay lists many basic
maintenance steps that owners can independently accomplish.

C. No, because the essay encourages readers
to go beyond learning about the features
of their car and actually perform some
of the basic upkeep.

D. No, because the essay does not discuss a
car's safety features in any detail.

IF YOU FINISH BEFORE TIME IS CALLED, YOU MAY CHECK YOUR WORK ON
THIS SECTION ONLY. DO NOT TURN TO ANY OTHER SECTION IN THE TEST.   STOP

MATH TEST

60 Minutes—60 Questions

Directions: Solve each of the following problems, select the correct answer, and then fill in the corresponding space on your answer sheet.

Don't linger over problems that are too time-consuming. Do as many as you can, then come back to the others in the time you have remaining.

Calculator use is permitted, but some problems can best be solved without a calculator.

Note: Unless otherwise noted, all of the following should be assumed.

1. Illustrative figures are *not* necessarily drawn to scale.
2. All geometric figures lie in a plane.
3. The term *line* indicates a straight line.
4. The term *average* indicates arithmetic mean.

1. Tanya used $3\frac{3}{8}$ yards of fabric to make her dress and she used $1\frac{1}{3}$ yards of fabric to make her jacket. What was the total amount, in yards, that Tanya used for the complete outfit of dress and jacket?

   A. $4\frac{1}{8}$

   B. $4\frac{1}{6}$

   C. $4\frac{4}{11}$

   D. $4\frac{1}{2}$

   E. $4\frac{17}{24}$

DO YOUR FIGURING HERE.

2. $5x^3y^5 \times 6y^2 \times 2xy$ is equivalent to:

   F. $13x^3y^7$

   G. $13x^4y^8$

   H. $60x^3y^7$

   J. $60x^3y^{10}$

   K. $60\,x^4y^8$

GO ON TO THE NEXT PAGE

3. Brandon puts 6 percent of his $36,000 yearly salary into savings, in 12 equal monthly installments. Jacqui deposits $200 every month into savings. At the end of one full year, what is the difference, in dollars, between the amount of money that Jacqui saved and the amount of money that Brandon saved?

A. 20
B. 24
C. 240
D. 1,960
E. 2,800

4. Mikhail has received bowling scores of 190, 200, 145, and 180 so far in the state bowling tournament. What score must he receive on the fifth game to earn an average score of 180 for his 5 games?

F. 179
G. 180
H. 185
J. 200
K. Mikhail cannot earn an average of 180.

5. For steel to be considered stainless steel, it must have a minimum of 10.5 percent chromium in the metal alloy. If there is 262.5 pounds of chromium available, what is the maximum amount of stainless steel, in pounds, that can be manufactured?

A. 27.56
B. 252
C. 262.5
D. 2,500
E. 25,000

DO YOUR FIGURING HERE.

GO ON TO THE NEXT PAGE

6. A homeowner wants to put a wallpaper border on the top edge of all the walls of his kitchen. The kitchen measures 6.5 meters by 4 meters. What is the required length, in meters, of the border?

F. 8

G. 10.5

H. 13

J. 21

K. 26

DO YOUR FIGURING HERE.

7. Which expression below is equivalent to $w(x-(y+z))$?

A. $wx - wy - wz$

B. $wx - wy + wz$

C. $wx - y + z$

D. $wx - y - z$

E. $wxy + wxz$

8. Solve for n: $6n - 4 = 3n + 24$

F. 28

G. $\dfrac{28}{3}$

H. $\dfrac{28}{9}$

J. $\dfrac{20}{9}$

K. $\dfrac{3}{28}$

9. What two numbers should be placed in the blanks below so that the difference between successive entries is the same?

26, _____, _____, 53

A. 36, 43

B. 35, 44

C. 34, 45

D. 33, 46

E. 30, 49

GO ON TO THE NEXT PAGE

10. What is the real number value of $m^3 + \sqrt{12m}$ when $5m^2 = 45$?

    F. 15

    G. 27

    H. 33

    J. 38.09

    K. 739.39

11. The radius of a sphere is $3\frac{3}{5}$ meters. What is the volume of the sphere, to the nearest cubic meter? Use the formula $V = \frac{4}{3}\pi r^3$.

    A. 42

    B. 45

    C. 157

    D. 195

    E. 3,429

12. There are 10 peanuts, 6 cashews, and 8 almonds in a bag of mixed nuts. If a nut is chosen at random from the bag, what is the probability that the nut is NOT a peanut?

    F. $\frac{5}{12}$

    G. $\frac{7}{12}$

    H. $\frac{5}{7}$

    J. 10

    K. 14

DO YOUR FIGURING HERE.

GO ON TO THE NEXT PAGE

13. The number of people in the electronics store is shown in the matrix below.

Adolescents	Adults	Senior Citizens
[75	100	30]

The ratio of people from each age group who will purchase a product to the number of people in that age group in the store is shown in the following matrix:

Adolescents	$\begin{bmatrix} 0.20 \\ 0.35 \\ 0.10 \end{bmatrix}$
Adults	
Senior Citizens	

Based on the matrices, how many people will make purchases?

A.　15

B.　41

C.　53

D.　133

E.　205

DO YOUR FIGURING HERE.

GO ON TO THE NEXT PAGE

Use the following table to answer questions 14 and 15:

The table below shows the genres of radio music, broken down by the medium, (AM, FM, or satellite) on which it is aired. In addition, the table shows the number of hours in which there is a "live" disc jockey.

Genre	Medium	# Of Hours Where There Is A "Live" Disc Jockey
Classical	AM	6
	FM	3
	Satellite	12
Country	AM	24
	FM	7
	Satellite	16
News	AM	24
	FM	24
	Satellite	24
Pop	AM	14
	Satellite	5
Rock	FM	12
	Satellite	24

14. What is the average number of hours, rounded to the nearest hour, that the Country genre has a "live" disc jockey?

    F.   3

    G.   7

    H.   14

    J.   16

    K.   24

DO YOUR FIGURING HERE.

GO ON TO THE NEXT PAGE

15. The time of day in which there is a "live" disc jockey does not matter, as long as there is a "live" disc jockey for the number of hours listed in the table. Assume that a disc jockey can switch from any genre and medium to another with the flip of a switch. Based on the table above, what is the minimum number of disc jockeys needed, if each works an 8-hour shift?

A.   5
B.   13
C.   24
D.   25
E.   195

16. In the table below, every row, column, and diagonal must have equivalent sums. What is the value of the lower left cell in order for this to be true?

m	$-4m$	$3m$
$2m$	0	$-2m$
	$4m$	$-m$

F. $-4m$
G. $-3m$
H. -3
J. 0
K. m

DO YOUR FIGURING HERE.

GO ON TO THE NEXT PAGE

17. The standard coordinate plane is shown
    below, with the four quadrants labeled. Point
    R, denoted by $R(x, y)$ is graphed on this plane,
    such that $x \neq 0$ and $y \neq 0$.

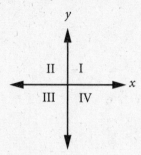

    If the product xy is a positive number, then
    point R is located in:

    A. Quadrant I only
    B. Quadrant II only
    C. Quadrant III only
    D. Quadrant I or IV only
    E. Quadrant I or III only

18. The cafeteria offers 7 different sandwiches, 3
    different soups, and 4 different drink choices
    on the luncheon menu. How many distinct
    meals are available if a meal consists of one
    sandwich, one soup, and one drink?

    F. 7
    G. 14
    H. 21
    J. 84
    K. Cannot be determined by the given
        information.

19. At the university there are 5 females for every
    3 males. If there are 6,000 male students, how
    many students are female?

    A. 10,000
    B. 12,000
    C. 16,000
    D. 18,000
    E. 30,000

DO YOUR FIGURING HERE.

GO ON TO THE NEXT PAGE

20. What is the length, in inches, of the diagonal of a rectangle whose dimensions are 16 inches by 30 inches?

DO YOUR FIGURING HERE.

F.   25
G.   23
H.   34
J.   578
K.   1,156

21. Which of the following expressions is NOT equivalent to $5n + 1$?

A. $\dfrac{1}{5n+1}$

B. $5(n + 2) - 9$

C. $\dfrac{1}{\dfrac{1}{5n+1}}$

D. $\dfrac{5n^2 + n}{n}$

E. $\dfrac{25n^2 - 1}{5n - 1}$

22. Which of the following equations is equivalent to $3x + 2y = 16$?

F. $y = -\dfrac{3}{2}x + 16$

G. $y = -\dfrac{2}{3}x + 8$

H. $y = \dfrac{3}{2}x + 8$

J. $y = -\dfrac{3}{2}x + 8$

K. $y = -\dfrac{2}{3}x + 8$

23. A solution to the equation $x^2 - 20x + 75 = 0$ is:

A. -15
B. -5
C. 0
D. 3
E. 5

GO ON TO THE NEXT PAGE

24. Given right triangle △*LMN* below, what is the value of cos *N*?

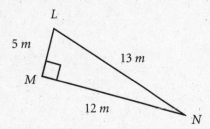

DO YOUR FIGURING HERE.

F. $\dfrac{5}{13}$

G. $\dfrac{5}{12}$

H. $\dfrac{12}{13}$

J. $\dfrac{13}{12}$

K. $\dfrac{12}{5}$

25. In the circle below, chord *AB* passes through the center of circle *O*. If the radius, *OC*, is perpendicular to chord *AB* and has length of 7 centimeters, what is the length of chord *BC*, to the nearest tenth of a centimeter?

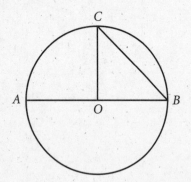

A. 5.3

B. 7

C. 9.9

D. 12.1

E. 14.0

GO ON TO THE NEXT PAGE

26. To convert a temperature in degrees Celsius to degrees Fahrenheit, the formula is $F = \dfrac{9}{5}C + 32$, where C is the degrees in Celsius. What temperature, to the nearest degree Celsius equals a temperature of 86 degrees Fahrenheit?

    F. 30
    G. 54
    H. 80
    J. 86
    K. 187

27. The Olympic-sized pool is 50 meters long, 25 meters wide, and holds 14,375 cubic meters of water. If the pool is the same depth in all parts, about how many meters deep is the water in the pool?

    A. Less than 9
    B. Between 9 and 10
    C. Between 10 and 11
    D. Between 11 and 12
    E. More than 12

28. In right triangle ΔDEF below, the measure of segment DE is 42 inches, and the tangent of angle D is $\dfrac{5}{8}$. What is the length of segment EF, to the nearest tenth of an inch?

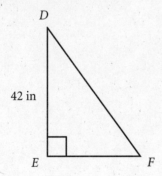

    F. 26.3
    G. 42.625
    H. 49.6
    J. 67.2
    K. 210

DO YOUR FIGURING HERE.

GO ON TO THE NEXT PAGE

29. The bar graph below shows the number of people at the spring prom, according to their grade level at the high school. According to the graph, what fraction of the people at the prom were sophomores?

Number of Prom Attendees, by Grade Level

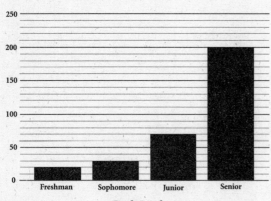

DO YOUR FIGURING HERE.

A. $\dfrac{1}{16}$

B. $\dfrac{3}{32}$

C. $\dfrac{3}{29}$

D. $\dfrac{3}{20}$

E. $\dfrac{3}{10}$

30. In the segment shown below, point X is the midpoint of segment WZ. If the measure of WY is 26 cm and the measure of WZ is 44 cm, what is the length, in centimeters, of segment XY?

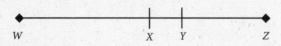

F. 70

G. 22

H. 18

J. 13

K. 4

GO ON TO THE NEXT PAGE

31. What is the *x*-coordinate of the intersection point, in the (x, y) coordinate system, of the lines $2x + 3y = 8$ and $5x + y = 7$?

DO YOUR FIGURING HERE.

A. −1

B. $\dfrac{1}{3}$

C. 1

D. 2

E. 3

32. For all pairs of real numbers *a* and *b*, where $a = 2b − 8$, $b = ?$

F. $a + 4$

G. $2a − 8$

H. $2a + 8$

J. $\dfrac{a − 8}{2}$

K. $\dfrac{a + 8}{2}$

33. What is the area, in square millimeters, of the parallelogram *RSTU* shown below?

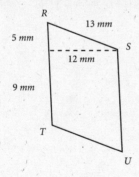

A. 30

B. 39

C. 54

D. 168

E. 182

GO ON TO THE NEXT PAGE

34. If $x = -(y + 3)$, then $(x + y)^3 = ?$

    F.   −27

    G.   −9

    H.   9

    J.   27

    K.   Cannot be determined from the given information.

35. Shown below is a partial map of Centerville, showing 80 square miles—a total of 8 miles of Main Street and a total of 10 miles of Front Street. There is a fire station at the corner of Main and Front St, shown as point F. The town wants to build a new fire station exactly halfway between the hospital, at H, and the school, at S. What would be the driving directions to get from the current fire station to the new fire station, by way of Main and Elm streets? All streets and avenues shown intersect at right angles.

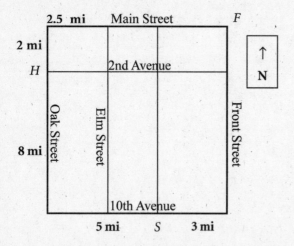

    A.   2.5 miles east, 4 miles north

    B.   2.5 miles west, 4 miles north

    C.   2.5 miles east, 6 miles south

    D.   5.5 miles west, 4 miles south

    E.   5.5 miles west, 6 miles south

DO YOUR FIGURING HERE.

GO ON TO THE NEXT PAGE

36. There are two consecutive odd integers. The difference between four times the larger and twice the smaller is 36. If x represents the smaller integer, which equation below can be used to determine the smaller integer?

F. $4x - 2x = 36$

G. $4(x + 1) - 2x = 36$

H. $4(x + 2) - 2x = 36$

J. $4(x + 3) - 2x = 36$

K. $36 - 4x = 2x$

37. A 15-foot supporting wire is attached to a telephone pole 12 feet from the ground. The wire is then anchored to the ground. The telephone pole stands perpendicular to the ground. How far, in feet, is the anchor of the supporting wire from the base of the telephone pole?

A. 3

B. 6

C. 9

D. 12

E. 15

38. In the figure below, the sides of the square are tangent to the inner circle. If the area of the circle is 100π square units, what is the unit length of a side of the square?

F. 400

G. 100

H. 20

J. 10

K. π

DO YOUR FIGURING HERE.

GO ON TO THE NEXT PAGE

39. The rectangles *ABCD* and *EFGH* shown below are similar. Using the given information, what is the length of side *EH*, to the nearest tenth of an inch?

A.   0.8

B.   1.3

C.   5.3

D.   7

E.   8

40. In the parallelogram *VWXY* below, points *U*, *V*, *Y* and *Z* form a straight line. Given the angle measures as shown in the figure, what is the measure of angle ∠*WYX*?

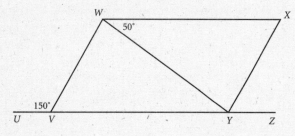

F.   25°

G.   30°

H.   50°

J.   100°

K.   150°

DO YOUR FIGURING HERE.

GO ON TO THE NEXT PAGE ▷

41. In the figure below, all interior angles are 90°, and all dimension lengths are given in centimeters. What is the perimeter of this figure, in centimeters?

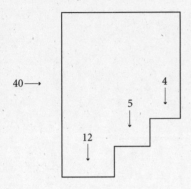

DO YOUR FIGURING HERE.

A. 40

B. 61

C. 82

D. 122

E. Cannot be determined from the given information.

42. In the mayoral election, $\frac{3}{4}$ of the eligible voters at one site cast a vote. Three-fifths of the votes at this site were for candidate Martinez. If there are 3,500 eligible voters at this site, how many of them voted for Martinez?

F. 417

G. 1,575

H. 2,100

J. 2,625

K. 4,725

GO ON TO THE NEXT PAGE

43. Given that a and b are positive integers, and the greatest common factor of a^4b^2 and a^3b is 54, what is a possible value for b?

    A. 2
    B. 3
    C. 6
    D. 9
    E. 27

44. If 40 percent of x is 70, then what is 160 percent of x?

    F. 28
    G. 45
    H. 112
    J. 175
    K. 280

45. Point M (2, 3) and point N (6, 5) are points on the coordinate plane. What is the length of the segment MN?

    A. $\sqrt{2}$ units
    B. $2\sqrt{3}$ units
    C. $2\sqrt{5}$ units
    D. 6 units
    E. 20 units

46. The ratio of the sides of two squares is 5:7. What is the ratio of the perimeters of these squares?

    F. 1:2
    G. 1:12
    H. 1:35
    J. 5:7
    K. 25:49

DO YOUR FIGURING HERE.

GO ON TO THE NEXT PAGE

47. What is the equation of a circle in the coordinate plane with center $(-2, 3)$ and radius of 9 units?

   A. $(x - 2)^2 + (y + 3)^2 = 9$
   B. $(x + 2)^2 + (y - 3)^2 = 9$
   C. $(x - 2)^2 + (y + 3)^2 = 81$
   D. $(x + 2)^2 + (y - 3)^2 = 3$
   E. $(x + 2)^2 + (y - 3)^2 = 81$

48. In the complex number system, $i^2 = -1$. Given that $\dfrac{3}{5-i}$ is a complex number, what is the result of $\dfrac{3}{5-i} \times \dfrac{5+i}{5+i}$?

   F. $\dfrac{3}{5+i}$

   G. $\dfrac{15 + 3i}{24}$

   H. $\dfrac{15 + 3i}{26}$

   J. $\dfrac{15 + i}{26}$

   K. $\dfrac{15 + i}{24}$

49. The figures below show regular polygons and the sum of the degrees of the angles in each polygon. Based on these figures, what is the number of degrees in an n-sided regular polygon?

   180°   360°   540°   720°

   A. $60N$
   B. $180n$
   C. $180(n - 2)$
   D. $20n^2$
   E. Cannot be determined from the information given.

DO YOUR FIGURING HERE.

GO ON TO THE NEXT PAGE

50. Fifty high school students were polled to see if they owned a cell phone and an mp3 player. A total of 35 of the students own a cell phone, and a total of 18 of the students own an mp3 player. What is the minimum number of students who own both a cell phone and an mp3 player?

    F.   0
    G.   3
    H.   17
    J.   32
    K.   53

51. What is the solution set of all real numbers n such that $-4n + 3 > -4n + 1$?

    A.   All real numbers
    B.   All positive numbers
    C.   All negative numbers
    D.   All numbers such that $n > -\dfrac{1}{2}$
    E.   All numbers such that $n < -\dfrac{1}{2}$

52. If 3 people all shake hands with each other, there are a total of 3 handshakes. If 4 people all shake hands with each other, there are a total of 6 handshakes. How many total handshakes will there be if 5 people all shake hands with each other?

    F.   7
    G.   9
    H.   10
    J.   11
    K.   12

DO YOUR FIGURING HERE.

GO ON TO THE NEXT PAGE

53. The chart below shows the percentages of the county budget expenses by category. The remainder of the budget will be placed in the category Miscellaneous. If this data is to be put into a circle graph, what will be the degree measure of the Miscellaneous wedge, rounded to the nearest degree?

DO YOUR FIGURING HERE.

Budget Category	Percentage of Budget
Salaries	23
Road Repair	5
Employee Benefits	22
Building Maintenance/ Utilities	18

A.   32

B.   58

C.   68

D.   115

E.   245

54. If $\tan\theta = -\dfrac{4}{3}$, and $\dfrac{\pi}{2} < \theta < \pi$, then $\sin\theta = ?$

F. $-\dfrac{4}{5}$

G. $-\dfrac{3}{4}$

H. $-\dfrac{3}{5}$

J. $\dfrac{3}{5}$

K. $\dfrac{4}{5}$

GO ON TO THE NEXT PAGE

55. Which of the following systems of inequalities is represented by the shaded region on the coordinate plane below?

DO YOUR FIGURING HERE.

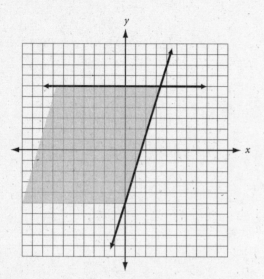

   A. $y < 6$ and $y > 3x - 5$

   B. $x < 6$ and $y > 3x - 5$

   C. $y < 6$ and $y < 3x - 5$

   D. $x < 6$ and $y < -3x - 5$

   E. $y < 6$ and $y > \dfrac{1}{3}x - 5$

56. If $f(x) = 2(x + 7)$ then $f(x + c) = ?$

   F. $2x + 2c + 7$

   G. $2x + c + 7$

   H. $2x + c + 14$

   J. $2x + 2c + 14$

   K. $2(x + 7) + c$

GO ON TO THE NEXT PAGE ⇨

57. Which graph below represents the solution set

for the equation $y = \dfrac{2x^2 - 8}{x - 2}$?

DO YOUR FIGURING HERE.

A.

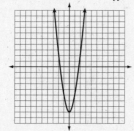

B.

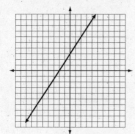

C.

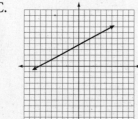

D.

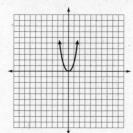

E.

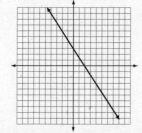

GO ON TO THE NEXT PAGE

58. What are the coordinates of Q', the reflection of the point Q(r, s) after a reflection over the y-axis?

    F. $(-r, s)$

    G. $(-r, -s)$

    H. $(s, -r)$

    J. $(r, -s)$

    K. $(-s, r)$

59. If $g = 4q + 3$ and $h = 2q - 8$, what is g in terms of h?

    A. $g = \dfrac{h+8}{2}$

    B. $g = \dfrac{4h+11}{2}$

    C. $2h + 19$

    D. $2h + 11$

    E. $h = \dfrac{g-3}{4}$

DO YOUR FIGURING HERE.

GO ON TO THE NEXT PAGE

60. Find the $\cos(75°)$ knowing that $\cos(75°) = \cos(30° + 45°)$. Use the formula $\cos(\alpha + \beta) = \cos(\alpha)\cos(\beta) - \sin(\alpha)\sin(\beta)$ and the table of values below:

θ	$\sin\theta$	$\cos\theta$	$\tan\theta$
30°	$\dfrac{1}{2}$	$\dfrac{\sqrt{3}}{2}$	$\dfrac{\sqrt{3}}{3}$
45°	$\dfrac{\sqrt{2}}{2}$	$\dfrac{\sqrt{2}}{2}$	1
60°	$\dfrac{\sqrt{3}}{2}$	$\dfrac{1}{2}$	$\sqrt{3}$

F. $\dfrac{\sqrt{3} - \sqrt{2}}{4}$

G. $\dfrac{\sqrt{3} - \sqrt{2}}{2}$

H. $\dfrac{\sqrt{6} - \sqrt{2}}{4}$

J. $\dfrac{\sqrt{6} - \sqrt{2}}{2}$

K. $\dfrac{3 - \sqrt{2}}{4}$

DO YOUR FIGURING HERE.

READING TEST

35 Minutes—24 Questions

> **Directions:** This test contains four passages, each followed by several questions. After reading a passage, select the best answer to each question and fill in the corresponding oval on your answer sheet. You are allowed to refer to the passages while answering the questions.

PASSAGE I

Emily couldn't help but grin broadly after answering the phone. She frequently called us "two peas in a pod," but I'd always felt like any
Line time we were mentioned outside of my presence
(5) he was "Bruce" and I was "Bruce's twin brother." Because of this, I wasn't surprised to hear my wife giggling uncontrollably and see her twirling the phone cord around her finger while talking to him. Despite the fact she was speaking to someone
(10) genetically identical to me, I couldn't help but wonder if she had ever responded so enthusiastically to one of my stories.

"Okay, I'll tell him. Talk to you soon." After Emily hung up, I watched her take a deep, almost
(15) wistful breath before walking over to me.

"Bruce seems well," I said, trying to sound casual. "He told me about the new job and everything. What did you guys talk about?"

"Not much." Emily replied. She walked behind
(20) my chair and patted my shoulder before sitting on the couch and opening her magazine. It didn't appear as if she was really reading. She seemed to stop and start, pausing and reflecting about something unrelated to the smiling celebrities featured
(25) in the article.

"It's funny to think that he knows some of these people," she said, pointing at her magazine.

I looked at the gleaming teeth and chiseled features of the actors, and then looked over at a
(30) picture of Bruce and me resting on the mantel. Looking closely at the photo always made my stomach turn; as with every picture of us, there was an unmistakable vitality in Bruce's face that wasn't present in mine. It was as if I was wearing a

(35) "Bruce" costume; I was trying to mimic one of his trademark smiles, but always seemed to produce a different failed attempt.

"You all right?" Emily asked, noticing my expression.
(40) I grabbed the picture from the mantel and brought it to her. She looked at it, and looked up at me, quizzically.

"Can you tell which one is me?" I asked.

She looked back at the picture and pushed her
(45) lip out as she looked from one face to the next. After about five seconds she pointed to my face, then turned and looked at me confidently.

"How could you tell?" I asked.

"Well, it wasn't very hard," she responded. "You
(50) are my husband, and I love the way you smile. Bruce looks exactly the same in every picture, it looks practiced, but for you it always seems like you're thinking about something, even concentrating, to make sure you smile right."
(55) "Really?" I was surprised by how much thought she had put into this.

She took the picture and put it back on the mantel. I could still see the perfection in Bruce's smile and hesitation in mine, but at least Emily found a
(60) way to compliment my insecurities.

Emily went back to perusing her magazine.

"At least you ended up with a Fairholm," I said, "even if it wasn't the famous one."

"Oh, was I supposed to pursue the famous one?"
(65) she shot back.

She closed her magazine and put it down on the coffee table. There wasn't an argument coming, but I saw her disappointment. The problem was not that she actually would have married my

GO ON TO THE NEXT PAGE ⟶

(70) brother before me; it was the simple fact that I couldn't help but believe that to be the case. I saw myself as second to him and always had. With embarrassing relatives, people will always point out that one can't choose his or her family, but
(75) when you're a twin, it's not the association that you fear, it's the comparison.

"Do you want to be where he is?" she inquired, with an empty tone.

"This is exactly where I want to be." I replied.

(80) "I just never know how to explain to people that I'm an insurance adjuster, not a Hollywood agent. They always want to know how it happened when we had the same upbringing and education. They look at me as if I did something wrong."

(85) "Do you ever call him?" she asked.

"I figure he's busy, and he calls enough," I said.

She cradled her chin in her hand, and looked at me in mild disbelief. "You realize that by not calling and turning down his invitations to visit you make
(90) him feel rejected, right?"

"Come on, Emily. He's surrounded by famous people, he doesn't need my approval."

"Maybe not," she sighed, "but his favorite stories to tell me aren't about Hollywood, they're about
(95) you two growing up."

"Well, he was popular then, too," I said, shrugging.

"He doesn't look at it that way," she responded. "He would give up a lot to have your approval, Dave.
(100) He wants to be your brother, not a competitor."

"It's okay, Emily. I'll call him soon, but I think that he'll be okay either way."

1. Dave would probably agree with which of the following statements regarding his relationship with Bruce?

   A. They would be better off not talking at all.
   B. Their phone conversations are vital to their relationship.
   C. Their bond as twins is stronger due to Emily's effort.
   D. Their competition makes it harder for them to get along.

2. Emily is best described as:

   F. aloof and ineffectual.
   G. needling and meddlesome.
   H. caring and diplomatic.
   J. pained and inconsolable.

3. Which of the following statements does NOT describe a feeling Dave has toward his brother?

   A. He is jealous of the reaction his brother gets from Emily during their phone conversation.
   B. He believes he would be better suited for his brother's type of work.
   C. He is resentful of his brother's superior social skills.
   D. He is skeptical of his brother's desire for his approval.

4. The primary focus of the first paragraph is:

   F. Emily's attempt to make her husband jealous.
   G. Emily's desire for the brothers to resolve their differences.
   H. Dave's hope to distance himself from his twin brother.
   J. Dave's feelings of inferiority to his twin brother.

GO ON TO THE NEXT PAGE →

5. Lines 85–102 ("Do you ever… either way.")
   suggest that Dave does not contact Bruce
   because Dave:

   A. believes that Bruce has great need for
      him, but does not want to admit to
      Emily that she is right.

   B. feels guilty about being distant toward
      Bruce, and worries that he will have to
      explain himself.

   C. wants to prove to Emily that he is not
      impressed by Bruce's high profile job.

   D. still harbors resentment over Bruce get-
      ting preferential treatment during their
      childhood.

6. According to the passage, when Dave looks at
   the photograph, he sees:

   F. his brother being cruel to him.

   G. two indistinguishable faces.

   H. a comparison unfavorable to him.

   J. his wife paying more attention to Bruce.

7. Which of the following best summarizes
   Dave's feelings when he asks Emily to pick him
   out in the picture?

   A. Dave is confident that Emily will prefer
      his image to Bruce's.

   B. Dave is insecure; he feels the picture
      compares him unfavorably to Bruce.

   C. Dave is worried, because he thinks Emily
      will want to talk more about Bruce after
      seeing a picture of him.

   D. Dave is angry, because he did not
      want to talk about the picture in the
      first place.

8. It can be logically deduced from the passage
   that Dave and Bruce:

   F. tell Emily different sounding stories
      about their shared childhood.

   G. are frequently at odds regarding their
      different professions.

   H. have often fought over Emily's attention.

   J. were much closer shortly before Bruce
      moved.

9. Both Emily and Dave conclude that when
   pictures are taken of the brothers:

   A. Bruce looks much better than Dave.

   B. Dave appears angry at Bruce.

   C. Pictures of Bruce are more consistent
      than those of Dave.

   D. Dave's expression makes a greater
      impression on the viewer than Bruce's.

10. According to the passage, the reason Emily
    tells Dave about the content of Bruce's stories
    is because Emily:

    F. wants to convince Dave that Bruce does
       not see himself as better than Dave.

    G. wishes to hear Dave's version of the
       stories.

    H. sees this as a way to make Dave more
       impressed with his brother.

    J. thinks that this will make Dave sympa-
       thetic to Bruce's loneliness.

GO ON TO THE NEXT PAGE ⇒

PASSAGE II

Large-scale media would likely be traced back to ancient tribes sharing information about the edibility of berries or the aggressiveness of animals. Despite

Line constant evolution, the information
(5) most sought after is that regarding personal safety, personal opportunity, and the triumphs and misdeeds of others—the larger the persona and more laudatory or despicable the act, the better. When a story is of continued national interest, however,
(10) the focus shifts even further from facts and more to theater. To step back and compose an objective plot of goings on is a distant possibility, but establishing the hero or villain of the day is paramount. Ultimately, the public's desire to have cold, dry
(15) and correct facts is virtually nonexistent.

Current newscasts exacerbate this by delivering an assault on the senses with meaningless graphics and theatrical music; meanwhile the monotone newscaster reads, verbatim from a teleprompter,
(20) often using identical phrases to those on other networks. Additionally, the viewer has probably already read the same story on the Internet earlier. When television was limited to three networks, rather than ubiquitous news-only channels, the
(25) newscaster was a national figure, audience members would eagerly await information that was new to them, and would expect a relatively thorough explanation of any complicated goings on. For example, to this day many people, in explain-
(30) ing the Watergate scandal to those too young to know of it, use Walter Cronkite's delineation as the basis for their understanding.

The objective, trustworthy anchorperson has also given way to vociferous demagogues promis-
(35) ing truth but delivering oversimplified, bias-driven sound bites. The idea of allowing individuals to draw their own conclusions is notably absent; in fact, many personalities mock those with opinions differing from those presented. The availability of
(40) neutral online sources mitigates this slightly, but not to any large degree. While the actual article may be impartial, electronic periodicals will still sensationalize headlines in order to attract casual readers, and those very headlines sway many read-
(45) ers to certain opinions before the article is even read. For example, if a headline mentions an "enraged public," the reader is far more likely to both read and take umbrage with the information than he or she would if the article mentioned a
(50) subject that "irked locals."

In truth, though, the public is as desirous for dry and objective facts as finicky children are for brussels sprouts. The personalities willing to shrug off accountability in favor of wild accusations and
(55) bombastic slogans captivate a large demographic, while one would be generous by saying that objective fact-based programs occupy even a niche market. This not only damages the general accuracy of so-called "news," but further polarizes the
(60) public. People now have the option to receive their news from hosts with a variety of political leanings, and one almost invariably chooses to watch the personality closest to one's own personal opinions. This is more harmful than convenient,
(65) because it allows viewers to simply parrot information they are given, eliminating any thought or scrutiny. It is this intellectual laziness that aids in distancing the general public from factual information: as a growing number become resigned to
(70) accept whatever their favorite host tells them, the more freedom networks have in passing sensationalist entertainment as news. It boils down to the unfortunate truth that most are far more likely to accept inaccurate information as fact rather than
(75) question the legitimacy of something that seems to fit with opinions a particular audience member holds.

Those who make the news also obfuscate objective facts. A legion of employees is designated
(80) solely for the purpose of making the decisions of political figures sound flawless. Oftentimes, important decisions are made, and throughout a lengthy press conference, not a single factual implication is discussed. The meeting becomes

GO ON TO THE NEXT PAGE ⟹

(85) nothing more than an opportunity for political employees to test their infallible sounding slogans, while the media dissects the semantics rather than the facts. Semantics, however, are all the media is presented with.

(90)   Despite all these methods of prevarication, people still are better informed than they were in the past. Public knowledge of events often occurs minutes after the fact, rather than days or weeks. The populace has a strong desire for news in general,

(95) and amid all the unscrupulous presentation methods, facts do exist. However, the profitability of news has made presentation premium, not trustworthiness. Complicating matters further is the populace's impatience; the standard consumer

(100) would rather be presented with a minute and potentially inaccurate statement—one that may or may not be retracted the following day—than suffer through a lengthy treatise comprised of all the known facts and nuances of a particular event.

(105) The desire to know still exists, however; it just happens to be overshadowed by the public's desire for personal consensus and the media's desire to reel in the public.

11. One of the primary points the author attempts to make regarding the current news media is that:

   A.   the media passes off made-up stories as facts.

   B.   the news anchors are not as opinionated as they were in decades past.

   C.   the media focuses more on presentation than substance.

   D.   the media goes directly against what news audiences truly desire to see.

12. The author makes what claim about impartial news stories?

   F.   They no longer exist.

   G.   They can be sensationalized in ways other than article content.

   H.   They often have headlines that correctly reflect the emotional level of the story.

   J.   They all have headlines that attempt to make the reader feel involved in the story.

13. The author brings up Walter Cronkite's coverage of Watergate in order to assert that:

   A.   Walter Cronkite was a particularly adept newsperson.

   B.   a previous standard for news rightly included clarification of complex issues.

   C.   current newscasters are far more forgettable than those before them.

   D.   the expanding number of television channels has made individual newscasters less famous.

14. By stating that "personal consensus" is of great importance to the public (line 107), the author is probably suggesting that members of the public:

   F.   do not want information that contradicts their own beliefs.

   G.   work hard to find the source closest to truth, despite the difficulties present.

   H.   wish to resolve any moral conflicts they may have with practices in news reporting.

   J.   have difficulty finding news sources reflecting their personal views.

GO ON TO THE NEXT PAGE

15. According to the passage, what type of news stories are sensationalized the most?

   A. Those with a fairly clear chain of events

   B. Those that stay in the public's consciousness for long periods of time

   C. Those that clearly support one political view

   D. Those with the most scandalous information

16. As used in line 12 (paragraph 1), the word *distant* most nearly means:

   F. separated

   G. different

   H. reserved

   J. unlikely

17. Based on the passage, which of the following headlines would the author be most likely to criticize?

   A. Earthquake Rocks Small Community, Arouses Questions Regarding Preparedness

   B. New Tax Protested by Idaho Farmers

   C. Parents Across Country Outraged at Offensive Song

   D. Governor Describes Proposed Legislation as 'Monstrous"

18. The author asserts that individuals will often accept potentially inaccurate information because they:

   F. believe that most newscasters are honest.

   G. have no way to research correct facts.

   H. are forced to translate the guarded words of political employees.

   J. have similar political beliefs to specific personalities.

19. In the fourth paragraph, the phrase "even a niche market" (lines 57–58) expresses the author's feeling that:

   A. media companies are influenced greatly by public demand.

   B. cable television networks are unwilling to present objective facts.

   C. factual news media should look into better marketing practices.

   D. factual news would be profitable with greater exposure.

20. The author argues that in searching for a news source audience members are most likely to choose the source that:

   F. features the most entertaining newscaster.

   G. validates the audience member's opinion.

   H. presents the shortest and simplest explanation for goings on.

   J. focus on big stories rather than local ones.

GO ON TO THE NEXT PAGE

PASSAGE III

My grandfather was born in a turbulent time
in Russia. His non-communist lineage made him
unwelcome, before he had left the womb. His
Line father, an officer in the Russian army, was consid-
(5) ered an enemy of the communist Bolsheviks, so
my grandfather lived less than a year in what was
his native Moscow, and spent most of his younger
years moving across Asia. Despite this, he had
pride in being Russian, associated with Russians
(10) throughout his life, and would frequently quiz me
on Russian history. This all in tribute to a country
that ended up under different rule during the time
his mother was pregnant with him.

As a child, exiled to Siberia, my great grand-
(15) father told his son of the greatness that existed
within the country that had forced the family into
exile. It was known that, first as a family, and later
as an adult, my grandfather was going to have to
seek a new place to call home, but despite this
(20) foregone conclusion, Russia was still romanticized,
and my grandfather learned to treat the country
with reverence. This was in contrast to the sentiments found in other recently exiled Russians,
who would not simply lament the actions taken by
(25) the country, but disparage all eight million square
miles. In my family's search for a place to settle,
attempting to forge a consistent identity was nearly
impossible, as no one knew if the next location
would hold for a month, let alone a year, all hoped
(30) for an unattainable "new Moscow."

The first elongated refuge was found, ironically,
in China, which would later have its own communist revolution. After several years of relative stability, the revolution precipitated the move to
(35) the United States. Upon arrival in San Francisco,
my grandfather, along with my grandmother and
their young son, my father, found other Russian
immigrants who were also new to the country.
"*Ya amerikanets*" people would say, and despite the fact
(40) that they were recent immigrants who associated
primarily with those of shared ethnicity and
circumstance, they would play the role they

desired, and repeat "*ya amerikanets*"— "I am
American." They would share many stories about
(45) their native land, but did not repeat "ya russkiy,"
because being Russian went without saying.

While it was clear that this would be the last
country my grandfather would reside in, and that
he wished to become more American, it was per-
(50) haps the most confusing of times. It was less of
a problem in acclimating to an adopted setting;
the problem was dealing with a permanent setting at all. The only consistency throughout the
first thirty years of my grandfather's life was the
(55) knowledge that every "home" was temporary, and
now this was no longer the case. I often wonder if
his successful career in the real estate business had
anything to do with what must have been a rare
transformation of circumstance.

(60) Not only was my grandfather interested in real
estate, he was ardent about the importance of ownership, a naturally discordant view to that of the
then Soviet Union, and thus selling homes became
a purpose in addition to an occupation.

(65) Part of his success in real estate was owed to
strategic compromise. Considering American
sentiments regarding Russia during the Cold War,
there were times that he was sure he lost certain house sales due to his last name and accent.
(70) However, to those willing to listen, he found
advantages informing people that he was an exiled
Russian, and ardently disagreed with the communist government. He would also point out his
pride in being a new American, and allow a poten-
(75) tial buyer to degrade Russia without blinking.

Fortunately, the 1950s were a time of settling
across the country, and this made real estate a
very lucrative profession. It wasn't just this that
attracted my grandfather, though; he also saw it as
(80) an opportunity to give tiny parts of the country to
other people, returning the favor, in a way.

Yet, it always seemed that something vital still
rested in the opposite hemisphere. Once communism fell, he began returning to Russia yearly, and

GO ON TO THE NEXT PAGE ⇒

(85) while he and my grandmother never showed the
family pictures from Russia the way they would
from the various cruise ships they traveled on, it
could be deduced that returning to Russia was
analogous to an adopted child traveling to meet his
(90) or her birth-parents: the journey is one of personal
necessity rather than pleasure, and the encounter is
one that elucidates one's very existence. In selling
real estate, my grandfather had worked to make this
unnecessary. I believe that he wished for people to
(95) keep those houses, and pass them down to later
generations, giving the space a sort of familial per-
manence, rather than a fleeting stay.

For most, the thought of real estate agents
conjures up images of smiling advertisements on
(100) benches and buses, and the skill of selling something so important. Many are wary of salespeople
in general, questioning the practice of convincing
people something is in their best interest when the
salesperson stands to personally benefit. My
(105) grandfather did financially benefit from sales, but
there was more to it; his realization of the
American dream only made him want to be a part
of others reaching for the same thing, whether
their native home was around the block or
(110) thousands of miles away.

21. One of the main points the author attempts to
convey in the passage is that:

A. immigrants would often rather live in
their native land.

B. American-born people tend not to be
able to understand how displacement
affects immigrants.

C. immigrants that acclimate well to
America still may have indelible ties to
their native land.

D. immigrants are often shocked by the stability offered to them in America.

22. Based on the first three paragraphs, which of
the following best describes the movements
of the author's grandfather, prior to his
emigration to America?

F. He grew up primarily in Siberia and
then moved to China during the Russian
revolution.

G. He grew up in Moscow, was exiled as an
adult, and rapidly moved through Asia.

H. He was born in Moscow, moved rapidly
through Asia, and settled for a while in
communist China.

J. He was born in Moscow, exiled to Siberia
with his family, and moved frequently
before settling for a somewhat longer
period in China.

23. The author's grandfather's "purpose" (line 64)
and desire to return "the favor" (line 81) are
best described as:

A. providing others with a sense of pride in
being American.

B. shedding light on injustices carried out
by other countries.

C. facilitating a stable situation for others.

D. providing well for his family.

GO ON TO THE NEXT PAGE

24. Which of the following actions contradicts a general attitude held by the author's grandfather?

   F. "He would also point out his pride in being a new American, and allow a potential buyer to degrade Russia without blinking" (lines 73–75)

   G. "They would share many stories about their native land, but did not repeat "*ya russkiy*," because being Russian went without saying" (lines 44–46)

   H. "he was ardent about the importance of ownership, a naturally discordant view to that of the then Soviet Union" (lines 61–63)

   J. "Once communism fell, he began returning to Russia yearly" (lines 83–84)

25. The author classifies a "new Moscow" as "unattainable" (line 30) because:

   A. the family believed Moscow to be the most desirable city in the world.

   B. it was unlikely that communism would fall shortly after the revolution.

   C. cities in other countries are entirely unlike those in Russia.

   D. it would not be possible to find a new home that could still be considered a native home.

26. When the author refers to Russians "playing the role" (line 42), he most likely means that the Russians were:

   F. convincing themselves that they were ready to acclimate.

   G. joking with each other.

   H. native to the way Americans tend to act with each other.

   J. still hopeful that they would see Russia again.

27. The "strategic compromise" applied by the author's grandfather (line 66) would most likely involve:

   A. agreeing with the potential buyer, no matter what.

   B. ignoring offensive statements.

   C. acting as American as possible.

   D. taking America's side in international disputes.

28. According to the passage, the grandfather's trip back to his native Russia provided him with:

   F. a greater understanding of the inner workings of his native land.

   G. greater motivation to sell homes in America.

   H. a greater sense of personal understanding.

   J. a necessary visit with estranged family members.

29. According to the first paragraph, the author's grandfather's birth happened:

   A. during the communist revolution.

   B. under communist rule.

   C. prior to the communist revolution.

   D. after the fall of communism.

30. When the author states that his grandfather "worked to make this unnecessary" (lines 93–94), he is suggesting that his grandfather's occupation could potentially:

   F. help his grandfather feel more connected to America through his success.

   G. oversee a transaction that could give others a sense of belonging.

   H. sell houses that would allow other recent immigrants stability.

   J. help others realize the American dream.

GO ON TO THE NEXT PAGE

PASSAGE IV

In both recorded and oral history, the rattlesnakes are categorized as malevolent beings.
Their lance-shaped heads and angular brow-lines
Line make them look the perfect villain, and their
(5) venom cements this classification. Publicized
reports of bite victims seem to prove their nefari-
ous nature.

Unlike mammalian predators like bears, rattlesnakes are not given the classification of an animal
(10) deserving human respect. One imagines the rattlesnake hiding in our backyards, waiting to strike.

In recent long-term studies, however, the
social behavior of rattlesnakes has been found
to be quite different than many would expect.
(15) Herpetologists, scientists who study snakes, had
long suspected a more complex and thoughtful existence for the reptiles, and now have hard
information to back up their theories. When
examined, the sinister opportunist lurking in
(20) the shadows better resembles a mild-mannered
domestic. Unlike the non-venomous kingsnake,
rattlesnakes are entirely non-cannibalistic, and
tend to spend their entire lives with a single mate.
The mating ritual in which two males will extend
(25) almost half of their bodies off the ground to
wrestle is not lethal, and, once bested, a rattlesnake
peacefully retreats to find a new den of eligible
mates. Female rattlesnakes give birth to live
young, and rattlesnakes often share their dens,
(30) even hibernating with tortoises without incident.

Sadly, it seems that only those with an existing
fascination with snakes are aware of this socially
functional rattlesnake. Another discovery that
made little stir in the public consciousness is an
(35) experiment in which herpetologists tracked snakes
with radio transmitters, and saw their behavior
when humans entered their habitat. While a few
snakes did hold their ground and rattle, most saw
or sensed a disturbance (snakes cannot hear) and
(40) immediately headed in the opposite direction.
Many of the snakes that were handled by herpetologists did not coil or strike. This is not to say

that a snake will not bite a human if disturbed,
but the tendency is to retreat first and give warn-
(45) ing second, before striking becomes a possibility.

Describing a more docile nature does not imply
that rattlesnakes would make good pets for children, but considering the aggressiveness often
displayed by a South American pit viper, the fer-de-
(50) lance, one familiar with both would have far fewer
trepidations in passing by a rattlesnake. For one
thing, rattlesnakes do coil and rattle, giving
humans an opportunity to move away, while
fer-de-lances will often strike at passersby without
(55) warning. Furthermore, when it comes down to
statistics, American hospitals report an average of
7,000 snakebite patients a year, generally more than
half are actually from non-venomous snakes
mistook by victims as venomous. On average,
(60) fewer than six people die of snake envenomation
annually, and the vast majority of the serious bites
are due to either handling the snake or stepping
on it; most people bitten by snakes they were not
engaging end up with very mild bites. Compare
(65) this with an average of over one million hospital
visits for dog bites and twenty annual deaths at
the jaws of man's best friend. With such miniscule
statistics regarding snakebites, it is curious why
they are still viewed as unfathomably dangerous,
(70) when bees, lightning—and yes, dogs—are far more
responsible for human fatalities. The fer-de-lance,
however, is responsible for thousands of annual
deaths in Central and South America.

If one is looking for proof that rattlesnakes do
(75) not intend to harm humans, one should consider
perhaps the most stunning evidence regarding
bite behavior. Over half of the bites rattlesnakes
administer to humans are "dry," meaning the rattlesnake purposely does not release venom. While
(80) I will not posit that this is due to rattlesnakes
possessing awareness for the well-being of its
non-food source bite victim, there is a great deal
of thought present. The snake acknowledges that
venom is needed for immobilizing and digesting

GO ON TO THE NEXT PAGE →

(85) prey (venom is actually saliva), producing venom takes time, and the human is not a food source. Therefore, if the snake is not surprised or fearing death, the damage of a rattlesnake bite will likely be far less severe than if the snake used all its

(90) venom. This has been known for some time, but in many cases, it is probably better for humans to believe that the snakes are more liberal with venom than they are, simply because a frightened and cornered rattlesnake is very dangerous.

(95) Unfortunately, some take the traditional role of the rattlesnake and use it as an excuse to harm the animals. People in various areas use the fearsome reputation of rattlesnakes, along with the more docile reality, for profit. Rattlesnake "round-ups"

(100) are held, where people collect snakes beforehand and join in a festival celebrating their conquest. The events are billed as both entertainment and as making surrounding residential areas safer for children, however the vast majority of snakes are

(105) collected from uninhabited areas, and people are frequently bitten at the festivals while handling the snakes for the audience. Eventually, the snakes are killed to make clothing or trophies, and these events are estimated to be responsible for 100,000

(110) rattlesnake deaths annually, in comparison to fewer than six for humans.

 Behavior like this provides a better reason for *crotalid* mythology. With statistics categorically showing a low level of danger from rattlesnakes to

(115) humans, and an extremely high level vice-versa, it would be a wonder to see what human-related folklore would be like if rattlesnakes were able to speak or write.

31. In relation to the entire passage, the phrase "the sinister opportunist lurking in the shadows better resembles a mild-mannered domestic" (lines 19–21) most likely implies that:

A. adult rattlesnakes are considerable less aggressive than juveniles.

B. recent studies regarding rattlesnakes found few incidents of aggressive behavior.

C. rattlesnakes are more similar to mammals than once thought.

D. rattlesnakes are entirely predictable in behavior.

32. The passage implies that the rattlesnakes fearsome reputation can be beneficial because:

F. it influences people to avoid or move away from rattlesnakes.

G. it protects the lives of rattlesnakes.

H. it inspires medical advancement in treating snakebites, despite a low mortality rate.

J. adventurous people may seek rattlesnakes as pets.

33. What evidence does the passage give regarding the social ability of rattlesnakes?

A. Rattlesnakes are aware of the uses of their venom.

B. Wrestling between males establishes a social hierarchy.

C. Rattlesnakes can share their habitat with other species.

D. Rattlesnakes rarely eat other snakes.

GO ON TO THE NEXT PAGE ⇨

34. The statement "it would be a wonder to see what human-related folklore would be like if rattlesnakes were able to speak or write" (lines 115–118) means that:

    F. humans and rattlesnakes both present great risks to each other's safety.

    G. humans and rattlesnakes behave in many similar ways.

    H. humans are a much greater threat to rattlesnakes than rattlesnakes are to humans.

    J. humans have traditionally assigned human emotions to rattlesnakes in folklore.

35. According to the passage, what is the correlation between human behavior and serious rattlesnake bites?

    A. There is no statistical relationship.

    B. Humans that move in quick motions attract strikes.

    C. Humans that actively seek interaction with snakes are less likely to receive a "dry" bite.

    D. Rattlesnakes deliver a variable amount of venom based on how threatening humans act.

36. What is suggested by lines 46–48 when the author states that the new evidence "does not imply that rattlesnakes would make good pets for children"?

    F. Only professional herpetologists should keep rattlesnakes.

    G. Dogs can also be dangerous pets.

    H. Non-aggressive behavior does not make a venomous animal harmless.

    J. Rattlesnakes in the wild are more docile than those in captivity.

37. The passage states that the relative likelihood of a human being killed by a rattlesnake bite is:

    A. greater than that of a dog bite.

    B. less than that of a bee sting.

    C. equal to that of a lightning strike.

    D. comparable to that of the South American fer-de-lance.

38. Which of the following correctly categorizes a rattlesnake's strategy in venom usage?

    F. The larger the prey or predator, the more venom is used.

    G. Even when threatened, a rattlesnake reserves venom to use on prey.

    H. Rattlesnakes are aware that they will wound larger animals.

    J. Rattlesnakes would rather use venom solely for prey.

39. The author states rattlesnake "round-ups" use contradictory logic because:

    A. children are rarely bit by rattlesnakes.

    B. the rattlesnakes that bite people at "round-ups" would have been far less likely to bite someone in their natural habitat.

    C. organizers use erroneous statistics to make the rattlesnakes seem more dangerous and the events more impressive.

    D. many that go to the events are unaware how many snakes are killed.

40. As used in line 113, the term *crotalid* is most likely:

    F. an unfavorable characterization of humans.

    G. a scientific word meaning "rattlesnakes."

    H. a word describing a herpetologist that specializes in rattlesnakes.

    J. a general word for a group unfairly accused of wrongdoing.

IF YOU FINISH BEFORE TIME IS CALLED, YOU MAY CHECK YOUR WORK ON THIS SECTION ONLY. DO NOT TURN TO ANY OTHER SECTION IN THE TEST.

SCIENCE TEST

35 Minutes—40 Questions

Directions: Each of the following seven passages is followed by several questions. After reading each passage, decide on the best answer to each question and fill in the corresponding oval on your answer sheet. You are allowed to refer to the passages while answering the questions. Calculator use is not allowed on this test.

PASSAGE I

Glaciers are large masses of ice that move slowly over the earth's surface due to the force of gravity and changes in elevation. Glacial *calving* occurs when one edge of a glacier borders a body of water. A calving glacier's *terminus* (the lower edge) periodically produces icebergs as they break away from the glacier and into the water.

STUDY 1

A computer was used to create a model of a typical calving glacier. It was hypothesized that a primary factor determining the calving rate is the glacier's velocity at its terminus. Figure 1 shows the calving rate, in meters per year, and length of the computer-generated glacier over a period of 2,000 years.

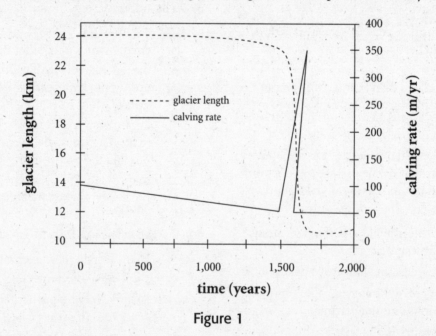

Figure 1

GO ON TO THE NEXT PAGE

STUDY 2

Four calving glaciers (A–D) were studied over a period of ten years. The average velocity at the terminus of each glacier was recorded for years 1–5, and again for years 6–10. The calving rate of each glacier was estimated for the same time periods. The results are recorded in Table 1.

Table 1

	Years 1–5		Years 6–10	
Glacier	Average velocity (m/yr)	Calving rate (m/yr)	Average velocity (m/yr)	Calving rate (m/yr)
A	72	72	63	64
B	51	52	45	47
C	98	106	256	312
D	160	189	53	54

STUDY 3

Meteorologists reported unusually high average temperatures in the regions of Glacier C and Glacier D during the same ten-year period examined in Study 2. It was hypothesized that the high temperatures were responsible for the relatively rapid variations in velocity and calving rate evident for Glacier C and Glacier D in Table 1.

1. If the glacier model used in Study 1 is typical of all calving glaciers, the scientists would draw which of the following conclusions about the relationship between glacier length and calving rate?

   A. As calving rate decreases, glacier length always increases.

   B. As glacier length decreases, calving rate always decreases.

   C. A sharp increase in calving rate results in a sharp decrease in glacier length.

   D. A sharp increase in calving rate results in a sharp increase in glacier length.

2. The meteorologists in Study 3 hypothesized that the faster the calving rate, the faster the sea level at a calving glacier's terminus would rise. If this hypothesis is correct, which of the following glaciers resulted in the fastest rise in sea level during years 6–10?

   F. Glacier A

   G. Glacier B

   H. Glacier C

   J. Glacier D

GO ON TO THE NEXT PAGE

3. Based on the results of Study 2, a calving glacier traveling at a velocity of 80 m/yr would most likely have a calving rate:

    A. between 72 m/yr and 106 m/yr.
    B. between 106 m/yr and 189 m/yr.
    C. between 189 m/yr and 312 m/yr.
    D. over 312 m/yr.

4. Which of the following statements best describes the behavior of the glaciers observed during Study 2?

    F. All of the glaciers observed traveled faster during the first five years than during the last five years.
    G. All of the glaciers observed traveled faster during the last five years than during the first five years.
    H. The calving rate is always less than the average velocity for all of the glaciers observed.
    J. The calving rate is always greater than or equal to the average velocity for all of the glaciers observed.

5. Which of the following graphs best represents the relationship between the calving rate and the average velocity of the glaciers observed in Study 2 for years 6–10?

A.
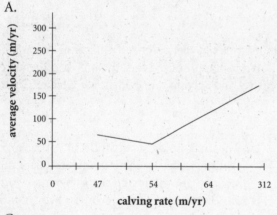

B.
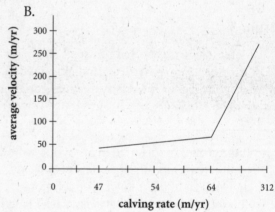

C.
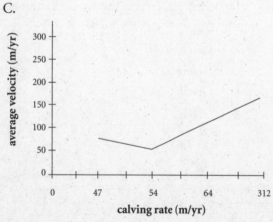

D.
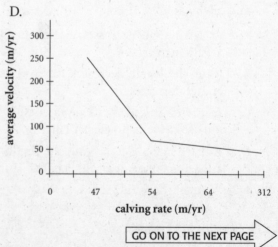

GO ON TO THE NEXT PAGE

6. If the hypothesis made by the meteorologists in Study 3 is correct, the glacier modeled in Study 1 most likely experienced unusually high temperatures at approximately what time during the simulated 2,000-year study?

F. 500 years

G. 1,000 years

H. 1,500 years

J. 2,000 years

Passage II

Allergic rhinitis refers to a person's nasal reaction to small airborne particles called *allergens*.

Table 1 shows the specific allergen, its type, and the approximate number of reported cases of allergic symptoms for a population of 1,000 people living in northern Kentucky during a single year.

Table 1

Month	Allergen Type / Specific Allergen — Pollen			Mold		
	Trees	Grass	Weeds	Alternaraa	Cladosporium	Aspergillus
January				⊛	⊛	⊛
February	⊛			⊛	⊛	⊛
March	⊛⊛			⊛	⊛	⊛
April	⊛⊛⊛⊛			⊛	⊛	⊛
May	⊛⊛⊛	⊛⊛⊛		⊛	⊛	⊛
June		⊛⊛⊛⊛		⊛	⊛	⊛
July		⊛⊛	⊛	⊛⊛	⊛	⊛
August			⊛⊛⊛	⊛⊛⊛⊛	⊛⊛⊛	⊛⊛⊛⊛
September			⊛⊛	⊛⊛⊛	⊛⊛⊛⊛	⊛⊛⊛
October			⊛⊛	⊛⊛⊛	⊛⊛	⊛⊛
November				⊛⊛	⊛	⊛
December				⊛	⊛	⊛

Note: Each ⊛ equals 100 reported cases of allergic rhinitis.

Weekly tree pollen and total mold spore concentrations were measured in grains per cubic meter (gr/m₃) for samples of air taken in southern Iowa for eight weeks. The pollen and mold spore counts are shown in Figures 1 and 2, respectively.

GO ON TO THE NEXT PAGE

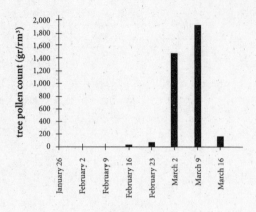

Figure 1

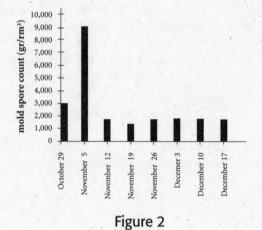

Figure 2

7. Based on Figure 1, the tree pollen count on March 2 was closest to:

A. 75 gr/m^3.

B. 150 gr/m^3.

C. 1,500 gr/m^3.

D. 1,900 gr/m^3.

8. According to Figure 2, the mold spore count in the weeks after November 5:

F. increased.

G. decreased.

H. varied between 1,000 gr/m^3 and 2,000 gr/m^3.

J. remained above 2,000 gr/m^3.

9. Based on the data in Figure 1, the tree pollen count increased the most between which two dates?

A. February 9 to February 16

B. February 23 to March 2

C. March 2 to March 9

D. October 29 to November 5

10. According to Figure 1, which of the following conclusions about the tree pollen count is most valid?

F. The tree pollen count was highest on March 9.

G. The tree pollen count was highest on March 16.

H. The tree pollen count was lowest on February 23.

J. The tree pollen count was lowest on March 16.

11. Based on Table 1, most of the cases of allergic rhinitis in May in northern Kentucky were caused by which of the following allergens?

A. Tree and grass pollen

B. Grass and weed pollen

C. Alternaria

D. Aspergillus

GO ON TO THE NEXT PAGE

PASSAGE III

Simple harmonic motion (SHM) is motion that is *periodic*, or repetitive, and can be described by a frequency of oscillation. Students performed three experiments to study SHM.

EXPERIMENT 1

The students assembled the pendulum shown in Diagram 1. The mass at the end of the arm was raised to a small height, *h*, and released. The frequency of oscillation was measured in oscillations per second, or Hertz (Hz), and the process was repeated for several different arm lengths. The results are shown in Figure 1.

EXPERIMENT 2

A spring was suspended vertically from a hook, and a mass was connected to the bottom of the spring, as shown in Diagram 2. The mass was pulled downward a short distance and released, and the frequency of the resulting oscillation was measured. The procedure was repeated with four different springs and four different masses, and the results are shown in Figure 2.

Diagram 2

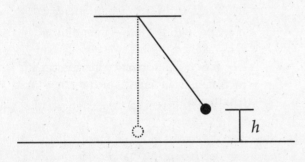

Diagram 1

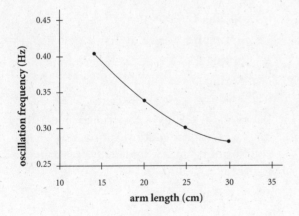

Figure 1

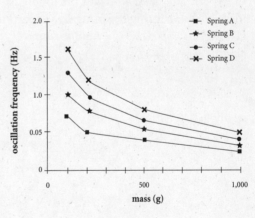

Figure 2

GO ON TO THE NEXT PAGE

EXPERIMENT 3

Using the apparatus from Experiment 2, the mass-spring system was allowed to come to rest, and the *equilibrium length* of the spring was measured. The same four masses and four springs were used, and the results are shown in Figure 3.

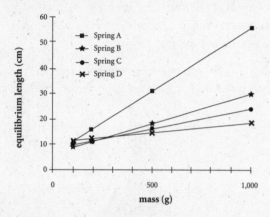

Figure 3

12. In Experiment 3, for which of the following masses would Spring B, Spring C, and Spring D have closest to the same equilibrium lengths?

   F. 100 g
   G. 270 g
   H. 500 g
   J. 1,000 g

13. A student has hypothesized that as the length of the arm of a pendulum increases, the oscillation frequency of the pendulum during SHM will decrease. Do the results of Experiment 1 support her hypothesis?

   A. Yes; the oscillation frequency of the pendulum observed in Experiment 1 decreased as the arm length increased.

   B. Yes; although the longest pendulum arm resulted in the highest oscillation frequency, the frequency decreased with increasing arm length for the other three lengths tested.

   C. No; the oscillation frequency of the pendulum observed in Experiment 1 increased as the arm length increased.

   D. No; although the longest pendulum arm resulted in the lowest oscillation frequency, the frequency increased with increasing arm length for the other three lengths tested.

14. Based on the results of Experiment 2, if an engineer needs a spring that oscillates most slowly after being stretched and released, which of the following springs should be chosen?

   F. Spring A
   G. Spring B
   H. Spring C
   J. Spring D

15. Based on the results of Experiment 3, if a 700 g mass was suspended from Spring A, at what equilibrium length would the system come to rest?

   A. Less than 20 cm
   B. Between 20 cm and 30 cm
   C. Between 30 cm and 50 cm
   D. Greater than 50 cm

GO ON TO THE NEXT PAGE

16. The students tested a fifth spring, Spring E, in the same manner as in Experiment 2. With a 100 g mass suspended from Spring E, the oscillation frequency was 1.4 Hz. Based on the results of Experiment 2, which of the following correctly lists the 5 springs by their oscillation frequency with a 100 g mass suspended from *fastest* to *slowest*?

F.   Spring E, Spring B, Spring C, Spring A, Spring D

G.   Spring D, Spring A, Spring C, Spring B, Spring E

H.   Spring A, Spring B, Spring C, Spring E, Spring D

J.   Spring D, Spring E, Spring C, Spring B, Spring A

17. Experiment 1 was repeated using a larger pendulum mass. Which of the following figures best expresses the comparison between the results found using the larger pendulum mass and using the original mass?

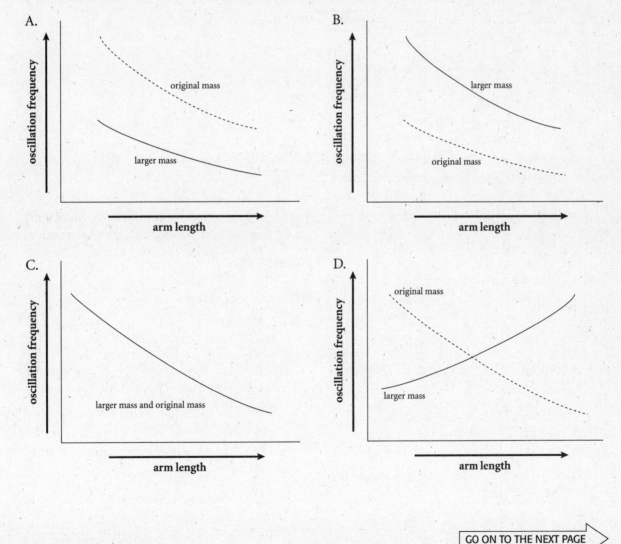

GO ON TO THE NEXT PAGE

PASSAGE IV

An *alloy* is a uniform mixture of two or more metals. When the melting point of an alloy is lower than the melting point of any of its metal components, the alloy is referred to as a *eutectic* system. Figure 1 is a *phase diagram* that illustrates the states of matter of the gold-silicon (Au-Si) eutectic system over a range of temperatures and alloy compositions. For the Au-Si system, 0 percent Si means pure Au, and 100 percent Si means pure Si.

Note: (Au) and (Si) represent the solid forms of gold and silicon, respectively.

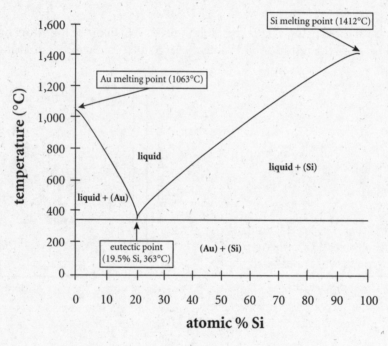

Figure 1

18. According to Figure 1, at what temperature will Au begin to boil?

F. 363°C

G. 1,063°C

H. 1,412°C

J. The boiling point of Au is not included on the figure.

19. Based on Figure 1, an alloy that is atomically 50% Si and 50% Au will be in what state at a temperature of 600°C?

A. Completely liquid

B. Liquid with some amount of solid Si

C. Liquid with some amount of solid Au

D. Completely solid

GO ON TO THE NEXT PAGE

20. A *solder* is a metallic material designed specifically to have a very low melting point. To make a solder out of a Au-Si alloy, what atomic percentages of Au and Si would be most appropriate?

    F. 0% Si, 100% Au

    G. 19.5% Si, 80.5% Au

    H. 80.5% Si, 19.5% Au

    J. 100% Si, 0% Au

21. Based on the information in Figure 1, one could generalize that for Au-Si alloy compositions containing atomically less than 10 percent Si, the temperature at which the alloy becomes completely liquid decreases with:

    A. increasing Si atomic percentage.

    B. decreasing Si atomic percentage.

    C. increasing Au atomic percentage.

    D. neither increasing nor decreasing Si atomic percentage. The melting point is constant for all alloy compositions.

22. A liquid Au-Si alloy of unknown composition is gradually cooled from an initial temperature of 1,500°C. Solid particles are observed to begin forming as the temperature drops to 1,200°C. The particles must consist of which material, and what must be the approximate atomic composition of the alloy?

    F. The particles are Au, and the atomic composition of the alloy is 10% Si, 90% Au.

    G. The particles are Au, and the atomic composition of the alloy is 19.5% Si, 80.5% Au.

    H. The particles are Si, and the atomic composition of the alloy is 73% Si, 27% Au.

    J. The particles are Si, and the atomic composition of the alloy is 90% Si, 10% Au.

GO ON TO THE NEXT PAGE

PASSAGE V

A person requires a certain percentage of oxygen in the blood for proper respiratory function. The amount of oxygen in the air varies enough with altitude that people normally accustomed to breathing near sea level may experience respiratory problems at significantly higher altitudes. Table 1 shows the average percentage of oxygen saturation in the blood, as well as the blood concentrations of three enzymes, GST, ECH, and CR, for three populations of high altitude (ha) dwellers and three populations of sea level (sl) dwellers. Enzyme concentrations are given in arbitrary units (a.u.). Figure 1 shows average oxygen partial pressure and average temperature at various altitudes.

Table 1

Population	Altitude range (m)	Oxygen saturation (%)	Enzyme concentration (a.u.)		
			GST	ECH	CR
ha1	3,500–4,000	98.1	121.0	89.2	48.8
ha2	3,300–3,700	99.0	108.3	93.5	45.6
ha3	3,900–4,200	97.9	111.6	91.9	52.3
sl1	0–300	98.5	86.7	57.1	44.9
sl2	0–150	99.2	79.8	65.8	53.1
sl3	0–200	98.7	82.5	61.4	47.0

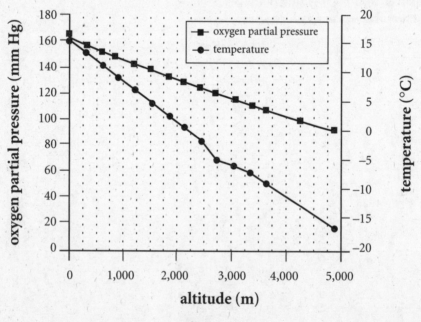

Figure 1

GO ON TO THE NEXT PAGE ⇒

23. Based on the data in Table 1, one would conclude that the blood of high altitude dwellers contains a higher concentration of:

    A. CR than ECH.

    B. CR than GST.

    C. ECH than GST.

    D. GST than CR.

24. Based on the information given, one would expect that, compared to the high altitude dwellers, the sea level dwellers:

    F. have blood with a lower percentage oxygen saturation.

    G. have blood with a lower GST concentration.

    H. can tolerate lower oxygen partial pressures.

    J. can tolerate lower temperatures.

25. According to Figure 1, an atmospheric sample found at an oxygen partial pressure of 110 mm Hg was most likely found at a temperature of about:

    A. 8.1°C.

    B. 0°C.

    C. −5.4°C.

    D. −12.5°C.

26. ECH is an enzyme that improves the efficiency of cellular energy production. Assume that people with higher ECH concentrations in the blood can function normally at higher altitudes without any respiratory difficulties. Based on Table 1, people from which population can function normally at the highest altitude?

    F. sl 1

    G. sl 2

    H. ha 2

    J. ha 3

27. Assume that a person's blood oxygen saturation percentage is determined only by the oxygen partial pressure at the location at which they live and the efficiency of the person's respiratory system at incorporating oxygen into the blood. Which of the following pieces of information supports the hypothesis that people from population ha 2 can incorporate oxygen into their blood more efficiently than people from population sl 1?

    A. Population ha 2 lives where the oxygen partial pressure is lower than that of where population sl 1 lives, yet population ha 2 has a higher blood oxygen saturation percentage than does population ha 1.

    B. Population ha 2 lives where the oxygen partial pressure is higher than that of where population sl 1 lives, yet population ha 2 has a lower blood oxygen saturation percentage than does population ha 1.

    C. Population ha 2 has a higher CR concentration than does population sl 1.

    D. Population ha 2 has an unusually high GST concentration.

GO ON TO THE NEXT PAGE

PASSAGE VI

Two students explain why lakes freeze from the surface downward. They also discuss the phenomena of the melting of ice under the blades of an ice skater's skates.

STUDENT 1

Water freezes first at the surface of lakes because the freezing point of water decreases with increasing pressure. Under the surface, *hydrostatic pressure* causes the freezing point of water to be slightly lower than it is at the surface. Thus, as the air temperature drops, it reaches the freezing point of water at the surface before reaching that of the water beneath it. Only as the temperature becomes even colder will the layer of ice at the surface become thicker.

Pressure is defined as *force* divided by the *surface area* over which the force is exerted. An ice skater exerts the entire force of her body weight over the tiny surface area of two very thin blades. This results in a very large pressure, which quickly melts a small amount of ice directly under the blades.

STUDENT 2

Water freezes first at the surface of lakes because the density of ice is less than that of liquid water. Unlike most liquids, the volume of a given mass of water expands upon freezing, and the density therefore decreases. As a result, the *buoyant force* of water acting upward is greater than the force of gravity exerted downward by any mass of ice, and all ice particles float to the surface upon freezing.

Ice melts under an ice skater's skates because of friction. The energy used to overcome the force of friction is converted to heat, which melts the ice under the skates. The greater the weight of the skater, the greater the force of friction, and the faster the ice melts.

28. According to Student 1, which of the following quantities is *greater* for water molecules beneath a lake's surface than for water molecules at the surface?

    F. Temperature

    G. Density

    H. Buoyant force

    J. Hydrostatic pressure

29. When two ice skaters, wearing identical skates, skated across a frozen lake at the same speed, the ice under the blades of Skater B was found to melt faster than the ice under the blades of Skater A.

    What conclusion would each student draw about which skater is heavier?

    A. Both Student 1 and Student 2 would conclude that Skater A is heavier.

    B. Both Student 1 and Student 2 would conclude that Skater B is heavier.

    C. Student 1 would conclude that Skater A is heavier; Student 2 would conclude that Skater B is heavier.

    D. Student 1 would conclude that Skater B is heavier; Student 2 would conclude that Skater A is heavier.

30. Which student(s), if either, would predict that ice will melt under the blades of an ice skater who is NOT moving?

    F. Student 1 only

    G. Student 2 only

    H. Both Student 1 and Student 2

    J. Neither Student 1 nor Student 2

GO ON TO THE NEXT PAGE ⟩

31. A beaker of ethanol is found to freeze from the bottom upward, instead of from the surface downward. Student 2 would most likely argue that the density of frozen ethanol is:

A. greater than the density of water.

B. less than the density of ice.

C. greater than the density of liquid ethanol.

D. less than the density of liquid ethanol.

32. A toy boat was placed on the surface of a small pool of water, and the boat was gradually filled with sand. After a certain amount of sand had been added, the boat began to sink. Based on Student 2's explanation, the boat began to sink because:

F. hydrostatic pressure became greater than the buoyant force of the water on the boat.

G. atmospheric pressure became greater than the buoyant force of the water on the boat.

H. the force of gravity of the boat on the water became greater than the buoyant force of the water on the boat.

J. the force of gravity of the boat on the water became less than the buoyant force of the water on the boat.

33. According to Student 2, if friction between the ice and the blades of an ice skater's skates is reduced, which of the following quantities simultaneously decreases at the point where the blades and the ice are in contact?

A. Pressure exerted by the blades on the ice

B. Heat produced

C. Force of gravity of the blades on the ice

D. Freezing point of water

34. Based on Student 2's explanation, the reason a hot air balloon is able to rise above the ground is that the balloon and the air inside it are:

F. less dense than the air outside the balloon.

G. more dense than the air outside the balloon.

H. at a higher pressure than the air outside the balloon.

J. less buoyant than the air outside the balloon.

GO ON TO THE NEXT PAGE

PASSAGE VII

In many communities, chemicals containing fluoride ions (F^-) are added to the drinking water supply to help prevent tooth decay. Use of F^- is controversial because studies have linked F^- with bone disease. Students performed two experiments to measure F^- levels.

EXPERIMENT I

Five solutions, each containing a different amount of Na_2SiF_6 (sodium silicofluoride) in H_2O were prepared. Five identical *electrodynamic cells* were filled with equal volumes of each of the five solutions, and a sixth identical cell was filled with a *blank* solution (one containing no added Na_2SiF_6). The cells were activated to measure the electrical *conductivity* for each. The conductivities were then corrected by subtracting the conductivity of the blank solution from each value (see Table 1 and Figure 1).

Table 1

Concentration of F^- (mg/L*)	Measured conductivity ($\propto$S/cm**)	Corrected conductivity ($\propto$S/cm**)
0.0	15.96	0.00
0.1	16.13	0.17
0.5	16.80	.084
1.0	17.63	1.67
2.0	19.30	3.34
4.0	22.64	6.68

* mg/L is milligrams per Liter

** $\propto$S/cm is microSeimens per centimer

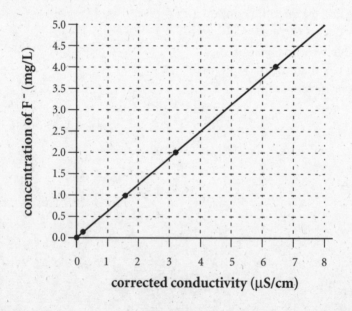

Figure 1

GO ON TO THE NEXT PAGE

EXPERIMENT 2

A water sample was taken directly from the drinking water supply of one community. An electrodynamic cell identical to those used in Experiment 1 was filled with water from this sample, and the cell was activated. The procedure was repeated for water samples from several communities, and the conductivities were measured (Table 2).

Table 2

Community	Measured conductivity ($\propto$S/cm**)	Concentration of F^- (mg/L)
Newton	22.31	3.8
Springfield	16.46	0.3
Lakewood	18.63	1.6
Reading	19.47	2.1

35. Based on the results of Experiment 1, if the concentration of F^- in a solution is doubled, then the corrected conductivity of the solution will approximately:

    A. remain the same.

    B. halve.

    C. double.

    D. quadruple.

36. A sample was also taken from the drinking water supply of the community of Bluewater in Experiment 2 and its conductivity was measured to be 20.69 μS/cm. Which of the following correctly lists the drinking water supplies of Newtown, Lakewood, and Bluewater in *increasing* order of F^- concentration?

    F. Lakewood, Newtown, Bluewater

    G. Bluewater, Newtown, Lakewood

    H. Newtown, Bluewater, Lakewood

    J. Lakewood, Bluewater, Newtown

37. Based on the results of Experiment 1, if a solution with a concentration of 3.0 mg/L F^- had been tested, the corrected conductivity would have been closest to which of the following values?

    A. 1.3 μS/cm

    B. 3.3 μS/cm

    C. 5.0 μS/cm

    D. 6.5 μS/cm

38. If Experiments 1 and 2 were repeated to measure the concentration of chloride ions (Cl^-) in drinking water, then which of the following changes in procedure would be necessary?

    F. The solutions in Experiment 1 should be prepared by adding different concentrations of NaCl (or another chemical containing Cl^-) to H_2O.

    G. The conductivity of the blank solution should be added to the measured conductivities.

    H. The electrodynamic cells should be set to measure resistivity instead of conductivity.

    J. Both NaCl and Na_2SiF_6 should be added to all of the samples.

39. Based on the results of Experiments 1 and 2, if the measured conductivities for the samples tested in Experiment 2 were compared with their corrected conductivities, the measured conductivities would be:

    A. lower for all of the samples tested.

    B. higher for all of the samples tested.

    C. lower for some of the samples tested, higher for others.

    D. the same for all of the samples tested.

GO ON TO THE NEXT PAGE ⟶

40. The presence of other negative ions, such as
Cl^-, results in an increase in the electrical
conductivity of a solution. If all of the
samples tested in Experiment 2 contained
trace concentrations of Cl^-, how would
the measurements have been affected?
Compared to the actual F^- concentrations,
the F^- concentrations apparently measured
would be:

F. higher.

G. lower.

H. the same.

J. higher for some of the samples, lower for
others.

IF YOU FINISH BEFORE TIME IS CALLED, YOU MAY CHECK YOUR WORK ON
THIS SECTION ONLY. DO NOT TURN TO ANY OTHER SECTION IN THE TEST.

STOP

WRITING TEST
30 Minutes—1 Question

Directions: This section will test your writing ability. You will have thirty (30) minutes to compose an essay in English. Prior to planning your essay, pay close attention to the essay prompt so that you understand exactly what you are supposed to do. Your essay's grade will be based on how well it expresses an opinion on the question in the prompt, as well as its logical construction, supporting evidence, and clarity of expression based on the standards of written English.

You may use the unlined space on the next page to plan your essay. Anything written in this space will not be scored by the graders. Your essay must be written on the lined pages. While you may not need all the space to finish, you should not skip lines. Corrections and additions may be written neatly in between lines but not in the margins. Be sure to write clearly. Illegible work will not receive credit.

If you finish in under thirty minutes, you may review your essay. When time is called, lay your pencil down immediately.

DO NOT CONTINUE UNTIL TOLD TO DO SO.

In some cities, laws have been proposed that would restrict licensed drivers under 18 to driving alone or with an adult in the car. Parents and lawmakers who favor such laws point to the high incidence of car accidents with 16- and 17-year-old drivers, and claim that not allowing teenagers under 18 to ride together will help newer drivers to focus on driving safely. Teenagers and parents who are against the restriction argue that teenagers riding together isn't necessarily the cause of accidents and that more comprehensive driver training is a better way to reduce accidents. In your opinion, should cities pass laws that ban teenagers from riding in a car that is driven by a driver under 18?

In your essay, take a position on this question. You may write about either one of the two points of view given, or you may present a different point of view on this question. Use specific reasons and examples to support your position.

Use this space to *plan* your essay. Your work here will not be graded. Write your essay on the lined pages that follow.

Practice Test Two: **Answer Key**

ENGLISH TEST			MATH TEST		READING TEST		SCIENCE TEST	
1. C	26. J	51. D	1. E	31. C	1. D	21. C	1. C	21. A
2. H	27. B	52. F	2. K	32. K	2. H	22. J	2. H	22. H
3. C	28. G	53. C	3. C	33. D	3. B	23. C	3. A	23. D
4. J	29. D	54. J	4. H	34. F	4. J	24. F	4. J	24. G
5. B	30. J	55. D	5. D	35. E	5. D	25. D	5. B	25. C
6. J	31. C	56. H	6. J	36. H	6. H	26. F	6. H	26. H
7. B	32. H	57. A	7. A	37. C	7. B	27. B	7. C	27. A
8. J	33. D	58. J	8. G	38. H	8. F	28. H	8. H	28. J
9. D	34. F	59. C	9. B	39. C	9. C	29. B	9. B	29. B
10. H	35. B	60. G	10. H	40. J	10. F	30. G	10. F	30. F
11. A	36. F	61. D	11. D	41. D	11. C	31. B	11. A	31. C
12. G	37. C	62. H	12. G	42. G	12. G	32. F	12. G	32. H
13. A	38. F	63. A	13. C	43. A	13. B	33. C	13. A	33. B
14. H	39. C	64. H	14. J	44. K	14. F	34. H	14. F	34. F
15. B	40. H	65. B	15. D	45. C	15. B	35. C	15. C	35. C
16. J	41. B	66. F	16. G	46. J	16. J	36. H	16. J	36. J
17. A	42. G	67. B	17. E	47. E	17. C	37. B	17. C	37. C
18. J	43. D	68. G	18. J	48. H	18. J	38. J	18. J	38. F
19. D	44. G	69. D	19. A	49. C	19. A	39. B	19. B	39. B
20. H	45. A	70. G	20. H	50. G	20. G	40. G	20. G	40. F
21. C	46. J	71. A	21. A	51. A				
22. G	47. D	72. G	22. J	52. H				
23. C	48. H	73. A	23. E	53. D				
24. J	49. D	74. H	24. H	54. K				
25. C	50. G	75. D	25. C	55. A				
			26. F	56. J				
			27. D	57. B				
			28. F	58. F				
			29. B	59. C				
			30. K	60. H				

ANSWERS AND EXPLANATIONS

ENGLISH TEST

The questions fall into the following categories, according to the skills they test. If you notice that you're having trouble with particular categories, review the following:

1. REDUNDANCY—English Workout 1
2. RELEVANCE—English Workout 1
3. VERBOSITY—English Workout 1
4. JUDGING THE PASSAGE—English Workout 2
5. LOGIC—English Workout 2
6. MODIFIERS—English Workout 2
7. READING-TYPE QUESTIONS—English Workout 2
8. STRUCTURE AND PURPOSE—English Workout 2
9. TONE—English Workout 2
10. VERB USAGE—English Workout 2
11. COMPLETENESS—English Workouts 2 and 3
12. IDIOM—English Workouts 2 and 3
13. PRONOUNS—English Workouts 2 and 3
14. SENTENCE STRUCTURE—English Workouts 2 and 3
15. PUNCTUATION—English Workout 3

PASSAGE I

1. (C)—Sentence Structure

Choice (C) forms a complete sentence by using the simple past tense *was*. Choice (A) creates a sentence fragment; an *-ing* verb needs a helping verb, such as *was* or *is*, to be the main verb in a sentence. Choice (B) incorrectly uses a comma to separate the subject from the main verb. Choice (D) omits the verb entirely, creating a sentence fragment.

2. (H)—Logic

The phrase *not only* in the beginning of the sentence is your clue to the correct answer. Logically, the phrase *not only* is always followed by *but also*. Here's another example: I *not only* studied math, *but* I *also* studied science. The other choices neither complete the idiom correctly nor convey the necessary contrast between the ideas in the two clauses.

3. (C)—Punctuation

Add an apostrophe and an *s* to a singular noun to show possession. The narrator and Gretchen attend one school, so choice (C) is correct. Choice (A) omits the apostrophe needed to show that the *swim team* belongs to the *school*. Choice (B) incorrectly treats *school* as a plural, placing the apostrophe after the *s*. Choice (D) incorrectly uses *ours* and does not make *school* possessive.

4. (J)—Verbosity

The test makers value simple and direct prose, so change passive constructions such as *it was with Gretchen that I* when you're given the opportunity. As is often the case on the English section of the ACT, the shortest answer—choice (J)—is correct. In addition to being verbose, choice (F) contains a sentence structure error: It is not clear who knows that the writer enjoyed swimming. Choices (G) and (H) are both also verbose.

5. (B)—Idiom

Slow down and carefully read the Nonstandard-Format questions. You just may see a question such as this that tests vocabulary. Choice (B) indicates that the narrator's mother recommended swimming lessons but did not decide that the narrator *must* take them. Choices (A), (C), and (D) all indicate that the mother's mind was made up.

6. (J)—Sentence Structure

If a sentence seems to have too many ideas, then it is probably a run-on. By itself, a comma cannot separate two clauses that could be independent sentences, as in choice (F). Choice (G) replaces *swimmers* with a pronoun but does not correct the run-on. Similarly, choice (H) removes the comma but does not address the problem of two complete thoughts that are incorrectly joined. Choice (J) solves the problem by using *whom*, which turns the second half of the sentence into a dependent clause that describes the *women*.

7. (B)—Punctuation

This sentence contains a parenthetical phrase. If you omitted *who had been swimming competitively since elementary school*, you would still have a complete sentence. Like all parenthetical phrases, this needs to be set off from the rest of the sentence. A comma is used at the beginning of the phrase, so a comma must also be used at the end of the phrase. This makes choice (D) incorrect. Choices (A) and (C) insert unnecessary commas within the parenthetical phrase.

8. (J)—Redundancy

When in doubt, take it out. *Giving up*, by definition, means *quitting* or *failing*. Choices (F), (G), and (H) create redundancies.

9. (D)—Verb Usage

Trust your ear. *Begin* is an irregular verb; the simple past tense *began* can be used by itself, but the past participle *begun* cannot. Instead, *begun* always appears with *has*, *have*, or *had*, as in "I *have begun* to

prepare for the ACT." Choice (D) correctly uses the simple past tense *began*. Choice (B) creates another verb usage error by inserting *been*. Choice (C) incorrectly uses *began* with *had*.

10. (H)—Pronouns

Don't panic if you see a question that tests the use of *who* and *whom*. The pronoun *who* refers to a subject, just like the pronouns *he* and *she* replace subjects. The pronoun *whom* refers to an object, just like the pronouns *him* and *her* replace objects. Here, *coach* is the subject of the sentence, so *who* (choice (H)) is correct. Never refer to a person as *which* (choice (J)).

11. (A)—Sentence Structure

Don't force a change where one isn't needed. The correct answer for some of the underlined portions will be NO CHANGE. The sentence *The hard work eventually paid off* is correct and concise as it is written. Choice (B) is verbose, and choices (C) and (D) create run-on sentences.

12. (G)—Relevance

Start by asking yourself, "Does this stuff belong here?" The question asks for a sentence that is relevant to the narrator's experience on the swim team. Only choice (G) is connected to the narrator and the swim team; the sentence explains that the narrator was one of the only swimmers on the team to be interested in the butterfly. The history of the stroke (F), the relative speed of the stroke (H), and an alternative name for the stroke (J) are not as related to the narrator's personal experience.

13. (A)—Relevance

The shortest answer is often, but not always, correct. Don't omit portions that add relevant information to the sentence. The sentence is about the narrator's swimming, so her participation in the medley relay is relevant. Choices (B) and (C) add descriptions of the medley relay that are not relevant to the topic.

14. (H)—Verb Usage

The four choices offer different tenses of the same verb. The clue *last year* indicates that the narrator earned the varsity letter in the past. Choice (H), the simple past tense, is correct. Neither the future tense (F) nor the present tense (J) makes sense with the clue *last year*. Choice (G) would only make sense if something had prevented the narrator from earning the varsity letter.

15. (B)—Structure and Purpose

Keep the main point of the passage in mind. Before beginning high school, the narrator had never thought of herself as an athlete. Then she joined the swim team and became successful at the sport. Choice (B) is most relevant to the central ideas of the passage. Choices (A) and (C) focus too narrowly on details in the passage, while choice (D) contradicts the main point of the passage.

PASSAGE II

16. (J)—Punctuation

Don't assume that a comma or semicolon is needed just because a sentence is long. Read the sentence aloud to yourself, and you should be able to hear that a comma is not needed in the underlined portion. A semicolon would only be correct if the second half of the sentence expressed a complete thought (choice (F)). Choices (G) and (H) both use an unnecessary comma.

17. (A)—Verb Usage

When a verb is underlined, check to see if it agrees with its noun. Watch out for descriptive phrases that separate a verb from its noun. Here, the verb *was*

agrees with the singular noun *tank*. NO CHANGE is needed. Choice (B) uses the present tense, but the surrounding sentences use the past tense. Choices (C) and (D) incorrectly use a verb in the plural form.

18. (J)—Sentence Structure

When the word *that* or *which* is underlined, watch out for an incomplete sentence. As it is written, this is a sentence fragment; a complete verb is missing. Removing *that*, as in choice (J), turns *made* into the main verb of a complete and correct sentence. Choice (G) does not address the sentence fragment error, and choice (H) also fails to provide a clear and appropriate sentence.

19. (D)—Redundancy

If you are *familiar* with a type of animal, then you have almost certainly *seen it before*. Choice (D) creates a concise sentence that does not lose any of the original meaning. The other choices are redundant. Choice (B) repeats *sights* when *view* has already been used, and choice (C) uses the unnecessarily repetitive phrase *to which I was no stranger*.

20. (H)—Structure and Purpose

Scan the paragraph for connecting words and phrases that you can use as clues to determine the most logical order of sentences. In sentence 5, the word *first* suggests that the sentence should be placed close to the beginning of the paragraph. Sentence 2 says "There were *also* animals I had never before glimpsed," which indicates that a preceding sentence discusses animals the writer had glimpsed. Sentence 5, which describes the writer's view of familiar animals, most logically belongs immediately after Sentence 1.

21. (C)—Verb Usage

If an underlined verb agrees with its noun, then determine whether the verb's tense makes sense in the context of the passage. The surrounding verbs are in the past tense, so this sentence should use the simple past tense *saw* (choice C). Choices (A) and (D) use the present tense, and choice (B) illogically uses the past progressive *had been seeing*.

22. (G)—Structure and Purpose

An effective first sentence for a paragraph will introduce the topic of the paragraph and connect that topic to ideas that have come before. Paragraph 3 focuses on the catfish, while Paragraph 4 describes the large alligator and snapping turtle in the bayou tank. Choice (G) is an effective connection between these paragraphs, referring to the catfish and introducing the idea that there were even bigger animals on display. Neither choice (A) nor choice (H) leads into the topic of Paragraph 4. Choice (J) doesn't provide a transition from the discussion of the catfish in Paragraph 3.

23. (C)—Structure and Purpose

The phrase in question provides a visual image; deleting the phrase would mean losing a description (choice C). The removal of the phrase would not affect the transition between sentences (choice A). Contrary to choice (B), the contrast between images would be decreased. The level of suspense may be somewhat decreased by the loss of the description, but it would not be increased (choice D).

24. (J)—Verb Usage

The verbs *slides* and *aims* agree with the singular subject *it*, but they are in the wrong tense. The rest of the paragraph describes actions that took place in the past. For the sentence to make sense in context, these verbs should also be in the past tense

(choice (J)). Choices (F) and (G) use present-tense verbs. Choice (H) creates a logically incomplete sentence.

25. (C)—Idiom

Ask yourself, "Does this stuff sound like English?" If something sounds awkward or unusual, there is probably an error. Most words that end in *-ly* are adverbs; they are used to modify verbs, adjectives, or other adverbs. Adverbs cannot be used to describe nouns, such as *moment* (choice (A)). Choice (C) correctly uses the adjective *slight* to modify *moment*. The sentences formed by choices (B) and (D) don't make sense.

26. (J)—Idiom

The phrase *much of the onlookers* probably sounds strange to you. That's because *much* is used with non-countable things or concepts (as in "There isn't much time") or quantities (as in "There isn't much pizza left"). You could count the number of *onlookers*, so *many*, choice (J), is correct. Choices (G) and (H) also create idiomatic errors.

27. (B)—Structure and Purpose

The question tells you that the writer's goal is to describe the appearance of the crayfish, so eliminate any sentences that do not have details about how crayfish look (choice (C)). Choice (A) suggests that crayfish look like lobsters, and choice (D) describes the crayfish as small. Neither of these sentences offers the descriptive detail that is given in choice (B).

28. (G)—Punctuation

Trust your ear. You naturally pause when a comma or semicolon is needed in a sentence. A pause between *all* and *I* just doesn't sound right; that's because the full introductory phrase *After seeing all I could inside the museum* should not be interrupted. A comma should not separate a verb ("seeing") from its object ("museum"). This eliminates choices (F) and (H). A comma is needed between an introductory phrase and the complete thought that follows, making choice (G) correct and choice (J) incorrect.

29. (D)—Verbosity

Say it simply. The shortest answer here is correct: it turns the passive construction *it was that* in choices (A) and (B) into the active *I had*. Choice (C) is unnecessarily wordy.

30. (J)—Completeness

A sentence must have a subject and verb and express a complete thought. The sentence that begins *And operates* does not have a subject. Removing the period (choice (J)) creates a grammatically incorrect sentence. Choice (G) is awkwardly worded. Choice (H) creates a run-on sentence; a coordinating conjunction such as *and* needs to be used along with a comma to link two complete thoughts.

PASSAGE III

31. (C)—Pronouns

When a pronoun is underlined, check to see that it agrees in number with the noun it replaces or refers to. In this sentence, the underlined pronoun refers back to the plural *secret identities and elaborate disguises*. Choice (C) uses the correct plural pronoun *they*. Choices (A) and (B) create pronoun agreement errors by using the singular pronoun *it*. Choice (D) creates a sentence fragment, since it makes the sentence into a dependent clause.

32. (H)—Punctuation

Many English questions will focus on the correct use of commas. Commas should be used to separate an appositive or descriptive phrase from the main

part of the sentence. The phrase *the restaurant critic for The New York Times* describes the noun *Ruth Reichl*, so the phrase should be set off with commas (choice (H)). Choices (F) and (J) fail to use both necessary commas. On the other hand, choice (G) incorrectly inserts a third comma.

33. (D)—Structure and Purpose

Only add sentences that are directly connected to the topic of a paragraph. Paragraph 2 discusses the importance of a *Times* review to restaurants in New York City. The suggested sentence provides a specific detail about one restaurant without explaining how the review from *The Times* affected business. Choice (D) best explains why the sentence should not be added.

34. (F)—Idiom

Trust your ear. We look *to* someone or something for advice. No change is needed. Choice (G) suggests that the paper is looking *along with* its readers, while choice (H) suggests that the readers are looking *near* the newspaper. Choice (J) uses an *-ing* verb without a helping verb, which creates a sentence fragment.

35. (B)—Verb Usage

Verbs must make sense in the context of the passage. The next sentence says that a negative review *can undermine* a restaurant. Because the two sentences discuss possible results of a review, the underlined verb in this sentence should be in the same tense— *can bring* (choice (B). Choice (A) illogically uses the conditional in the past tense, while choices (C) and (D) do not use the conditional at all.

36. (F)—Punctuation

The subject of the sentence is *restaurant owners and workers*, and the verb is *have*. There isn't a descriptive phrase or clause separating the subject and verb, so no comma is needed. A semicolon should be used to connect two complete thoughts (choice (G)). Choice (H) incorrectly treats *restaurant* as the first item in a list; instead, *restaurant* identifies the type of *owners* and *workers*.

37. (C)—Pronouns

To whom does the meal belong? It belongs to the *writer*, so the possessive pronoun *whose* is correct. *Who's* is always a contraction for who is or who has (choice (B)). Choices (A) and (D) introduce sentence structure errors.

38. (F)—Verbosity

The shortest answer is often correct. The sentence is concise and direct as it is written. Each of the other choices adds unnecessary words to the underlined portion.

39. (C)—Redundancy

On the ACT, there's no need to say the same thing twice. *Common, ordinary, representative,* and *average* all have very similar meanings; choices (A) and (B) use redundant language. Choice (C) makes the sentence concise by using only *typical*. Choice (D) uses a word that does not make sense in the context of the sentence.

40. (H)—Redundancy

If you have *decided* to do something to solve a problem, you have found a *solution*—there's no need to use both words. Choice (H) eliminates the redundancy and verbosity errors of the other choices.

41. (B)—Modifiers

As a rule, modifying words, phrases, and clauses should be as close as possible to the things or actions they describe. For instance, the list beginning *such as an attractive blonde named Chloe* describes the

different personas. Therefore, *different personas* should come right before the list. This eliminates choice (A). Choice (B) correctly uses an introductory phrase and makes *Reichl* the subject of the sentence. Choice (C) is a sentence fragment; a complete verb is missing. Choice (D) inserts an unnecessary comma between *clothing* and *that*, and the pronoun *herself* is incorrect in context.

42. (G)—Structure and Purpose

The most logical and effective sentence will be connected to the main topic of the paragraph and make a transition to the following sentence. Paragraph 4 describes how Reichl turned herself into different characters, and Paragraph 5 describes the result of reviewing a restaurant while in disguise. The best link between these ideas is choice (G). Choice (F) is a narrow detail that does not connect the two paragraphs, while choices (H) and (J) move completely away from the topic of Reichl's disguises.

43. (D)—Modifiers

Sometimes it helps to rephrase a question in your own words. For example, how this question could be rewritten: "What does the phrase *of a restaurant* describe?" Reichl focuses on the quality of a restaurant, so the best placement is (D). The phrase does not describe *developed, view,* or *person*.

44. (G)—Structure and Purpose

The word *occasionally* means sometimes; its placement in this sentence indicates that sometimes Reichl was sometimes treated very differently when she was in disguise, and sometimes she wasn't. Removing the word *occasionally* would indicate that Reichl always or typically had a different experience as one of her personas (choice (G)).

45. (A)—Structure and Purpose

Paragraph 6 describes the effect of Reichl's use of disguises when she reviewed restaurants. Logically, this effect should follow the explanation of why and how Ruth dined as different people, the topics of Paragraphs 3 and 4. Paragraph 6 should remain where it is.

PASSAGE IV

46. (J)—Punctuation

Trust your ear. A comma indicates a short pause, which you won't hear when you read this part of the sentence aloud. No comma is needed (choice (J)). A comma can be used to separate a descriptive phrase from the rest of the sentence (choices (F) and (H)), but neither *would develop into prize-winning vegetables* nor d*evelop into prize-winning vegetables* is a descriptive phrase. Choice (G) incorrectly treats the underlined portion of the sentence as part of a list.

47. (D)—Structure and Purpose

The paragraph describes events in chronological order, from the last freeze of the year to the time that spring *truly arrived*. Sentence 3 describe thinning out the plants and pulling weeds so the new plants would grow; it would only make sense to do this *after* the seeds have been planted and have started to grow. Sentence 4 is about planting seeds, so Sentence 3 must come after Sentence 4 (choice (D)).

48. (H)—Punctuation

When you read this sentence aloud, you should be able to hear a short pause between *burden* and *less*. This pause indicates that the conjunction *and* is needed to separate the two descriptions (choice (H)). Choice (G) is wrong because a colon is used to introduce a brief definition, explanation, or list.

Choice (J) uses the inappropriate conjunction but, which doesn't make sense in context.

49. (D)—Relevance

When *OMIT the underlined portion* is an option, consider whether the underlined portion is relevant to the topic of the sentence or paragraph. Paragraph 2 is about the writer's failure to maintain her garden, not about the weather in July and August. Choice (D) is correct.

50. (G)—Logic

Always read the questions carefully! This one asks for the choice that would NOT work in the sentence. In other words, three of the answer choices would make sense in the sentence. The first sentence of Paragraph 3 contrasts with Paragraph 2, so the contrasting transitions in (F), (H), and (J) are all possible substitutions for the underlined word. *Indeed*, (choice (G)), however, is a word used to show emphasis, not contrast.

51. (D)—Relevance

The shortest answer is often correct. Choices (A), (B), and (C) all refer to large-scale farming, which is only loosely related to the topic of gardening. Choice (D) keeps the sentence focused on the topic of Paragraph 3.

52. (F)—Structure and Purpose

Before you answer this question, read enough of Paragraph 4 to identify its main idea. Paragraph 3 introduces the topic of square foot gardening, and Paragraph 4 describes several of its advantages. The best link between these ideas is the original sentence (choice (F)). Paragraph 4 doesn't mention the history of square foot gardening or the writer's neighbor, so choices (G) and (J) don't make sense. Choice (H) is a detail about square foot gardening, but it does not function as a topic sentence for the paragraph.

53. (C)—Idiom

If an underlined word ends in -*ly*, you can be pretty sure that it is an adverb. Remember that adverbs can be used to describe verbs, adjectives, and other adverbs, but not nouns. The word *garden* is a noun, so choices (A) and (B) are incorrect. The adjective *traditional* (choice (C)) is correct. The phrase *tradition garden* (choice (D)) does not make sense.

54. (J)—Pronouns

Who spends hours thinning each row? From this sentence it's unclear: you have no idea who *they* are. Other sentences in Paragraph 4 use the pronoun *you*, so it makes sense to use *you* here.

55. (D)—Redundancy

OMIT the underlined portion is an option, so check to see if the information is irrelevant to the topic or repetitive. This sentence begins with the phrase *In a square foot garden*, so it is unnecessary to repeat *in the garden*. Choice (D) is correct.

56. (H)—Completeness

OMIT the underlined portion isn't always the correct answer. As it is written, the sentence does not express a complete thought. To correct the error, remove *which could* so that *make* becomes the main verb of the sentence. Choices (G) and (J) create sentence fragments.

57. (A)—Verb Usage

Don't look too hard for an error—many of the English questions will require NO CHANGE. The present tense and the pronoun *you* is used throughout Paragraph 4, so this sentence is correct as it is written.

58. (J)—Redundancy

Remember that the ACT values economy. If you can express an underlined portion in fewer words without changing or losing the original meaning, then the shortest answer is probably correct. The only choice that does not use redundant language is (J).

59. (C)—Verb Usage

The verb in this sentence is separated from its singular subject *One season* by the phrase *of using the square garden techniques*. Choice (C) corrects the subject-verb agreement error of the original sentence. Incorrect choices use the plural form of the verb (A and B) or the future tense (D), which does not make sense in the context of the sentence.

60. (G)—Judging the Passage

This question asks about the passage as a whole, so take a moment to think about the main idea of the passage. Paragraphs 1 and 2 describe the writer's failed attempts at a traditional garden, while Paragraphs 3, 4, and 5 focus on the writer's success with a square foot garden. The essay is not instructive; instead, it compares two types of gardens, choice (G).

PASSAGE V

61. (D)—Punctuation

When a coordinating conjunction such as *but* or *and* combines two independent clauses (complete thoughts), a comma must come before it. In this sentence a comma should be inserted after *light* (choice (D)). Choice (C) incorrectly places a comma in a compound and fails to add one before the coordinating conjunction, and choice (B) incorrectly uses a semicolon between an independent and a dependent clause. You'll likely see at least one semicolon question on the ACT, so remember that a semicolon is used to separate two complete thoughts or to separate items in a series or list when one or more of those items already contains commas.

62. (H)—Verb Usage

The answer choices present different forms of the verbs *improves* and *decreases*, so you know the issue is subject-verb agreement. The two underlined verbs need to agree with the plural subject *steps*; only choice (H) puts both *improve* and *decrease* in the correct form.

63. (A)—Verbosity

The simplest way to say something is often the most correct way to say something. The original sentence is the most concise and correct version. Choice (B) is redundant, using both *problem* and *trouble*. Choices (C) and (D) are both unnecessarily wordy in comparison to (A), which expresses the same meaning.

64. (H)—Sentence Structure

An *–ing* verb needs a helping verb, such as *is*, to function as the main verb in a clause or sentence. Changing *being* to *is*, as in choice (H), corrects the sentence structure error. Choice (G) inserts an incorrect comma between *vision* and *has*, while choice (J) creates a new sentence structure error by omitting the verb *being*.

65. (B)—Modifiers

Something that is *set* is established or predetermined. For the sentence to make sense, *set* should describe *time*; the wiper blades should be replaced at an *established* time each year. Choice (B) is correct. It does not make sense for the *blades* (choice (A)), the *year* (choice (C)) or the *risk* to be *set* or established.

66. (F)—Idiom

Trust your ear. With some idiom questions, you have to rely on your ear to hear what sounds correct. *In general* is an introductory phrase used to mean usually or typically. Choice (F) provides the correct idiom for this context. The other choices contain idioms that are not typical of spoken English and do not fit this context.

67. (B)—Structure and Purpose

To pick the best first sentence for Paragraph 4, you must be able to identify the main idea of the paragraph. If you scan a few sentences of Paragraph 4 before you answer the question, you'll see that the topic of the paragraph is changing a car's oil and oil filter. Only choice (B) introduces this topic. Choice (A) is too general, while choices (C) and (D) refer to car maintenance procedures that are not discussed in Paragraph 4.

68. (G)—Logic

The connecting word *so* is underlined, so consider the relationship between the two parts of the sentence. There is a slight contrast—the first part of the sentence explains what you *do* need, while the second part identifies what you *don't* need. The contrasting conjunction *but* (choice (G)) makes the most sense in context. The other choices indicate a cause-and-effect relationship that is not present in the sentence.

69. (D)—Punctuation

Information that is key to the main idea of a sentence should not be set off by commas. Here, it's important to know that the *section* is *in your owner's manual*, so commas are incorrect. Choice (D) is correct. Choice (C) incorrectly uses a semicolon; a complete thought is not expressed by *and collect all of the tools you need*.

70. (G)—Structure and Purpose

Carefully read the question so that you understand the writer's purpose. If the writer wants to explain how to change oil, then the sentence should explain at least one specific step in the process. Choice (G) provides the most detailed information about how to go about changing oil.

71. (A)—Punctuation

Use a semicolon to introduce or emphasize what follows. The warning *you do not want to risk being crushed by a car* is certainly worthy of emphasis, so the sentence is correct as it is written. The other choices create run-ons, as the sentence expresses two complete thoughts; additionally, (D) incorrectly separates a subject noun from its verb with a comma.

72. (G)—Structure and Purpose

Paragraph 4 uses the informal *you* and *your*, while the rest of the essay uses the more formal third person. Therefore, eliminating the second-person pronouns from Paragraph 4 would make the paragraph match the tone and voice of the rest of the essay (choice (G)). Choices (H) and (J) are opposite answers: eliminating *you* and *your* would make the advice less direct and would make the essay more formal.

73. (A)—Redundancy

Watch out for redundant language! A *qualified mechanic* will do a *professional* job, just as a *qualified mechanic* is likely *certified*; choices (B) and (C) use repetitive language. Choice (D) introduces a sentence structure error. The best version of the underlined portion is choice (A).

74. (H)—Structure and Purpose

Knowing the general topic of each paragraph will help you quickly answer a question like this one. The sentence refers to *these different fluids*, so look for a part of the passage that discusses fluids. The second and third sentences of Paragraph 3 refer to different fluids (*coolant, oil, brake fluid*, and *transmission fluid*), so the most logical placement for the sentence is at the end of Paragraph 3 (choice (H)). Paragraph 2 and Paragraph 4 each only refer to one fluid, so choices (F) and (J) are incorrect.

75. (D)—Judging the Passage

Use your Reading Comp skills to answer this question. Does the main idea of the passage fit with this purpose? Not really, as the passage focuses solely on basic maintenance that car owners can do themselves. The passage doesn't discuss the need to learn about a car's safety features. Choice (D) is correct.

MATH TEST

1. (E)—Adding/Subtracting Fractions

100 Key Math Concepts for the ACT, #22. To determine the total amount of fabric used, add the mixed numbers. To add mixed numbers, add the whole number parts, and then add the fractions. The whole number parts add to 4. To add the fractions, find the least common denominator of 8 and 3, which is 24. Convert each fraction to an equivalent fraction with a denominator of 24: $\frac{3 \times 3}{8 \times 3} = \frac{9}{24}$, and $\frac{1 \times 8}{3 \times 8} = \frac{8}{24}$. Now, add the numerators, and keep the denominator: $\frac{9}{24} + \frac{8}{24} = \frac{17}{24}$. The total fabric used is $4\frac{17}{24}$.

If you chose (B), you found a common denominator, but you did not add the numerators to get a total numerator of 4. A common error when adding fractions would result in choice (C). This fraction was obtained by the incorrect procedure of adding the numerators, and then adding the denominators.

2. (K)—Multiplying and Dividing Powers/ Multiplying Monomials

100 Key Math Concepts for the ACT #47, #55. To simplify this expression, first multiply the numerical coefficients to get $5 \times 6 \times 2 = 60$. To multiply the variable terms, keep the base of the variable and add the exponents. Remember that x denotes x^1. Multiply the x variable terms: $x^3 \times x = x^{3+1} = x^4$. Multiply the y variable terms: $y^5 \times y^2 \times y = y^{5+2+1} = y^8$. The resultant expression is $60x^4y^8$.

If your answer was (J), you fell into the common trap of multiplying the exponents instead of the correct method of adding the exponents. If your answer was either (F) or (G), you added the numerical coefficients instead of multiplying. If your answer was (H), you did not include the exponents of 1 for the single terms of x and y.

3. (C)—Percent Formula

100 Key Math Concepts for the ACT, #32. First, find the amount each person saves yearly. Brandon puts 6% of his $36,000 salary, or $0.06 \times 36,000 =$ $2,160 each year. Jacqui puts $200 every month, or $12 \times 200 = \$2,400$ each year. The difference, in dollars, of their savings is therefore $2,400 - 2,160 = \$240$.

Answer choice (A) reflects the *monthly* difference in their savings. If you chose answer choice (D), you incorrectly found the difference between Brandon's yearly savings and Jacqui's *monthly* savings. Choice (E) indicates Brandon's monthly *salary*, minus Jacqui's monthly savings.

4. (H)—Average Formula/Using the Average to Find the Sum/Find the Missing Number

100 Key Math Concepts for the ACT, #41, #43, #44. An average is found by taking the total sum of the terms and dividing it by the total number of terms. Therefore, the sum = (average) × (number of terms). For Mikhail to have an average for the 5 games to be 180, the sum = $180 \times 5 = 900$. The first four scores total $190 + 200 + 145 + 180 = 715$. Therefore, his score for the 5th game must be $900 - 715 = 185$.

Answer choice (F) is just the average of the first four scores. Choice (G) is the average of the first four scores added and averaged with 180.

5. (D)—Percent Formula

100 Key Math Concepts for the ACT, #32. The amount of chromium is a part of the whole alloy.

Use the formula Part = Percent × Whole. There are 262.5 pounds of chromium available, which must reflect at least 10.5% of the whole. Let w represent the whole amount of alloy that can be manufactured and write the algebraic equation: $262.5 = 10.5\%$ w or $262.5 = 0.105w$. Divide both sides of the equation by 0.105: $w = \dfrac{262.5}{0.105}$ pounds of steel. Choice (A) represents 10.5% of 262.5. If you chose answer choice (B), you simply subtracted 10.5 from 262.5, without regard to the percent or the whole amount. Answer choice (C) is simply the amount of chromium. If you chose answer choice (E), you set up the problem correctly, but incorrectly converted 10.5% to the decimal 0.0105.

6. (J)—Special Quadrilaterals

100 Key Math Concepts for the ACT, #86. A wallpaper border is a strip that surrounds the perimeter of the kitchen. The perimeter of a rectangle = 2(length + width). The kitchen has a length of 6.5 meters and a width of 4 meters, so the amount of border needed is $2(6.5 + 4) = 2(10.5) =$ 21 meters.

Answer choice (G) is a common mistake made when calculating perimeter. This answer would result from just adding the two dimensions, and not multiplying by 2. Answer choice (K) is the area, not the perimeter, of the kitchen.

7. (A)—PEMDAS

100 Key Math Concepts for the ACT, #7. To find an equivalent for the given expression, use the distributive property. First, evaluate the inner parentheses according to the order of operations, or PEMDAS. Distribute the negative sign to $(y + z)$ to get $w(x - y - z)$. Next, distribute the variable w to all terms in parentheses to get $wx - wy - wz$.

Answer choice (B) fails to distribute the negative sign to the z term. Answer choices (C) and (D) only distribute the w t to the first term. Choice (E) incorrectly distributes wx to the $(y + z)$ term.

8. (G)—Solving a Linear Equation

100 Key Math Concepts for the ACT, #63. This is an equation with a variable on both sides. To solve, work to get the n terms isolated on one side of the equation, and the numerical terms on the other side. Subtract $3n$ from both sides to get $6n - 3n - 4 = 3n - 3n + 24$. Combine like terms: $3n - 4 = 24$. Now, add 4 to both sides: $3n - 4 + 4 = 24 + 4$, or $3n = 28$. Finally, divide both sides by 3: $n = \dfrac{28}{3}$.

Answer choice (F) reflects a common trap: forgetting to divide by 3. If you chose answer choice (H) or (J), you incorrectly added $6n$ and $3n$, and possibly subtracted 4 from 24 instead of adding 4. Dividing incorrectly at the last step would have led you to answer choice (K).

9. (B)—Translating from English into Algebra/ Solving a Linear Equation

100 Key Math Concepts for the ACT, #63, #65. In this arithmetic sequence, you can think of the terms as 26, $26 + s$, $26 + s + s$, and $26 + s + s + s$. In this example, s represents the difference between successive terms. The final term is 53, so set up an algebraic equation: $26 + s + s + s = 53$. Solve this equation for s, by first combining like terms: $26 + 3s = 53$. Subtract 26 from both sides to get $26 - 26 + 3s = 53 - 26$, or $3s = 27$. Divide both sides by 3 to find that s, the difference between terms, is 9. Therefore, the terms are 26, $26 + 9$, $26 + 9 + 9$, 53, or 26, 35, 44, 53.

Answer choice (D) results from taking 53 − 26, dividing by 4, adding this value to each term, and rounding. In answer choices (A), (C), and (E), there is a common difference between 2nd − 1st and then 4th − 3rd, but it is different than the difference between the 3rd and the 2nd terms.

10. (H)—Evaluating an Expression/Solving a Linear Equation

100 Key Math Concepts for the ACT, #52, #63. First, solve the equation $5m^2 = 45$ for m. Once a value is obtained for m, substitute this into the expression to evaluate and find the answer. To solve the equation, divide both sides of the equation by 5 to get $m^2 = 9$. Take the square root of each side to get $m = 3$, or $m = -3$. Now, evaluate the expression. Because the expression contains the radical $\sqrt{12m}$, and the expression must be a real number, reject the value of $m = -3$. When a radicand, the expression under the radical sign, is negative, the number does not have a value in the set of real numbers. Substitute 3 for m in the expression:

$$(3)^3 + \sqrt{12(3)} = 27 + \sqrt{36} = 27 + 6 = 33.$$

If you chose answer choice (G), you just found the value of m^3. You might have selected answer choice (J) if you interpreted the $12m$ under the radical sign as the number 123 instead of 12×3. If you chose answer choice (K), you probably failed to take the square root of 9 when solving the equation and used the value of 9 for m.

11. (D)—Converting Fractions to Decimals/Volume of Other Solids

100 Key Math Concepts for the ACT, #29, #95. First, convert the mixed number radius to a decimal: $3\frac{3}{5} = 3.6$.

Substitute 3.6 into the formula to get $V = \frac{4}{3} \times \pi \times (3.6)^3$. Use the π key on your calculator. If your calculator has fractional capability and follows the correct order of operations, type the entry in as listed above. Otherwise, first find 3.6 to the third power. Multiply the result by 4, and then divide by 3. Finally, multiply by π. In either case, the result is approximately 195.43, or 195 to the nearest cubic meter.

If you chose answer choices (A) or (B), you multiplied the radius by 3, instead of taking the radius to the third power. For choice (C), as well as choice (A), you incorrectly converted $3\frac{3}{5}$ to 3.35, a common trap. If you arrived at answer choice (E), you first multiplied $\frac{4}{3} \times \pi \times (3.6)$, and then raised this value to the third power.

12. (G)—Probability

100 Key Math Concepts for the ACT, #46. Probability is a ratio that compares the number of favorable, or desired, outcomes to the total number of outcomes. Probability is always a number between 0 and 1, and is never greater than 1. In this question, the favorable outcome is the number of nuts that are NOT peanuts, or $6 + 8 = 14$. The total number of outcomes is $10 + 6 + 8 = 24$. The probability that the nut is NOT a peanut is $\frac{14}{24} = \frac{7}{12}$, in lowest terms. Choice (F) is the probability that the nut IS a peanut. Choice (H) is the ratio that compares peanuts to other nuts.

13. (C)—Percent Formula

100 Key Math Concepts for the ACT, #32. The matrices outline the corresponding number of people in the store to the ratio, written as a decimal, of the number of people making purchases, *with*

reference to their age group. A ratio written as a decimal is essentially a percentage. So following the correspondence yields $75 \times 0.20 = 15$ adolescent purchases, $100 \times 0.35 = 35$ adult purchases, and $30 \times 0.10 = 3$ senior-citizen purchases. This is a total of $15 + 35 + 3 = 53$ people making purchases.

Answer choice (A) represents the adolescent purchases. If you chose choice (B), you took the total number of people in the store, 205, and multiplied by the ratio for adolescents, 0.20. Choice (D) adds the total number of people, 205, multiplies by the sum of the ratios, 0.65, and then rounds. Choice (E) is the total number of people in the store, not the total number of purchases.

14. (J)—Average Formula

100 Key Math Concepts for the ACT, #41. To find an average, calculate the sum of the data and then divide by the total number of data items. According to the table, the number of hours that the Country genre has a "live" disc jockey is 24, 7 and 16. $24 + 7 + 16 = 47$. Divide: $47 \div 3 = 15.67$, which is 16 to the nearest hour.

Answer choice (F) is the number of *entries*, not hours, for the Country genre. Choice (G) is the average number of hours for the Classical genre. Answer choice (K) is the average number of hours for the News genre.

15. (D)

This problem tests your ability to read a table of information. You must study the wording in the problem and study the table to understand its structure. To determine the minimum number of disc jockeys needed given the information in the problem, add up all of the hours (the last column) and then divide by 8 (the number of hours a disc jockey works). From the table, the number of hours

is: $6 + 3 + 12 + 24 + 7 + 16 + 24 + 24 + 24 + 14 + 5 + 12 + 24 = 195$ total hours. $195 \div 8 = 24.375$, which means you must have 25 disc jockeys, because you cannot have a fraction of a person.

A common trap would be answer choice (C), because the answer would round down to 24 disc jockeys, but this would fall short of the requirement to fulfill all of the hours.

Choice (E) reflects the total number of hours needed. Answer choice (A) is the number of 24-hour segments that require a "live" disc jockey.

16. (G)—Adding and Subtracting Signed Numbers/ Adding and Subtracting Monomials

100 Key Math Concepts for the ACT, #5, #53. To find the missing value, add the monomials in the first row: $m + -4m + 3m = 0$. This first row sums to zero. To be sure, check the rightmost column: $3m + -2m + -m = 0$. Every row, column, and diagonal must sum to 0, The first column must therefore be $m + 2m + \square = 0$, or $3m + \square = 0$. Isolate the missing term on one side of the equation by subtracting $3m$ from both sides: $\square = -3m$.

If your choice was (H), you ignored the m variable in the term. If your choice was (F), (J) or (K), you may have just looked at the first column and the last row and found a value that would work with those, without considering the other rows, columns, and diagonals.

17. (E)—Multiplying/Dividing Signed Numbers

100 Key Math Concepts for the ACT, #6. The algebraic expression xy means to multiply the point's x value by its y value. If the product is positive, then the x and y factors are either both positive or both negative, according to the rules for multiplying signed numbers. Positive x-coordinates are to the

right of the origin. Positive *y*-coordinates are above the origin. In quadrant I, both coordinates are positive, and in quadrant III, both coordinates are negative. In quadrant II, the *x*-coordinate is negative (to the left of the origin) and the *y*-coordinate is positive (above the origin). In quadrant IV, the *x*-coordinate is positive (to the right of the origin), and the *y*-coordinate is negative (below the origin).

18. (J)—Counting the Possibilities

100 Key Math Concepts for the ACT, #45. The number of distinct lunches is determined by the fundamental counting principle. The counting principle directs you to multiply the different choices together to find the total number of combinations: $7 \times 3 \times 4 = 84$. If you consider just the sandwiches and soups alone, each sandwich can be paired with one of three soups, so there would be $7 \times 3 = 21$ different alternatives. These 21 alternatives would then become $21 \times 4 = 84$ different meals, because each of these 21 meals could be combined with 4 different drink choices.

A common trap answer is choice (G), where the numbers are added together, instead of multiplied. Choice (F) is the number of sandwiches available, not the number of distinct meals. Choice (H) reflects the number of distinct choices of just sandwich and soup.

19. (A)—Setting Up a Ratio/Solving a Proportion

100 Key Math Concepts for the ACT, #36, #38. The question describes a comparison of the number of female to male students. This is a ratio—the ratio of female to male students is 5 to 3, or $\frac{5}{3}$. Let *n* represent the number of female students. Set up the proportion $\frac{5}{3} = \frac{n}{6,000}$ and cross multiply to get $3n = 5 \times 6,000$, or $3n = 30,000$. Divide both sides by 3 to get $n = 10,000$ females.

If you chose answer choice (B), you may have used rounding and incorrectly considered the ratio to be twice as many females as males. Answer choice (C) represents the total number of students at the university. If you chose choice (D) or choice (E), you may have stopped after multiplying 6,000 by 3 or by 5, respectively.

20. (H)—Pythagorean Theorem/Special Quadrilaterals

100 Key Math Concepts for the ACT, #84, #86.

Draw a diagram of a rectangle:

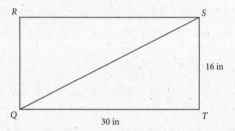

Because a rectangle has 4 right angles, you can treat the diagonal, *QS*, as the hypotenuse of a right triangle with legs of 16 and 30 inches. Use the Pythagorean theorem to solve for the length of the hypotenuse. If *c* represents the length of the hypotenuse and *a* and *b* represent the length of the legs, then $a^2 + b^2 = c^2$. Substitute into the formula:

$$c^2 = 16^2 + 30^2$$
$$c^2 = 256 + 900$$
$$c^2 = 1,156$$

Take the square root of both sides of the equation to find that $c = 34$ inches.

If you chose (F), you used 30 inches for *c* (the hypotenuse) in the formula, and then solved for one of the legs. Choice (G) adds the two dimensions and divides by 2. If you chose choice (J), you incorrectly divided by 2 instead of taking the square root; for choice (K) you added the squares but did not take the square root of the sum.

21. (A)—Simplifying an Algebraic Fraction

100 Key Math Concepts for the ACT, #62. Answer choice (A) is not equivalent to $5n + 1$—it is the reciprocal. If you chose answer choice (B), you may have incorrectly simplified by not multiplying 5×2. The expression simplifies as $5n + 10 - 9$, or $5n + 1$. Answer choice (C) is also equivalent to $5n + 1$—when you divide fractions, you multiply by the reciprocal of the denominator, and $\frac{1}{1} \prod \frac{1}{5n - 1} = \frac{1}{1} \times \frac{5n + 1}{1} = 5n + 1$. If you chose either choice (D) or (E), you may have thought that they could not be equivalent because they have a squared variable. But when choice (D) is factored and simplified, you can see it is equivalent: $\frac{n(5n + 1)}{n} = 5n + 1$. The same is true for choice (E): $\frac{(5n + 1)(5n - 1)}{5n - 1} = 5n + 1$.

22. (J)—Solve "In Terms Of"

100 Key Math Concepts for the ACT, #64. Each of the answer choices is in the form "$y = \ldots$", so solve for y in terms of x. Isolate y on one side of the equation. First, subtract $3x$ from both sides: $3x - 3x + 2y = -3x + 16$. Combine like terms to get $2y = -3x + 16$. Now, divide all terms on both sides by 2: $y = -\frac{3}{2}x + 8$.

In answer choice (F) the numeric term 16 is not divided by 2. Answer choices (G) and (K) have the reciprocal of the coefficient of x. In answer choice (H), $3x$ was added to both sides of the equation instead of subtracted, to get the incorrect term of $+\frac{3}{2}x$.

23. (E)—Factoring Other Polynomials/Solving a Quadratic Equation

100 Key Math Concepts for the ACT, #61, #66. To solve a quadratic equation, first factor the trinomial in the form $ax^2 + bx + c$. Since the "c" term is positive, and the "b" term is negative, the factors will be $(x - \#)(x - \#)$. Look for factors of 75 that when added together will equal 20, the "b" coefficient. Some factor possibilities for 75 are 1 and 75, 3 and 25, and 5 and 15. Only the factors 5 and 15 will add to 20. The equation, after factoring, becomes $(x - 5)(x - 15) = 0$. The solutions are the values of x that result in either of the factors equaling 0: $x = 5$ or $x = 15$.

The common error traps are choices (A) or (B), where you might have quickly looked at the factors and thought the answers were either -5 or -15. If you chose choice (D), you may have thought the only factors of 75 were 3 and 25, and therefore chose 3 as a solution. If you chose answer choice (C), you may have ignored the term of 75, and found a solution of 0.

24. (H)—Sine, Cosine, and Tangent of Acute Angles

100 Key Math Concepts for the ACT, #96. The cosine (cos) ratio is the ratio of the side adjacent to angle N, to the hypotenuse of the right triangle. The N $= \frac{12}{13}$.

Answer choice (F) is the sine (sin) ratio of angle N. Choice (G) is the tangent (tan) ratio of angle N. Choice (J) is the secant (sec), or the reciprocal of the cos to angle N. Choice (K) is the cosecant (csc), or the reciprocal of the sin to angle N.

25. (C)—Special Right Triangles

100 Key Math Concepts for the ACT, #85. Since chord AB passes through the center, it is a diameter

of the circle, and segment OB is a radius, equal to 7 cm. Because OC is perpendicular to AB, a right angle is formed. To find the length of chord CB, note that it is the hypotenuse of right triangle $\triangle COB$, with legs that each measure 7 cm. Because the legs have the same measure, this is a special right triangle, the 45°-45°-90° right triangle, and the sides are in the ratio of $n:n:n\sqrt{2}$. Chord BC is therefore $7\sqrt{2} \approx 9.899$, or 9.9 to the nearest tenth of a centimeter. Alternately, you could have used the Pythagorean theorem, $a^2 + b^2 = c^2$, where $a = b = 7$:

$$7^2 + 7^2 = c^2$$
$$49 + 49 = c^2$$
$$c = \sqrt{98} \approx 9.9 \text{ cm}$$

If your answer was choice (A), you used the Pythagorean theorem, but evaluated 7^2 as 7×2, instead of 7×7. This is a common trap. Choice (B) is the length of the legs, not the hypotenuse. Choice (D) is $7\sqrt{3}$. Answer choice (E) is the length of the diameter of the circle.

26. (F)—Solving a Linear Equation

100 Key Math Concepts for the ACT, #63. Substitute the value of 86 into the formula for F, the degrees in Fahrenheit, to get $86 = \frac{9}{5}C + 32$. Subtract 32 from both sides:

$$86 - 32 = \frac{9}{5}C + 32 - 32$$
$$54 = \frac{9}{5}C$$

Now, multiply both sides by the reciprocal of $\frac{9}{5}$ to isolate C:

$$\frac{5}{9} \times 54 = \frac{5}{9} \times \frac{9}{5} \times C$$
$$30 = C$$

If you chose answer choice (G), you forgot to multiply by the reciprocal to get rid of the fraction on the right side of the equation. Choice (H) makes the same error, but adds 32. Choice (J) is the degrees in Fahrenheit. Choice (K) would be the degrees in Fahrenheit of 86 degrees Celsius.

27. (D)—Volume of a Rectangular Solid

100 Key Math Concepts for the ACT, #94. A swimming pool that is the same depth in all parts is a rectangular solid. The amount of water in the pool is the volume of the water. Use the formula $V = lwh$, and substitute in the volume, length, and width given in the problem. $14,375 = 50 \times 25 \times h$, or $14,375 = 1,250h$. Divide both sides of the equation by 1,250, to get $11.5 = h$. The depth is between 11 and 12 meters.

28. (F)—Sine, Cosine, and Tangent of Acute Angles

100 Key Math Concepts for the ACT, #96. The tangent is the ratio of the side opposite to the given angle over the side adjacent to the given angle. Segment EF is the side opposite to angle D, so call this side m. Segment DE, the adjacent side to angle D, equals 42 inches. Set up the equation:

$$\frac{5}{8} = \frac{m}{42}$$
$$(42)(5) = 8m$$
$$210 = 8m$$
$$m = 26.3$$

If you chose (G), you added 42 and $\frac{5}{8}$. Answer choice (H) reflects the length of side DF, the hypotenuse of the right triangle. Answer choice (J) incorrectly uses 42 as the opposite side and side EF as the adjacent side.

29. (B)—Setting Up a Ratio

100 Key Math Concepts for the ACT, #36. The fraction of the people who were sophomores would be the ratio of the number of sophomores to the total number of people at the prom. There were 30 sophomores, and a total of $20 + 30 + 70 + 200 = 320$ people at the prom. The fraction is $\frac{30}{320} = \frac{3}{32}$. Answer choice (A) is the fraction of the attendees who were freshman. Answer choice (C) is the ratio of sophomores to those who are NOT sophomores. Answer choice (D) is the ratio of sophomores to seniors. Answer choice (E) is a common trap—it compares the number of sophomores to 100, instead of to the total number of students in attendance.

30. (K)

This problem requires you to understand that the sum of the parts of a segment is equal to the whole segment. It is given that X is the midpoint of segment WZ. Because the length of $WZ = 44$ cm, the length of WX is one half of this or 22 cm. From the relative positions of the points in the segment, $WX + XY = WY$, or alternately, $WY - WX = XY$. It is given that $WY = 26$ and calculated that WX is 22. Therefore $XY = 26 - 22$, or 4 centimeters.

If you chose choice (F), you just added the two numbers given in the problem. Answer choice (G) is the length of one half of segment WZ, or the length of WX. If you answer was choice (H), you subtracted the two numbers given in the problem. Choice (J) is one half of segment WY.

31. (C)—Solving a System of Equations

100 Key Math Concepts for the ACT, #67. Find the point of intersection of two lines by solving the system of equations. Use the elimination method, by lining up the equations by like terms:

$$5x + y = 7$$
$$2x + 3y = 8$$

The problem asks for the x-coordinate, so look at the equations, and multiply one of them so that when the equations are combined, the y values are eliminated. If you multiply all terms in the top equation by -3, when you combine them, the y values will be eliminated:

$$-3(5x + y = 7) \Rightarrow -15x - 3y = -21$$
$$2x + 3y = 8 \Rightarrow 2x + 3y = 8$$

Combine like terms in the resulting equations: $(-15x + 2x) + (-3y + 3y) = -21 + 8$, or $-13x = -13$. Now, divide both sides of this simpler equation by -13 to get $x = 1$.

If you chose answer (A), you probably divided the negative numbers incorrectly to get -1. Answer choice (B) may have resulted from only multiplying *the* y by 3 and not multiplying the terms of $5x$ and 7, and getting the result of $3x = 1$, or $x = \frac{1}{3}$. Answer choice (D) is the y-coordinate of the intersection of the two lines.

32. (K)—Solving "In Terms Of"

100 Key Math Concepts for the ACT, #64. To solve the equation for b, isolate b on one side of the equation. First, add 8 to both sides of the equation: $a + 8 = 2b - 8 + 8$, or $a + 8 = 2b$. Now, divide both sides by 2 to get $b = \frac{a + 8}{2}$.

If your answer was choice (F), you forgot to divide a by 2. In choice (G), you exchanged the variable a for the variable b, instead of solving for b. Answer choice (H) is similar to choice (G), but the subtraction was changed to addition. In choice (J), you may have subtracted 8 from both sides instead of adding 8.

33. (D)—Areas of Special Quadrilaterals

100 Key Math Concepts for the ACT, #87. The area of a parallelogram is $A = bh$, where height is the h is the length of the perpendicular segment to one of the sides of the parallelogram. In the figure, segment RT, of length $9 + 5$, or 14 mm, is the base and the dotted segment, of length 12 mm, is the height. The area is $14 \times 12 = 168$ mm^2.

Answer choice (A) is the area of the little triangle at the top, not the parallelogram. If you chose answer choice (B), you added the given numbers, without recognizing that the problem is asking for area. Answer choice (C) is the perimeter of the parallelogram. Answer choice (E) reflects a common error, where you multiplied the sides together, instead of the base times the height.

34. (F)—Evaluating an Expression/Solving an Equation

100 Key Math Concepts for the ACT, #52, #63. The problem asks for you to evaluate $(x + y)^3$, so manipulate the given equation to isolate $x + y$ on one side of the equation. Once you have this value, cube it to find the answer to the problem. For the given equation $x = -(y + 3)$, first distribute the negative sign on the right hand side to get $x = -y - 3$. Now, add y to both sides of the equation: $x + y = -y + y - 3$. Combine like terms to arrive at $x + y = -3$. Now substitute -3 for $(x + y)$ in the expression to get $(-3)^3 = -3 \times -3 \times -3 = -27$.

Answer choice (G) is a common trap: evaluating $(-3)^3$ as $-3 \times 3 = -9$. Answer choices (H) and (J) result from not applying integer multiplication rules for negative numbers.

35. (E)—Special Quadrilaterals

100 Key Math Concepts for the ACT, #86. Because all streets and avenues shown intersect at right angles, the map is a rectangle in which opposite sides have the same measures. To find the location half way from H and S, first think of the corner of Oak and 10th to be the origin, or (0, 0). Just as in coordinate geometry, the first ordered pair represents the east-west direction and the second ordered pair represents the north-south direction. The distance from the origin at Oak Street to the school is 5 miles east. The distance from the origin at 10th Avenue to the hospital is 8 miles north. The new station will be halfway between these coordinates, or $\frac{5}{2} = 2.5$ miles east of the origin and $\frac{8}{2} = 4$ miles north of the origin. To drive from F to the new fire station, you would have to drive $8 - 2.5 = 5.5$ miles west on Main Street, and then $10 - 4 = 6$ miles south on Elm Street (the first two miles south to get to 2nd Avenue, and then the 4 more miles south to be halfway from the hospital and the school).

Choice (A) is the directions of the new fire station starting from the origin at Oak and 10th. Choice (B) is the directions of the new fire station starting from the school. Choice (C) is the directions from the corner of Main and Oak to the new station. If your answered choice (D), you forgot to add in the 2 miles on Elm Street to get from Main to 2nd Avenue.

36. (H)—Translating from English into Algebra

100 Key Math Concepts for the ACT, #65. Consecutive integers are integers that differ by 1, such as 3, 4, 5... Consecutive odd integers are odd integers that differ by 2, such as 7, 9, 11, 13...

Because the answer choices use the variable x, let x represent the smaller of the consecutive odd integers, so $(x + 2)$ would be the larger of the integers. Four times the larger is represented by $4(x + 2)$, and twice the smaller by $2x$. The key word *difference* means to subtract the smaller from the larger, and the key word *is* means equals. The equation is $4(x + 2) - 2x = 36$.

Choice (F) represents four times a number, minus twice the same number. Even though answer choices (G) and (J) are odd integers, they differ by an odd number, which would make the next number even. Choice (K) is an equation for the difference between 36 and four times the smaller integer.

37. (C)—Pythagorean Theorem

100 Key Math Concepts for the ACT, #84. The question states that the telephone pole is perpendicular to the ground and a wire is attached to the pole. This will result in a right triangle. It helps to draw a quick figure to represent the situation. The thicker side of the triangle represents the telephone pole, and the hypotenuse is the wire:

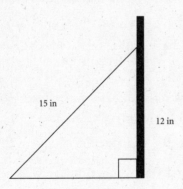

To find out how far the anchor of the supporting wire is from the base of the telephone pole, solve for the length of the missing leg. Use the Pythagorean

theorem, which is $a^2 + b^2 = hypotenuse^2$. Let b represent the missing leg and substitute in the given values to get $12^2 + b^2 = 15^2$, or $144 + b^2 = 225$. Subtract 144 from both sides: $b^2 = 81$. To solve for b, take the square root of both sides: $\sqrt{b^2} = \sqrt{81}$, so $b = 9$ or -9. A length cannot be negative, so the length is 9 ft.

Answer choice (A) subtracts $15 - 12$ to get 3. If you chose answer (B), you may have thought that 15^2 meant 15×2, and calculated $30 - 24 = 6$. Choice (D) is the length up the pole, and choice (E) is the length of the wire.

38. (H)—Area of a Circle

100 Key Math Concepts for the ACT, #91. The area of a circle is $A = \pi r^2$, where r is the radius of the circle. Use the equation $100\pi = \pi r^2$ and solve for r by dividing both sides by π: $100 = r^2$. If you take the square root of both sides then $r = 10$ or -10. Reject the -10 value, because a radius length cannot be negative. The radius of the circle is 10, so the diameter of the circle, which is the same as the length of a side of the square, is $2 \times 10 = 20$ units.

Answer choice (F) is the area of the square. Choice (G) is r^2. Choosing choice (J) is a common error that mistakes the radius of the circle for the side of the square.

39. (C)—Setting Up a Ratio/Solving a Proportion

100 Key Math Concepts for the ACT, #36, #38. When figures are similar, the side lengths are in proportion. Let x represent the missing side length and set up the proportion of shorter side to longer side: $\frac{3}{8} = \frac{2}{x}$. Cross multiply to get $3x = 16$. Divide both sides by 3 to get $x = 16 \div 3 \approx 5.3$, to the nearest tenth of an inch.

If you chose answer choices (A) or (B), you set up the proportion incorrectly—make sure to match up the long sides and the short sides on the same side of the fraction. Answer choice (D) is the most common error made with similar figures, by assuming that since $3 - 1 = 2$ that the missing side would be $8 - 1 = 7$. Similar figures have sides that are in proportion, which is not an additive relationship.

40. (J)—Parallel Lines and Transversals

100 Key Math Concepts for the ACT, #79. The figure shown is a parallelogram. Extend the top side out to make a parallel line to line *UZ*. Line *WY* is a transversal to the parallel lines, forming alternate interior angles, $\angle XWY$ and $\angle WYV$, which have the same measures of 50°. Line *WV* is another transversal line to the parallel lines, forming alternate interior angles $\angle UVW$ and $\angle VWX$. Because they have the same measure, $\angle VWX = 150°$. In addition, $\angle VWX$ and $\angle VYX$ have the same measure—they are opposite angles in a parallelogram. Now, $\angle VYX - \angle WYV = \angle WYX$, or $150 - 50 = 100°$.

If your answer was choice (H), you incorrectly thought that $\angle WYX$ had the same measure as $\angle XWY$. Answer choice (K) is the measure of $\angle VYX$, not $\angle WYX$.

41. (D)—Special Quadrilaterals

100 Key Math Concepts for the ACT, #86. The key to solving this problem is to simplify the drawing, knowing that you are looking for the perimeter. This figure, for perimeter purposes, can be thought of as a rectangle—just "lower" all the bottom pieces and move all left pieces to the right and you have a rectangle, with side lengths of 40 centimeters, and top/bottom lengths of $12 + 5 + 4 = 21$ centimeters:

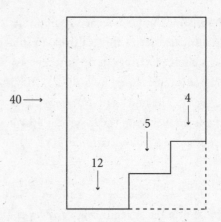

The perimeter is two times the length plus two times the width, or $2(40) + 2(21) = 80 + 42 = 122$ centimeters.

Choice (A) is the measure of the length. Choice (B) is just the measure of two sides of the figure (just the numbers that are shown).

42. (G)—Convert Fractions to Decimals/Translating from English into Algebra

100 Key Math Concepts for the ACT, #29, #65. Convert the fractions into decimal equivalents, and remember that the key word *of* means to multiply. Because $\frac{3}{4}$ of the 3,500 eligible voters cast a vote, this is $0.75 \times 3,500 = 2,625$ votes that were cast at the site. Three-fifths of these votes were for Martinez, or $0.6 \times 2,625 = 1,575$ votes for Martinez.

If you answered choice (F), you followed the correct procedure, but incorrectly converted the fractions. Choice (H) is $\frac{3}{5}$ of all the eligible voters. Choice (J) is $\frac{3}{4}$ of the eligible voters. Answer (K) is the sum of choices (H) and (J).

43. (A)—Greatest Common Factor/Evaluating an Expression

100 Key Math Concepts for the ACT, #15, #52.
To find the greatest common factor, find all factor pieces that the two expressions have in common. In this case, the factors in common are a, a, a, and b, or a^3b. It is given that the greatest common factor is 54, so think of a cubic number that is a factor of 54. The first cubic numbers are 1^3 (1), 2^3 (8), and 3^3 (27). Twenty seven is a factor of 54: $27 \times 2 = 54$, so a possible value for b is 2.

Answer choice (B) is the value of the variable a. Answer choice (C), 6, is a factor of 54, but that leaves the value of 9 for a, and 9 is not a perfect cube. The same reasoning would eliminate choice (D). Choice (E) is the value of a^3.

44. (K)—Percent Formula

100 Key Math Concepts for the ACT, #32. To tackle this problem, break it up into its parts. First, find the value of x, given that 40 percent of x is 70. The key word *of* means to multiply. Write this as the equation $0.40x = 70$; divide both sides by 0.4 to get $x = 175$. Now find 160 percent of x, or $1.60 \times 175 = 280$.

Answer choice (F) is 40% of 70. Choice (G) is 160% of 28, the incorrect value from choice (F). Answer choice (H) is 160% of 70. A common trap is answer choice (J), which is the value of the variable x.

45. (C)—Simplifying Square Roots/Finding the Distance Between Two Points

100 Key Math Concepts for the ACT, #49, #71.
To find the length of segment MN, use the distance formula: $d = \sqrt{(x_2 - x_1)^2 + (y_2 - y_1)^2}$. Substitute in the point values:

$$d = \sqrt{(6 - 2)^2 + (5 - 3)^2}$$
$$d = \sqrt{4^2 + 2^2}$$
$$d = \sqrt{20} = \sqrt{4} \times \sqrt{5} + 2\sqrt{5}$$

If you chose answer choice (A), you may have used the distance formula incorrectly, using $(y_1 - x_1)$ and $(y_2 - x_2)$ instead of finding the difference between the x and y coordinates. Answer choice (B) multiplies by 2 instead of raising to the second power in the formula. Choice (D) is just the sum of the differences between the x and y coordinates. If your answer was choice (E), you forgot to take the square root of 20, as indicated by the distance formula.

46. (J)—Setting Up a Ratio/Special Quadrilaterals

100 Key Math Concepts for the ACT, #36, #86. If the sides are in the ratio of 5:7, the perimeter will also be in this exact same ratio. When finding a perimeter, you add up the sides. Perimeter is measured in single units, just as is the side length. Therefore, the ratio will not change. If you are unsure about this fact, assign values and actually calculate the perimeters. Consider the smaller square to have sides $5s$ in length and the larger square to have sides $7s$ in length. The smaller square has a perimeter of $4 \times 5s = 20s$, and the larger $4 \times 7s = 28s$. The ratio $20s:28s$ is equivalent to 5:7, after dividing both terms of the ratio by $4s$.

If you chose answer (F), you may have thought you needed to subtract $7 - 5 = 2$, to get the (incorrect) ratio 1:2. Likewise, answer (G) adds $7 + 5 = 12$. Answer choice (H) multiplies $7 \times 5 = 35$. Answer choice (K) confuses area and perimeter—the ratio of the *areas* is 25:49.

47. (E)—Equation for a Circle

100 Key Math Concepts for the ACT, #75. The equation of a circle, when given the coordinates of

the center (h, k) and the radius (r) is obtained by $(x - h)^2 + (y - k)^2 = r^2$. Substitute in the given values to get $(x - (-2))^2 + (y - 3)^2 = 9^2$. This simplifies to $(x + 2)^2 + (y - 3)^2 = 81$.

There are two common traps when finding the equation of a circle. One trap is to forget to square the radius, as in answer choice (B). The other common trap is adding h and k to x and y, instead of subtracting, as in answer choice (C). Answer choice (A) is both of these traps together. Choice (D) incorrectly takes the square root of the radius, instead of squaring the radius.

48. (H)—Adding and Subtracting Signed Numbers/ Multiplying Fractions

100 Key Math Concepts for the ACT, #5, #23. In the complex number system, i^2 is defined to be equal to -1, as you are told in the question stem. Use the distributive property to multiply the fraction:

$$\frac{3}{5 - i} \times \frac{5 + i}{5 + i} = \frac{(3 \times 5) + 3i}{5^2 + 5i - 5i - i^2}$$

$$= \frac{15 + 3i}{25 - (-1)} = \frac{15 + 3i}{26}$$

If your answer was choice (F), you may have cancelled incorrectly to simplify. Answer choice (G) reflects a common error when multiplying complex numbers— $25 - i^2$ was incorrectly interpreted to be $25 - 1 = 24$.

In choice (J), the 3 in the numerator was not distributed to the i term. Choice (K) is the result of two errors—the common error described in choice (G) and the error in choice (J).

49. (C)—Interior Angles of a Polygon

100 Key Math Concepts for the ACT, #88. One way to solve this problem is to make a table. Each time the number of sides goes up by 1, the sum of the angles goes up by 180°. Make a third column in the table to discover a relationship.

Number of Sides	Sum of the Angles	
3	180°	180° × 1
4	360°	180° × 2
5	540°	180° × 3
6	720°	180° × 4

Notice that to find the sum of the angles, you can multiply 180 times 2 less than the number of sides of the polygon. This is choice (C).

If you chose choice (A), you may have just considered the triangle, and assumed that the relationship was $60n$. If your answer was choice (B), you may have noticed that the number of degrees rose by 180°, but did not consider the sides of the polygons. Choice (D) is a relationship that works for the 3-sided and 6-sided polygons, but not the other two.

50. (G)—Logic

This problem is a method of logical thinking. The key to solving this problem is to first assume that there are no students who have both a cell phone and an mp3 player. If this were the case, then there would be $35 + 18 = 53$ students polled. The problem states that 50 students were polled, so therefore at least 3 students have both electronic devices. This is the minimum number of students who own both.

If you chose answer choice (F), you may have ignored the fact that 50 students were polled. Choice (H) is the difference between the number of cell phone owners and mp3 owners. Answer choice (J) is a possible number of students who own *only* a cell phone. Choice (K) is the sum of 35 and 18.

51. (A)—Solving an Inequality

100 Key Math Concepts for the ACT, #69. To solve this inequality, attempt to get the variable on one side of the inequality by adding $4n$ to both sides: $-4n + 4n + 3 > -4n + 4n + 1$. Combine like terms to get $3 > 1$. This inequality is always true for the set of real numbers.

If you chose answer (B) or (C), you may have thought that the term $-4n$ would limit the set of solutions. If your answer was choice (D) or choice (E) you may have mistakenly added $-4n$ to both sides and added 3 to both sides to get $-8n > 4$, and then solved for n.

52. (H)—Problem Solving

This question tests your problem solving strategies. Make a diagram of the situation in order to understand. In the diagram, the people are represented as diamonds, and the handshakes as connecting lines:

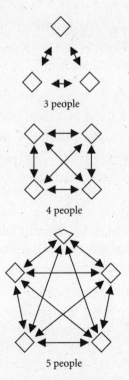

3 people

4 people

5 people

From the diagram, there are 10 total lines for 5 people, which represent 10 handshakes.

If you chose answer (F), you may have considered that 4 people have 2 more handshakes than people, and assumed this was the pattern for more people. If your answer was (G), you may have incorrectly thought that the pattern in handshakes was multiples of 3. The key to the correct solution is to draw the picture.

53. (D)—Setting Up a Ratio/Solving a Proportion

100 Key Math Concepts for the ACT, #36, #38. First, determine the percentage in the category Miscellaneous. The total percentage must sum to 100%, so the percentage for Miscellaneous is $100 - 23 - 5 - 22 - 18 = 32\%$. To find the number of degrees in a circle graph that corresponds with 32%, set up the ratio, where x represents the number of degrees for the Miscellaneous category. Recall that there are 360° in a circle: $\frac{32}{100} = \frac{x}{360}$. Cross multiply to get $32 \times 360 = 100x$, or $11{,}520 = 100x$.

Divide both sides by 100 to get $x = 115°$, rounded to the nearest degree.

Choice (A) is a common trap that represents the percentage, not the number of degrees in a circle graph. If your answer was choice (B), you thought that there were 180° in a circle. Answer choice (C) is the percentage categories that are *not* Miscellaneous, and choice (E) is the number of degrees that are *not* Miscellaneous.

54. (K)—Special Right Triangles/Sine, Cosine, and Tangent of Acute Angles

100 Key Math Concepts for the ACT, #85, #96. The information that $\frac{\pi}{2} < \theta < \pi$ tells you that the angle is in quadrant II of the coordinate plane. In quadrant II,

the sin values are positive. So the answer must be positive. Eliminate (F), (G), and (H). You are given the value of tan θ, which is the ratio of the opposite side to the adjacent side of a right triangle. Sketch this triangle, using leg lengths of 4 and 3:

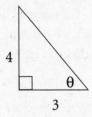

This is a special right triangle, the 3-4-5 Pythagorean triple, so the hypotenuse is 5 units in length. The sin of an angle is the ratio of the length of the opposite side to the length of the hypotenuse, or $\frac{4}{5}$.

If you chose choice (F), you may have ignored the fact that the angle is in quadrant II, and thought that the sin value would be negative. Choice (G) is the cotangent of the angle. Choices (H) and (J) are cosine values for the angle for quadrants II and I, respectively.

55. (A)—Using an Equation to Find the Slope/ Using an Equation to Find an Intercept

100 Key Math Concepts for the ACT, #73, #74. Look at the graphed boundary lines for the inequalities. Find the equation for these boundary lines and then determine if the shading represents less than or greater than these boundary lines. The horizontal line has a slope of 0 and a y-intercept (where the line crosses the y-axis) of 6, so the equation of this boundary line is $y = 6$. It is shaded below this line, so the inequality is $y < 6$. The slanted line has a slope with a change in y values of 3 and a change in x values of 1, so the slope is $\frac{3}{1} = 3$. The

y-intercept is −5. The line is increasing, so the slope is positive. The shading is greater than, or above, this boundary line, so the inequality is $y > 3x − 5$.

If you chose answer choice (B), you fell into a common trap of interpreting the horizontal boundary line equation to be $x < 6$. Answer choice (C) is another common error, thinking that the shading represents less than, or below, the slanted line. Answer choice (D) interprets the slope as −3. Negative slopes decrease, or slant downwards, when going from left to right. Answer choice (E) represents a slope of $\frac{1}{3}$, not the correct slope of 3. A slope of $\frac{1}{3}$ would mean for every change of 1 in the y values, the x values would change by 3.

56. (J)—Evaluating an Expression

100 Key Math Concepts for the ACT, #52. The question asks you to evaluate the function f(x), replacing x with ($x + c$). Replace any instance of x in the function definition with $x + c$: $2(x + 7)$ will be $2(x + c + 7)$. Use the distributive property and multiply each term in parentheses by 2 to get $2x + 2c + 2 \times 7$, or $2x + 2c + 14$.

In choice (F), the 2 was not distributed to the constant term 7. Choice (G) only multiplies the 2 by the first term in the parentheses. In choices (H) and (K), the c term was just added onto the end of the function definition, instead of replacing the x with ($x + c$).

57. (B)—Simplifying an Algebraic Fraction/Using an Equation to Find the Slope/Using an Equation to Find an Intercept

100 Key Math Concepts for the ACT, #62, #73, #74. First, simplify the equation by simplifying

the fraction on the right hand side. Factor the numerator and then cancel the $(x - 2)$ factor from the numerator and denominator:

$$\frac{2x^2 - 8}{x - 2} = \frac{2(x^2 - 4)}{x - 2} = \frac{2(x + 2)(x - 2)}{x - 2} = 2(x + 2)$$

The simplified equation is $y = 2(x + 2)$, or $y = 2x + 4$. This equation is now in slope-intercept form, where the y-intercept is 4 and the slope is $\frac{2}{1}$. Choice (B) is the correct graph that has a slope of 2 and crosses the y-axis at 4.

If you ignored the denominator in the given equation, then you would have incorrectly chosen answer choice (A), the graph of the quadratic $y = 2x^2 - 8$. Answer choice (C) is the graph of the equation $y = \frac{1}{2}x + 4$. If this was your choice, you may have misinterpreted the slope of a line. Choice (D) is the graph of a quadratic function, not the correct linear function. You cannot assume a function is a quadratic just because you see a variable that is squared; you must first try to simplify the equation. Choice (E) is the graph of the linear function $y = -2x + 4$.

58. (F)—Line Reflections

This problem tests your knowledge of line reflections in the coordinate plane.

When you reflect a point or a figure over the y-axis, the x-coordinate of each point is the opposite sign and the y-coordinate stays the same. The reflection of the point Q(r, s) after a reflection over the y-axis is therefore Q'($-r, s$).

Answer choice (G) would be the result of a reflection over the y-axis, followed by a reflection over the x-axis. Choice (H) is incorrect—the x and y coordinates were switched. Answer choice (J) is

a common trap that represents a reflection over the x-axis.

59. (C)—Solving "In Terms Of"

100 Key Math Concepts for the ACT, #64. The problem is asking what is the value of g in terms of h. The two given equations do not show a direct relationship between g and h, so you must solve for q in the second equation, to get q in terms of h, and then substitute this value in for q in the first equation. To solve for q in the second equation, isolate q by first adding 8 to both sides of the equation: $h + 8 = 2q - 8 + 8$, or $h + 8 = 2q$. Divide both sides by 2 to get $\frac{h + 8}{2} = q$. Use this value of q in the first equation: $g = 4q + 3$ becomes $g = \frac{4(b + 8)}{2} + 3$. Factor out a 2 from the numerator and the denominator of the first term to get $g = 2(h + 8) + 3$. Multiply the terms in parentheses by 2, or $g = 2h + 16 + 3$, or $g = 2h + 19$.

Answer choice (A) is the value of q in terms of h, from the second equation. In choice (B) the constant term 3 in the first equation was incorrectly added to the numerator of the transformed first equation, and the 4 was not distributed to both terms of h and 8. In answer choice (D), the 2 was factored out correctly, but the remaining 2 was not distributed to the constant term of 8. Choice (E) is the value of q, not h, in terms of g from the first equation.

60. (H)—Evaluating an Expression/Trigonometric Functions of Other Angles

100 Key Math Concepts for the ACT, #52, #98. In this problem, you are asked to use the formula $\cos(\alpha + \beta) = \cos(\alpha)\cos(\beta) - \sin(\alpha)\sin(\beta)$ and the table of values, to find the value of $\cos(75°) = \cos(30° + 45°)$. Substitute in 30° for α and 45°

for β to get: $\cos(30°)\cos(45°) - \sin(30°)\sin(45°)$. Now, use the table to replace each sin or cos with the corresponding values in the table:

$\frac{\sqrt{3}}{2} \times \frac{\sqrt{2}}{2} - \frac{1}{2} \times \frac{\sqrt{2}}{2}$. Using order of operations, multiply and then add the numerators and keep the denominator: $\frac{\sqrt{6}}{4} - \frac{\sqrt{2}}{4} = \frac{\sqrt{6} - \sqrt{2}}{4}$. Alternately, you could use your calculator to find the value of the $\cos(75°) \approx 0.2588$, and then test each answer choice to find the answer closest to this value. Choice (H) will be the only value to equal the $\cos(75°)$.

If you chose answer choice (F) or choice (K), you probably used the wrong values in the table. In answer choice (G), you used the wrong values in the table, and also forgot to multiply the denominators, resulting in a denominator of 2 instead of 4. Answer choice (J) is the common trap—you correctly used the table, but did not multiply the denominators to get a denominator of 4.

READING TEST

PASSAGE I—PROSE FICTION

This is a Prose Fiction passage, so remember to ask yourself the three important questions:

Who are these people?

Dave is the narrator and an insurance adjuster. Emily is his wife. Bruce is Dave's twin brother.

What is their state of mind?

Dave is rattled because he sees his wife talking so enthusiastically to his brother. This incident leads Dave to think further about the ways in which he always felt inferior to his brother. Emily is disappointed that Dave is so down on himself, and also hopeful that Dave will eventually realize that Bruce is upset by the fact that Dave does little to contact his brother.

What's going on?

Because Bruce is very successful now and was always more popular that Dave when the two were growing up, Dave is insecure whenever Bruce is the subject of conversation. He is especially insecure because his wife is so excited to talk to Bruce. This leads him to ask Emily to identify him in a photograph. Emily identifies Dave correctly, and tries to calm him down. Emily also attempts to convince Dave to make more of an effort to stay in contact with his brother, suggesting that Bruce feels rejected by Dave, but Dave does not see this as a possibility, because Bruce is so successful.

1. (D)—Inference Question

The question is asking about Dave's opinion specifically. Throughout the passage Dave describes the problems with comparison between twins, and many of his comments to Emily are also focused on comparing himself to his twin. Choice (D) is correct because it mentions this competition and implies that it makes their relationship more difficult. Choice (A) is extreme, choice (B) implies that their relationship is stronger than it is, and choice (C) is not supported by the text, because Emily doesn't seem to be able to convince Dave to make more of an effort.

2. (H)—Inference Question

Emily has a good relationship with both brothers; she has an enjoyable conversation with Bruce and works to make Dave feel better. Also, she wants the brothers to be closer than they are. Because it reflects these details, choice (H) is the correct answer. Choice (F) is the opposite; Emily is very attentive, and choices (G) and (J) are both extreme and negative distortions of Emily's desire to help relations between the brothers.

3. (B)—Detail Question

This question is asking for an answer that is not found in the passage, so the first step is to eliminate choices that are contained in the passage. In the first paragraph, Dave is envious of the reaction his wife has when talking to Bruce, eliminating choice (A). The paragraph about Dave's reaction to the picture captures his negative feelings regarding the difference in their popularity, eliminating choice (C). The final conversation shows Dave as doubtful of Bruce's need for his approval, eliminating choice (D). This leaves choice (B), which is not found in the passage, and is therefore the correct answer.

4. (J)—Big Picture Question

The first paragraph starts with a description of Emily on the phone, but the focus quickly shifts to Dave's reaction. It then moves to Dave making some points about his brother's popularity and questioning if his own wife ever reacted so favorably to him. Choice (J) summarizes this well. Choices (F) and (H) are not found in the passage, and choice (G) occurs much later.

5. (D)—Inference Question

Emily attempts to make Dave believe that he is important to Bruce, but Dave still feels he is in Bruce's shadow. It is unclear whether or not Dave entirely believes Emily, but when she brings up Bruce's desire to talk about the brothers' childhood, Dave's response suggests that he does not want to talk about it because it again reminds him of how Bruce has always been the more popular of the two. This makes choice (D) the correct answer. Choice (A) is out of scope; the passage does not suggest that Dave does anything to spite Emily. Choice (B) is incorrect because Dave does not feel guilty; he sees Bruce's success as proof that it doesn't matter whether he calls Bruce or not. Choice (C) is out of scope; Dave's reasons for not calling Bruce have to do with his feelings towards his brother, not any feelings related to Emily.

6. (H)—Detail Question

In lines 32–34, Dave explicitly talks about how Bruce's image has positive aspects (vitality) that his image lacks. This is a perfect match for choice (H), which restates this generally. Choices (F) and (J) are not found in the passage, and choice (G) is contradicted by the fact that both Dave and Emily can tell the difference between the twins.

7. (B)—Inference Question

Dave is uncomfortable at this point, because Emily is clearly thinking about Bruce. The previous paragraph describes the picture as a source of insecurity for Dave, suggesting that he is nervous and seeking reassurance that Emily is with him for reasons other than his connection to Bruce. Only choice (B) describes these feelings. Choice (A) is the opposite of what Dave is feeling, and neither choice (C) nor (D) can be deduced from the information in the passage.

8. (F)—Inference Question

With an open-ended question like this, the answer choices must be individually tested. Choice (F) can be logically deduced, especially from the last exchange: Emily mentions that Bruce tells her stories about their childhood, and when Dave makes a comment about Bruce's popularity, Emily responds that "[Bruce] doesn't look at it that way" (line 98). This suggests that there is a difference between each brother's childhood stories. Choice (G) is too extreme and better describes the reaction other people have to the different professions of Bruce and Dave. Choice (H) is also too extreme: Dave feels competitive with Bruce, but that does not imply that they have fought. Choice (J) is not supported by the text; their childhood is the only time where it is stated that they spent time together.

9. (C)—Detail Question

Dave and Emily have different opinions regarding the picture. Dave is displeased with his image, while Emily professes to like his smile. However, Dave describes Bruce's smile as "trademark" and Emily says that Bruce looks "exactly the same" in every picture. This makes choice (C) correct. Choices (A) and (D) depict opinions that are strictly Dave's and Emily's, respectively, and choice (B) is not supported by the passage at all.

10. (F)—Detail Question

Emily follows her comment about Bruce's stories by dismissing Dave's comment about Bruce's popularity, saying that Bruce "doesn't look at it that way" (line 98). This is in reaction to Dave's frequent comments suggesting that Bruce has been more successful socially, and Dave's implication that Bruce feels superior to Dave. This matches choice (F), which correctly restates this idea. Choice (G) is not supported by the passage; choice (H) is opposite, because Emily wants Dave to focus less on his brother's successes; and choice (J) is extreme, since Bruce wants more attention from his brother but is not necessarily lonely.

PASSAGE II—SOCIAL SCIENCES

This editorial passage describes the author's opinions on a lack of factual accuracy in the current news media and the sources of these problems.

The **first paragraph** introduces the issue the author has with the news media.

The **second paragraph** provides historical context and makes it clear that the author preferred the media trends of the past.

The **third paragraph** describes specific flaws the author sees in the current news media.

The **fourth paragraph** details the public's fault in perpetuating the current news trends; the author believes that the public looks for opinions to agree with rather than forming their own.

The **fifth paragraph** describes factors beyond the media, namely political spin, that make it difficult for the media to be wholly accurate in the first place.

The **sixth paragraph** restates some of the flaws the author sees, but also describes how there are some advantages in the current way news is delivered.

11. (C)—Big Picture Question

The author is critical of the media throughout the passage, and focuses mostly on ways in which the current media is not concerned enough with factual accuracy. Choice (C) matches this nicely. Choice (A) is too extreme; the author talks about distorting facts, not making them up. Choice (B) contradicts paragraph 2, which characterizes some news personalities as "demagogues" with biased views. Choice (D) contradicts paragraph 4; the public's desire for this type of news is one of the reasons for its existence.

12. (G)—Detail Question

In paragraph 3, the author mentions how impartial stories can sway the opinions of readers through headlines rather than content. Choices (H) and (J) both mention headlines, but choice (H) makes the opposite point, and (J) is far too specific, using the example as a basis for a point that the author does not explicitly make. Choice (F) is contradicted by the passage. Choice (G) is general, but correct; the headline is another method used to sensationalize the story, as illustrated by the example of the "enraged public" versus the "irked locals."

13. (B)—Inference Question

The sentence preceding the Walter Cronkite example states that audience members expected to have complicated events explained to them; the Cronkite example follows this logic. Choice (B) matches this perfectly. Choice (A) may be inferred, but it is not the point the author is making—the author's concern is the treatment of the news, not specific news personalities. This reasoning also eliminates choice (C). Choice (D) is never mentioned in or suggested by the passage.

14. (F)—Inference Question

In order to research this statement, it is a good idea to look back at paragraph 3, because it details the public. "Personal consensus" applies to the author's point about people looking for news reported with a political opinion similar to their own. Choice (F) matches this. Choices (G) and (J) are both contradicted by information given in paragraph 3. Choice (H) is not supported by the passage, and contradicts the author's main point.

15. (B)—Detail Question

In paragraph 1, the author states that in stories of "continued national interest" the focus shifts from facts to "theater." Choice (B) is the best match. Choices (A), (C), and (D) are not explicitly mentioned as more or less likely to be sensationalized.

16. (J)—Detail Question

The sentence describes objective reporting as a "distant possibility." Questions like this are made easier if you pick a word that means the same thing in context. In this case, you can predict "improbable" or something similar. This matches choice (J) perfectly. Choices (F), (G), and (H) do not address the likelihood of objective reporting.

17. (C)—Inference Question

The author is most likely to criticize a headline that sensationalizes or makes a value judgment, and the end of paragraph 3 gives an example. Choices (A), (B), and (D) are all basically factual, and specific. Choice (C) is correct, because it uses a very inclusive group, like the example in paragraph 3 does, makes a value judgment by calling the song offensive, and uses emotional language.

18. (J)—Detail Question

The fourth paragraph focuses on the flaws of the public and states that individuals who agree with certain politically biased hosts are unlikely to question the validity of the "facts" presented. This matches choice (J) perfectly. Choices (F) and (G) are not explicitly stated by the author. Choice (H) describes accuracy problems for the media, not the public.

19. (A)—Inference Question

The author makes the point that fact-based news only captures a small minority of the news audience. Also, the beginning of paragraph 4 states that the public is not interested in dry facts. Choice (A) can be inferred, because the media companies are providing the type of programs that the public seems to want. Choice (B) is extreme—in fact, it could be inferred that if the greater public was interested in objective facts, the media (including cable) would provide programs of that sort. Choices (C) and (D) cannot be deduced from the passage; the author seems to believe that factual news will not draw a large audience no matter what.

20. (G)—Detail Question

Because this question deals with the audience, paragraph 4 is a good place to look. The author states that audience members look for hosts who share their political opinions. Choice (G) is a general restatement of this idea, so it is correct. Choice (F) is not stated in the passage. Choice (H) distorts a detail from the last paragraph; audience members prefer short to lengthy, but there is no statement about audience members gravitating toward the shortest or most simple stories. Choice (J) misuses the detail about headlines from paragraph 3.

PASSAGE III—HUMANITIES

This passage focuses mostly on the life and experiences of the author's grandfather, a Russian immigrant, and the greater themes existing within his experiences.

Paragraph 1 describes the goings on in Russia at the time of the author's grandfather's birth.

Paragraph 2 describes the way the author's great grandfather praised Russia even though he had been exiled.

Paragraph 3 describes the turbulent goings on that led to the immigration to America, and the struggle with identity upon arrival.

Paragraph 4 and the short paragraph 5 further discuss the acclimation process and bring up the author's grandfather's work in real estate.

Paragraph 6 describes difficulties associated with working as a Russian immigrant, and how they were dealt with.

Paragraph 7 mentions the grandfather's success in real estate.

Paragraph 8 details the lasting effects of leaving one's native country, and related themes.

Paragraph 9 ties the grandfather's work in real estate to his heritage and history.

21. (C)—Big Picture Question

The author frequently describes his grandfather's actions and describes their relationship to his heritage. Choice (C) fits this, as the other Russians in paragraph 3 are also characterized as being naturally tied to Russia. Choice (A) distorts the grandfather's later visits to Russia; the passage does not imply that immigrants would prefer to be elsewhere. Choice (B) cites the opinions of American-born people, while the passage does not focus on those opinions. Choice (D) refers only to the grandfather, who was perpetually displaced; his story is addressed as being unique.

22. (J)—Detail Question

The three specific locations mentioned are Moscow, Siberia, and China, in that order. Also, the author mentions that that China was the longest stay. Choices (F), (G), and (H) all have errors: (F) puts the Russian revolution in the wrong time period, (G) says he was exiled from Russia as an adult, and (H) says he settled in communist China, when he left during the revolution.

23. (C)—Inference Question

These line references both have to do with his work in real estate. You can deduce that he sees real estate as providing stability for people, something he did not have earlier in his life. Choice (C) matches this very well. Choice (A) is part of his sales strategy, not his purpose. Choices (B) and (D) are never discussed as tasks he specifically attempts.

24. (F)—Big Picture Question

The grandfather is proud to be Russian, and deeply influenced by his heritage, but is also proud to do his job and be a successful American. Choice (F) contradicts the grandfather's attitude, because while he criticizes the government, he loves the country itself. Choice (G) suggests an unspoken pride between Russians, which is in line with the grandfather's characterization. Choices (H) and (J) both fit, because he is critical of the communist government but still reverent regarding the country.

25. (D)—Inference Question

The passage deals heavily with displacement, and its implications, along with its effects on people. Since Moscow was where the family was originally from, you can deduce that the answer will have something to do with belonging. Choice (D) fits this classification well; Moscow is the family's native home, and all feel tied to Russia, but are searching for places to live outside of Russia. Choices (A) and (C) are not implied at all in the passage. Choice (B) may be factually true, but does not apply to the desires of the family.

26. (F)—Inference Question

This selection refers to Russians saying, "I am American" in Russian. It is contrasted with points about the fact that they are speaking Russian with other Russians, therefore suggesting that "playing the role" must mean becoming more accustomed to their new country. Choice (F) matches this perfectly. Choices (G) and (H) cannot be deduced from the information given, and choice (J) may be true, but does not apply to "playing the role."

27. (B)—Inference Question

"Strategic compromise" applies to the grandfather's desire to sell homes, in spite of the current stigma against Russians. The tactics mentioned by the author are informing the customer he was exiled and disagreed with the current Russian government, and not responding to negative remarks regarding the entire country of Russia. Choice (B) fits this final part, as negative statements about Russia as a whole would offend the grandfather. Choices (A) and (D) are too extreme and specific. Choice (C) is not mentioned.

28. (H)—Detail Question

According to the passage this sort of trip "elucidates one's very existence." This is the only result given; the rest of the details apply to the emotional strain involved. Choice (H) is the only choice that applies to this. Choices (F) and (G) are not even implied by the text, and choice (J) applies to the adoption analogy rather than the grandfather.

29. (B)—Detail Question

The last sentence in the first paragraph states that the country came under new rule during the time his mother was pregnant with him. He was therefore born after the revolution, and under communist rule. Choice (B) is correct. The other choices contradict that factual sentence.

30. (G)—Inference Question

The need to rediscover a lost native land is what would be made unnecessary, so the correct answer would have to describe the opposite situation. Choice (G) fits this very well; having a sense of belonging would alleviate the need to search for it. Choice (F) is incorrect because the grandfather embodies the feelings he is potentially making "unnecessary." Choice (H) describes people that may still desire to revisit their roots. Choice (J) describes a totally unrelated achievement possible in real estate.

PASSAGE IV—NATURAL SCIENCE

The author, who is fascinated by rattlesnakes, makes an argument against the negative reputation of rattlesnakes by comparing actual snake behavior to general myths.

Paragraphs 1, 2, and 3 present a negative opinion of the rattlesnake, and introduce an argument against it.
Paragraph 3 presents evidence from a study.

Paragraph 4 states that most people are not aware of these facts.
Paragraph 5 compares the danger of rattlesnakes to those of other animals.
Paragraph 6 describes a snakebite from a snake's point of view.
Paragraphs 7, 8, and 9 point out the amount of danger rattlesnakes are in due to human behavior, specifically rattlesnake "round-ups" detailed in paragraph 8.

31. (B)—Inference Question

The passage is most concerned with discrediting the myth that rattlesnakes are aggressive and very dangerous, and the selection refers to exactly that: the "sinister opportunist" is the myth, while the "mild-mannered domestic" is closer to fact. Choice (B) can be deduced from this. Choice (A) is incorrect, as juvenile snakes are not even mentioned. Choice (C) misuses the detail about rattlesnakes giving live birth, which is not treated as a recent discovery. Choice (D) is too extreme; the author describes rattlesnakes as fairly docile, but not entirely predictable.

32. (F)—Inference Question

At the end of paragraph 6, the author states that the reputation is good because a frightened and cornered rattlesnake is dangerous. Choice (F) fits this, because if people did not avoid or move away from rattlesnakes, there would be more dangerous interaction between humans and snakes. Choices (G) and (J) are contradicted by the passage; in rattlesnake round-ups their reputation costs the snakes their lives, and the author, who is aware of their docile nature, would certainly never believe a rattlesnake should be a pet. Choice (H) misuses the detail about snakebite deaths.

33. (C)—Detail Question

The passage gives quite a few examples of the social behavior of rattlesnakes, so be prepared to find a restated fact among the answer choices. Choice (C) fits this nicely, because the passage states that rattlesnakes have been known to hibernate with tortoises. Choice (A) is not a social behavior. Choice (B) goes beyond the text; the wrestling is used to claim a mate, but the losing snake will leave, rather than take a place within a hierarchy. Choice (D) also misuses a detail; rattlesnakes are described as "entirely" non-cannibalistic, meaning they never eat other snakes.

34. (H)—Inference Question

The mythology referred to is that of the heartless, aggressive rattlesnake. This relates to rattlesnake "round-ups" to which the author clearly objects, so it would follow that the author sees this particular human behavior as heartless and aggressive. Choice (H) matches this perfectly, and the statistical comparison in paragraph 8 supports this. Choice (F) contradicts the author's belief that rattlesnakes are not as dangerous as commonly thought. Choices (G) and (J) do not relate to the point the author is making.

35. (C)—Detail Question

It is stated that serious bites can usually be traced to people that either handle or step on snakes, in contrast to those who were not engaging the snakes. Choice (C) fits this nicely, specifically focusing on those handling snakes, an example of individuals purposefully seeking interaction. Choice (A) is incorrect because a relationship is mentioned. Choice (B) is not mentioned in the text. Choice (D) is a distortion, because rattlesnakes deliver venom based on how threatened they feel, not necessarily based on how threatening humans act.

36. (H)—Inference Question

The selection's sentence starts with describing the docile behavior of rattlesnakes, as a follow up to scientific findings in the previous paragraph. The implication is that snakes, while not as dangerous as often thought, can still be dangerous. Choice (H) matches this perfectly. Choice (F) is outside the scope of the passage; there is no mention of herpetologists keeping snakes. Choice (G) misuses a later detail; the author is not comparing the rattlesnake as a pet to dogs. Choice (J) states a comparison that is never made.

37. (B)—Detail Question

In paragraph 5, the author lists various statistics, and states that dogs, bees, and lightning are all responsible for more annual deaths, and that the fer-de-lance is responsible for substantially more. Choice (B) is the only answer that fits; every other choice is contradicted by the facts given.

38. (J)—Detail Question

In paragraph six, the author explains that the rattlesnakes knows that it needs its venom for food, and goes on to state that the only situations in which a rattlesnake would release all of its venom is when it feels threatened. Choice (J) fits with this; the rattlesnake wishes to conserve its venom, specifically for prey. Choice (F) is incorrect because humans are large in comparison, and receive mostly "dry" bites. Choice (G) contradicts the statement about rattlesnakes potentially using all their venom if threatened. Choice (H) contradicts the statement that rattlesnakes are not aware of the well-being of non-food sources.

39. (B)—Detail Question

The author examines two pieces of contradictory logic. The first is that the organizers use the reputation of the rattlesnake to promote interest, but rely on the more docile nature of the snakes. The second is the fact that most of the snakes are taken from areas without people, and put into contact with people, thus making for a more dangerous situation. Choice (B) matches the second piece of information. Choice (A) is not stated as fact in the text. Choice (C) brings up erroneous statistics, when really it is the rattlesnake's erroneous reputation that is used. Choice (D) is not mentioned in the passage.

40. (G)—Vocabulary in Context Question

The answer lies in the last sentence, which speculates on the status of humans in rattlesnake folklore "if rattlesnakes were able to speak or write." This makes it clear that *crotalid* must have something to do with actual rattlesnakes. Choice (G) is the only choice that fits, because the sentence is mocking the way that humans have characterized rattlesnakes within human mythology. Choices (F), (G), and (H) all are incorrect, because they mention groups that are not specifically rattlesnakes.

SCIENCE TEST

PASSAGE I

The first passage requires a little basic understanding of the scientific method and a lot of figure interpretation. You don't need to grasp all of the details of the passage or the diagrams, but do take note of obvious trends or extremes in the given data. For example, the large changes in the data in Figure 1 at around 1,500 years are particularly worth noting.

1. (C)

Be careful of extreme language, such as the use of "always" in choices (A) and (B). While the general trend is that decreasing glacier length corresponds to decreasing calving rate, the opposite is true at the sharp peak in calving rate at around 1,500 years, which choice (C) correctly describes.

2. (H)

This question asks you to find the glacier with the largest calving rate for years 6–10 in Table 1. Make sure you are looking in the right place, which in this case is the far right column of Table 1.

3. (A)

This question requires a little deeper understanding of the data presented Table 1. For all four glaciers during both time periods, the calving rate is slightly greater than or equal to the average velocity. To predict the calving rate of a glacier with a velocity of 80 m/yr, you must look for glaciers traveling at similar velocities. The closest values come from glaciers A and C during years 1–5, which had velocities of 72 m/yr and 98 m/yr, respectively. The corresponding calving rates for these two glaciers are

72 m/yr and 106 m/yr. The correct answer should fall within this range, as described by choice (A).

4. (J)

With open-ended questions like this one, simple process of elimination is usually most efficient. Comparison of each choice with the data in Table 1 reveals that only choice (J) accurately reflects the "behavior of the glaciers."

5. (B)

Don't be too concerned with the strange scale of the horizontal axis of each choice. The values on the axis correspond exactly to the calving rates for years 6–10 given in Table 1. Simply find the graph that correctly plots the four points given by the data in the last two columns of Table 1.

6. (H)

The meteorologists in Study 3 hypothesized that high temperatures cause rapid variations in velocity and calving rate. Figure 1 shows a rapid change in calving rate at around 1,500 years. If the hypothesis is true, then the glacier modeled in Study 1 experienced a rapid change in temperature approximately 1,500 years ago, and choice (H) is correct.

Passage II

This passage is consists almost entirely of Table 1 and Figures 1 and 2, with very little descriptive language. Fortunately, the more complicated the diagram, the more likely the questions referring to that diagram will be straightforward. In other words, don't waste too much time trying to interpret Table 1 right away. As it turns out, only one question requires you to refer to Table 1.

7. (C)

Sometimes, you will be asked to simply read information directly from a graph. If you are careful to refer to the right part of the right graph, you will find correct answers to these kinds of questions very quickly. The bar for March 2 on Figure 1 rises to approximately 1,500 gr/m^3, as in choice (C).

8. (H)

You are asked to describe a trend in the data in Figure 1 beyond the high value given for November 5. After this value, the data maintains no discernable trend, but does stay within a relatively small range of values, as is correctly described in choice (H).

9. (B)

Be careful to answer the correct question. "Increased the most," doesn't necessarily mean the count increased to its largest value, which is the trap set in choice (C). Choice (D) is also a trap, set for those who refer to the wrong figure.

10. (F)

This question asks about the tree pollen count, so you should refer to Figure 1. Process of elimination reveals that only choice (F) correctly reflects the data shown in the figure.

11. (A)

You are finally asked to refer to the rather complicated Table 1. Find the row for the month of May, and look for the corresponding column(s) containing the most reported cases of allergic rhinitis. In this case, that means the most ⊛ symbols. Tree and grass pollens account for six of the nine total ⊛ symbols in the May row, which indeed constitute "most" of the cases.

PASSAGE III

When a passage includes multiple experiments designed to study the same topic, look for key similarities and differences between the experiments. In Experiment 1, oscillation frequency of a pendulum is measured, and the only variable is the length of the pendulum arm. In Experiment 2, the oscillation frequencies of several springs are measured, and there are two variables: the spring and the suspended mass. Experiment 3 involves the same springs as does Experiment 2, but measures equilibrium length instead of oscillation frequency.

12. (G)

Notice that in Figure 3, the lines plotted for Springs B, C, and D intersect at approximately the same mass. The exact mass value is not completely clear from the figure, but it is definitely larger than choice (F) and smaller than choice (H), which leaves choice (G) as the only possibility.

13. (A)

According to Figure 1, oscillation frequency does indeed decrease with increasing arm length, so you can eliminate choices (C) and (D). The second part of choice (B) is simply false, which leaves only choice (A).

14. (F)

This question requires a couple of steps of logic. First, you must realize what "slowly" means in terms of oscillation frequency. Recall from the passage that oscillation frequency is measured in "oscillations per second." The faster the spring oscillates, the more oscillations it will complete per second. Therefore, you are looking for the spring with the lowest value for oscillation frequency, which is Spring A.

15. (C)

Refer to the line plotted for Spring A in Figure 3. On that line, a mass of 700 g corresponds to an equilibrium length of just less than 40 cm. Only choice (C) includes this estimate.

16. (J)

According to Figure 2, an oscillation frequency of 1.4 Hz at a mass of 100 g would be represented by a data point that would fall in between the frequency values for Spring C and Spring D at that mass. Only choices (H) and (J) place Spring E correctly between Springs C and D, and only choice (J) correctly lists the springs in order of *decreasing* oscillation frequency.

17. (C)

The effects of mass are not mentioned in Experiment 1. Only the pendulum arm length affects the oscillation frequency, so the plots for the original mass and the larger mass should be identical, as in choice (C).

PASSAGE IV

This passage is based almost entirely on Figure 1, which contains a great deal of information and deserves a few moments of your attention before attacking the questions. As always, it is important to understand what is represented on each axis. In this case, the vertical axis is straightforward, but the horizontal axis is a bit unconventional. The last sentence in the passage should help you to grasp that the horizontal axis represents the composition of the alloy, where the value (0–100%) is the atomic percentage of Si in the alloy. The further to the right on the Figure, the more Si and less Au there is in the alloy. The lines on the graph separate the different phases of the alloy, from completely solid at the bottom of the graph to completely liquid at the top. Play close attention to any notes included to help describe a figure. The note in this case tells you that parentheses around an element indicate that element's solid state.

18. (J)

Be careful to not confuse melting point with boiling point. Only the melting points are shown in Figure 1, so choice (J) is correct.

19. (B)

Draw a vertical line from the 50% mark on the horizontal axis and a horizontal line from the 600°C mark on the vertical axis. These lines intersect in the region of the diagram labeled "liquid + (Si)," which the note tells you means liquid plus Si in its solid state.

20. (G)

The lowest melting point is indicated by the section of the graph labeled "liquid" that reaches the furthest down on the graph. An arrow on the graph labels this point the "eutectic point" and gives the exact alloy composition there, which is reproduced correctly in choice (G).

21. (A)

The question asks you to look at compositions with less than 10% Si, which means you can draw a vertical line from the 10% mark on the horizontal axis and ignore everything to the right of that line. In the portion of the graph to the left of this line, the temperature required for the alloy to become completely liquid decreases with increasing Si atomic percentage. Choice (D) is a trap set for those drawn to the wrong line on the figure. The horizontal line at a temperature of 363°C indicates the temperature

at which the alloy becomes completely solid, not liquid.

22. (H)

Draw a horizontal line from 1,200°C on the y-axis to where it intersects the plot. Draw a line down from that point to the x-axis. It intersects somewhere between 70 and 80% Si. According to the figure, solid Si particles would also begin to form at this temperature. Choice (H) encompasses this information and is correct.

PASSAGE V

Don't be intimidated by unfamiliar language like the biological terms in this passage. Remember that no advanced scientific knowledge is assumed. As usual, here the important task is to be able to locate the appropriate information from the given figures. Note the trends in both figures, namely the decreases in temperature and oxygen partial pressure with increasing altitude in Figure 1 and the elevated GST and ECH concentrations of the high altitude dwellers in Table 1.

23. (D)

Make sure you refer to the correct part of Table 1 for the enzyme concentration values of populations ha 1, ha 2, and ha 3. The table shows that for all three high altitude populations, GST levels are highest, CR levels are lowest, and ECH levels are intermediate. Only choice (D) does not violate this relationship.

24. (G)

The process of elimination works best here. Choice (F) is not universally true; the oxygen saturation percentages are pretty similar for high altitude and sea level dwellers. Neither Table 1 nor

Figure 1 show a comparison between high or low altitude populations and temperature or partial oxygen pressure, so choices (H) and (J) cannot be correct. Only choice (G) is directly supported by the values in the table.

25. (C)

The answer to this question comes directly from Figure 1, but you must be careful to not confuse the two data sets. You can draw a horizontal line from 110 mm Hg on the left vertical axis until it intersects with the oxygen partial pressure data (open squares). That intersection happens at about 3,200 m. To find the temperature at this altitude, draw a horizontal line from the temperature plot (closed circles) at 3,200 m to the right axis. It intersects at just under $-5°C$, choice (C). Accidentally reversing the two data sets likely results in selecting trap answer (A).

26. (H)

You are asked to find the highest ECH concentration for any of the six populations, which occurs for population ha 2.

27. (A)

Only choices (A) and (C) agree with the information in Table 1. You can eliminate choice (C), though, because nothing in the passage or data suggests that CR concentration has anything to do with efficiency at incorporating oxygen into the blood.

PASSAGE VI

On passages that present two conflicting viewpoints, make sure you read the first passage and answer the questions associated with it before reading the second passage and answering the remaining questions. Note the fundamental similarities and differences between the two viewpoints. In this case,

Student 1 attributes the fact that lakes freeze from the surface downwards to the effects of pressure, while Student 2 credits a change in density. Both students are able to apply their explanations to the ice skating situation as well. You are not asked to determine the validity of either viewpoint, but instead to follow each argument separately and be able to apply each student's reasoning.

28. (J)

Recall that Student 1 credits pressure with the freezing phenomenon. Choices (G) and (H) reflect elements of the viewpoint of Student 2, and can therefore be eliminated. If choice (F) were true, the temperature and pressure effects would work against each other, so only choice (J) makes sense.

29. (B)

According to Student 1, pressure causes the ice to melt, and pressure increases with increasing weight. Student 2 states that friction causes the ice to melt, and that the force of friction increases with increasing weight. Therefore, the students would agree that ice would melt faster under the heavier skater, as in choice (B).

30. (F)

In the explanation of Student 2, ice melts when heat is generated as the skater overcomes the force of friction by moving across the ice. If the skater is not moving, then, no heat should be generated. Student 1, though, explains that ice melts due to pressure, which is present whether or not the skater is moving, making choice (F) correct.

31. (C)

Student 2 explains that less dense materials float above more dense materials. Since the frozen ethanol remains below the liquid ethanol, choice (C) must be true.

32. (H)

You can eliminate choices (F) and (G) due to the mention of pressure in both, which is a concept only Student 1 contemplates. Student 2 describes floating as the case in which the buoyant force exceeds the force of gravity, so the sinking boat is evidence of the opposite situation described in choice (H).

33. (B)

Eliminate choice (A), because only Student 1 considers pressure, and eliminate choice (D), because the only possible support for this explanation also comes from Student 1. Eliminate choice (C), because the force of gravity will only change as the mass of the skater changes. Student 2 states that heat is produced by overcoming friction, so less friction would mean less heat, as in choice (B).

34. (F)

Recall that the viewpoint of Student 2 focuses on a difference in *density*, and eliminate choice (H). Choices (G) and (J) both actually mean the same thing, but the term "buoyant" is included in choice (J) to entice the unwary test taker. In either case, the balloon would remain on the ground. The less dense balloon described in choice (F) would indeed rise above the ground.

PASSAGE VII

The first paragraph of this research summary passage explains that the experiments were conducted to study F^- concentrations in water. Experiment 1 tested solutions prepared by the students to have specific F^- concentrations, and the solutions'

electrical conductivities were measured. Table 1 shows a direct relationship between F^- concentration and conductivity, and Figure 1 further emphasizes the linearity of this relationship. Be careful to notice the difference between *measured* and *corrected* conductivities and that it is the corrected conductivities that are plotted in Figure 1. Don't worry if you don't recognize the units given for conductivity; knowledge of these units is not required to answer the questions.

Experiment 2 tested solutions taken from various communities' drinking water supplies. The direct relationship between F^- concentration and conductivity seen in Experiment 1 is confirmed.

35. (C)

Either Table 1 or Figure 1 can provide the answer here. Table 1 contains numerical examples of cases where the F^- concentration is indeed doubled (from 0.5 mg/L to 1 mg/L, for example), and gives the corresponding change in conductivity. Taking care to look the *corrected* conductivity column, you can see that 2 times the concentration results in 2 times the corrected conductivity. Likewise, Figure 1 makes it clear that relationship between the two quantities is linear, which means that any multiplication of the concentration results in the same multiplication of the conductivity.

36. (J)

Compare the new conductivity value to those given in Table 2, specifically those for Newtown and Lakewood, and recall the direct relationship between conductivity and F^- concentration. Noticing that Bluewater's conductivity value lies between the values for Newtown and Lakewood allows you to eliminate choices (F) and (G). Taking care to list the towns in order of *increasing* F⁻ leads you to choice (J).

37. (C)

Refer to Table 1 to see where a value of 3.0 mg/L would fit in. This new concentration is between the 2.0 mg/L and 4.0 mg/L values given in the table, so the corrected conductivity should lie between 3.34 μS/cm and 6.68 μS/cm. Choices (B) and (D) are too close to the extremes of this range, but choice (C) is exactly in the middle as it should be. Alternatively, you could read the corrected conductivity for a concentration of 3.0 mg/L directly from Figure 1.

38. (F)

Questions that ask you to change the procedure of an experiment usually require you to review the original experiment before answering. In this case, the description of Experiment 1 tells you that F⁻ is added in the form of dissolved Na_2SiF_6. To study Cl⁻ concentrations, the students must use a chemical that contains Cl⁻ when preparing the solutions, as in choice (F).

39. (B)

Experimental data is not required to answer this question. The last sentence of the description of Experiment 1 explains that the corrected conductivity is calculated by *subtracting* the measured conductivity of the blank solution. This always results in the corrected conductivity being less than the measured conductivity, as in choice (B).

40. (F)

You are told that Cl⁻ results in an increase in conductivity, and the data shows that F⁻ results in an increase in conductivity. Therefore, in a solution containing both F⁻ and Cl⁻, it would be impossible to distinguish the contributions to conductivity from each ion given only conductivity measurements. Conductivity would be increased by the presence of Cl⁻, and the apparent values for F⁻ concentration would be falsely high, as in choice (F). If you miss this point, you could at least eliminate choice (J), since the question asks only about the case where *all* of the samples have Cl⁻ concentrations. The effect of the Cl⁻ should not be different for different solutions.

WRITING TEST

MODEL ESSAY

Below is an example of what a high-scoring essay might look like. Notice the author states her position clearly in the introductory paragraph and supports that position with evidence in the following paragraphs. The essay also uses transitions, some advanced vocabulary, and an effective "hook" to draw in the reader.

The elevated rate of automobile accidents that occur when teenaged drivers are behind the wheel has driven some parents and legislators to lobby for laws that would ban drivers under 18 from driving with other teenagers in the car. Those who support these laws believe that driving alone or with an adult would minimize distraction for new drivers, helping them to drive more safely. Others disagree, pointing to the lack of evidence that groups of teenagers riding together are actually the cause of these accidents.

Everyone benefits from having more safe drivers on the road, but efforts to curb the freedoms of drivers under 18 are misguided and unfair. For example, elderly drivers may have impaired vision or motor skills, but are not subject to additional restrictions based only on their age. Male drivers are more prone to car accidents than female drivers, but one can only imagine the outcry if a restriction on the driving privileges of all men were proposed! A driver's license should provide the same responsibilities and freedoms to each person who receives one. If we don't believe that 16-year-olds are as capable of operating a car safely as 18-year-olds, we should not issue them driver's licenses at all.

If we want to promote safe driving, there are more evenhanded methods of doing so. In our state, all drivers who take their license exam must have completed 40 hours of classroom training, regardless of age. These classes are an effective way to ensure that everyone who takes the driver's exam has the same base level of knowledge about traffic laws, operation of a motor vehicle, and the importance of driving safely. This information is important for all new drivers. A requirement for licensed drivers to take a refresher course every five years could help to ensure that more drivers remain aware of new laws and safety issues.

Proponents of this law claim that preventing teenagers from riding in cars together will help to lower the number of accidents. However, no studies have been released that can isolate the presence of other teenagers in the car as a cause of accidents. Having a conversation with a friend in the passenger seat could certainly be distracting, but talking on a cell phone, or listening to loud music, might be equally or even more distracting—and again, all of these distractions can occur when an older person is driving, as well.

Safety and responsibility are important for drivers of all ages. The proposed laws target younger drivers unfairly, and there is no evidence that they would prevent accidents. Measures that attempt to promote safe driving should be aimed at all drivers, not the small percentage of them who are under 18 years old.

You can evaluate your essay and the model essay based on the following criteria, covered in chapter 16.

- Does the author answer the question?
- Is the author's position clearly stated?
- Does the body of the essay support and develop the position taken?
- Are there at least three supporting paragraphs?
- Is the relevance of each supporting paragraph clear?
- Is the essay a reasonable length?
- Is the essay organized, with a clear introduction, middle, and end?
- Did the author use one paragraph for each new idea?
- Is each sentence in a paragraph relevant to the point made in that paragraph?
- Are transitions clear?
- Is the essay easy to read? Is it engaging?
- Are sentences varied?
- Is vocabulary used effectively? Is college-level vocabulary used?

Compute Your Score

1 **Figure out your score in each section.** Refer to the answer keys to figure out the number right in each test section. Enter the results below:

Raw Scores

	TEST 1	TEST 2	TEST 3		TEST 1	TEST 2	TEST 3
English:				Reading:			
Math:				Science:			

2 **Find your practice test scores.** Find your raw score on each section in the table below. The score in the far left column indicates your estimated scaled score if this were an actual ACT.

SCALED SCORE	RAW SCORES			
	Test 1 English	Test 2 Mathematics	Test 3 Reading	Test 4 Science
36	75	60	40	40
35	74	60	40	40
34	73	59	39	39
33	72	58	39	39
32	71	57	38	38
31	70	55–56	37	37
30	69	53–54	36	36
29	68	50–52	35	35
28	67	48–49	34	34
27	65–66	45–47	33	33
26	63–64	43–44	32	32
25	61–62	40–42	31	30–31
24	58–60	38–39	30	28–29
23	56–57	35–37	29	26–27
22	53–55	33–34	28	24–25
21	49–52	31–32	27	21–23
20	46–48	28–30	25–26	19–20
19	44–45	26–27	23–24	17–18
18	41–43	23–25	21–22	16
17	39–40	20–22	19–20	15
16	36–38	17–19	17–18	14
15	34–35	15–16	15–16	13
14	30–33	13–14	13–14	12
13	28–29	11–12	12–13	11
12	25–27	9–10	10–11	10
11	23–24	8	9	9
10	20–22	7	8	8
9	17–19	6	7	7
8	14–16	5	6	6
7	12–13	4	5	5
6	9–11	3	4	4
5	7–8	2	3	3
4	4–6	1	2	2
3	3	1	1	1
2	2	0	0	0
1	1	0	0	0

KAPLAN

	TEST 1	TEST 2	TEST 3		TEST 1	TEST 2	TEST 3
Scaled Scores English:				Reading:			
Math:				Science:			

3 **Find your estimated composite score.** To calculate your estimated composite score, simply add together your scaled scores on each subsection and divide by four.

Composite Score:

TEST 1	TEST 2	TEST 3

100 KEY MATH CONCEPTS
FOR THE ACT

NUMBER PROPERTIES

1. **UNDEFINED**

   On the ACT, *undefined* almost always means **division by zero.** The expression $\dfrac{a}{bc}$ is undefined if either b or c equals 0.

2. **REAL/IMAGINARY**

   A real number is a number that has a **location on the number line.** On the ACT, imaginary numbers are numbers that involve the square root of a negative number. $\sqrt{-4}$ is an imaginary number.

3. **INTEGER/NONINTEGER**

   Integers are **whole numbers;** they include negative whole numbers and zero.

4. **RATIONAL/IRRATIONAL**

   A **rational number** is a number that can be expressed as a **ratio of two integers. Irrational numbers** are real numbers—they have locations on the number line—they just **can't be expressed precisely as a fraction or decimal.** For the purposes of the ACT, the most important **irrational numbers** are $\sqrt{2}$, $\sqrt{3}$, and π.

5. **ADDING/SUBTRACTING SIGNED NUMBERS**

   To **add a positive and a negative,** first ignore the signs and find the positive difference between the number parts. Then attach the sign of the original number to the larger number part. For example, to add 23 and −34, first we ignore the minus sign and find the positive difference between 23 and 34—that's 11. Then we attach the sign of the number with the larger number part—in this case it's the minus sign from the −34. So, 23 + (−34) = −11.

   Make **subtraction** situations simpler by turning them into addition. For example, think of −17 − (−21) as −17 + (+21).

   To **add or subtract a string of positives and negatives,** first turn everything into addition. Then combine the positives and negatives so that the string is reduced to the sum of a single positive number and a single negative number.

6. **MULTIPLYING/DIVIDING SIGNED NUMBERS**

   To multiply and/or divide positives and negatives, treat the number parts as usual and **attach a negative sign if there were originally**

an odd number of negatives. To multiply −2, −3, and −5, first multiply the number parts: 2 × 3 × 5 = 30. Then go back and note that there were three—an odd number—negatives, so the product is negative: (−2) × (−3) × (−5) = −30.

7. PEMDAS

When performing multiple operations, remember PEMDAS, which means **Parentheses** first, then **Exponents,** then **Multiplication** and **Division** (left to right), then **Addition** and **Subtraction** (left to right).

In the expression $9 - 2 \times (5 - 3)^2 + 6 \div 3$, begin with the parentheses: $(5 - 3) = 2$. Then do the exponent: $2^2 = 4$. Now the expression is: $9 - 2 \times 4 + 6 \div 3$. Next do the multiplication and division to get $9 - 8 + 2$, which equals 3.

8. ABSOLUTE VALUE

Treat absolute value signs a lot like **parentheses.** Do what's inside them first and then take the absolute value of the result. Don't take the absolute value of each piece between the bars before calculating. In order to calculate $|(-12) + 5 - (-4)| - |5 + (-10)|$, first do what's inside the bars to get: $|-3| - |-5|$, which is $3 - 5$, or -2.

9. COUNTING CONSECUTIVE INTEGERS

To count consecutive integers, **subtract the smallest from the largest and add 1.** To count the integers from 13 through 31, subtract: $31 - 13 = 18$. Then add 1: $18 + 1 = 19$.

DIVISIBILITY

10. FACTOR/MULTIPLE

The **factors** of integer n are the positive integers that divide into n with no remainder. The **multiples** of n are the integers that n divides into with no remainder. 6 is a factor of 12, and 24 is a multiple of 12. 12 is both a factor and a multiple of itself.

11. PRIME FACTORIZATION

A **prime number** is a positive integer that has exactly two positive integer factors: 1 and the integer itself. The first eight prime numbers are 2, 3, 5, 7, 11, 13, 17, and 19.

To find the prime factorization of an integer, just keep breaking it up into factors until **all the factors are prime.** To find the prime factorization of 36, for example, you could begin by breaking it into 4 × 9:

$$36 = 4 \times 9 = 2 \times 2 \times 3 \times 3$$

12. RELATIVE PRIMES

To determine whether two integers are relative primes, break them both down to their prime factorizations. For example: $35 = 5 \times 7$, and $54 = 2 \times 3 \times 3 \times 3$. They have **no prime factors in common,** so 35 and 54 are relative primes.

13. COMMON MULTIPLE

You can always get a common multiple of two numbers by **multiplying** them, but, unless the two numbers are relative primes, the product will not be the least common multiple. For example, to find a common multiple for 12 and 15, you could just multiply: $12 \times 15 = 180$.

14. LEAST COMMON MULTIPLE (LCM)

To find the least common multiple, check out the **multiples of the larger number** until you find one that's **also a multiple of the smaller.** To find the LCM of 12 and 15, begin by taking the multiples of 15: 15 is not divisible by 12; 30's not; nor is 45. But the next multiple of 15, 60, is divisible by 12, so it's the LCM.

15. GREATEST COMMON FACTOR (GCF)

To find the greatest common factor, break down both numbers into their prime factorizations and take **all the prime factors they have in common.** $36 = 2 \times 2 \times 3 \times 3$, and $48 = 2 \times 2 \times 2 \times 2 \times 3$. What they have in common is two 2s and one 3, so the GCF is $= 2 \times 2 \times 3 = 12$.

16. EVEN/ODD

To predict whether a sum, difference, or product will be even or odd, just **take simple numbers like 1 and 2 and see what happens.** There are rules—"odd times even is even," for example— but there's no need to memorize them. What happens with one set of numbers generally happens with all similar sets.

17. MULTIPLES OF 2 AND 4

An integer is divisible by 2 if the **last digit is even.** An integer is divisible by 4 if the **last two digits form a multiple of 4.** The last digit of 562 is 2, which is even, so 562 is a multiple of 2. The last two digits make 62, which is not divisible by 4, so 562 is not a multiple of 4.

18. MULTIPLES OF 3 AND 9

An integer is divisible by 3 if the **sum of its digits is divisible by 3.** An integer is divisible by 9 if the **sum of its digits is divisible by 9.**

The sum of the digits in 957 is 21, which is divisible by 3 but not by 9, so 957 is divisible by 3 but not 9.

19. MULTIPLES OF 5 AND 10

An integer is divisible by 5 if the **last digit is 5 or 0.** An integer is divisible by 10 if the **last digit is 0.** The last digit of 665 is 5, so 665 is a multiple of 5 but not a multiple of 10.

20. REMAINDERS

The remainder is the whole number left over after division. 487 is 2 more than 485, which is a multiple of 5, so when 487 is divided by 5, the remainder will be 2.

FRACTIONS AND DECIMALS

21. REDUCING FRACTIONS

To reduce a fraction to lowest terms, **factor out and cancel** all factors the numerator and denominator have in common.

$$\frac{28}{36} = \frac{4 \times 7}{4 \times 9} = \frac{7}{9}$$

22. ADDING/SUBTRACTING FRACTIONS

To add or subtract fractions, first find a **common denominator,** and then add or subtract the numerators.

$$\frac{2}{15} + \frac{3}{10} = \frac{4}{30} + \frac{9}{30} = \frac{4+9}{30} = \frac{13}{30}$$

23. MULTIPLYING FRACTIONS

To multiply fractions, **multiply** the numerators and **multiply** the denominators.

$$\frac{5}{7} \times \frac{3}{4} = \frac{5 \times 3}{7 \times 4} = \frac{15}{28}$$

24. DIVIDING FRACTIONS

To divide fractions, **invert** the second one and **multiply.**

$$\frac{1}{2} \div \frac{3}{5} = \frac{1}{2} \times \frac{5}{3} = \frac{1 \times 5}{2 \times 3} = \frac{5}{6}$$

25. CONVERTING A MIXED NUMBER TO AN IMPROPER FRACTION

To convert a mixed number to an improper fraction, **multiply** the whole number part by the denominator, then **add** the numerator. The result is the new numerator (over the same denominator). To convert $7\frac{1}{3}$, first multiply 7 by 3, then add 1, to get the new numerator of 22. Put that over the same denominator, 3, to get $\frac{22}{3}$.

26. CONVERTING AN IMPROPER FRACTION TO A MIXED NUMBER

To convert an improper fraction to a mixed number, **divide** the denominator into the numerator to get a **whole number quotient with a remainder.** The quotient becomes the whole number part of the mixed number, and the remainder becomes the new numerator—with the same denominator. For example, to convert $\frac{108}{5}$ first divide 5 into 108, which yields 21 with a remainder of 3. Therefore, $\frac{108}{5} = 21\frac{3}{5}$.

27. RECIPROCAL

To find the reciprocal of a fraction, switch the numerator and the denominator. The reciprocal of $\frac{3}{7}$ is $\frac{7}{3}$. The reciprocal of 5 is $\frac{1}{5}$. The product of reciprocals is 1.

28. COMPARING FRACTIONS

One way to compare fractions is to re-express them with a **common denominator.**

$\frac{3}{4} = \frac{21}{28}$ and $\frac{5}{7} = \frac{20}{28}$, $\frac{21}{28}$ is greater than $\frac{20}{28}$, so $\frac{3}{4}$ is greater than $\frac{5}{7}$.

Another way to compare fractions is to convert them both to **decimals.** $\frac{3}{4}$ converts to .75, and $\frac{5}{7}$ converts to approximately .714.

29. CONVERTING FRACTIONS TO DECIMALS

To convert a fraction to a decimal, **divide the bottom into the top.** To convert $\frac{5}{8}$, divide 8 into 5, yielding .625.

30. REPEATING DECIMAL

To find a particular digit in a repeating decimal, note the **number of digits in the cluster that repeats.** If there are 2 digits in that cluster, then every 2nd digit is the same. If there are 3 digits in that cluster, then every 3rd digit is the same. And so on. For example, the decimal equivalent of $\frac{1}{27}$ is .037037037. . . , which is best written $.\overline{037}$.

There are 3 digits in the repeating cluster, so every 3rd digit is the same: 7. To find the 50th digit, look for the multiple of 3 just less than 50—that's 48. The 48th digit is 7, and with the 49th digit the pattern repeats with 0. The 50th digit is 3.

31. IDENTIFYING THE PARTS AND THE WHOLE

The key to solving most fractions and percents story problems is to identify the part and the whole. Usually you'll find the **part** associated with the verb *is/are* and the **whole** associated with the word *of.* In the sentence, "Half of the boys are blonds," the whole is the boys ("*of* the boys), and the part is the blonds ("*are* blonds").

PERCENTS

32. PERCENT FORMULA

Whether you need to find the part, the whole, or the percent, use the same formula:

$$\text{Part} = \text{Percent} \times \text{Whole}$$

Example: What is 12% of 25?
Setup: Part = .12 × 25

Example: 15 is 3% of what number?
Setup: 15 = .03 × Whole

Example: 45 is what percent of 9?
Setup: 45 = Percent × 9

33. PERCENT INCREASE AND DECREASE

To increase a number by a percent, **add the percent to 100%,** convert to a decimal, and multiply. To increase 40 by 25%, add 25% to 100%, convert 125% to 1.25, and multiply by 40. 1.25 × 40 = 50.

34. FINDING THE ORIGINAL WHOLE

To find the **original whole before a percent increase or decrease,** set up an equation. Think of a 15% increase over x as $1.15x$.

Example: After a 5% increase, the population was 59,346. What was the population *before* the increase?

Setup: $1.05x = 59{,}346$

35. COMBINED PERCENT INCREASE AND DECREASE

To determine the combined effect of multiple percents increase and/or decrease, **start with 100 and see what happens.**

Example: A price went up 10% one year, and the new price went up 20% the next year. What was the combined percent increase?

Setup: First year: 100 + (10% of 100) = 110. Second year: 110 + (20% of 110) = 132. That's a combined 32% increase.

RATIOS, PROPORTIONS, AND RATES

36. SETTING UP A RATIO

To find a ratio, put the number associated with the word *of* **on top** and the quantity associated with the word *to* **on the** bottom and reduce. The ratio of 20 oranges to 12 apples is $\frac{20}{12}$ which reduces to $\frac{5}{3}$.

37. PART-TO-PART AND PART-TO-WHOLE RATIOS

If the parts add up to the whole, a part-to-part ratio can be turned into two part-to-whole ratios by putting **each number in the original ratio over the sum of the numbers.** If the ratio of males to females is 1 to 2, then the males-to-people ratio is $\frac{1}{1+2} = \frac{1}{3}$ and the females-to-people ratio is $\frac{2}{1+2} = \frac{2}{3}$. Or, $\frac{2}{3}$ of all the people are female.

38. SOLVING A PROPORTION

To solve a proportion, **cross multiply:**

$$\frac{x}{5} = \frac{3}{4}$$
$$4x = 5 \times 3$$
$$x = \frac{15}{4} = 3.75$$

39. RATE

To solve a rates problem, **use the units** to keep things straight.

Example: If snow is falling at the rate of 1 foot every 4 hours, how many inches of snow will fall in 7 hours?

Setup:

$$\frac{1 \text{ foot}}{4 \text{ hours}} = \frac{x \text{ inches}}{7 \text{ hours}}$$
$$\frac{12 \text{ inches}}{4 \text{ hours}} = \frac{x \text{ inches}}{7 \text{ hours}}$$
$$4x = 12 \times 7$$
$$x = 21$$

40. AVERAGE RATE

Average rate is *not* simply the average of the rates.

$$\text{Average } A \text{ per } B = \frac{\text{Total } A}{\text{Total } B}$$
$$\text{Average Speed} = \frac{\text{Total distance}}{\text{Total time}}$$

To find the average speed for 120 miles at 40 mph and 120 miles at 60 mph, **don't just average the two speeds.** First figure out the total distance and the total time. The total distance is $120 + 120 = 240$ miles. The times are 3 hours for the first leg and 2 hours for the second leg, or

5 hours total. The average speed, then, is $\frac{240}{5} = 48$ miles per hour.

AVERAGES

41. AVERAGE FORMULA

To find the average of a set of numbers, **add them up and divide by the number of numbers.**

$$\text{Average} = \frac{\text{Sum of the terms}}{\text{Number of terms}}$$

To find the average of the five numbers 12, 15, 23, 40, and 40, first add them: $12 + 15 + 23 + 40 + 40 = 130$. Then divide the sum by 5: $130 \div 5 = 26$.

42. AVERAGE OF EVENLY SPACED NUMBERS

To find the average of evenly spaced numbers, just **average the smallest and the largest.** The average of all the integers from 13 through 77 is the same as the average of 13 and 77.

$$\frac{13 + 77}{2} = \frac{90}{2} = 45$$

43. USING THE AVERAGE TO FIND THE SUM

$$\text{Sum} = (\text{Average}) \times (\text{Number of terms})$$

If the average of ten numbers is 50, then they add up to 10×50, or 500.

44. FINDING THE MISSING NUMBER

To find a missing number when you're given the average, **use the sum.** If the average of four numbers is 7, then the sum of those four numbers is 4×7, or 28. Suppose that three of the numbers are 3, 5, and 8. These numbers add up to 16 of that 28, which leaves 12 for the fourth number.

POSSIBILITIES AND PROBABILITY

45. COUNTING THE POSSIBILITIES

The fundamental counting principle: if there are **m ways** one event can happen and **n ways** a second event can happen, then there are **$m \times n$ ways** for the two events to happen. For example, with 5 shirts and 7 pairs of pants to choose from, you can put together $5 \times 7 = 35$ different outfits.

46. PROBABILITY

$$\text{Probability} = \frac{\text{Favorable outcomes}}{\text{Total possible outcomes}}$$

If you have 12 shirts in a drawer and 9 of them are white, the probability of picking a white shirt at random is $\frac{9}{12} = \frac{3}{4}$. This probability can also be expressed as .75 or 75%.

POWERS AND ROOTS

47. MULTIPLYING AND DIVIDING POWERS

To multiply powers with the same base, **add the exponents:** $x^3 \times x^4 = x^{3+4} = x^7$. To divide powers with the same base, **subtract the exponents:** $y^{13} \div y^8 = y^{13-8} = y^5$.

48. RAISING POWERS TO POWERS

To raise a power to an exponent, **multiply the exponents.** $(x^3)^4 = x^{3 \times 4} = x^{12}$.

49. SIMPLIFYING SQUARE ROOTS

To simplify a square root, **factor out the perfect squares** under the radical, unsquare them and put the result in front. $\sqrt{12} = \sqrt{4 \times 3} = \sqrt{4} \times \sqrt{3} = 2\sqrt{3}$.

50. ADDING AND SUBTRACTING ROOTS

You can add or subtract radical expressions only if the part under the radicals is the same.

$$2\sqrt{3} + 3\sqrt{3} = 5\sqrt{3}$$

51. MULTIPLYING AND DIVIDING ROOTS

The product of square roots is equal to the square root of the product:

$\sqrt{3} \times \sqrt{5} = \sqrt{3 \times 5} = \sqrt{15}$. The quotient of square roots is equal to the **square root of the quotient:**

$$\frac{\sqrt{6}}{\sqrt{3}} = \frac{\sqrt{6}}{3} = \sqrt{2}.$$

ALGEBRAIC EXPRESSIONS

52. EVALUATING AN EXPRESSION

To evaluate an algebraic expression, **plug in** the given values for the unknowns and calculate according to PEMDAS. To find the value of $x^2 + 5x - 6$ when $x = -2$, plug in -2 for x:

$$(-2)^2 + 5(-2) - 6 = 4 - 10 - 6 = -12.$$

53. ADDING AND SUBTRACTING MONOMIALS

To combine like terms, **keep the variable part unchanged while adding or subtracting the coefficients.** $2a + 3a = (2 + 3)a = 5a$

54. ADDING AND SUBTRACTING POLYNOMIALS

To add or subtract polynomials, **combine like terms.**

$$(3x^2 + 5x - 7) - (x^2 + 12) =$$
$$(3x^2 - x^2) + 5x + (-7 - 12) = 2x^2 + 5x - 19$$

55. MULTIPLYING MONOMIALS

To multiply monomials, **multiply the coefficients and the variables separately.**

$$2a \times 3a = (2 \times 3)(a \times a) = 6a^2$$

56. MULTIPLYING BINOMIALS—FOIL

To multiply binomials, use **FOIL**. To multiply $(x + 3)$ by $(x + 4)$, first multiply the **F**irst terms: $x \times x = x^2$. Next the **O**uter terms: $x \times 4 = 4x$. Then the **I**nner terms: $3 \times x = 3x$. And finally the **L**ast terms: $3 \times 4 = 12$. Then add and combine like terms: $x^2 + 4x + 3x + 12 = x^2 + 7x + 12$.

57. MULTIPLYING OTHER POLYNOMIALS

FOIL works only when you want to multiply two binomials. If you want to multiply polynomials with more than two terms, make sure you **multiply each term in the first polynomial by each term in the second.**

$$(x^2 + 3x + 4)(x + 5) =$$
$$x^2(x + 5) + 3x(x + 5) + 4(x + 5) =$$
$$x^3 + 5x^2 + 3x^2 + 15x + 4x + 20 =$$
$$x^3 + 8x^2 + 19x + 20$$

FACTORING ALGEBRAIC EXPRESSIONS

58. FACTORING OUT A COMMON DIVISOR

A factor common to all terms of a polynomial can be **factored out.** All three terms in the polynomial $3x^3 + 12x^2 - 6x$ contain a factor of $3x$. Pulling out the common factor yields $3x(x^2 + 4x - 2)$.

59. FACTORING THE DIFFERENCE OF SQUARES

One of the test maker's favorite factorables is the **difference of squares**.

$$a^2 - b^2 = (a - b)(a + b)$$
$$x^2 - 9, \text{ for example, factors to } (x - 3)(x + 3).$$

60. FACTORING THE SQUARE OF A BINOMIAL

Learn to recognize polynomials that are squares of binomials:

$$a^2 + 2ab + b^2 = (a + b)^2$$
$$a^2 - 2ab + b^2 = (a - b)^2$$

For example, $4x^2 + 12x + 9$ factors to $(2x + 3)^2$, and $n^2 - 10n + 25$ factors to $(n - 5)^2$.

61. FACTORING OTHER POLYNOMIALS— FOIL IN REVERSE

To factor a quadratic expression, **think about what binomials you could use FOIL on to get that quadratic expression.** To factor $x^2 - 5x + 6$, think about what **F**irst terms will produce x^2, what **L**ast terms will produce $+6$, and what **O**uter and **I**nner terms will produce $-5x$. Common sense—and trial and error—lead you to $(x - 2)(x - 3)$.

62. SIMPLIFYING AN ALGEBRAIC FRACTION

Simplifying an algebraic fraction is a lot like simplifying a numerical fraction. The general idea is to **find factors common to the numerator and denominator and cancel them.** Thus, simplifying an algebraic fraction begins with factoring.

To simplify $\dfrac{x^2 - x - 12}{x^2 - 9}$ first factor the numerator and denominator: $\dfrac{x^2 - x - 12}{x^2 - 9} = \dfrac{(x - 4)(x + 3)}{(x - 3)(x + 3)}$

Canceling $x + 3$ from the numerator and denominator leaves you with $\dfrac{x - 4}{x - 3}$.

SOLVING EQUATIONS

63. SOLVING A LINEAR EQUATION

To solve an equation, do whatever is necessary to both sides to **isolate the variable.** To solve $5x - 12 = -2x + 9$, first get all the x's on one side by adding $2x$ to both sides: $7x - 12 = 9$. Then add 12 to both sides: $7x = 21$, then divide both sides by 7 to get: $x = 3$.

64. SOLVING "IN TERMS OF"

To solve an equation for one variable **in terms of** another means to **isolate the one variable on one side of the equation,** leaving an expression containing the other variable on the other side. To solve $3x - 10y = -5x + 6y$ for x in terms of y, isolate x:

$$3x - 10y = -5x + 6y$$
$$3x + 5x = 6y + 10y$$
$$8x = 16y$$
$$x = 2y$$

65. TRANSLATING FROM ENGLISH INTO ALGEBRA

To translate from English into algebra, look for the key words and systematically turn phrases into algebraic expressions and sentences into equations. Be careful about order, especially when subtraction is called for.

Example: The charge for a phone call is r cents for the first 3 minutes and s cents for each minute thereafter. What is the cost, in cents, of a call lasting exactly t minutes? ($t > 3$)

Setup: The charge begins with r, and then something more is added, depending on the length of the call. The amount added is s times the number of minutes past 3 minutes. If the total number of minutes is t, then the number of minutes past 3 is $t - 3$. So the charge is $r + s(t - 3)$.

INTERMEDIATE ALGEBRA

66. SOLVING A QUADRATIC EQUATION

To solve a quadratic equation, put it in the $ax^2 + bx + c = 0$ form, **factor** the left side (if you can), and set each factor equal to 0 separately to get the two solutions. To solve $x^2 + 12 = 7x$, first rewrite it as $x^2 - 7x + 12 = 0$. Then factor the left side:

$$(x - 3)(x - 4) = 0$$
$$x - 3 = 0 \text{ or } x - 4 = 0$$
$$x = 3 \text{ or } 4$$

Sometimes the left side might not be obviously factorable. You can always use the **quadratic formula.** Just plug in the coefficients a, b, and c from $ax^2 + bx + c = 0$ into the formula:

$$\frac{-b \pm \sqrt{b^2 - 4ac}}{2a}$$

To solve $x^2 + 4x + 2 = 0$, plug $a = 1$, $b = 4$, and $c = 2$ into the formula:

$$x = \frac{-4 \pm \sqrt{4^2 - 4 \times 1 \times 2}}{2 \times 1}$$
$$= \frac{-4 \pm \sqrt{8}}{2} = -2 \pm \sqrt{2}$$

67. SOLVING A SYSTEM OF EQUATIONS

You can solve for two variables only if you have two distinct equations. Two forms of the same equation will not be adequate. **Combine the equations in such a way that one of the variables cancels out.** To solve the two equations $4x + 3y = 8$ and $x + y = 3$, multiply both sides of the second equation by -3 to get: $-3x - 3y = -9$. Now add the equations; the $3y$ and the $-3y$ cancel out, leaving: $x = -1$. Plug that back into either one of the original equations and you'll find that $y = 4$.

68. SOLVING AN EQUATION THAT INCLUDES ABSOLUTE VALUE SIGNS

To solve an equation that includes absolute value signs, **think about the two different cases.** For example, to solve the equation $|x - 12| = 3$, think of it as two equations:

$$x - 12 = 3 \text{ or } x - 12 = -3$$
$$x = 15 \text{ or } 9$$

69. SOLVING AN INEQUALITY

To solve an inequality, do whatever is necessary to both sides to **isolate the variable.** Just remember that when you **multiply or divide both sides by a negative number,** you must **reverse the sign.** To solve $-5x + 7 < -3$, subtract 7 from both sides to get: $-5x < -10$. Now divide both sides by -5, remembering to reverse the sign: $x > 2$.

70. GRAPHING INEQUALITIES

To graph a range of values, use a thick, black line over the number line, and at the end(s) of the range, use a **solid circle** if the point **is included** or an **open circle** if the point is **not included.** The figure here shows the graph of $-3 < x \le 5$.

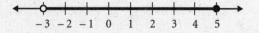

COORDINATE GEOMETRY

71. FINDING THE DISTANCE BETWEEN TWO POINTS

To find the distance between points, **use the Pythagorean theorem or special right triangles.** The difference between the xs is one leg and the difference between the ys is the other leg.

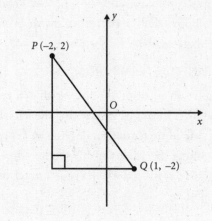

In the figure above, $\overline{PQ}$ is the hypotenuse of a 3-4-5 triangle, so $PQ = 5$.

You can also use the **distance formula:**

$$d = \sqrt{(x_2 - x_1)^2 + (y_2 - y_1)^2}$$

To find the distance between $R(3, 6)$ and $S(5, -2)$:

$$d = \sqrt{(5 - 3)^2 + (-2 - 6)^2}$$
$$= \sqrt{(2)^2 + (-8)^2}$$
$$= \sqrt{68} = 2\sqrt{17}$$

72. USING TWO POINTS TO FIND THE SLOPE

In mathematics, the slope of a line is often called m.

$$\text{Slope} = m = \frac{\text{Change in } y}{\text{Change in } x} = \frac{\text{Rise}}{\text{Run}}$$

The slope of the line that contains the points $A(2, 3)$ and $B(0, -1)$ is:

$$\frac{y_2 - y_1}{x_2 - x_1} = \frac{-1 - 3}{0 - 2} = \frac{-4}{-2} = 2$$

73. USING AN EQUATION TO FIND THE SLOPE

To find the slope of a line from an equation, put the equation into the **slope-intercept** form:

$$y = mx + b$$

The slope is m. To find the slope of the equation $3x + 2y = 4$, reexpress it:

$$3x + 2y = 4$$
$$2y = -3x + 4$$
$$y = -\frac{3}{2}x + 2$$

The slope is $-\frac{3}{2}$.

74. USING AN EQUATION TO FIND AN INTERCEPT

To find the y-intercept, you can either put the equation into $y = mx + b$ **(slope-intercept)** form—in which case b is the y-intercept—or you can just plug $x = 0$ into the equation and solve for y. To find the x-intercept, plug $y = 0$ into the equation and solve for x.

75. EQUATION FOR A CIRCLE

The equation for a circle of radius r and centered at (h, k) is:

$$(x - h)^2 + (y - k)^2 = r^2$$

The following figure shows the graph of the equation $(x - 2)^2 + (y + 1)^2 = 25$:

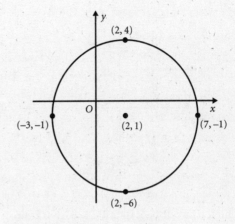

76. EQUATION FOR A PARABOLA

The graph of an equation in the form $y = ax^2 + bx + c$ is a parabola. The figure below shows the graph of seven pairs of numbers that satisfy the equation $y = x^2 - 4x + 3$:

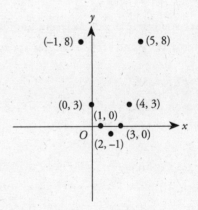

77. EQUATION FOR AN ELLIPSE

The graph of an equation in the form

$$\frac{x^2}{a^2} + \frac{y^2}{b^2} = 1$$

is an ellipse with $2a$ as the sum of the focal radii and with foci on the x-axis at $(0, -c)$ and $(0, c)$, where $c = \sqrt{a^2 - b^2}$. The following figure shows the graph of $\frac{x^2}{25} + \frac{y^2}{16} = 1$:

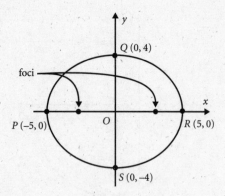

The foci are at $(-3, 0)$ and $(3, 0)$. $\overline{PR}$ is the **major axis,** and $\overline{QS}$ is the **minor axis.** This ellipse is symmetrical about both the x- and y-axes.

LINES AND ANGLES

78. INTERSECTING LINES

When two lines intersect, **adjacent angles are supplementary** and **vertical angles are equal.**

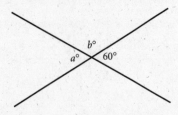

In the figure above, the angles marked $a°$ and $b°$ are adjacent and supplementary, so $a + b = 180$. Furthermore, the angles marked $a°$ and $60°$ are vertical and equal, so $a = 60$.

79. PARALLEL LINES AND TRANSVERSALS

A transversal across parallel lines forms **four equal acute angles and four equal obtuse angles.**

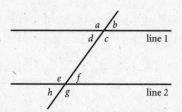

Here, line 1 is parallel to line 2. Angles a, c, e, and g are obtuse, so they are all equal. Angles b, d, f, and h are acute, so they are all equal.

Furthermore, **any of the acute angles is supplementary to any of the obtuse angles.** Angles a and h are supplementary, as are b and e, c and f, and so on.

TRIANGLES—GENERAL

80. INTERIOR ANGLES OF A TRIANGLE

The three angles of any triangle **add up to 180°.**

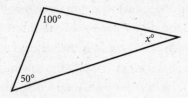

In the figure above, $x + 50 + 100 = 180$, so $x = 30$.

81. EXTERIOR ANGLES OF A TRIANGLE

An exterior angle of a triangle is equal to the **sum of the remote interior angles.**

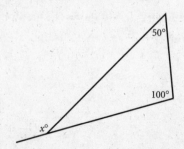

In the figure above, the exterior angle labeled $x°$ is equal to the sum of the remote interior angles:

$$x = 50 + 100 = 150$$

The three exterior angles of any triangle add up to 360°.

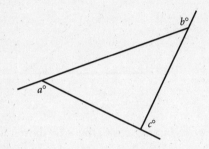

In the figure above, $a + b + c = 360$.

82. SIMILAR TRIANGLES

Similar triangles have the same shape: **corresponding angles are equal and corresponding sides are proportional.**

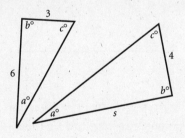

The triangles above are similar because they have the same angles. The 3 corresponds to the 4 and the 6 corresponds to the s.

$$\frac{3}{4} = \frac{6}{s}$$
$$3s = 24$$
$$s = 8$$

83. AREA OF A TRIANGLE

$$\text{Area of Triangle} = \frac{1}{2}(\text{base})(\text{height})$$

The height is the perpendicular distance between the side that's chosen as the base and the opposite vertex.

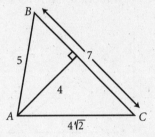

In the triangle above, 4 is the height when the 7 is chosen as the base.

$$\text{Area} = \frac{1}{2}bh = \frac{1}{2}(7)(4) = 14$$

RIGHT TRIANGLES

84. PYTHAGOREAN THEOREM

For all right triangles:

$$(\text{leg}_1)^2 + (\text{leg}_2)^2 = (\text{hypotenuse})^2$$

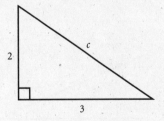

If one leg is 2 and the other leg is 3, then:

$$2^2 + 3^2 = c^2$$
$$c^2 = 4 + 9$$
$$c = \sqrt{13}$$

85. SPECIAL RIGHT TRIANGLES

• *3-4-5*

If a right triangle's leg-to-leg ratio is 3:4, or if the leg-to-hypotenuse ratio is 3:5 or 4:5, then it's a 3-4-5 triangle and you don't need to use the Pythagorean theorem to find the third side. Just figure out what multiple of 3-4-5 it is.

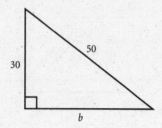

In the right triangle above, one leg is 30 and the hypotenuse is 50. This is 10 times 3-4-5. The other leg is 40.

• *5-12-13*

If a right triangle's leg-to-leg ratio is 5:12, or if the leg-to-hypotenuse ratio is 5:13 or 12:13, then it's a 5-12-13 triangle and you don't need to use the Pythagorean theorem to find the third side. Just figure out what multiple of 5-12-13 it is.

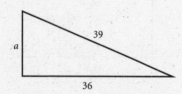

Here one leg is 36 and the hypotenuse is 39. This is 3 times 5-12-13. The other leg is 15.

• *30°-60°-90°*

The sides of a 30°-60°-90° triangle are in a ratio of $1:\sqrt{3}:2$. You don't need to use the Pythagorean theorem.

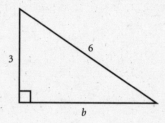

If the hypotenuse is 6, then the shorter leg is half that, or 3; and then the longer leg is equal to the short leg times $\sqrt{3}$, or $3\sqrt{3}$.

• *45°-45°-90°*

The sides of a 45°-45°-90° triangle are in a ratio of $1:1:\sqrt{2}$.

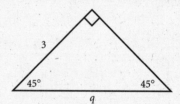

If one leg is 3, then the other leg is also 3, and the hypotenuse is equal to a leg times $\sqrt{2}$, or $3\sqrt{2}$.

OTHER POLYGONS

86. SPECIAL QUADRILATERALS

• *Rectangle*

A rectangle is a **four-sided figure with four right angles.** Opposite sides are equal. Diagonals are equal.

Quadrilateral *ABCD* above is shown to have three right angles. The fourth angle therefore also measures 90°, and *ABCD* is a rectangle. The perimeter of a rectangle is equal to the sum of the lengths of the four sides, which is equivalent to 2(length + width).

• *Parallelogram*

A parallelogram has **two pairs of parallel sides.** Opposite sides are equal. Opposite angles are equal. Consecutive angles add up to 180°.

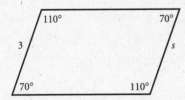

In the figure above, *s* is the length of the side opposite the 3, so *s* = 3.

• *Square*

A square is a **rectangle with 4 equal sides.**

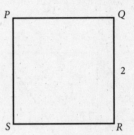

If *PQRS* is a square, all sides are the same length as *QR*. The perimeter of a square is equal to four times the length of one side.

• **Trapezoid**

A **trapezoid** is a quadrilateral with one pair of parallel sides and one pair of nonparallel sides.

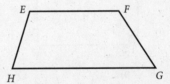

In the quadrilateral above, sides $\overline{EF}$ and $\overline{GF}$ are parallel, while sides $\overline{EH}$ and $\overline{FG}$ are not parallel. *EFGH* is therefore a trapezoid.

87. AREAS OF SPECIAL QUADRILATERALS

Area of Rectangle = Length × Width

The area of a 7-by-3 rectangle is 7 × 3 = 21.

Area of Parallelogram = Base × Height

The area of a parallelogram with a height of 4 and a base of 6 is $4 \times 6 = 24$.

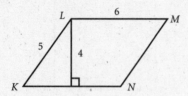

Area of Square = (Side)^2

The area of a square with sides of length 5 is $5^2 = 25$.

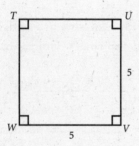

$$\text{Area of Trapezoid} = \left(\frac{\text{base}_1 + \text{base}_2}{2} \right) \times \text{height}$$

Think of it as the average of the bases (the two parallel sides) times the height (the length of the perpendicular altitude).

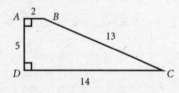

In the trapezoid $ABCD$ above, you can use side $\overline{AD}$ for the height. The average of the bases is $\frac{2 + 14}{2} = 8$, so the area is 5×8, or 40.

88. INTERIOR ANGLES OF A POLYGON

The sum of the measures of the interior angles of a polygon is $(n - 2) \times 180$, where n is the number of sides.

Sum of the Angles = $(n - 2) \times 180$ degrees

The eight angles of an octagon, for example, add up to $(8 - 2) \times 180 = 1,080$.

To find **one angle of a regular polygon,** divide the sum of the angles by the number of angles (which is the same as the number of sides). The formula, therefore, is:

$$\textbf{Interior Angle} = \frac{(n - 2) \times 180}{n}$$

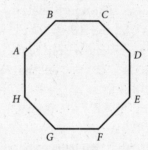

Angle A of the regular octagon above measures $\frac{1,080}{8} = 135$ degrees.

CIRCLES

89. CIRCUMFERENCE OF A CIRCLE

Circumference of a Circle = $2\pi r$

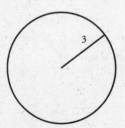

Here, the radius is 3, and so the circumference is $2\pi(3) = 6\pi$.

90. LENGTH OF AN ARC

An **arc** is a piece of the circumference. If n is the measure of the arc's central angle, then the formula is:

$$\text{Length of an Arc} = \frac{n}{360}(2\pi r)$$

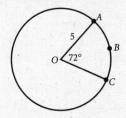

In the figure above, the radius is 5 and the measure of the central angle is 72°. The arc length is $\frac{72}{360}$ or $\frac{1}{5}$ of the circumference:

$$\left(\frac{72}{360}\right)2\pi\,(5) = \left(\frac{1}{5}\right)10\pi = 2\pi$$

91. AREA OF A CIRCLE

$$\text{Area of a Circle} = \pi r^2$$

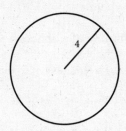

The area of the circle above is $\pi(4)^2 = 16\pi$.

92. AREA OF A SECTOR

A **sector** is a piece of the area of a circle. If n is the measure of the sector's central angle, then the formula is:

$$\text{Area of a Sector} = \left(\frac{n}{360}\right)(\pi r^2)$$

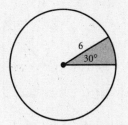

In the figure above, the radius is 6 and the measure of the sector's central angle is 30°. The sector has $\frac{30}{360}$ or $\frac{1}{12}$ of the area of the circle:

$$\left(\frac{30}{360}\right)(\pi)\,(6^2) = \left(\frac{1}{12}\right)(36\pi) = 3\pi$$

SOLIDS

93. SURFACE AREA OF A RECTANGULAR SOLID

The surface of a rectangular solid consists of 3 pairs of identical faces. To find the surface area, find the area of each face and add them up. If the length is l, the width is w, and the height is h, the formula is:

$$\text{Surface Area} = 2lw + 2wh + 2lh$$

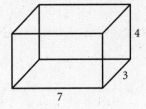

The surface area of the box above is:
$2 \times 7 \times 3 + 2 \times 3 \times 4 + 2 \times 7 \times 4 = 42 + 24 + 56 = 122$

94. VOLUME OF A RECTANGULAR SOLID

Volume of a Rectangular Solid = *lwh*

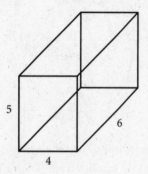

The volume of a 4-by-5-by-6 box is
$4 \times 5 \times 6 = 120$.

A cube is a rectangular solid with length, width, and height all equal. The volume formula if e is the length of an edge of the cube is:

Volume of a Cube = e^3

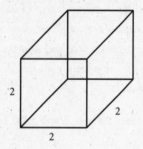

The volume of the cube above is $2^3 = 8$.

95. VOLUME OF OTHER SOLIDS

Volume of a Cylinder = $\pi r^2 h$

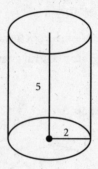

The volume of a cylinder where $r = 2$, and $h = 5$ is $\pi(2^2)(5) = 20\pi$.

Volume of a Cone = $\dfrac{1}{3}\pi r^2 h$

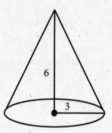

The volume of a cone where $r = 3$, and $h = 6$ is:

$$\text{Volume} = \frac{1}{3}\pi(3^2)(6) = 18$$

Volume of a Sphere = $\dfrac{4}{3}\pi r^3$

If the radius of a sphere is 3, then:

$$\text{Volume} = \frac{4}{3}\pi(3^3) = 36\pi$$

TRIGONOMETRY

96. SINE, COSINE, AND TANGENT OF ACUTE ANGLES

To find the sine, cosine, or tangent of an acute angle, use SOHCAHTOA, which is an abbreviation for the following definitions:

$$Sine = \frac{Opposite}{Hypotenuse}$$

$$Cosine = \frac{Adjacent}{Hypotenuse}$$

$$Tangent = \frac{Opposite}{Adjacent}$$

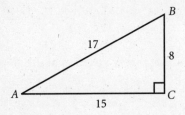

In the figure above:

$$\sin A = \frac{8}{17}$$

$$\cos A = \frac{15}{17}$$

$$\tan A = \frac{8}{15}$$

97. COTANGENT, SECANT, AND COSECANT OF ACUTE ANGLES

Think of the cotangent, secant, and cosecant as the reciprocals of the SOHCAHTOA functions:

$$Cotangent = \frac{1}{Tangent} = \frac{Adjacent}{Opposite}$$

$$Secant = \frac{1}{Cosine} = \frac{Hypotenuse}{Adjacent}$$

$$Cosecant = \frac{1}{Sine} = \frac{Hypotenuse}{Opposite}$$

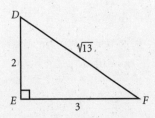

In the preceeding figure:

$$\cot D = \frac{2}{3}$$

$$\sec D = \frac{\sqrt{13}}{2}$$

$$\csc D = \frac{\sqrt{13}}{3}$$

98. TRIGONOMETRIC FUNCTIONS OF OTHER ANGLES

To find a trigonometric function of an angle greater than 90°, sketch a circle of radius 1 and centered at the origin of the coordinate grid. Start from the point (1, 0) and rotate the appropriate number of degrees counterclockwise.

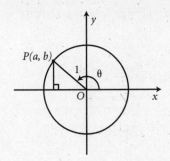

In the "unit circle" setup above, the basic trigonometric functions are defined in terms of the coordinates a and b:

$$\sin \theta = b$$
$$\cos \theta = a$$
$$\tan \theta = \frac{b}{a}$$

Example: $\sin 210° = ?$

Setup: Sketch a 210° angle in the coordinate plane:

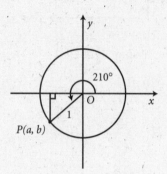

Because the triangle shown in the figure above is a 30°-60°-90° right triangle, we can determine that the coordinates of point P are $-\dfrac{\sqrt{3}}{2}, -\dfrac{1}{2}$. The sine is therefore $-\dfrac{1}{2}$.

99. SIMPLIFYING TRIGONOMETRIC EXPRESSIONS

To simplify trigonometric expressions, use the inverse function definitions along with the fundamental trigonometric identity:

$$\sin^2 x + \cos^2 x = 1$$

Example: $\dfrac{\sin^2 \theta + \cos^2 \theta}{\cos \theta} = ?$

Setup: The numerator equals 1, so:

$$\frac{\sin^2 \theta + \cos^2 \theta}{\cos \theta} = \frac{1}{\cos \theta} = \sec \theta$$

100. GRAPHING TRIGONOMETRIC FUNCTIONS

To graph trigonometric functions, use the x-axis for the angle and the y-axis for the value of the trigonometric function. Use special angles—0°, 30°, 45°, 60°, 90°, 120°, 135°, 150°, 180°, etc.—to plot key points.

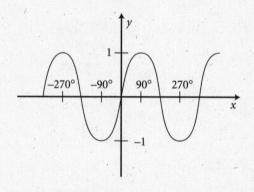

The figure above shows a portion of the graph of $y = \sin x$.